And Then It Was Winter

A biographical novel — more truth than fiction
Volume One

Loy VanNatter

A Tribute to Mom

Published by Wheatmark®
610 East Delano Street, Suite 104
Tucson, Arizona 85705 U.S.A.
www.wheatmark.com

ISBN: 978-1-60494-297-2 (paperback)
ISBN: 978-1-60494-439-6 (hardcover)
LCCN: 2009943626

"Now is the time to love all living things
for
All living things there is a season
There is a time to be born
There is a time to live
and
There is a time to die."

Author's Note:

As I ATTEMPT TO PLACE the story of my life in written form I do so with no regrets. My life has been enriched with the loving care and nourishment from total strangers who became friends plus a multitude of people whose lives touched mine that paved the road leading to my destiny.

In writing this saga it has been necessary to create many events from imagination inasmuch as part of the record is based on hearsay. Therefore this accounting of my life would fall under the category of a "biographical novel" although most of the text is more truth than fiction.

An ancient Chinese proverb states:

"Water and words are easy to pour
"But impossible to recover."

Dedicated to my wife, Jane
my teachers and mentors
and many friends
All who have made this journey possible.

My Father—Abe VanNatter.

CHAPTER 1

SOUNDS OF WHAT MIGHT HAVE been the closing of metal doors broke the silence between two worlds—one known and one unknown. The spirit of the man lying on the cold floor of the hospital was no longer housed within the ailing, crumpled vessel. A rising spirit hovering over the stilled body revealed the presence of a youthful, young man. For one fleeting moment the spirit gazed down upon the lifeless body; then as a dim light filtered through a small window opening onto the roof of the hospital, a stream of light beckoned the spirit to come. Moving toward the light, a sable blackness enveloped the youthful spirit, cradling him in a blanket of soft, velvety comfort. There was no fear, no pain—only a restful peace.

Was it real? Was it hallucinations from the effects of medications? Or was it a near-death experience?

Lying on a hospital bed next to the nurse's station, the ill man's fever-ravaged body had called for help (but no one heeded the crying man's plea). Desperate, the patient climbed over the bed railings hoping he could conjure enough strength to get to the bathroom to answer nature's calling. When his feet touched the cold, bare floor, his body collapsed. Intravenous tubes pulled away from his arms and blood flowed like geysers from his wrists. The metal stands holding life-saving fluids came crashing down upon the man's weakened body. Supporting himself against the only chair in the room, he made every effort to rise to his feet. Dragging all the medical paraphernalia across the room, he reached the entry into the bathroom then he fell again, his body crumbling against the ceramic tiled floor. Then there was nothing but blackness. Looking down upon the crumpled vessel lying on the stone floor stood a young man. That young man knew it was his own aged earthly body lying before him.

The sound of metal doors clanging would be the last earthly sound the youthful spirit would hear as he was beckoned to move toward an open window leading onto the roof of the hospital. A sable darkness enveloped the young spirit, wrapping him in soft, velvety comfort, then proceeded to transport him toward a dim light in the distance. The light grew brighter and brighter until the journey brought the young man to the edge of sable blackness to where the man's spiritual body stood gazing into a world as bright as a noonday sun. The sky was cloudless and crystal blue. Before the young man's eyes the beauty of the eternal world he was about to step into surpassed all earthly visions of beauty he had ever experienced during his long, earthly sojourn.

A voice spoke. "I'm happy to see you, Van, but you must not step into the light." The young man felt the touch of a woman's hand as she spoke. "Time will bring us together again, but now you must return." For a brief moment, two souls bonded for a second time as they had during the brief years they shared before being separated by an untimely death.

The return journey to the land of the living would set forth a lifetime, long before accepting the human form of a newborn babe. From infancy to maturity, an earthly existence would be relived.

That event, or what some might describe as a "near-death" experience, would erase all fear of death when the journey of life begins its final voyage to the edge of darkness then makes the eternal step into a peaceful world where there is no return.

Icy, Midwestern winter winds were as cold and formless as the young spirit who stood in an old barnyard staring at the flickering light from a kerosene lamp in the upstairs window of the unpretentious farmhouse. The unsteady beam of light piercing the early morning darkness beckoned the spirit to come closer. Slowly, the spirit moved with the light as it guided him into the house and up the stairs to a small bedroom on the second floor.

The dead body of a woman in her twenties lay on a straw mattress which overlapped the iron frame bed. Three sobbing children knelt beside the bed. A tall, muscular man with sandy, wavy hair stood emotionless behind them. No tears flowed from the man's cold, steel blue eyes. Many moons would pass before the unseen guest would become a seed within the body of the recently widowed man and that seed would become his youngest son.

Abraham VanNatter was the eldest of four children. He was the firstborn to join the house of James VanNatter, a respected landowner and farmer who toiled the Illinois soil as his forefathers had done from generation to generation. After the birth of Abe, James VanNatter and his wife, Virginia, enlarged their family to include two more boys and one girl—Spencer, Mattie, and Marion.

It was a 13-year-old girl by the name of Clara Russell with whom Abe became infatuated and began to court. For three years he wooed Clara, during which time he erected a small house, a barn, and a woodshed on his newly acquired land. When the house was completed and Clara was 16 years of age, Abe and Clara married. Abe was a happy man.

The farm flourished—even to the point of being lucrative, and the young farmer could afford the services of hired hands. Within a year after the wedlock between Abe and Clara, the teenage wife gave birth to a baby girl they named Marie. The pregnancy did not go well. When time came for deliverance, Clara drew her last breath as Marie drew her first.

The death of Clara and the loss of his first love turned Abe into an embittered man. He wanted his baby, but Clara's mother insisted it was best for the health and welfare of the infant that she take Marie and raise her as her own child. Abe never saw his firstborn again—not until she became a grown woman.

Abe didn't remain a widower long. Within three months following Clara's death, he began courting a neighboring farmer's daughter by the name of Josephine Armstrong. The side of the bed which Clara shared with Abe barely cooled before he chose Josephine to be his second wife.

The union between Abe and Josephine produced three daughters, Urith, Helen, and Mildred. All was well within the house of Abe until that fateful day—the day Josephine went away.

The influenza epidemic in the late 1800s would long be remembered. No one escaped the dreaded illness. The sickness spread throughout the farm community like a giant hand determined to snuff out the life of everyone it touched. Josephine VanNatter was just another victim of the disease.

Josephine's death occurred at the peak of one of the Midwest's harshest winters. Snow blanketed the farm lands from early November. Although the advent of spring was near, heavy clouds threatened more winter and more snow. Even on the day the body of Josephine was placed in the frozen earth, white crystals softly drifted downward from the gray sky, dusting the mourners standing by the open grave site.

Abe never cried. His hurt was buried as deep as the grave in which his beloved wife was laid to rest. When the last words were spoken, he quietly led his three daughters to the horse and buggy that would return them to their motherless home. As Abe's horse, Jenny, pulled the carriage over the rutted country road, the bereaved father was deep in thought. He knew he must find someone to care for his motherless children.

Ola Grace Jordan Ellison VanNatter. My mother.

CHAPTER 2

NOTHING MOVED ON THE DESERTED streets in the early morning fog blanketing the village of West Lebanon, except the shadow of a drunken man weaving his way from gaslight to gaslight. The town's only saloon had closed its doors for the night. The second floor of the watering hole housed the local prostitutes where an occasional red light penetrated the thick fog from one of the upstairs windows. This was a signal a prostitute was ready to accommodate another customer. The staggering, inebriated man gave an occasional glance toward the red light, then proceeded onward to Fourth Street.

Harry Ellison was born and raised in West Lebanon. His mother and father had never traveled more than a few miles beyond the outskirts of the town. They too had been conceived and born in this Midwestern farming village. Like all generations before him, Harry Ellison was aware of his future. No other world would exist beyond the confines of this small town.

The drunken staggering and blurry eyes of the intoxicated man miscalculated the first step onto the wooden porch of the small, yellow frame house. The thud of his body hitting the deck of the porch awakened his young, pregnant bride.

Ola Grace Jordan Ellison quickly opened the door and helped the incapacitated man to his feet.

"Where ya been, Harry? I've been worried about ya."

Harry's watery, swimming eyes glared at his wife. "It's none of yer goddamn business where I've been—so—shut yer fuckin' mouth, ya fuckin' bitch!"

As the word "bitch" sputtered from Harry Ellison's booze-soaked lips, a closed fist sped through the air making a direct contact on the side of Ola Grace's face. Her youthful, pregnant body hit the bare floor of the porch. She could see Harry's heavy boots stepping over her as consciousness faded and she was rocketed into blackness. She had no recollection how long she lay there. It was the light of a new day which brought her back to reality. Her head throbbed and her body ached. She remained on the floor until she regained enough strength to stand. She knew then she must put an end to this brutal marriage to a man she never loved.

The spring rains came and the earth turned green. Daffodils and irises broke through the fertile soil in the flower bed Mother Ellison diligently nurtured. Colorful sweet peas clung to the back fence. The baby inside Ola Grace Jordan Ellison grew.

Summertime brought the usual Midwestern hot, humid weather to the town of West Lebanon. On July 6, 1905, Ola Grace delivered her firstborn son, Ralph Burton Ellison.

The firstborn from the seed of Harry Ellison was the result of human passion gone amok. Ola Grace had no intention of permitting the forceful man to violate her body. It had been an amiable meeting where they met and he offered to take her home. As the young, teenage girl prepared to disembark from the horse-drawn carriage, strong, unanticipated arms wrapped themselves around her youthful figure.

His strength forced her legs apart. The man then mounted the young girl, forcing his penis into her body. At the very moment Harry Ellison reached a climax, the young woman knew she had conceived.

The Jordan clan were a proud family of Irish stock. They migrated from Ireland sometime during the 1600s and settled in upstate New York and in North Carolina. Apparently, they came to this country with enough wealth to consider them an affluent family. According to the history of the Jordan clan, they at one time owned a number of slaves. Mike Jordan met and married a girl of French descent by the name of Martha Lape. After the marriage, Michael and his new bride decided to move to the fertile plains of the Midwest. Michael Jordan sired eight children, Ola Grace being the third child to be born and the Jordan family's first girl.

The news of their daughter becoming pregnant out of wedlock was far from acceptable, especially with Ola Grace's mother, Martha Lape Jordan. The woman not only forced Ola Grace into marriage, but proceeded to disown her as her own flesh and blood. Ola Grace had no alternative but to move into the Ellison home. It was in this home that she would give birth to her first child.

Ralph was a healthy child. Upon the advent of their first grandson, the elder Mother Ellison became obsessed — obsessed to the point where Ola Grace's position within the Ellison household became no more than that of a surrogate mother. Every cry and every whimper from the child was cause for Grandma Ellison to rush to the baby then cuddle him in her arms for consolation. Only at feeding time did Ola Grace have the opportunity to hold and caress her newborn child.

At the time of Ralph's birth, Harry Ellison was sharing

a bed with West Lebanon's most notorious prostitute. From his wedding day, he felt trapped in a situation whereby society forced him to marry someone he didn't love. Seldom did the disturbed man make an appearance at the house on Fourth Street. If he did return, it was always in the wee hours of the morning, then he would make his bed on the davenport in the parlor. So it was, on an early morning his drunken footsteps could be heard as he stumbled up the stairs onto the porch. Curses flowed from his mouth as though he were having a private conversation with demons from hell.

The baby's cries for his 2:00 a.m. feeding awakened Ola Grace. She had just taken the infant to her breast and sat in the rocking chair in the parlor when she became aware of Harry's crazed, alcoholic eyes focused on her and the infant resting in her arms.

"What the hell are ya doin', Oley? Where in the goddamn shit did that thing come from?"

Calmly, the young mother uncovered the baby's head revealing the infant nursing from her full breast.

"It's yer son, Harry."

Without uttering another word, Harry staggered then let his booze-soaked body collapse on the davenport in the parlor. The new mother snuggled her newborn next to her breast. Throughout the night, Ola Grace sat in the rocking chair waiting for dawn.

The union between Ola Grace and Harry Ellison did not improve. As Ralph grew, Grandma Ellison became more and more possessive of her grandson. Harry would only make his presence known when he wished to flaunt his surliness and physical abuse upon his young wife. With each verbal and physical abuse, the more determined the young mother became to escape the clutches of a situation she had not for herself chosen.

"I'm gittin' out a this marriage, Mother Ellison. Your son hates me and I hate him. He's not the man I care to have raisin' my son and I do mean—my son. Harry has hit me fer the last time and I'm gonna leave him and takin' my son with me."

"Fergit it, Missy," the elder woman retorted. "Ya ain't goin' ta drag our family through a lot of mud jes' cause ya ain't happy with Harry. Ya married my son, ya made yer bed! Now—lay in it!" Sarcastically, Grandma Ellison continued. "And somethin' else, Missy—didn't that preacher say somethin' like 'fer better or worse?'"

"We'll see, Mother Ellison!" As Ola Grace uttered her statement to the elder woman's proclamation, she slammed the dish she was drying to the floor. Tiny pieces of a broken plate scattered across the bare, wooden planks. The shattered dish proved to be a symbolic omen that would end a marriage that should never have been. Without bothering to pick up the pieces, Ola Grace fled from the kitchen into her lonely room.

Ralph reached his first birthday. As the infant struggled to take his first steps, he would fall. Grandma Ellison was first to pick the baby up in her arms then once again place him upright. Trial and error soon brought about success, and Ralph was able to walk on two feet. As he grew, his personality became more acute, revealing a lovable child and one who delighted in displaying individuality. This of course pleased the Ellisons, and it also met with Ola Grace's approval. Harry, although never showing anything but hatred toward his wife, would often smile at the progress his son was making. Occasionally, he would take the baby in his arms, throw him into the air, and actually laugh when the tot screamed with glee, knowing his dad was going to catch him on the way down.

When Harry decided to spend the night on Fourth Street instead of sharing the bed with a prostitute in a room over the town's watering hole, he would make up his bed on the davenport in the parlor. Ola Grace would take her young son to her bed in the small bedroom adjacent to the living room. It was one of the few times, other than feeding time, the distraught mother could cuddle her baby without interference from the Ellison clan. She would lay awake for hours hoping to come up with a plan for escape from the hell she did not want and was subjected to. Her determination to leave this small village and the Ellison household preyed constantly on her mind until it became an obsession. Awake or sleeping, Ola Grace anxiously awaited her day of deliverance.

The old mantel clock had just struck midnight. Awakened from a sound sleep, Ola Grace felt the presence of a naked man lying beside her. He placed his hand over her mouth in an attempt to muffle a scream. An immediate flashback of that fateful night while riding home in Harry Ellison's buggy was being repeated. Harry mounted his young wife, forced her legs apart, then proceeded to penetrate his penis into her body. Deeper and deeper the man's appendage worked its way inside his victim. Reaching his climax, the man's penis softened and he withdrew from Ola Grace's vagina. Quickly, he climbed off his frightened wife then stood beside the bed. He stared down at Ola Grace with a crazed look like she had never seen in the man either sober or drunk. "I hate ya, Oley! Ya know, Oley—I could kill ya and never give it another thought."

With a sudden burst of strength, Ola Grace jumped from the bed and faced her rapist like a cornered tigress. "I hate you, Harry Ellison. I'm gonna make ya pay for this and yer gonna pay plenty. If ya ever come near me or this bed again while my baby and me are in this house, I swear, I'll kill ya. Do you hear!? I'll kill ya! Now—git out!"

Harry turned and walked toward the door. As he exited the room, Ola Grace slammed the door behind him. To further secure the door, she placed a chair under the doorknob. Returning to the bed, she cuddled her infant son next to her used body. Throughout the remaining hours of darkness, thoughts of escape never left her tumultuous mind.

It was a sleepless night for the young mother. She rose from her bed, then quietly opened the door to see if Harry Ellison was still in the house. She took Ralph to her breast then sat in the old wooden rocking chair, tightly holding her son to her bosom and wondering what her next move should be. Thoughts of having been impregnated again rushed through her mind. What could she do? If there was a God, why had he so totally abandoned her?

A distinct demanding sound of Mother Ellison's Midwestern twang interrupted Ola Grace's deep thoughts. "Ya gotta earn yer keep, Oley. Ya ain't even started breakfast yet."

Ignoring Grandma Ellison's sharp tongue, the young mother arose from the chair then sat Ralph on the floor just as the old woman entered the parlor.

"What ya doin', Oley? Ya know I cain't stand ya settin' him on the floor. He jes' might catch his death of cold."

Ignoring Mother Ellison's comments, Ola Grace went into the kitchen. She stoked the range with some fresh kindling, then walked to the cabinet and began taking dishes from the shelves for the purpose of setting the breakfast table. Mother

Ellison picked Ralph up from the floor then followed Ola Grace into the kitchen.

"Fer the life of me, Oley, I don't know what's gittin' into ya. You've been so quiet these last few days, I jes' cain't figure out what's goin' on in yer head."

Stored bitterness since the night Ralph was conceived suddenly spouted forth in sharp, dagger-pointed words from Ola Grace's mouth. "I'll tell ya, Mother Ellison, what's wrong—I hate 'im. I hate every bone in yer son's body and I'm gittin' out of this marriage. The only thing I'm good fer around here is to nurse my son and be yer unpaid servant. I jes' hope yer good fer nothin' son didn't git me pregnant again last night. He came into the bedroom—woke me from a sound sleep and proceeded to rape me! I hate 'im! I hate 'im!" Angry tears flowed from Ola Grace's eyes.

Taken aback by Ola Grace's outburst, the elder Mrs. Ellison made a feeble attempt to smooth the anger of her irate daughter-in-law. "Well—Oley—ya know as well as I do, ya ain't got no right to refuse yer husband. Ya jes' hafta be ready when he is. As fer gittin' out of your marriage to my son, that ain't gonna be easy. Ya got a kid to think about and as I told ya before, ya ain't gonna drag this family through a lot of mud jes' cause ya ain't happy with Harry!"

Like a determined soldier headed off to war, Ola Grace turned on her heels. As she left the kitchen, her final statement in response to her mother-in-law could only be, "We'll see, Mother Ellison." The teenage mother knew the time had come to put an end to a persistent living hell in which she had been doomed.

Suicide passed through the young mother's mind. The second month of her menstrual cycle passed, and with no sign of a monthly period, her dreaded suspicion had come to pass. She knew she was pregnant again by a man whom she despised. There was no place to run to—no escape from the torment that had so totally engulfed her entire being. Her own mother had disowned her. Martha Lape Jordan was a feisty creature and for some unknown reason was an embittered woman. There had never been a time when Ola Grace needed the kind compassion, understanding, and love from her father as she needed it now. She had no skills. A woman's duty was to remain at home, clean house, have kids, and make sure the food was on the table. Ola Grace rarely spoke. She listened.

It was a time when Harry Ellison made one of his rare appearances and joined the family at the dinner table. As the innocuous chit-chat was uttered from the mouths of all except Ola Grace, Harry, in his sadistic and sarcastic manner, directed a statement to Ola Grace.

"Oley—the whores are lookin' fer a cleanin' woman. Why don't ya apply fer the job? That's about all yer good fer is to clean up after some whore."

Ola Grace projected a cold stare at her abusive husband. His suggestion, however, didn't go unheeded. Throughout the day, she mulled Harry's sick suggestion over in her mind. She needed money. She no longer found it necessary to nurse her young son. If she had a job, she might be able to put aside enough money to get a lawyer. A ray of light began to pierce the darkness. It just might be an answer for a way out of the Ellison's clutches.

The following morning, Ola Grace made her way to the town brothel. The madam greeted her in a friendly manner and was more than willing to give the young woman a job as a char woman. The women of the night liked her. They were aware of Harry Ellison's sadistic bent. They often paid

Ola Grace a little extra for sewing and repairing their gowns, clothing that was often torn by oversexed, insensitive, uncaring men. As Ola Grace's belly grew and cleaning became more difficult, the prostitutes extended themselves further by keeping her on as a dressmaker, work she could easily do at home.

Summer moved into autumn, then came the chill of winter, and the new life within the womb of the young mother grew. Winter snows covered the ground. It was an early winter, and as the earth became cloaked in an ermine blanket of white, Ola Grace knew the time had come for the birth of her second baby. On December 6, 1906, Cecil Alvin Ellison left the safety of his mother's womb.

Cecil Alvin Ellison was destined to be an unwanted and an unloved child except for the love of his mother. He was never accepted as the son of Harry Ellison, nor was he ever considered a member of the Ellison clan. Ola Grace and her newborn infant were alone.

Days turned into weeks, and months passed with little or no dialogue between Ola Grace and Mother Ellison. It was always thought Grandpa Ellison was deaf. No one ever gave it a thought that he might be a very good listener.

After the birth of Cecil, Harry Ellison rarely made an appearance at the yellow house on Fourth Street. If there was anything for which to be grateful, it was his absence. Every penny Ola Grace earned working for the whores was carefully stashed away, leaving only enough to pay for her keep while residing within the Ellison household. Each day she secretly planned her escape.

The Ellisons housed Harry's horse, Maude, in a small barn next to the outdoor privy. The horse was the only source of transportation for the Ellison family, yet, like Ola

Grace, the animal was not loved or cared for except to make certain there was food in her bin and water in a rusty watering trough just outside the barn door. Ola Grace took over the duty caring for Maude. She brushed her daily, then she would take her out of the barn for a short period of exercise. The horse became the young mother's only friend. They were able to communicate even though no audible words were ever spoken. The horse seemed to know every thought going through Ola Grace's mind, and the young woman had a knack for understanding the thoughts projecting from the mind of the horse.

"My four-legged friend jes' might be a way of me gittin' outta here. If she could git me to Williamsport, I jes' might git myself a lawyer." Throughout the remainder of the day and far into the night, Ola Grace pondered over her plans. By morning, she was ready to take the first step toward an escape. She performed her usual morning tasks by stoking the fire in the old cast iron kitchen range, setting the breakfast table, baking biscuits, heating the teakettle, and preparing breakfast. The only words spoken would be to summon the elder Ellisons for the first meal of the day. No one spoke, not even a sound from the mouth of three-year-old Ralph.

It was a fortunate morning for Ola Grace. Harry's absence and oral abuse would not hamper the goal the young mother hoped to accomplish on this red-letter day. Once the meal was completed and the elders left the table, Ola Grace cleared the dishes and the remains of the silent meal. A large dishpan filled with boiling water was ready to receive the soiled dishes. Once the last plate was washed, dried, and put away, the young mother quickly swept the wooden floor. The time had come. Excitement and anticipation flowed through her veins.

Taking Cecil in her arms, Ola Grace took Ralph's hand then led the way from the parlor into the bedroom. Through the bedroom window she could see Mother Ellison making her way to the privy. The timing was perfect. Quickly, she closed the door separating the bedroom from the parlor. Once the money she saved from sewing for the whores was safely tucked inside her small leather purse, she began bundling Ralph into his winter coat.

"Where we goin', Mama?" Ola Grace gently placed her hand over the youngster's mouth. "Shh—it's a secret—we're gonna take a buggy ride. You must be very, very quiet."

Taking a warm woolen blanket from the crib in Cecil's bed, she wrapped it around her infant son. With Cecil in her arms and Ralph firmly grasping his mother's hand, the young mother and her two sons hurried to the barn. Ralph jumped into the buggy, and once he was settled, Ola Grace placed Cecil on his lap. Without hesitation, she pulled the buggy through the open barn door. Earlier that morning, she had pre-harnessed Maude. It was only a matter of attaching the reins to the harness and connecting Maude to the single tree. Ola Grace had to move quickly before Mother Ellison would become suspicious. The young mother hurriedly boarded the buggy. Taking the reins in her hands, she gently tapped Maude on the back. "Giddy up, Old Girl. Ya can do it! We gotta git outta here before anyone sees us."

It was as if the horse knew Ola Grace's plan. The buggy lurched forward. "We're goin' fer a ride kids. I'm jes' hopin' this trip will at least be a start to gittin' us outta this mess."

Old Maude anticipated the thoughts running through the mind of Ola Grace. Until this moment, the aged horse had not experienced the youthful spring in her stride since she was a young filly.

The sound of buggy wheels rolling over the rutted yard brought a sudden end to Mother Ellison's visit to the privy. She opened the outhouse door at the exact moment Ola Grace and her family left the front yard and began rolling onto the gravel road. Frantic thoughts passed through the woman's head. "Where's Oley takin' my grandson? Oley! Oley!" she screamed. The shrill voice of Mother Ellison echoed through the cold crisp air. The reverberating sound penetrated Ola Grace's ears until the moment she turned onto Main Street and headed out of town. Faster and faster Maude pulled the buggy. At last, only the purring sound of buggy wheels rolling over the graveled road to Williamsport and the steady rhythm of Maude's feet could be heard. There was peace. The journey was so quiet, Ralph and his baby brother drifted off to sleep. It was not until the street noises of Williamsport interrupted the quiet journey did the youngsters awaken.

The streets of Williamsport were void of heavy traffic, even on Main Street. Ola Grace guided Maude toward the nearest hitching post at Main and Elm. As she tied the reins to the post, the young mother happened to glance at a large sign etched in gold on a window directly in front of her.

GEORGE W. DAY, ESQ. ATTORNEY AT LAW

A quiet inner voice seemed to speak to the young mother. "This is it! I jes' hope Mr. Day will see me."

Snuggling Cecil in one arm then grasping the hand of Ralph, Ola Grace shyly opened the door into the warmth of a new and different world. The offices of George W. Day were about to introduce a man whose compassion and understanding would be the beginning of a new life for Ola Grace Jordan Ellison. Row upon row of leather-bound books were neatly placed in mahogany bookcases lining the wood-paneled walls. A well-dressed, middle-aged woman seated behind a small desk greeted her.

"May I help you?" she politely asked as she carefully observed the young mother holding the small infant in one arm and the hand of Ralph in the other.

Words did not come easily for Ola Grace. "I—I—hope I'm in the right place, ma'am. I believe I'm in bad need of a lawyer. My name is Ola Grace Ellison, and I live in West Lebanon. You see—I'm married to a man who's a drunk. Not only is he always drunk—he's mean. I'm jes' scared he might hurt my babies. He gives me no money and I jes' have ta find a way to raise these youngins' by myself."

Before she could finish her story, the secretary rose from her chair. "Please be seated over there for a moment." She pointed toward the large sofa next to the entry into the reception room of the office. "I believe Mr. Day does have some time today, but at the moment he's with a client. As soon as he's finished, I'll ask him to see you. Perhaps he can advise you in this matter."

The receptionist, seeing Ola Grace was comfortable, disappeared behind a heavy door leading into an adjacent office. As the door closed to the inner office, thoughts of doubt flooded the mind of Ola Grace. Had she done the right thing by coming here? She had no money. How did she expect to pay for a lawyer with the few shekels she saved working for the whores? Every second of waiting seemed like an eternity. There were thoughts of leaving the warmth of the lawyer's office, but as she rose to her feet, the door to the inner office opened.

A tall, silver-haired, distinguished looking gentleman stood in the open doorway. As he spoke, there was compassion, and the sound of his voice was similar to words that might have come from the mouth of the young mother's father.

"Come on in, Mrs. Ellison and bring those two lively youngsters with you. I just might have something for them." Attorney Day led the way into his large, spacious office. He pointed to a lush leather chair in front of his desk and motioned Ola Grace to be seated. The man then moved toward the swivel chair positioned behind his large desk. Once seated, he reached into a crystal bowl filled with an assortment of candies. He brought forth a handful of tasty treats as he spoke directly to Ralph. "Here, young man—why don't you take your little brother and sit on that couch over there. Your mother and I are going to have a little chat so you must be very quiet. We won't be long."

The attorney then leaned back in his swivel leather chair. "Now—Mrs. Ellison, your problem must be very serious for you to drive so far in this winter weather to seek the advice of a lawyer."

Ola Grace's throat was dry. She tried to speak, but her voice was barely audible.

"Don't be afraid, young lady. I'm here to listen. There comes a time in everyone's life when it is necessary to unload some of our troubles onto a friend, and I'd like to be your friend."

"Mr. Day—I—I—ain't got no money to pay fer a lawyer, but, I know the only way I can git outta this mess I'm in, I jes' hafta git some help." Ola Grace's opening statement opened the door for communication, and the words began to flow. It was the first time since her marriage to Harry Ellison that she could unburden the heavy load she carried.

"Ya see, Mr. Day—I'm married to the town of West Lebanon's worst and meanest drunk. He ain't been sober since the day we got married. He's hit me and knocked me down to the floor and has raped me. I'm afraid he's gonna hurt my babies—maybe even kill us. If he ever works, any money he makes from pitching hay or some odd job, he spends on booze and whores. My babies and me are livin' with his mom and dad, or we wouldn't have a roof over our heads. In many ways, the Ellisons are good people, especially when it comes to their first grandson, Ralph over there—he's my first—but, since my baby Cecil was born, they have showed nothin' but hatred for the little feller. I ain't had nothin' to do with my husband since Ralph was born until one time in the middle of the night, Harry Ellison come into the bedroom and forced himself on me. It's the same thing the man did before Ralph was born, and we weren't even married then." Tears welled in Ola Grace's eyes as she tried to continue. "That awful, terrible night is when he made me pregnant with my youngest one here." She pointed to Cecil snuggled next to his elder brother on the couch.

The kind lawyer held onto every word spoken by the young mother. He had heard the story time and time again. He knew how brutal and evil a person could be whose entire life was totally consumed by Barleycorn. Ola Grace's story was not a new one. It had nothing to do with being rich or poor; every case followed the same path of self-destruction, many times destroying an entire family. Patiently, the attorney waited until he was certain Ola Grace had completed her story.

"I ain't got no money, Mr. Day. I can't afford what it's gonna cost me to git a divorce unless I git a job. I've been sewin' fer the whores in West Lebanon, but they don't pay much. I don't know how I'm gonna feed my babies."

Tears welled in Ola Grace's eyes, then turned to sobs. The kind man rose from his chair then stood behind the bereaved woman. Gently, he placed his hand on her shoulder. "Please, Mrs. Ellison. I'm here to help you. We won't worry about money. You are living in a bad situation, and you were right when you say you fear for the life of your children and yourself. I have children of my own. I would not wish to subject my youngsters to the brutality or have them witness the sadistic tactics some men display toward their wives, whether they are under the influence of alcohol or whether it's just their nature. Harsh and unkind words are oftentimes more damaging and cruel than a physical beating. There is no reason why you should even consider remaining in your present environment. You are endangering the lives of your children and yourself. I do not believe God would ever condone the hell that has befallen upon you, and I would suggest you seek a divorce immediately. I'm not going to charge you for my services, Mrs. Ellison. There are costs to file with the courts, but even that is immaterial. I believe those fees can be waived in your particular case."

Attorney Day marked the beginning of dissolving the catastrophic union between Ola Grace Ellison and the town drunk of West Lebanon. There was nothing to gain financially by getting the divorce. Harry had no assets, except he could lay claim to his horse, Maude. The rickety, covered buggy had been in the Ellison family since the day Harry was born.

Mr. Day reached for a small bell on his desk. He rang and his secretary responded immediately to Mr. Day's summon. "Miss Price—I wish to prepare a Motion for Dissolution to present to the court tomorrow morning. I'm going to request the court demand Harry Ellison pay his wife and his two children the sum of $15 a month. I'm also asking the court to award this young mother total custody of their children plus the horse and the buggy which, as I understand, is the only monetary possession belonging to Mr. Harry Ellison."

Ola Grace rose from her chair. She placed Cecil in her arms then reached for Ralph's hand. As she did so, the attorney spoke. "Here children, take a little more candy. While you and your mother wait in the reception room, this will keep you busy." The kind man reached into the crystal bowl and withdrew another handful of delectable sweets. "This will not take long, Mrs. Ellison. My secretary will put together the necessary documents for the court."

Next to the sofa in the reception room, the *Williamsport Gazette* lay on a small table. Ola Grace reached for the newspaper and, while she was leafing through its pages, her eyes suddenly focused on an ad.

"Housekeeper wanted. Wages $1.50 a week plus room and board. Contact Abraham VanNatter, Route 1, State Line, Indiana.

Contemplating the ad, Ola Grace began to fantasize what it might be like to get away from West Lebanon and Harry Ellison. "Maybe this is the answer. I wonder if I could have my two youngins' with me. God knows, I'm a good housekeeper." Taking her eyes away from the ad, Ola Grace interrupted the secretary. "Miss—can I ask ya somethin'? Have ya got a penny postcard I can buy?"

The secretary opened the top drawer of her desk and withdrew a penny postcard. Ola Grace reached in her weathered purse hoping to find a penny. "No, no—please, Mrs. Ellison. I'm sure Mr. Day is only too happy to help you get a job, and if a one-penny postcard does it, I'm happy too. By the way, when you're finished answering that ad, I'll be only too glad to mail the postcard for you." Ola Grace quickly replied to the ad then handed the card to the secretary.

Ola Grace Ellison thanked the kind woman. Bundling her two children, the relieved mother climbed aboard the buggy and began the return journey to West Lebanon.

CHAPTER 3

BUGGY WHEELS ROLLING INTO THE front yard of the yellow house on Fourth Street was cause for the elder Mrs. Ellison to come running from the parlor onto the porch and down into the yard. Words and questions spewed from the woman's mouth even before Ola Grace could bring Maude to a halt.

"Well—Oley—where have ya been? Did ya find yerself a lawyer? I suppose yer hell bent fer leather on divorcin' my son and draggin' this family through a lot of mud! What ya goin' do with yer kids, Oley? Ya goin' move away and take 'em with ya?"

Ola Grace wasted no time answering the flood of questions asked by the excited mother-in-law. "Yes, Mother Ellison. I did see a lawyer—and yes—I'm divorcin' yer son. As far as my kids are concerned I'm goin' take 'em with me—jes' as soon as I git a job." The jubilant mother lightly touched the reins to Maude's back. The horse moved the carriage forward toward the barn, leaving Mother Ellison to ponder over things to come.

Divorces were few within the farm community of West Lebanon. When word passed from one gossipy person to another, the news had an instant impact on the entire community. It was an unwritten law that the wife was to be subservient to her husband, and that vow she took on her wedding day, "for better or for worse," was the law. Ola Grace's effort to separate herself from the verbal and physical abuse of Harry Ellison showered upon the young mother a wrath from the community beyond comprehension. It further added to the hell she had already been subjected to. Even the town whores had to admit the young mother had to have a lot of courage to defy those sacred vows taken in marriage. The petite woman from Irish stock continued to endure hell without dying.

Securing Maude in her stall, Ola Grace removed the harness from the old Mare's back. "We did it, Maude, and my deepest thanks to ya," she spoke as she patted the horse then pressed her lips next to the horse's nose. She reached for Ralph's hand, helping him down to the ground, then reached for Cecil, taking him to her bosom. The family of three entered the Ellison household. No words were spoken as they passed Mother Ellison sitting in the rocking chair. Ola Grace proceeded into the bedroom, removed Ralph's coat, placed Cecil in his crib then, as she always had done in the past, went into the kitchen to prepare supper.

Ola Grace continued to sew for the prostitutes. She added more cleaning chores to her routine, thus making a bit more money. Most of the monies earned were given to Mother Ellison in payment for part of her financial responsibility for having a roof over her head. The money with which she did not part was safely tucked away for the move she knew would be in the near future.

Harry Ellison, having been advised of the dissolution, made it his business to stay away from the house on Fourth Street. This action on his part was most welcome to the young mother. She had an inner peace and a sense of security she had not enjoyed since before the night of her firstborn's conception.

The days were long as the young woman waited for the postman to bring an answer to her response to the ad in the *Williamsport Gazette*. She knew should Mother Ellison collect the mail, she would never know if an answer to her application for the job at State Line was delivered to the West Lebanon address.

One week from the day the young mother made her infamous journey to Williamsport and Mr. Day's office, a reply arrived.

> *Dear Mrs. Ellison:*
>
> *I have three daughters, the oldest one is ten. The second daughter is eight and my youngest is six. My children lost their mother this past winter and they are in dire need of a woman's guidance in our home. Our house is small. As much as I would like to have both yer small youngins', particularly since they are boys and useful around the farm, I'm afraid we can only take one of 'em. Bring the youngest with ya. Well see how it works out, then maybe we can bring the other boy later.*
>
> *Yours truly,*
> *Abe VanNatter*

Ola Grace folded the letter, then tucked it inside the envelope. Cecil had awakened from his afternoon nap and was calling for his mother's attention. Without thinking, she laid the envelope and its contents on top of the library table, then proceeded to the bedroom to take care of her infant's needs. On her way to the bedroom, she passed Mother Ellison coming in from the kitchen. She had not intended to leave Abraham VanNatter's letter within reach of Mother Ellison.

The elder Mrs. Ellison immediately spied the unsealed letter. Quickly, she opened the envelope and became involved with its contents. She was so engrossed with Abe's reply she wasn't cognizant of Ola Grace's presence until she heard her voice.

"What are you doin', Mother Ellison!" Ola Grace screamed. In a lightning flash, she grabbed the letter from the woman's hands. By now her anger was uncontrollable. She wanted to strike the old woman, but something told her to remain calm.

"Well—Oley—ya cain't take Ralph with ya. I jes' won't let ya! Yer future boss says ya cain't have both kids." Her voice grew into a high pitch which would have been the envy of any cultured *coloratura* soprano. "That letter says yer future boss cain't take both yer kids. I don't care what ya do with Cecil, but Ralph—he's my grandson! He's all I got!"

The anger in the sound of the elder woman's voice now turned into a pathetic plea. Her eyes which had always been cold and lacked all compassion filled with tears. The acid tongue always ready and capable of spewing sarcasm changed into humility and humble pie.

"I know'd Harry ain't been good to ya, Oley. I cain't say I blame ya fer leavin' him, but, please don't take Ralph away." Uncontrollable sobs shook the elder woman's body.

Calmly and firmly, Ola Grace began to speak. There was a coolness in her voice that the young mother couldn't believe was coming from her mouth. "Mother Ellison—these are my children. My two boys are brothers and I have every intention of havin' them raised that way. I will wire Mr. Van-Natter now and inform him I will be leavin' on the train for State Line tomorrow mornin'."

It was a sleepless night for Ola Grace. Before sunrise, she

bundled Cecil in a warm blanket. She packed a bit of food to eat during the journey, then placed all the clothing she and Cecil possessed into a small bag. Ralph was sleeping soundly on a small cot next to her bed. Quietly, she knelt down for a brief farewell moment next to her firstborn son. Tenderly, she placed a kiss on his forehead. As she did so, Ralph opened his eyes.

"Mama's gotta go away, Ralph. Grandma Ellison will take good care of ya and when I git settled, I'm comin' fer ya. Be a good boy and don't cause no trouble."

Unleashed tears flowed freely over Ola Grace's cheeks. The tiny arms which had placed themselves around the neck of the sad mother were released. Rising to her feet and one more gentle kiss on the forehead of her firstborn, the young mother moved toward the open door, leaving Ralph in the darkened room.

Grandpa Ellison was already seated in the buggy, reins in hand, as Ola Grace and Cecil boarded the old carriage for the last time. He rarely spoke, but as Ola Grace was firmly seated beside him, the man whom all thought deaf and even considered dumb spoke. "Oley—my son's no good. I never had much say in raisin' him. It got so when I did tried to say somethin', I was told to shut up. Fer years I shut up and let 'em think I didn't hear a thing bein' said. I'm so sorry my son hurt ya so bad and I want ya to know I don't blame ya fer leavin' him. Don't ya worry about Ralph. I'll see to it the same thing don't happen to him that happened to my son."

Sadly, Maude gently pulled the buggy onto the graveled road. There was a heaviness and already a loneliness in her gait. She had been a faithful servant to the Ellisons since the time she was a young mare. The time had come now when her earthly journey must come to an end. Within a few days after Ola Grace's departure, the horse took one last breath and gave up the ghost.

*Grandma Ellison, Ralph (Ola Grace's firstborn),
and Grandpa Ellison.*

Ola Grace Jordan and Cecil B. Ellison, second born.

A family Jordan portrait. The Mike Jordan Clan.

CHAPTER 4

THERE WAS SOMETHING ABOUT THE old oak kitchen table covered with a worn oilcloth that encouraged communication from the youngest of Abe's daughters to the oldest. Around the table, as in times past, Abe would play his French Harp, or what is commonly known as a harmonica, while the kids would join in a sing-along. Abe would often alternate from playing the harmonica to the Jew's Harp and then the comb. When he wasn't accompanying with one of those three instruments, his high tenor voice would join in the sing-along, and the rafters of the old farmhouse would ring with music. It was a happy home.

The day Josephine died and was laid to rest in the frozen earth, a bitterness and gloom infiltrated the man's being and he was no longer a fun-loving man. He was lonesome and he was angry. He rarely smiled or spoke. At mealtimes, the three girls and their bereaved father gathered around the table, but each meal was consumed in silence.

Through all the bitterness life had dealt the farmer, he knew the welfare of his daughters must have first consideration. He must find a woman who would in some small way bring a semblance of motherly love to his growing daughters. Since Abe was not a churchgoing man, the local parish barely recognized his existence. It was the urgency of the situation that forced the widowed father to place an ad in the *Williamsport Gazette*.

Anticipation and certain doubt flooded his mind when he received a response to his ad. She was a mother. She had two children and she was in the process of getting a divorce. "What kind of woman must she be?"

For well over a week, Abe carried Ola Grace's postcard in the pocket of his bib overalls. He said nothing to the children about advertising for a housekeeper. There might be a sense of resentment. The girls had done well taking over the household chores after the death of their mother, Josephine.

It was the day before Ola Grace Ellison's arrival that Abe broke his silence at breakfast. There was something different on this particular morning. The deep bitterness engulfing Abe's soul disappeared like ice melts with the first signs of spring. He waited until the entire family was seated before he spoke.

"I have something to say to you girls this morning. It might be good news and it might not be so good. You need a woman to look after ya. I don't know how to be a mother and a dad, so I placed an ad in the newspaper. A few days ago, I received a postcard from a woman in West Lebanon who has two sons, one's about three years old and the other boy is only a small tyke, just a little over one year. I answered the woman's postcard and told her we could only accommodate one child. She was welcome to bring the baby with her. I also told her we might be able to take in the older boy at a later time. I expect the woman and her baby to arrive tomorrow. If we're goin' to have strangers in this house, I think we'd better git busy and make room for 'em."

In unison the girls shouted. "Papa!—Papa! It's wonderful!" One by one each girl left her place at the table and ran to her father's side, planting a kiss on his cheek and embracing him with the love and affection only children can give.

Urith, being the oldest of the three girls, was first to have a suggestion. "Papa—why don't we fix up the room off the kitchen. That's where Mama stored all the food she canned from last summer's harvest. It's not very big but I think we can put a couple small beds in there and maybe we can git that old chest out of the attic. She could put her clothes and the baby's things in it."

Abe was grateful for Urith's suggestion. "I have some straw in the barn," Abe chimed in. "We can fill the mattress ticks with fresh straw." The House of Abe excitedly began the chore of making room for the new arrivals.

At the break of a new day, a young uniformed lad riding a bicycle rapped on the kitchen door. Still in his long johns, Abe sleepily opened the door. The messenger boy handed a telegram to Abe. Abe quickly opened the yellow envelope then glanced at the message. He had learned how to read a few words but was never capable of understanding all the written words. Nevertheless, he knew the message was from the housekeeper that applied for the job. Laying the wire on the table, he proceeded to get dressed then went to the barn to take care of the morning chores before breakfast.

Urith was first to rise from her warm bed. She dressed and prepared to ready herself for school before awakening the other children. Entering the kitchen, she noticed the telegram lying on the table. Nervously, she opened the envelope. The telegram was from Ola Grace Ellison, the woman they hoped would be a replacement for their mother. All the girls waited for this moment, but the anticipation flowing through Abe's veins was more than noticeable.

"Will arrive on morning train stop
Be at State Line by 11:00 o'clock stop Signed Ola Grace
Jordan Ellison"

Holding the telegram in her hand, Urith rushed to the barn to read the contents of the wire to her father. In Abe's hurried excitement, he shortchanged the cow he was milking. He didn't slop the hogs, and knowing time was of the essence, he came into the house, shaved, washed his face, donned a clean shirt, then removed his one and only suit including the vest from its hanger. It was only on special occasions, like going to funerals, that Abe would make a pretense of dressing up in a respectable manner. As soon as the morning meal came to an end, the farmer rushed to the barn to hitch Jenny to the buggy. As the horse-drawn carriage moved from the barn toward the gate opening onto the gravel road, Abe yelled to his three daughters standing on the porch. "Her name is Mrs. Ellison kids. The youngin she's bringin' with her is still a baby, not much over a year old. It'll give ya girls somethin' to do by helpin' Mrs. Ellison take care of 'im!"

All the way to State Line Abe's mind was in constant turmoil. "Jes' hope this woman is right to care for my youngins'."

There was plenty of time to spare when Abe pulled the buggy next to a hitching post at the train's depot. He tied Jenny to the post then walked up and down the train's platform, nervous as a man about to be married to a mail-order bride. Thoughts that perhaps he had been too hasty in accepting the first reply to his ad crept into his mind.

There was no delay in the arrival time of the train. Ola Grace and Cecil were the only passengers to disembark at

State Line. Under one arm, the mother held her infant son, and with the other arm she struggled with the small suitcase. Before she could reach the last step from the train, Abe quickly took her bag and reached out his hand in a gesture of helping Ola Grace step onto the platform.

When the sun comes out and the storm clouds dissipate, turning the heavens into an azure blue sky, so it was with Abe. He had not seen such a beautiful woman since the day he married Clara. Gently, he helped Ola Grace and Cecil into the buggy. Although it was springtime, the air continued to have a bit of a chill. Abe came prepared. He brought extra blankets to keep the mother and baby warm. After tucking the blankets around Ola Grace and Cecil, he untied Jenny from the hitching post. He took the reins in hand, and Jenny moved forward onto the gravel road that would lead the newcomers to Abe's farm.

Abe wanted to talk—he wanted to laugh. "If this woman, even if she's younger than myself, can bring the love and warmth this house shared with Josephine, I certainly made a right decision." Ola Grace's beauty reminded him of his first love, the teenage girl he courted, wed, and who gave birth to his first child, Marie.

The sound of the horse's hoofs and the buggy entering the open gate at the farm was cause for Abe's three daughters to rush onto the back porch in anticipation of meeting the new housekeeper. Abe helped Ola Grace and Cecil disembark from the carriage, then proceeded to the barn where he unharnessed Jenny. The children took an immediate liking to Ola Grace—it was an immediate bonding that would endure a lifetime. As for Cecil, it was as if they had suddenly been blessed with a baby brother.

Ola Grace found her new environment a welcome relief from the tortuous years spent with Harry Ellison. For the first time since Ralph was born, she felt safe, and even though Abe was old enough to be her father, she admired him. He had no bad habits. He hated vulgarity or swearing and he didn't drink. There was no pipe tobacco smoke polluting the air and staining the plaster walls. The house of Abe again rang with laughter and song.

CHAPTER 5

IT WASN'T THAT ABE HAD any objections to people who went to church or chose to worship that way, his solace came from working with the earth and farming the land. He did however, once his housekeeper was settled, ask as to whether she attended church. Josephine and his children had been regular churchgoing people at the small country church only a mile or so down the road from the farm.

"I always went to church, Abe. But when I married Harry Ellison, it jes' didn't seem like goin' to church was gonna change anything. I do miss the fellowship though. If you want me to go with the kids to Sunday school and church on Sunday morning, I'd be glad to accommodate ya."

Ola Grace was blessed with an infectious laugh. Her wit and good humor infiltrated the minds of each one of Abe's children. It took no prodding to get the youngsters off to school or prepare them to go to church on Sunday morning.

On the seventh day of the week, Abe would crowd his family into the buggy, deliver them to the house of worship, then return to the farm to putter around the barn, repair weatherbeaten fences, or clean manure out of the barn stalls. When these chores were done, he returned to the church to pick up his family. The rest of the day Abe rested. Certain

Biblical traditions, the farmer respected. Number one, only the most menial tasks were to be performed on the Sabbath.

Abe's children had the greatest love and devotion for their father. Life was calm and happy in the house of Abe, providing his rules were followed and never broken. It was when Abe's rules were violated that a different man emerged.

It happened on a cold, winter morning when the breakfast meal came to a close. Abe had been very solemn during the entire meal, saying nothing to the children or to Ola Grace. He rose from the table then spoke to Helen.

"Helen git in the woodshed. I don't have any respect for thieves or people who tell lies, and I believe you stole and ya lied. Tears welled in Helen's eyes. She ran from the house, out through the kitchen door and into the woodshed. Abe followed.

When the door to the woodshed closed, screaming and the sound of a freshly cut switch swished through the cold, crisp air and down upon the young girl's buttocks. The father was sparing no mercy in what he thought was just punishment.

"Please I—Papa!—Don't Papa! Please don't hit me again. I didn't steal Ethel's hat, Papa. We traded hats! Ethel and me. Ya can ask Urith! My ear hurts, Papa, and Ethel's hat keeps my ear warm."

"Yer ear hurts?!" Abe retorted as the switch brought another stinging blow to Helen's body. "I'll show ya a sore ear!" The irate father held the switch in one hand and with the other his open palm slapped the sobbing child on the side of the head. "You're gonna end up in the house of correction, that's what's gonna happen to ya. If ya can't live by my rules, then maybe ya can live by the rules of them women dressed in black over at the nunnery!"

Helen put her hand over her throbbing ear as Abe thrust open the woodshed door. "Git in the house!" he shouted.

Ola Grace could see Helen running, holding one hand over her ear. She quickly opened the door and as the child entered, the young housekeeper protectively placed her arms around the sobbing youngster. Abe's steel blue eyes focused immediately toward the open kitchen door. He bolted like an enraged bull as he charged into the kitchen. "Git yer hands off my youngin! I'll do the whippins'. No kid of mine is gonna steal! There's no place fer liars or thieves in this house!"

Gently Ola Grace released the child's arms wrapped around her waist. "She didn't do nothin', Abe. Ya ought'nt whip yer kids like that."

Before Ola Grace could utter another word, Abe shouted, "Keep yer nose where it belongs, Oley. These are my kids—not your'n!"

Unsteadily Cecil toddled toward his mother with outstretched baby arms. He reached for the hem of Ola Grace's apron.

Switching his icy eyes away from the young housekeeper, Abe glared at Cecil. "What are you? A mama's boy? I ain't got no room fer sissies around here either." Abruptly, Abe turned toward the open kitchen door then stomped his way toward the barn.

The house of Abe no longer rang with music and laughter. Silence replaced the happy sounds of chatter around the supper table. Ola Grace pondered on just how long Abe would contain his anger and unforgiving attitude toward his daughter. More than a week passed since the time Abe doled his severe punishment upon Helen. The thought of his daughter stealing plagued the man. His hatred for the act he thought his daughter committed the more intense the evil thoughts passing through his mind seemed to multiply.

It was sometime during the night or early morning hours, a heavy snow fell. It was before the break of a new day that Abe left his room and went to the barn. Ola Grace heard him closing the kitchen door. She rose from her warm bed, changed Cecil's diaper, then added wood to the hot embers in the kitchen stove. A satanic presence seemed to fill every crevice of the room. There had been no words spoken to Ola Grace nor the children since the day of Helen's beating.

Quietly, Ola Grace climbed the stairs leading to the second floor of the house. Entering the room where the children were sleeping, she gently touched each child, telling them it was time to get up for breakfast and prepare for school.

Abe harnessed the horse then hitched the old mare to the sleigh. Taking hold of the reins, he guided the open sleigh toward the back porch and the kitchen door. Entering the kitchen, Abe spoke for the first time.

"Helen ain't goin' to school today. As soon as she eats her breakfast, I'm takin' her to the nunnery."

Ola Grace stared at Abe in disbelief. Tears welled in Helen's eyes. She knew her fate was decided and there was no way to change her father's mind. "I jes' hope ya know what yer doin', Abe," the young housekeeper uttered.

Abe glanced at his young housekeeper with a cold stare. The die was cast. Ola Grace bowed her head in prayer as she had done so many times before. The children closed their eyes and clasped their hands before them. In unison, the housekeeper and the three children uttered the usual blessing before partaking of food.

"Thank ya, Lord Jesus, for the food we are about to partake." Ola Grace continued the prayer. "Please good Lord, watch over Helen. Please keep her from any more harm. Amen."

With each attempt Helen made to raise her fork to her mouth in an effort to eat the food on her plate, the more she could feel the piercing eyes of her father.

"Hurry up, Helen," Abe ordered. "We gotta git goin'. Those women at the nunnery ain't gonna wait fer us all day."

Helen quickly rose from the table. She grabbed her coat and as Abe stood up, Helen rushed by him. Not another word was spoken as she climbed onto the sleigh. She had resigned herself to whatever would be her fate.

The sounds disrupting the early morning stillness came from the long, black habits brushing against the flagstone floor of the convent as the devoted religious sisters entered the chapel to celebrate morning Mass. Standing at the arched entrance leading into the small sanctuary stood a tall, austere woman. Like the other Nuns, she wore the same habit. All women dressed in black had taken their final vows to be a Carmelite, except for the presence of a few noviciates, young women who had either made a decision to one day take their final vows as a Carmelite or some who were placed in the care of the Nuns as a disciplinary measure for some wrongful act not pleasing to the child's parents or society. There also were young girls who, after their parents left them orphaned and no other family member was willing to take the responsibility of rearing the departed's offspring, were placed in the care of the Carmelite Nuns. The inhabitants of the convent would never leave the stone walls or the cloistered grounds surrounding the parklike setting housing the Carmelite Order.

Sister Angelica's stern, austere figure in black moved only

her eyes as she searched the soul of every Nun and Noviciate passing into the most holy place of worship. She was the Mother Superior who dominated the Holy Order contained within the stonewalls of the Carmelite's sacred convent.

Prayer books clutched to their breasts, the devoted 'brides' of Christ and the noviciates dipped the tips of their fingers into the holy water fount containing water cleansed and blessed by the priest during the previous Lenten season. Reverently each silent figure genuflected before the crucifix, then knelt on the prayer bench in front of their respective pew. Rosaries dangled from their delicate hands as there silent moving lips offered "Our Father's" and "Hail Mary's" up to the heavens for the redemption of sinners in the outside world.

Altar boys approached the altar to light the long, tapered candles on the ornate altar then genuflected before the crucifix. The sound of the altar bell signified the beginning of early morning Mass. As the priest entered the altar and knelt before the crucifix, in unison, the Nuns rose to their feet. Latin prayers chanted by the parish priest would be the only vocal sounds the Nuns would hear throughout the day. At Communion, the women in black rose then moved silently toward the altar to accept the sacred body of Christ. The priest placed the holy wafer on each outstretched tongue with the acknowledgment each participant had accepted the sacred body of Christ, accompanying his words with the admonition—"Serve ye the Lord with fear, and rejoice unto Him with trembling; embrace discipline, lest you perish from the just way."

Hands clasped, their souls cleansed, prayerfully, each Nun returned to her pew, once again genuflecting before the crucifix then kneeling on her respective prayer bench. As the priest chanted the benediction, the Nuns rose to their feet, knelt, genuflected, crossed themselves, then quietly departed the holy sanctuary as they had entered. They were prepared to fulfill their daily duties in prayer and in silence.

Mother Angelica led the way into the dimly lit dining room of the convent. Each Nun took her place behind a pre-assigned chair as they waited for the Reverend Mother to be seated at the head of the table. With hands clasped before them, the Nuns seated themselves then waited for the Reverend Mother to offer grace. Only two lighted antique kerosene lamps placed in the center of the long table broke the darkness of the early morning. Flickering flames inside the spotlessly polished lamp globes reflected moving shadows on the bare walls. Only a crucifix mounted on the wall above and behind the head of Mother Superior and an oil portrait of the reigning Pope on the opposite wall broke the sterility of the room.

The eyelids of the Reverend Mother never blinked or closed. Her bird-like beady eyes, even in prayer, seemed to search the soul's depth of each Nun seated at the table. Only a slight movement of Mother Angelica's rigid lips were visible as she gave thanks for the food each member of her flock was about to receive. Her long, beak-like nose served as a pointer toward any Nun or Noviciate who might in some small way disobey the rules of the Order. Any unkempt habit or action on the part of a young Noviciate or Nun was cause for dismissal. The offender would be forbidden to eat. She must return to her cell to do penance for the rest of the day.

Mother Superior maintained her office to the left of the ancient, solid wooden door leading into the convent. The four walls of the office were paneled in rich mahogany matching a large walnut desk which faced an oversized leaded window. Here Sister Angelica had an unobstructed view of the grounds and entrance into her realm. She could clearly observe any stranger or foe who might dare to enter onto these hallowed grounds. Long before the intruder could pull the rope attached to the bell hanging over the entry door, the sharp eyes of the Reverend Mother had already observed the presence of any newcomer.

This cold, snowy, morning was no exception. She watched as a small child and a man disembarked from a sleigh as it pulled to a halt in front of the massive wooden door that would remain closed or opened only at the discretion of the Nun.

The beady eyes of the Nun silently watched as Abe grabbed Helen's arms and led her toward the forbidding door. Before Abe could ring the bell, Mother Angelica opened the door just far enough to see and talk to the strangers.

"Yes?" she questioned. "What do you want?"

The cool, stern reception caused Abe to stammer. "I—I— have a youngin' here that's a thief. I can't make her mind. I've whipped her and she still ain't learnin' nothin'. It's my thinkin' you women here in this place might be able to do a better job raisin' her than I can."

Mother Angelica opened the door a bit wider. She looked down upon the frightened child. "How old are you? And what is your name?"

Helen chokingly tried to respond. "My name is Helen and I'm—I'm ten."

The Nun then opened the door far enough for Abe and Helen to enter into the massive entry hall of the convent. "Come in—and close the door." Directing her next questions to Abe, she continued. "And—what did you say your name was Mr.—"

"I'm Abe VanNatter and this girl here is my daughter." My wife died a few months ago and other than the help from my housekeeper, I've been tryin' to raise my three girls by myself. Helen here is the only one I've had a bit of trouble raisin'."

Turning away from Abe and Helen, the Nun moved toward the open corridor. "Let's go into my office and we'll discuss this matter further. You realize Mr. VanNatter, should you leave Helen in our care, you must sign certain papers permitting us to keep your child. You also must realize she will belong to us. You will be giving up all parental rights to your daughter. Helen will be treated like all our Noviciates who have chosen the solitary life of a Nun. It will only be at our discretion as to when or how often you may visit your daughter."

Mother Superior continued her chatter all the way into her spacious office. She walked to her desk then sat in a large leather chair. As Abe listened to the Nun's chatter, serious doubts began to cross his mind. Had he committed a terrible wrong by bringing Helen to this place?

The Nun opened the top drawer of her desk and withdrew a lengthy document. As she handed the paper to Abe she spoke. "Mr. VanNatter, read this carefully. We would not wish you to give up all your rights to your child unless you are absolutely certain and aware of our stipulations."

Abe's life had always consisted of total honesty and trust. The written word meant nothing to this farmer other than his ability to sign his name. He lived a life believing in other people's spoken word and he expected them to trust his. The only formal education the man received amounted to the first two years of grammar school. "She thinks I can read," he thought as he glanced through each page of the document. At the bottom of the last page, his eyes were drawn to a line which the Nun had marked with an "X". Quickly Abe signed his name at the appointed place. He handed the document to the Nun. Abe took one last glance at Helen, then turned abruptly toward the door leading to the corridor, the entry hall, and the heavy door. Moist tears filled his steel blue eyes as the door opened and chilly air brushed against his face. Boarding the sleigh, he motioned for the horse to move forward. For many weeks and months to come, Abe would be haunted by that final glance into the sad, hurt eyes of his daughter Helen.

CHAPTER 6

IT WAS A SMALL ROOM on the first floor of the convent. The only outside light filtering into the room came from a transom over the door and a small window high above a cot pushed against a bare wall. The room was furnished with a writing table and a straight back chair placed next to the cot. The thick plaster walls were void of any decor except for the suffering figure of Christ mounted on a cross. This emaciated, tortured being hung directly above the pillow where Helen would lay her head.

Mother Angelica gently took Helen's hand. "Come—I'll show you to your room, Helen. We refer to our rooms here at the convent as our cells. It's a place where we think about things we have done that are not pleasing to God. In the quietness of our cell, we ask God to forgive us for all those evil, unkind, and hurtful things we have done to ourselves and all those people who are close to us. As Carmelites, we have taken a solemn vow of silence, therefore, we do not speak. If you wish to speak, you must speak only to me.

Mother Angelica removed a large ring of keys from her habit. Finding the right key, she placed it into the door that led into the small cubicle. "This is your home now, Helen. I trust you will enjoy being one of us. Our day at the convent begins at 5:00 a.m. Inasmuch as our waking hours are devoted to our Lord and Savior, we open our day by attending Holy Mass in the chapel. Each morning you will rise no later than 4:30 a.m. At that time, you are expected to wash and dress yourself then one of the other Noviciates will come to escort you to the chapel. I will leave you now, Helen. When I return, I will bring you the proper clothing you must wear at all times here at the convent. Since you are a new member of our community, you will be referred to as a "Noviciate," meaning you have not taken a final vow in our order as condoned by our Holy Father the Pope who reigns in a far away land called Rome. Many young women, such as yourself, who arrive here at the convent join in taking their final vows to become the true bride of Jesus Christ. We trust, you too, someday, will become a member of our sacred order. A part of each day will be devoted to instructing you in the only true faith of our Lord. You will spend a part of your day continuing your studies as you did in public school. The remaining time before retiring at night will be spent performing duties assigned you by a supervising Nun. Those duties must be carried out to absolute perfection. Our discipline here at the convent can be most severe."

Turning toward the door and saying nothing further, the Nun left the room. Helen could hear the key turn inside the lock as the footsteps of the stranger left a lonely child plummeted into a solitary world she had not chosen.

Helen let her body fall upon the small cot. Sobbing uncontrollably, she buried her head in the pillow. "Why am I here? I didn't do nothin'." Her thoughts turned to running away, but how could she escape? The window was much too high for her to reach, and the door remained locked from the outside to her cell. Only when she was summoned for duty or given special instructions would she have contact with another human being.

The heavy sound of Mother Angelica's high button shoes could be heard approaching Helen's cell. The young girl could see the large key enter the keyhole and turn inside the lock. Over the Nun's arms, she carried a black habit similar to her own and a simple white scarf that would cover Helen's head. In her hands she carried a pair of high-button shoes which would reach far above the young girls's ankles.

"Remove your clothing, Helen. I will help you don the proper attire for our convent and that of a Carmelite."

Slowly, Helen unfastened her shoes and removed all her clothing except her panties. As Mother Angelica handed the young girl the bloomers she carried over her arm she spoke. "You must take your panties off, Helen. You will wear these bloomers under your habit."

Turning away from the Reverend Mother, Helen slowly slipped out of her panties and reached for the bloomers. As she did so, the Nun could plainly see the red, fiery stripes across Helen's buttocks as a result of a recent beating. Offering no comment as to what she had observed, the Nun took the long black habit and slipped it over Helen's head then helped her lace the heavy, leather shoes. She then placed a white scarf over the young girl's shoulder-length, black hair. "You are now one of us, Helen. You will be referred to as Sister Helen, the youngest sister to join the Carmelites."

Mother Superior departed Helen's cell. Once again, the ten-year-old faced the realization that the convent and the cell would be her home and her prison for the rest of her life. There was no escape from the punishment she must endure for a crime she never committed.

*   *   *

ABE NOT ONLY IMPRISONED HELEN, he incarcerated himself into his own solitary hell. No one could reach the tortured man nor would he permit another person to trespass into his troubled mind. Constant thoughts of Helen ceased to leave his conscience. Her pathetic cries often awakened him from a deep sleep. When he chopped wood, she was there. He could still hear her pathetic cries as the freshly cut switch slashed against the tender skin of her buttocks and across her back. Memories haunted him with an indelible mental picture of Helen being abandoned and the frightened look of the child as she stood alone in the presence of the woman in black. He had committed a terrible wrong. His evil actions were unforgivable. His memory refused to let go of the mind's imprint of a Nun resembling a huge hawk prepared to take flight carrying his daughter away never to be seen again. The reality of his unforgiving deed became a reality when the heavy door leading into the solitary world of the Carmelites closed and he sealed his daughter's fate.

Springtime rains turned snow into slush, and new blades of grass crept through the soggy earth. With the approaching summer, Abe's long period of silence began to fade. An occasional smile broke across his stoic face, and there were times one could hear him whistling a tune echoing from the barn. Although few words were spoken at mealtime, a noticeable twinkle in the father's tired, blue eyes would react to remarks passed between Ola Grace and the children.

For weeks and months, the young housekeeper had taken great care not to mention Helen's name. Like springtime ushers in the sunshine and the kitchen table was set for the morning meal, a different, smiling Abe opened the kitchen door. With a quick stretch of his arm, he grabbed Mildred, gently tickling her in the ribs. For the first time since Helen's departure there was laughter in the house of Abe.

"I'm goin' to see Helen today, Oley. Do ya wanna go? I'd be very much obliged if you'd go with me."

A surprised look flooded the face of the loyal house-keeper and the children. There was little doubt as to the response Ola Grace was going to give. "Are ya gonna bring Helen home, Abe? We've missed her so very much. I missed her and I know'd her sisters have too."

"I jes' might, Oley. I jes' hope they'll let me see her and we ain't gonna have no trouble. Helen's learned her lesson by now and it's time she comes home. I did sign some papers, though, the day I took Helen in there, and I've been wondering what signed. I know'd I ain't been very agreeable since the day I took her there, and I know'd I made a terrible mistake puttin' Helen there, but—dag gummit!" Abe's voice choked. He barely controlled his tears as he made an attempt to continue.

Ola Grace rose from her chair then walked to the back of Abe's chair. Gently and compassionately, she laid her hand on his shoulder. "I think, Abe, you'd better go git Helen by yerself. I'll stay here with the girls. If they let ya visit Helen, I know'd yer gonna have lots to talk about. You jes' don't need someone else taggin' along."

Mildred was always Abe's little princess. She could do no wrong and if she did err, then it had to be due to the influence of her older sisters. Oftentimes, when Urith and Mildred were alone in their beds, they would look at the cot Helen always shared with Mildred. Now Mildred slept alone. The sisters, in the quiet of the night would talk, wondering if the right thing to do was to tell their father the truth. They were well aware that if their father knew his youngest daughter had lied when she said, "Helen stole the hat," Abe's wrath would no doubt break forth on his fair-haired child. She would receive the most deadly beating of her entire life.

When Abe announced he was going to see Helen and he might bring her home, Mildred decided to confess. She could only hope she would not be the next victim to be sent to the woodshed. "Papa—" Mildred spoke as Abe stood and prepared to leave the table. "Yes, Angel—what is it?" Abe returned to his seat. He reached out toward Mildred and as he did so, she climbed on his lap. "Now—what is it that's so dag burn important ya gotta tell me now? If I'm gonna git yer sister, I gotta git goin'."

Frightened, not because she had told a lie, but of the consequences once her father knew the truth, Mildred began to speak. "Papa—ya know ya always told us to tell the truth no matter what and I'm gonna tell ya now. I saw Helen take her hat off and give it to Ethel. Ethel then took her hat off and give it to Helen. She didn't steal the hat, Papa. It was nothin' like that. Ethel give the hat to Helen. I lied Papa! As Mildred tried to speak, her eyes filled with tears and her voice sobbed from the inner pain of confession. "I know'd I deserve a lickin' Papa, but please don't put me in that place where ya put Helen."

In cold disbelief Abe stared at his youngest daughter. She was no longer the apple of his eye. He wanted to slap her, but instead, he quickly removed her from his lap. Instead of punishment, he focused his attention toward Urith "Is that right, Urith? Is Mildred telling me the truth?"

"Yes, Papa." Urith quickly responded. "It's true. I wanted to tell ya, but you were so mad and I know'd ya never believe me. We know'd Mildred is yer favorite and you'd believe her before you'd believe me or Helen."

Abe's entire body trembled with anger as he rose from the table. Without another word, he grabbed his coat. As he walked through the kitchen door into the barnyard, one could hear him mumble. "I'm gittin' Helen outta there—now!"

Ola Grace, Urith, and Mildred watched from the kitchen window as the sound of rolling buggy wheels passed the kitchen door then disappeared through the open barnyard gate.

Helen was coming home!

MOTHER ANGELICA SAT BEHIND HER desk marveling at the trees whose branches were now cloaked in rich shades of green. Blades of grass that had slept through the long winter under the deep snows carpeted the grounds of the convent in a richness only God could create. She was pleased with Helen's progress and was certain the young girl was a perfect candidate for becoming a Carmelite. She had taken well to the Catechism and a time was set for the young girl to be baptized and confirmed as a member of God's only true church. The Reverend Mother's thoughts were suddenly interrupted when her eyes focused on a horse and buggy entering the grounds of the convent at great speed. She could hear the voice of Abraham VanNatter as he brought his horse to a halt directly in front of the convent door.

"Whoa—Jenny. This ain't gonna take long. I'll be back in a minute." Abe jumped from the buggy and seemed to levitate above the three or four steps leading to the front door of the convent. Firmly, he grabbed the rope attached to the doorbell.

Frozen into a fixed stare at the figure standing on the doorstep of her convent, Mother Angelica hesitated, wondering how the man had the audacity to return and just what did he want?

Abe pulled the rope again and again. When there was no response, he began to pound on the door with his iron, weatherbeaten fist.

Through the closed door, the Reverend Mother's voice pierced through the heavy door. "What is it you want, Mr. VanNatter? I believe I made it quite clear you are not to come here unless you have been invited." The Nun's voice not only penetrated the heavy door but it also echoed throughout the long corridors of the convent like a second-rate opera singer.

"I wanta see my daughter!" Abe angrily yelled.

Slowly, the Nun unlocked the great door. She opened it just far enough to stare into the angry eyes of Abe. "You cannot see Helen. You gave her to us many months ago and she now belongs to God. I was certain you understood when you signed those papers requesting we raise your daughter, you no longer had parental claim. Now go away! No, you may not see Helen nor may you visit her."

The Nun's announcement turned Abe into the angry rage of a cornered animal. "Listen woman—and ya listen good! I ain't here to cause no trouble but—I'm here to see my youngin' and I'm gonna see her now! Ya either let me in this place or I'll knock the dag burn door down!"

In a semblance or an attempt to calm the irate father, the Nun replied. "All right—you may see Helen, but you will not speak with her. There is a small glass in the door leading into her cell. I am only permitting you this privilege so you will see your daughter is well and has adjusted to our way of living."

The great door opened and the Nun permitted Abe to

enter. Without further dialogue, the sister led the irate father down the wide corridor toward a tiny cubicle. Through a small glass in the locked door opening into Helen's cell, Abe could see his young daughter sitting at her desk writing. She was totally unaware she had a visitor. No longer was she the little girl Abe abandoned many months prior. Her long beautiful black hair which had draped around her shoulders had been cut short, and a white headdress covered her head. Her childlike body was clothed in black, her garment reaching to the floor. On her feet were black shoes laced above her ankles. Her face was pale and expressionless. It revealed a face of total resignation to her fate.

"She's one of them!" Abe's thoughts caused an irretrievable anger to flood his body and blood to rush to his face. His mouth was dry and with a husky voice he spoke. "I want my daughter outta here! I'm takin' Helen home! Now!"

"Oh, no! Mr. VanNatter!" Focusing her dagger-like beady eyes toward Abe, the Nun's sweet, saint-like aura sent her halo for a loop replacing the woman's holy presence into one of Satan's own angels. "You signed those papers! Remember? Your daughter belongs to us and to God!" The Nun's voice reverberated higher and higher as she shouted her caustic remarks toward the irate father. Suddenly, she realized she was out of control. She had succeeded in lighting a fuse that turned Abe's anger into an erupting volcano.

"Unlock this door, woman or I'll tear it down!" Abe ordered. "I want my youngin' outta here and I want her out now!" Abe's voice raged and roared throughout the empty, wide corridors. "Ya either let me have my youngin' now or I'll git the law into this! Ya stole my youngin'! I'm sure the judge will have somethin' to say."

The Reverend Mother had underestimated the man. She was of a firm conviction he cared little about the welfare of his child. She did know she wanted nothing to do with the law or any outside authorities trespassing into her world or the world of the Carmelites.

"All right! — You may take your daughter! But — not before you sign papers releasing her from our care." Nervously, the Nun took a ring of keys from the pocket of her habit. Finding the correct key to Helen's cell, she placed it in the lock of the door. The latch turned and the door opened. As Abe and the Reverend Mother entered Helen's prison, Abe ordered, "Git those clothes off my daughter! Where are the clothes Helen wore when I brought her to this pit of hell?"

Helen turned her eyes away from her desk. "Papa?" she questioned. "Papa—Papa! I didn't think you'd ever come for me." Abe opened his arms and Helen ran toward him wrapping her small arms around his waist. "I missed ya, Papa! I missed ya awful bad! Take me home, Papa."

Abe's voice choked as he spoke. I'm takin' ya home, Helen. I'm mighty sorry for what I did to ya. I'm takin' ya home and they're all waitin' for ya back at the farm. I hope ya can forgive me, Helen. Mildred told me this mornin' she was the one that lied.

Mother Angelica wasted no time exiting Helen's cell. "I'll get Helen's things," she muttered as she angrily turned on her heels then passed through the open door.

A young Nun approached the Reverend Mother, curious about the upsetting argument echoing throughout the open corridors of the convent. Before the Nun could speak, Mother Angelica's mouth blurted out an order. "Get Helen's belongings she wore at the time of her arrival. She's leaving the convent!"

The sunshine of spring broke through the white clouds as Helen and Abe boarded the buggy. To leave the convent was the feeling a prisoner must feel when he has been declared innocent and freed from the gray walls of a prison. All the way back to the farm, Helen chatted like a magpie determined to tell her story and the entire world had come to listen. Ola Grace and Mildred waited at the open gate, rushing out of the house at the first sound of a horse's hoof echoing against the graveled road. The house of Abe once again rang with laughter and song as Ola Grace placed the main meal of the day on the old table, said her usual prayer of thanksgiving, then it was fun, laughter, and singing as Abe reached in his bib overall pocket and withdrew his harmonica.

All was well in the house of Abe. There was always music and song. Summers passed, then fall and winter marking the years Ola Grace was an employee in the house of Abe. With each season there was growth to Abe's daughters. All the girls were in their teens. Cecil too, had grown and was now capable of doing small chores around the farm to help earn his keep. Then there was the advent of spring one year that did not arrive like a gentle lamb. The Ides of March charged across the open Midwestern prairies like a roaring lion. The old adage about the month of March was as true then as it is now—in like a lion and out like a lamb.

The remaining scars and wounds caused by Helen's incarceration at the convent were never reopened or mentioned. The passing years had given Ola Grace a sense of security and well-being, almost to the point of blocking out the darkest period of her life. She had more than fulfilled Abe's expectation as a housekeeper. She had learned to love Abe's daughters as if they were her very own. The children matured rapidly, including her own son, Cecil. He remained a quiet youngster, always listening but rarely speaking. If he did speak, it was never to Abe. Even at his tender age, he knew the man of the house only tolerated his presence.

CHAPTER 7

THE TOWN OF WEST LEBANON hadn't changed nor had the habits of Harry Ellison. He appeared, however, more often at the yellow house on Fourth Street after Ola Grace's departure, but rarely showed any love or affection toward his son, Ralph. The town's saloon and the brothel on the second floor of the town's watering hole remained Harry's world.

Flo Barnham joined West Lebanon's ladies of the night at the youthful age of 17. As far back as she could remember, her body had been used as a sex tool for her dad and her brothers. It was no coincidence, when she reached maturity and could leave the confines of her parents' custody, she realized those sexual favors she had been forced to give away could now be used as a source for earning a living. Within a short time after her arrival in the village of West Lebanon, Flo Barnham was known as the most notorious and most sought after prostitute in town.

Harry Ellison was the last customer to leave the saloon on that fateful night in March. Stepping out on the dirt and graveled street, violent wind pushed against the intoxicated man like a giant earth mover. He tried to reach the stairway leading from the street to the second floor above the saloon, but the force of the wind became an impenetrable wall.

From her window in the brothel on the second floor, Flo Barnham watched the struggling intoxicated man as he pushed his drunken body against the wind. Harry Ellison's body could no longer endure the force of the wind and he fell to the ground. The prostitute rushed down the stairs. Her voice pierced the swirling wind. "Harry! Harry! Are ya okay, Harry?" There was no response. Pushing herself against the force of the wind until she reached the unconscious man, she screamed, "Please! Please! somebody help me!"

The compassionate whore locked her arms into Harry's armpits, and with all the strength her delicate feminine body could muster, she pulled Harry toward the two steps leading from the graveled rutted street to the door of the saloon. She rapped and pounded on the door, hoping the bartender, Joe, was still there.

The pounding on the saloon door rose above the noise of the wind whipping around the building. Joe quickly unlocked the tightly closed door. Against the force of nature's rampage, he and Flo Barnham dragged the stilled body of Harry Ellison inside. Flo felt for a pulse in the man's neck, there was none. West Lebanon's town drunk was dead!

Harry Ellison's passing from this life to the next exuded relief instead of sadness. His earthly journey had totally been immersed in an alcoholic torture to a point of no return and now it had come to an end. It was a welcome relief not only for Ola Grace, the man's elderly mother and father, but also his son.

Under the care of his grandparents, Ralph flourished. He had more than filled the deep void left by their own wayward son. Mother Ellison had long since reconciled her differences with Ola Grace. There was more respect for the woman who had borne her son's children than at any time Ola Grace's relationship with the Ellison clan existed.

Ola Grace, over the passing years, visited Ralph. Abe was kind and would often encourage his housekeeper to visit the Ellisons. Ralph and Cecil were closely bonded together. Even though the one family the young mother desired never came to pass, the fleeting years would cement a firm relationship between the two brothers that time and distance would never destroy.

JESSIE ARMSTRONG WAS JOSEPHINE'S YOUNGEST sister. It was never given a thought the spinster lady would marry. Not because she wasn't good looking, in fact, her petite figure and cheerful personality should have been a catch for any eligible bachelor. She settled in Attica, Indiana, shortly after Abe married Josephine. As each one of Abe's daughter's were born, Jessie took a possessive attitude toward the children, believing Josephine had brought them into this world more as a surrogate mother on behalf of her sister, Jessie.

After the severe winter and the influenza plague that swept the farm belt away from the house of Abe, Jessie just assumed Abe would let her raise the three girls as her own. That was not the case. Abe stood firm in his commitment to his three daughters, to raise them as best he could as a single parent. He was often haunted by the circumstances that took away his first daughter, Marie. Over the years, his mind wondered about his firstborn. What did she look like? Did she resemble his first love, Clara, and was she having a safe, secure life? With the death of Josephine, Abe was determined to keep his family intact. In spite of the pressures Jessie placed on the devoted father, Abe refused to be swayed as to Jessie's persistence.

Many times, during those formative years of Abe's daughters, Jessie had written and pleaded with Abe to at least let the girls get away from the farm during part of the summer months, but it was always the same refusal. "No, they were needed to help out on the farm." Jessie did finally accept Abe's rejections after he hired a housekeeper and it was certain the girls would have a semblance of a male and female influence to balance their growing years.

Another letter arrived from Jessie. She had gotten married. She lived in a big house and would be most pleased if Abe would consider giving his daughters a taste of city life by permitting them to visit she and her new husband in Attica.

Jessie was always involved with her church. That was the extent of her social existence. There was a problem, however; all the men who might be a good catch had spouses and to lure a man away from his spouse was an unforgivable sin.

This all changed on a Sunday morning when a German immigrant entered Jessie's church. It was only a coincidence there was enough space on the pew to permit one more body to squeeze into the empty seat next to Jessie. Jessie's body and the German's body touched. Not only did their bodies touch, but a chemical reaction rushed through each person's body that was definitely positive. The foreign stranger took advantage of the shy, spinster lady sitting next to him by inviting her to dine. That was the beginning of a new existence for Jessie Armstrong. Karl Schultz asked Jessie to marry him.

Foreigners were not readily accepted in the provincial

town of Attica, Indiana. Any person with a strong, foreign accent when he spoke was always suspect of being some kind of spy for an alien nation. Karl Schultz was soon referred to as "Dutch." The man with a heavy German accent caused eyebrows to raise, and the town gossip immediately became food for imaginations to run wild whenever the new amour of Jessie Armstrong was mentioned. Nevertheless, regardless of the wave of suspicions and the wagging of vicious tongues inside the church and throughout the community, Jessie said, "Yes," to Dutch's proposal. Jessie was a happy woman.

No one ever knew how or why Dutch Schultz entered Jessie's church on that particular Sunday morning. No one knew how or why Dutch Schultz had money as his neatly dressed appearance always indicated along with the fancy team of horses and streamlined buggy he comfortably rode in as he traveled the streets of Attica. When the nuptials were announced between Karl Schultz and Jessie Marsh, Dutch chose to purchase for his new bride one of the finest houses in the best residential section of Attica. It was a large house, much bigger than any place Jessie had ever lived. Jessie longed to share the big house with her beloved sister's children. It was shortly after the marriage, Jessie, with Dutch's approval, wrote to Abe in an another attempt to have his permission to let the three girls come to Attica just for the summer months.

The note bothered Abe. He couldn't read the contents of the letter, so he confided in Ola Grace about the situation and she read the note to him outside the hearing of the three girls. Thoughts of perhaps it might be good for the girls to get away from the farm ran through his mind. They were maturing rapidly, and Jessie's invitation sounded reasonable.

There were problems, however. Would his devoted housekeeper agree to stay on after his girls left the nest? If she should decide she had fulfilled her duties and there was no further need for her services, how was he going to cope without her? Ola Grace had become indispensable.

After reading the letter to Abe, Ola Grace, too, had second thoughts. She was concerned about the girls' leaving. Abe would have no more need for her service and she had her son to care for until he was old enough to face the world on his own.

A worried Abe took his place at the supper table. He waited for Ola Grace before he spoke. He had not mentioned Josephine's name at the table or in general conversation since her death. At suppertime, for the first time since the demise of his wife and the mother of his children, he began by saying how they had been so blessed the day Ola Grace entered their lives. How she had made a good home for his motherless family. He spoke of her unselfishness and how Josephine would have been proud to know her daughters were in such good care.

"Now—" He treaded lightly on the subject of Jessie's invitation. "A few days ago, girls, I received a letter from your Aunt Jessie. I believe I may have told you about her marrying that foreigner from across the sea. We always called them Germans 'Krauts.' I suppose it's cause they invented 'Sauerkraut,' which we've all eaten plenty. Your Aunt Jessie apparently lives in a big house now and she wants all three of you girls to spend the summer with her. Now—it's up to you girls. If ya wanna go to Attica and Ola Grace approves, then I'll consent to lettin' you go."

Excitement rattled the rafters of the large kitchen. Of course, the girls wanted to go. They loved their Aunt Jessie.

They had never been to a big city. Their small world had never extended much further than the farm. The anticipation of living in a town as big as Attica on the other side of State Line was beyond containment.

Careful not to show her concern, it was a grave matter confronting Ola Grace. Supposing the girls remained in Jessie's care for the summer and did not want to return to the farm? There would no longer be need for her services. Thoughts of having to search for another job were frightening. Cecil was in school. She had to support her son. She knew to remove her son from school and his chance to get an education would be unthinkable. Education would be the boy's only salvation for surviving in a world that had been so cruel to him. She never understood why Abe didn't like Cecil, other than the fact he was not his own flesh and blood. She also knew Abe needed a wife, not just a housekeeper. With the girls no longer under his roof, he was free to go courting. He was still handsome and virile. He would have no difficulty finding another mate. It was a sleepless night for Ola Grace.

The school year came to a close. Summer vacation occupied the minds of every youngster from elementary grades through high school. Some finished their senior year and the time had come for their entry into the adult world. Urith was one of those teenagers. She anticipated leaving the farm and the excitement of living in the big city. Helen had one more year of schooling, and Mildred was close behind ready to enter her sophomore year when school resumed in mid-August.

At daybreak the following Saturday morning after the closing of the school semester, Abe, the three girls, Ola Grace, and Cecil climbed aboard the horse-drawn carriage. Before noontime, Abe's daughters would be on their way to Attica. Abe allotted plenty of time for arriving at the depot at State Line. It was a time of joy and also sadness as everyone stood on the open platform waiting for the train. When the wailing train whistle interrupted the stillness of the morning air, everyone knew the time of separation had come. Tears filled the eyes of each girl as they paid their farewells to the only person who filled what would have been an unthinkable void in their lives had it not been for Ola Grace and Cecil. They had accepted Cecil as more of a brother than a child who did not belong. Each girl embraced Ola Grace, placing a tender kiss on her cheek. Through the tears, each of Abe's daughters whispered into the young mother's ear. "Thank you, Mama—we love you." Ola Grace Jordan Ellison would never again be referred to as Mrs. Ellison.

The conductor stood on the steps leading onto the train. "All Aboard!" he shouted. As each girl stepped aboard the train, a heavy sadness remained with those left standing on the platform. Abe knew and Ola Grace knew there could be no retrieving the past. No longer would the idle chatter and teenage giggles be heard around the kitchen table or would the walls of the farmhouse echo the happy sounds of Abe's children.

Silently, Abe, Ola Grace, and Cecil stood on the platform until the train began to move and only the caboose could be seen as the train turned the curve then disappeared in the distance. In silence, Abe, Ola Grace, and Cecil walked toward the buggy. Cecil climbed into the backseat. Gentlemanly, Abe assisted Ola Grace onto the seat next to where he would sit then he untied the horse from the hitching post.

Boarding the driver's side of the horse driven carriage, he lightly touched the reins against Jenny's back. There was no need for a command from Abe. The horse seemed to know the time had come to move on.

"Ya know, Oley, we don't hafta git back to the farm. State Line ain't so far from Danville; why don't we jes' keep goin' and see what the town is like? I don't know about you, but it's been a long time since I've been there and I jes' bet ya there's a million and one changes in that town."

The streets of Danville bustled with traffic. Even though it was a time when the horse and buggy reigned as man's main source of transportation, a new era for travel was born. Instead of the sound of horses' hooves digging into the dirt roads, a din of purring engines filled the air to the tune of Henry Ford's Model T.

Abe's fascination with the new invention had endured since the first model came off the line. Many neighboring farmers had already invested in one of those new horseless carriages. Abe loved his aging, four-legged friend, but he also was conscious of her gait getting slower. She could still pull a plow and till the soil, but it was only a matter of time before she would have to be replaced with a younger horse, so, like his progressive neighbors, he would have to join the horseless carriage age.

"Oley—how'd ya like to take a look at them new horseless contraptions everyone's gittin' and talkin' about? I think it's about time we git a little modern, don' you?"

In all the years Oley had served the house of Abe, she had never been a part of his decision making. She was only an employee and there was no reason to ask her opinion on anything. In fact, when she offered her opinion at the time he so brutally punished Helen, Abe wasted no time telling her to keep her nose out of his business. Not since that day had she permitted herself to become involved in any of Abe's concerns.

Abe continued. "We don't hafta git home right away, Oley. Jes' so we git there before dark and I can git the pigs slopped and the milkin' done."

Abe guided Jenny toward Main Street. On the corner of Main and First Avenue, a new two-story building replaced the aged brick building that had stood on that corner for a hundred years. A large, leaded picture window faced numerous hitching posts where visiting farmers could easily secure their horses. Looking from the street side through the huge glass window, the presence of Henry Ford's latest creation stood for all to see. Shining and new, the Model T Ford resting just inside the door of this magnificent showroom sparkled like a priceless jewel.

"Ain't that a beauty, Oley?" Abe questioned excitedly pointing toward the new Ford. "It ain't gonna cost nothin' to go in and take a look."

Cecil jumped up and down in the back seat of the buggy with an unrestrained excitement. "Let's go in and see it, Mom. Abe jes' said, it ain't gonna cost nothin' to take a look."

Abe brought Jenny to a halt then waited for a farmer to untie his horse directly in front of the showroom. As he tied Jenny to the vacated post, a sophisticated man dressed in an immaculate white suit suddenly appeared. Without waiting for an introduction or for the passengers of the buggy to disembark, the stylishly dressed gentleman rushed toward the buggy. His broad smile and over-bearing self-confidence was like a dog running after a rabbit. Like a first-class gigolo, he quickly went to the side of the buggy where Ola Grace was sitting. Holding out his hand in a gesture of helping her step from the buggy to the ground, he spoke. "I jes' know you people are gonna love taking a close look at that beauty sittin' there in our showroom. That baby is replacin' the horse, Mr.___?"

"VanNatter," was Abe's quick response. Without inhaling another breath, the salesman continued. "Now—you good folks jes' follow me. I wanna give ya a demonstration as to just what this beautiful girl can do."

Entering the showroom and standing next to the most recent model of a car to come off the line, the salesman removed a tool from under the front seat. He referred to the tool as a crank then placed it in a small hole just below the radiator at the front of the car. With one turn of his wrist, the engine engaged and began to purr like a contented kitten.

"How'd ya like to take a ride? Mr.?" Not waiting for Abe to answer, the salesman continued. "I have another one of these babies just like the one ya see here sittin' out there on our back lot. It's bigger than a buggy and can easily seat six people. Jes' follow me."

Abe, Ola Grace, and Cecil followed the tall, lanky salesman through the back door of the building.

"There! Would ya take a look at that beauty!" The salesman pointed to an open-air, topless vehicle a few steps from the back door. "I'd like to give ya folks the thrill of yer life. How about it? Now—come on! Git in there and make yerself comfortable. If ya don't decide to buy this baby after I take ya fer a ride, ya haven't lost a thing. It ain't gonna cost ya nothin' to experience and git a taste of man's greatest creation." The salesman opened the door to the back seat. Standing aside, he guided Ola Grace and Cecil into the vehicle. He then motioned for Abe to take his place in the front passenger's seat. As Abe obeyed the high-powered salesman's orders, the never-ceasing yakking vendor rushed around the car to the driver's side. Certain all his passengers were comfortable, the red hot salesman removed the crank from under the front seat as he had done with the vehicle on the floor inside the showroom, placed the crank into the crankshaft and with one easy turn, the motor began to purr. The salesman then hurried to the driver's side, replaced the crank under the seat, then took his place behind the wheel.

"Now—folks—hold onto yer hats!" The driver placed the car in reverse then slowly backed away from the parking area. Moving forward, the motor revved and the Ford took off like a nervous horse. Abe held onto his hat and Ola Grace grabbed the side straps fastened to the doors in the back. They had never traveled at such speed. It must have been at least 10 miles an hour, maybe more. The back wheels of the car sent up a cloud of dust that would easily blind anyone following the vehicle. After they traveled a few short blocks, the driver slowed the car to a halt. "Now, Mr.___ Mr.___, what did ya say yer name was?"

"Jes' call me Abe and that's Oley and her son in the back seat. She's my housekeeper. She's been takin' care of my youngins' who left for Attica this mornin'. The boy there is Oley's son, Cecil."

The salesman pulled the car to the side of the road then came to a complete stop.

"Now—Abe—yer gonna have the pleasure of drivin' this beauty. I'm gonna sit on that side where you sittin' and ya come over here and git behind the wheel."

Abe suddenly became a child who had just been presented a new toy. He jumped from the vehicle with the lightness of a gazelle and as the salesman scooted over to the passenger side of the car, Abe took his place behind the wheel.

"Jes' take yer time, Abe. Don't give it too much gas. This creature has the power of 20 horses, so start off slow."

Patiently, the salesman showed Abe where the clutch and brake were located on the floor. "Yer throttle control—that gauges the amount of gas yer givin'—is up here on the steering wheel."

Abe took to driving the car like he always owned one. The speedometer read 10 miles an hour, then 20. He knew he could easily go 30 but didn't dare take the chance. With ease, he drove the vehicle back to the dealership. He brought the car to a halt, then turned to Oley. "If we buy this thing Oley, do ya think you and Cecil could drive Jenny back to the farm?"

"Sure Abe—I think we can make it home. But—but—ya be careful with this thing—do ya hear?" She sounded like a concerned mother warning an adventurous son.

Abe turned toward the salesman. "Ya just made yerself a deal, Mr. Salesman."

Ola Grace and Cecil had just reached the outskirts of the city when they heard the sound of a horseless carriage behind them. The horn on the newfangled machine sent a nervous jolt through Jenny's aged body. Ola Grace tightened the reins, guiding the horse to the side of the road. A grin from ear to ear flashed across the face of the pushy driver in his man-made horseless carriage as he passed the stopped horse and buggy.

"Come on Oley—ya can do better than that! I'll beat ya home!"

THE SUMMER OF 1908 WAS a lucrative year for the farmer. The crops yielded an abundance of food, and the overall economy was at its highest peak. Indian summer was rapidly fading into a chilly fall. Abe's daughters were happy living with Jessie. A letter arrived pleading with their father to allow them to stay in the city a bit longer. They felt they could take advantage of a better education as well as having access to more opportunities. Abe was not elated over the girls not returning to the farm. That was not the agreement he had with Jessie; nevertheless, he finally reconciled himself to the fact it was probably best for his daughters. The news from Attica didn't say exactly what the opportunities were, such as meeting the opposite sex, for which there was a variety of male species to choose from in the big city. Nor did the letter mention Urith was quite stuck on a young hunk from the hills of Southern Indiana.

CHAPTER 8

OLA GRACE CONTINUED TO BE a great source of companionship to Abe, and there was nothing he desired more than to ask her to marry him. He needed a wife much more than just a housekeeper. The fact, however, his being 20 years older than his faithful servant haunted him. Night after night he tossed and turned, longing for someone to share the empty bed in which his three girls were conceived. Negative thoughts flooded his thinking as the idea of proposing passed through his mind. What if he proposed and she refused? If she did accept, she was in the prime of her child bearing years. Abe was not amiable to siring more children. Then there was Cecil. How could he deal with a kid who didn't belong to him? He could feel Cecil's animosity. He could feel Cecil's deep resentment. He never really liked Cecil. He only tolerated the child's presence in his house because he was Ola Grace's son. Whenever he attempted to chastise the lad, Ola Grace's feathers would ruffle and she immediately came to her son's defense. Time and time again she made it clear to Abe that he was never to lay a hand on her second born.

"He's got to earn his keep, Oley. Now ya jes' quit pamperin' that boy. Nobody owes him a livin' and he might as well start learnin' young," Abe would say.

Days passed into weeks and then a couple of months passed before Abe decided to approach his youthful housekeeper for a serious discussion about their relationship.

"Oley—I wanna have a talk with ya alone. There's somethin' on my mind that's been botherin' me ever since the girls went to Attica. It's Sunday mornin' and when ya git the vittles cleaned up, let's take a ride. Cecil's old enough to stay by himself and what I must say won't take long."

Unsettled thoughts rushed through Ola Grace's mind. Whatever Abe wished to say, she saw no reason why it couldn't be said at the kitchen table. Was he gonna tell her she was no longer needed? Perhaps, without her knowing, he could have found some woman he wants to marry. If that were the case, she would have to go searching for other employment. Maybe he decided he saw no reason why he should continue to support her and her son. Thoughts of ever marrying again had long since been tossed out of her mind. After her terrible ordeal as a wife to Harry Ellison, she resigned her self to living alone. She knew Abe didn't like Cecil. It was a two-way street; Cecil hated him. If it were a matter of choosing between some man and her son, her son would come first. She saved a little money from the salary Abe consistently paid, and even though it wasn't much, it was enough to sustain her and Cecil until she found other employment.

Ola Grace had great respect for Abe. She appreciated his honesty, but the manner in which he disciplined his children was totally unacceptable.

Abe completed the necessary Sunday morning chores in the barn. When he returned to the kitchen, Ola Grace had already prepared a large wash tub with warm water so he could take a bath. He usually took his bath on Saturday night before retiring, but on this particular occasion he decided to delay this weekly routine until Sunday morning. While Abe removed his clothing in preparation for the bath, Ola Grace and Cecil left the kitchen.

Sitting in the tub mulling over in his mind as to what he was going to say to Ola Grace, the water began to cool, then Abe stepped from the tub onto a towel to dry his nude body. He then shaved his overnight growth of beard and proceeded to dress in his only suit, dress shirt, and tie Ola Grace had previously draped over the kitchen chair. Fully dressed, he then called for Ola Grace and Cecil to come into the kitchen. "Are ya ready to go, Oley?" Abe said as Ola Grace removed her apron and hung it on the doorknob of the kitchen door.

"Yes, Abe, I'm ready."

Hatred flashed from Cecil's eyes like daggers into the eyes of the man whose steel blue eyes looked directly into his. The idea of Abe taking his mom away without him only added another layer of distrust and vehemence for his mom's employer.

"Cecil." Abe directed his comment to the young lad whose only security he ever had was about to be taken away. "What I gotta say to yer mom ain't gonna take long. It's jes' a matter of a little business I gotta git settled."

Ola Grace, not waiting for Cecil's response, spoke. "All right, Abe. I'd hoped to go to church this mornin', but I'm sure whatever ya gotta say might be more important than goin' to church."

Ola Grace placed a sweater around her shoulders that hung on a nail near the kitchen door. "Okay, Abe—Let's go."

Abe left the house to crank the Model T. Ola Grace put her arms around her son. "I'll be back soon, Cecil. Now don't ya worry and don't git into any trouble. We'll soon know what Abe has on his mind."

Neither Abe nor Ola Grace spoke as she climbed into the car next to Abe. The Model T rolled through the gate and onto the gravel road. Silently, they rode through the country-side, neither one speaking until Abe pulled the Ford to the side of the road, then turned off the engine.

"Oley—I've been thinkin'. Have ya ever thought about gittin' hitched again?" There was a cold silence to Abe's question. After a few seconds passed, Ola Grace got up the courage to speak. "Yes, Abe. I thought about it a lot. I thought many times how nice it'd be to have a man put his arms around me, but, when I think what I went through with Harry, I git scared. It makes me wonder if all men ain't that way. Once ya marry them, they think they own ya and can treat ya jes' like they'd treat a dog, like somethin' they own and ya cain't do nothin' about it. When those thoughts come into my mind, the idea of gittin' hitched disappears fast and in my heart I jes' know I'm better off alone."

Abe scooted closer to Ola Grace. Gently, he placed his arm on the back of Oley's seat, gradually letting it slide downward till it touched her shoulders.

"Please—Please, Abe. I ain't ready for that kind of stuff. I ain't never been with another man except Harry and I'm not jes' sure I wanta be."

"I'd like ya to marry me, Oley. I've learned to love ya an awful lot and you were mighty good to my girls. They couldn't a had a better mother." As Abe spoke, he reached for Ola Grace's hand.

"I gotta have time to think about it, Abe. I'm not gonna say yes and I ain't gonna say no. I jes' hafta think about it."

Abe gently removed his hand from the hand of Ola

Grace. Saying nothing further, he reached under the seat and removed the crank. Stepping out of the Ford, he inserted the crank into the crankcase and with two turns, the motor responded. Taking his seat beside Ola Grace, they began to move. Each person deep in their own thoughts, Abe, wondering if Ola Grace was going to refuse his proposal and Ola Grace confronting all the doubts rushing through her mind. In silence, they rode. The divorced, widowed mother retrogressed into the unpleasant memories of Harry Ellison and his sadistic ways. She never completely buried into nothingness the night Harry Ellison raped her and even though he was dead, she was haunted by his constant presence. She could feel and see his body the night he forced himself on her in the buggy when Ralph was conceived. Thoughts of how she was forced into marriage, all because she became pregnant against her will. Mental flashbacks of how her own mother rejected her. She could still feel the pain from Harry Ellison's beatings during his drunken stupors. Then there was that horrible night he came to her bed forcing himself inside her, again causing her to conceive another child.

The young mother lived in the house of Abe long enough to know just how good a man Abe was. He possessed many good qualities Harry Ellison never had. Even Harry's own mother and dad admitted he was a bad seed. Abe was good to her. Age difference never entered her mind. When Abe was happy, the whole world became a happy place. But— Abe had a dark side. She dreaded his mood swings. When this part of his personality turned from a pleasant, happy man to long periods of sulking and pouting, those times were unbearable. It was during those periods that the man had no interest in communicating with anyone, neither herself or his neighboring farmers. She had grave doubts about coping with these traits belonging to an individual with whom she would share the same house and the same bed. She was uneasy in her trust as far as her son or any children they might conceive. As for love, she did love Abe in a platonic sort of way. But—how could she be sure? For the second time in her life, she felt cornered. There was no place to run. Only destiny would decide her fate.

Hours passed into days and days passed into a week. Still, Ola Grace had not given Abe an answer. The farmer remained in good spirits and noticeably transmitted amorous glances at his faithful housekeeper. At times, he would try to reach Cecil with his present good humor. Cecil refused to be entertained.

Abe, although nonreligious, decided he would go to church with Ola Grace. After the bare necessities, such as milking the cows and feeding the livestock, he entered the kitchen, washed his face and hands, shaved his overnight growth of beard, then donned his one and only suit of clothes. When he seated himself at the kitchen table, Ola Grace and Cecil joined him to partake of the first meal of the day. Ola Grace and Cecil sat in amazement at the dressed up farmer, wondering what his next move was going to be. "Oley—I've decided I'm goin' to church with ya and Cecil this mornin'." Abe had no use for church—why the sudden change? These thoughts rushed through Ola Grace's mind.

When breakfast was over and Ola Grace had cleaned the dishes, she and Cecil put on their best Sunday clothes to go to church. Both Cecil and Ola Grace could hear Abe cranking the Model T. Mother and son said nothing as they left the house of Abe to board Henry Ford's horseless carriage. Abe was the first to speak.

"Oley—have ya been thinkin' about what I asked ya? It's

been a week now and ya ain't said nothin' about gittin' married."

A pain beyond anything Cecil ever experienced flooded his body. He wanted to jump out of the Model T and run. How could his mom even think of marrying this horrible man? He hated him and he would always hate him.

There was a patience and kindness in Abe's voice the young woman hadn't heard during all the years she spent with Harry. Ola Grace sat in silence, then spoke. "Yes, Abe—I've been thinkin' about it. I know'd ya need a wife and I need someone to care about me and my son. I loved yer girls like they were my own flesh and blood, and I'm thankful ya give us a roof over our heads when there was no place to go. But—I jes' couldn't stand to see ya whippin' Cecil or any youngins' we might have like ya did Helen."

Ola Grace opened a deep wound Abe thought had healed. "Ya know, Oley, the good book says, 'Spare the rod and spoil the child.' My dad lived by those rules. I can't tell ya how many lickins' I got. I got many a lickin' for doin' things not half as bad as what I thought Helen did. I know'd I did wrong, but there's nothin' I can do about that now. The past is past and I don't wanna bring it back. I promise ya, Oley, I can only say I'd be the best husband I can to ya. I would never hit or hurt ya like Harry did. He should have been horse whipped, tarred and feathered, and run out of town for what he did to ya. Maybe that's what should have happened to me when I whipped Helen and put her in that horrible nunnery. But—it jes' didn't happen and I was given a second chance to right that awful wrong."

When Abe, Oley, and Cecil arrived at the church and they parked the Model T, Abe spoke again. Gently, Abe placed his arm around Oley's shoulder. "I'll be good to ya, Oley. I jes' hope yer gonna say yes."

Cecil listened. Far back in the recesses of his young mind, he recalled the day Helen was beaten and taken away. Maybe that was the reason he hated the man so much. Since he and his mom arrived on the farm, they shared the same room and for a long time, the same bed. Now she would be sleeping in Abe's room and in Abe's bed if she agrees to marry him. The young lad had to think. He wanted to run. He wanted to be alone.

He rushed passed Ola Grace and Abe, then into the church where he took a seat in the very last row. Halfway through the church service, Cecil rose from the pew and ran out of the church. He wanted to keep running, running so far no one would ever see him again. Abe's proposal to his mom was something he wanted to totally block from his thoughts, but they were indelibly printed. Some day—some day—he would run away. Just as soon as he was old enough to take care of himself.

When the service came to an end and the preacher finished the Benediction, all the churchgoing members began to leave the church. Ola Grace's eyes searched for Cecil, but he wasn't there. Her concern didn't abate until she noticed her son sitting in the back seat of the horseless carriage.

Throughout the day, Ola Grace pondered Abe's proposal. It was at suppertime when she decided to give her employer an answer. She knew the hurt raging within Cecil. She could feel all the anger the lad felt like it was taking place within herself.

Placing a bowl of mashed potatoes before Abe and after serving himself, he passed the bowl to Cecil. It was only when she seated herself that she spoke.

"Abe—after I say grace, I'm gonna give ya my answer." Reverently, Ola Grace folded her hands. Her eyelids closed, she began to give thanks for the goodness bestowed upon her from her heavenly father. At the very end, she said, "and please good Lord, give me the right answers to these things that's botherin' me. God bless my good son, Cecil, and please protect him. God bless Abe for givin' us a roof over our heads all these years. Amen."

Her prayerful hands relaxed, she placed them on her lap then quietly turned her eyes toward Abe. "I've decided to marry you Abe. I jes' hope we're makin' the right decision. I suppose if love has anything to do with the years we spent here under yer roof then in a way, I guess I learned to love ya."

Abe's anxious look relaxed and turned into a broad grin. "I'll take good care of ya, Oley, and I'll be good to Cecil, too. Ya know'd if I earn a penny, I'll share it with ya. I'm gonna try to make ya a good home, Oley."

Abe pushed his chair away from the table then stood directly behind Ola Grace's chair. He placed his arms around her and gently kissed her on the neck. "Thank ya for sayin' you'd marry me. I'm mighty proud."

Cecil was alone on the small cot in the room he shared with his mom. He wanted to run away, but he knew he was much too young. He was alone and that loneliness would be his lot for the rest of his life.

CHAPTER 9

CLAUDE RAINBOLT WAS HANDSOME, WELL over six foot, and a country boy from the hills of Southern Indiana. Why his hillbilly upbringing brought him to Attica, Indiana, I don't know. He was a descendant of a Holland Dutch family who landed on these shores many generations before he was born or even a thought in the mind of Josh Rainbolt. It was in the hills of Southern Indiana near the Kentucky border the family settled and it was here that Josh Rainbolt, in a two-room mountain cabin, propagated the race by siring three daughters and two sons, Claude being the firstborn.

How Josh Rainbolt earned a living in these forsaken hills is an unknown quantity, but at some time during the period of their growing up, Claude Rainbolt and his sister Nellie believed there had to be something better in the great country of America than spending an entire lifetime overlooking the Ohio River into the blue grass meadows of Kentucky.

Why the virile, handsome young hillbilly migrated north to the provincial town of Attica, I don't know. I do know it was shortly after his arrival that he met Urith June VanNatter. Urith was the right age, and like a mature flower ready to be plucked, Claude Rainbolt was at the right place at the right time to do the plucking.

*Abe VanNatter's daughters June and
Helen by his second wife, Josephine.*

Abe's daughter Mildred by his second wife, Josephine.

Urith June's Aunt Jessie was steeped in her religious beliefs. She made certain as long as Abe's girls resided under her roof they would also abide by her rules to attend all meetings at the church, including Sunday morning services. Wednesday night prayer meetings and at least once-a-year revival meetings where every night of the week for a period of two weeks involved spending the evening hours at the church listening to excited evangelists indoctrinating the flock on the road to hell and the road to heaven. Having sex outside of marriage was strictly forbidden and an unforgivable sin. Marriage was the only answer for relieving the jumping hormones of those who were young and single. Sometimes the unions worked and sometimes they turned into a worse hell than the description provided by the visiting evangelists.

Claude Rainbolt attempted to pacify Urith by accompanying her to church, but, like a stubborn horse that refuses to budge, when the altar call was announced asking those sinners in the congregation to come to the altar and be born again, the young hillbilly quietly walked out of the church and waited for the sound of the final Amen and for Urith June to join him.

The social life of Jessie and Karl Schmidt was totally consumed with church attendance and church activities. Wayward and worldly young men and women were frowned upon as sinners. Until they changed their ways, they were destined to spend eternity in an unquenchable lake of fire. The church was where young people met and married. Any child born outside the sanction of wedlock was considered a bastard. That label would follow that child for his or her entire life.

Urith June VanNatter, although petite and the top of her

head barely reached the waistline of her intended spouse, was fully developed. She was pretty and it was no coincidence the relationship bloomed. She became Mrs. Claude Rainbolt.

Claude was a good provider. He worked hard but always as a laborer. Their marriage was consummated in a small apartment not far from the home of Jessie and Karl. During the first year of the union between Urith June and Claude, the young bride became pregnant and in the natural course of things, nine months later she bore Claude his first son. He was named Claude Rainbolt, Jr.

Two years would pass, then the Rainbolts were blessed with another baby, a girl, whom they named Lenora.

In the early 1900s, having babies was as common and natural as eating a good meal, providing it happened under the name of "marriage." It was totally expected marriage meant having children and if the children did not come, it was never the fault of the man. The woman was considered the barren one; consequently, the wedlock was looked upon with pity and compassion.

It was soon after the birth of Lenora that another Rainbolt decided to make her escape from the hillbilly environment of Southern Indiana. A penny postcard arrived at the already crowded apartment of Claude and Urith Rainbolt. It was from Claude's oldest sister, Nellie Rainbolt. Nellie Rainbolt not only hated her father, but like Claude, she knew there must be a better life than the crowded two-room house in the hills and the domineering lifestyle of Josh Rainbolt. Urith and Claude generously offered space for the newcomer until she could make it on her own. In fact, Claude sent Nellie a one-way train ticket from Evansville to Attica. Nellie arrived.

Nellie was an attractive young teenager with natural curly, sandy colored hair that framed her freckled face. Like Claude, she was big for her age, but not ungainly so. A teenager in the early 1900s, especially girls born into meager circumstances, had two choices. They could marry young and begin the chore of having babies, or they could find work that would support them whereby they might have a certain amount of independence. In Nellie's case, independence was far more important than the life of a married woman. She had no skills other than perhaps the job of a domestic, which involved scrubbing floors, cooking, cleaning house, and being an extra hand at watching over the more well-to–do folks' offspring so they could enjoy the freedom of single living totally independent from the care of their birthlings that usually came with married life.

Nellie was lucky. Upon the second day of her arrival, an ad appeared in the *Attica Gazzette*.

COMPANION AND FULL-TIME MAID WANTED

ACCEPTING PERSONAL INTERVIEWS FRIDAY 9:00 A.M.

That ad was about to transform Nellie Rainbolt's destiny from being a poor, poverty stricken youngster into Attica's most distinguished socialite.

Attica was a working man's town. No one among the blue collar laborers could afford a maid, no one except one family who owned most of the grain elevators throughout the State of Indiana. The name Vandeventer was as prominent throughout the Midwest as the nationally known names Rockefeller and Vanderbilt.

The Vandeventer mansion was secluded behind large

trees enclosed by a heavy, tall wrought iron fence and gate. It wasn't exactly the type of dwelling one would expect within the confines of the provincial town of Attica. The park-like lawn was neatly manicured, and on the balcony of the huge house above the main entrance a lacy, delicate green fern draped over the iron railing of the balcony displayed more of a tropical environment than one associated with the heavy winters familiar to the Midwest.

Nellie Rainbolt was the first person to respond to the help-wanted ad. Arriving at the address depicted in the ad, the waif from the hills shyly reached for the bell that hung alongside the huge iron gate. Just touching the chain to ring the bell, she heard the loud ringing sound of the bell echoing in her ears as she stood outside the iron gate that opened onto a walkway leading to the massive main door of the mansion. When the door opened a distinguished looking gentleman dressed in a cutaway suit with striped wool trousers let his well-trained voice speak so the unseen unexpected visitor was quite aware the bell had successfully announced their arrival.

"Yes," the man coolly spoke as his eyes suddenly focused on the simply dressed young girl standing at the gate.

Nellie was so much in awe of the place where she was standing and the sound of the man's voice she could hardly speak. "My name—my name is Nellie Rainbolt. The ad said ya needed a maid and I know how to clean. I need a job, Mister."

The man in the cutaway suit began to walk down the nar-row walkway. He could see Nellie through the wrought iron gate. After scrutinizing Nellie as if she might be a good piece of merchandise, he opened the gate and invited Nellie to en-ter. "Follow me, Miss. I will see if Mrs. Vandeventer will see you."

Nellie had never seen such grandeur. She obeyed the man's orders and followed him as he opened the massive door opening into the entry hall where a winding stairway led to the second floor. "Wait here," the man said as he began ascending the winding stairway. Standing alone, Nellie felt as if an eternity passed as she waited for the butler's return. Doubts flooded her mind. How could she ever believe the people living in this world of wealth could even think of giving her a job? She wanted to run—run and never come back to the only mansion in Attica.

The voice of the butler spoke as he stood at the top of the stairs. "Miss Rainbolt, Mrs. Vandeventer will see you now. Would you please follow me?"

Each step on the stairway seemed steeper as Nellie began the long climb from the entry hall to the landing on the second floor. Without uttering another word, the butler politely ushered the young girl down a long hallway to an open door.

Realizing the newcomer to the Vandeventer home had arrived, the rich dowager looked away from her desk and let her eyes focus on the teenage girl standing in the doorway. Peering over her pince-nez glasses, the kind woman spoke. "Come in child. Please sit there so I can get a good look at you." Mrs. Vandeventer pointed to a chair directly in front of the writing desk.

"Well—so you're Nellie Rainbolt. I'm glad to meet you, Nellie. You are much younger than I envisioned the person who would answer my ad. We were hoping, however, whoever responded to the ad would be a young girl and one just like you."

Quietly studying Nellie as she spoke, Adrian Vandeventer continued. "Do you think you would like to live here,

Nellie? We do need some young life in this drafty old barn. You see, Nellie, we were never privileged to have children. If you think you would like to join our family then we would be most happy to have you come and live with us. I'm sure Mr. Vandeventer would be very pleased too."

The arrival of Nellie to the Vandeventer mansion was an unexpected gift. Charles Vandeventer's fondness for the waif from the hills was as deep and profound as his adored wife's. From the beginning of that first moment of acceptance into the Vandeventer family, the young girl was never considered a maid or companion. She became the daughter Charles and Adrian Vandeventer desired but could never have.

Adrian Vandeventer began grooming the young hillbilly girl into the image befitting the Vandeventer's social status. Special tutors were summoned to the house to teach Nellie how to speak properly and to privately educate her in subjects she had not learned in the provincial public school. Nellie responded well to her new environment, and her newly adopted family showed great pride in her rapid progress. As time passed from one month to another, Adrian and Charles, during their private moments often spoke of adopting Nellie. They wanted Nellie as their very own. Unfortunately, this was never to be consummated. A tragic accident on a warm Sunday afternoon would forever change the life of Nellie Rainbolt.

It was the usual Sunday morning routine of going to church then returning back to the Vandeventer estate when Adrian decided instead of lunching at home, the sunny day was ideal for a picnic in the country.

The butler immediately began preparing a picnic lunch, one that could easily be packed and placed in the trunk of the large Hudson sedan. Without changing from their Sunday clothing to more casual attire, the family boarded the luxurious car and the chauffeur took his place behind the wheel.

The gravel country road leading from the city was narrow. Automobiles, particularly those luxurious vehicles that could only be afforded by the rich, were few. The progress of transportation and a faster way of travel was slow. The farmer and the ordinary citizen continued to rely on horses not only as a means of travel but also for hauling wagons loaded with hay.

It was during the casual ride along the country road as the chauffeur searched for an open meadow to have a picnic, a team of horses pulling a wagon load of hay encountered the horseless carriage. Hearing the sound of the man-made machine, the horses freaked. The chauffeur lost control of the car as he made an attempt to come to a stop on the grassy edge of the road. The horses bolted! Before the driver of the car could bring the vehicle to a stop, the wheels of the Hudson slid into a deep ditch bordering the gravel road causing the car to toss and turn then roll over twice.

The car came to a complete stop as it rolled over and landed in the middle of a cornfield. Moans and cries for help rose from the occupants of the vehicle. Only one passenger failed to respond with a cry for help. It was Adrian Vandeventer.

The farmer restrained his team of horses then jumped from the wagon to the ground. He ran to the turned over car. He was able to release Nellie from the vehicle. She was badly bruised but she could stand. Charles Vandeventer was unconscious. The chauffeur was also injured. When he tried to open the driver's side door, he realized his hand and arm were useless. His right arm was broken. The farmer managed to get the door to the car open then he helped the disabled chauffeur out of the car. Charles Vandeventer was beginning to regain consciousness. With the help of Nellie, both Nellie and the farmer were able to free the man from the wreckage. Nellie and the farmer attempted to release Adrian from where she was tightly trapped in the back seat of the car. At that time, they became aware no sign of life was noticeable within the body of the woman who made Nellie a permanent member of the Vandeventer family and a surrogate mother to the poorest of poor waifs from Southern Indiana.

The accident totally crushed the legs of Charles Vandeventer. His crippled body would forever be confined to a wheelchair. Charles Vandeventer, as Adrian became her mother, was the father Nellie longed for. During her early years and prior to the Vandeventer encounter, she spent her first few years harboring nothing but hate and disgust for her natural father.

Charles Vandeventer moved around the big house with the aid of a wheelchair and was able to regain a certain comfortable lifestyle all due to the tender care and devotion Nellie Rainbolt bestowed on the man who had become her admired and loved father figure.

Nellie developed into a mature young woman, and her devotion and love for the disabled widower never faltered.

It was one morning after the first meal of the day Nellie was asked to come into the library. Charles Vandeventer was conversing with a dignified gentleman whom Nellie had seen before but never knew his relationship to Charles Vandeventer. As Nellie entered the room, Charles Vandeventer spoke. "Nellie—this is Mr. Thompson. He is my attorney.

Throughout the passing years he has guided all my business ventures and personal family affairs. According to the doctor's diagnosis, I have been informed there is not much time left for me. There is, however, an entire lifetime ahead for you. My darling wife and I have often spoken of wishing to adopt you and making you our own legitimate daughter. Our only drawback was the fact we feared we might run into opposition from your own maternal parents. You are, Nellie, and have become the daughter we always wanted. My attorney and I have come to the conclusion, Nellie, providing it meets with your approval if you are to inherit your rightful place as heiress to this estate and to avoid any and all legal entanglements, the only alternative would be for you to become my wife. Now, mind you, my dear child, the marriage would be in name only. As you can readily see, I am in no condition to provide you with anything other than my name and my good fortune. If you would consent to this proposal to become my wife, I would be most grateful."

Nellie was shocked. She loved the Vandeventers. Adrian Vandeventer had become a second mother she loved as much if not more than her own mother. Charles Vandeventer was the father Nellie longed for during her entire young life. Without hesitation, Nellie Rainbolt accepted and became the second Mrs. Vandeventer.

Nellie nursed her husband as tenderly as if they had been predestined to spend their lives together. If there was a quality of life for Charles Vandeventer, it was Nellie who made that possible. It was in the early hours of a certain morning that Charles A. Vandeventer drew his final breath as Nellie tenderly held him in her arms.

Nellie never remarried. She lived alone in the big mansion except for the few remaining loyal servants who continued on as a permanent fixture to the Vandeventer mansion. The woman who began as a poor waif from the hills of Southern Indiana remained mostly a recluse, imprisoned within her own palace. She seldom was seen in public.

CHAPTER 10

ON SEPTEMBER 23, 1908, OLA Grace Jordan Ellison became the third wife to Abraham VanNatter. The couple left the farm at dawn, leaving Cecil alone to feed the livestock, milk the cows, and gather the eggs from the nests occupied by the laying hens.

It was nightfall when the Model T rolled into the outskirts of Gaston. Without explaining to Ola Grace, Abe suddenly turned onto a dirt road leading to a farmhouse far off the main road. Without questioning, Ola Grace let her eyes focus on a sign neatly printed on the side of the mailbox, "John F. Curley, County Justice of Peace."

"I guess this is jes' as good a place as any to git hitched, Oley." Abe spoke as the Model T approached a small, white frame house nestled in a clump of trees, a white picket wooden fence separating the house from the surrounding forest.

Ola Grace was tired from the long day's journey. She was deep in thought wondering if she were making the right decision. She worried about Cecil left alone on the farm. Abe had trained him well to handle responsibility, but still, Cecil was a young boy. Her freshly laundered and ironed dress, her only "goin' to meetin'" clothes, she donned as her wed-

ding dress, had lost much of its freshly starched and wrinkle-free appearance. Abe's Sunday suit was wrinkled and
looked disheveled as only those who have taken long jour-
neys in a Model T could understand. Nevertheless, the point
of no return arrived and Ola Grace would soon become Mrs.
Ola Grace Jordan Ellison VanNatter.

A short, balding, stocky fellow with pince-nez glasses
suspiciously responded to Abe's rap on the door.

"Are ya the Justice of Peace for this County?" Abe asked.
The unimpressive man nodded in the affirmative. "Well—
this beautiful woman here and me wanna git married. Do ya
suppose ya can do that fer us?"

The Justice of Peace glanced at Ola Grace then focused
his eyes on Abe. Thoughts of why a young woman would
marry a man old enough to be her father rushed through the
JP's mind. "Well—" the man stammered as if he wasn't too
sure the ceremony should be performed. "It's a bit late, but
if ya two whippersnappers are so dag burned determined to
take that final step before tomorrow morning, I guess I can
accommodate ya. Come in and make yerself at home, while
my Mrs. and me finish eatin' our supper."

The parlor of the public servant's home was arranged
more like a wedding chapel than a living room. There was a
podium and next to the podium rested an ornate reed pump
organ.

The Justice of Peace disappeared into another room leaving Abe and Ola Grace to wait in the parlor. Ola Grace withdrew a small bag from her purse and withdrew a couple
sandwiches she prepared before leaving the farm that morning. The couple had just finished eating when the Justice of
Peace returned to the parlor. The JP put his judge's robe over
his small stature then took his place behind the podium. As

Ola Grace and Abe rose from the sofa to stand in front of the judge, the man in the black robe bellowed out his wife's name. "Maybeline!—Maybeline! Come in here and stand up for these two upstarts. They wanna git married!"

A petite, shy little creature entered the parlor. She removed her apron, placing it over the back of the ancient, wooden rocking chair. Routinely, she greeted the two lovers, then said, "Before ya git hitched, would ya like a little music? I can play the organ and I can sing ya a little song. It'll kinda help ya git off to a good start."

Without waiting for an answer, the timid wife sat on the swivel stool placed in front of the ornate musical instrument. Her feet began pumping the bellows of the organ and her tiny fingers began to play a short introduction to a wedding song. A high, squeaky voice sent a chill up the spines of Abe and Ola Grace, closely resembling the sound of fingernails scratching on a piece of tin.

When the final strains of a love song came to an end, the elf-like housewife rose from the organ bench and took her place beside Ola Grace and Abe. The man who substituted for a preacher for many weddings quickly read the do's and don'ts of marriage and finally, he came to the part which read, "I now pronounce you man and wife."

Following the ceremony, the petite housewife returned to the organ and played a little more music while the two newlyweds signed the license. Finishing the final chord, she rose from the spiral organ stool, then waddled over to the small writing desk to add her signature to the marriage license as having witnessed the union. Abe and Ola Grace were man and wife.

Wedding day for Ola Grace Jordan and Abe VanNatter.
September 23, 1908.

CHAPTER 11

ABE'S DAUGHTERS BY JOSEPHINE MATURED into adulthood. As with all generations, as the young girls became mature, the opposite sex was predominate in their minds and the desire to have babies prevailed. It was a dashing young man from West Lebanon who would turn the eyes of Helen. His name was Bill Reynolds. How the two young lovers meeting came about, I am not privy to know, but it was soon after the birth of Lenora, Urith's second child, Bill Reynolds made his way to Attica. It was here he would accidentally meet Helen as he tied the reins of his horse to a hitching post and prepared to enter a feed store.

Bill was built a bit on the heavy side, and as people are often cruel, he was given the nickname of "Fatty." That name would follow him for his entire life, although he was far from what one would be inclined to think of as obese. Bill had a steady job at the grain elevator in West Lebanon. He could well afford to support a wife, and as the chemistry between Helen and Bill was mutual, the meeting of the two soulmates evolved into a wedding. West Lebanon would be the new home for Helen, and it would be here she would give birth to her first child, a daughter they named Dorothy.

Mildred was now the remaining sole unmarried daughter sired by Abe with Josephine. She had always been Abe's most cherished one of the three girls and always the apple of his eye. It was shortly after the birth of Dorothy that Bill Reynolds introduced a colleague to Mildred who worked alongside him at the grain elevator. His name was Loy Kiser. Mildred was the beauty of the county and Loy Kiser was equally as handsome. Bill Reynolds' introduction brought about a union between Loy Kiser and Mildred. Helen and Bill as well as Loy Kiser and Mildred would create their marriage nest in West Lebanon and that would be where the two sisters and their spouses were destined to raise their families. It was here Helen would give birth to her second child, a son they named Robert. Mildred would give birth to her first child, Loy Allen Kiser.

At the time Ola Grace accepted Abe's proposal of marriage, the welfare of his three daughters was no longer his concern. He was convinced they had married well and were ready to create their own nest and their own families.

Ola Grace and Abe, without allowing time for a honeymoon, returned to the farm.

When the newlyweds arrived home, Cecil's resentment and hatred for Abe grew like a fast-growing cancer cell. Whenever Abe outwardly showed affection for his new bride with a tender embrace or caress, the young lad's anger seethed to the point of wanting to kill the man who had taken over the life of his mother. Passage of time ceased to erase the hatred seething in the very soul of Ola Grace's son toward his stepfather. He often would listen to the wailing sound of freight trains rumbling through the countryside, and his one desire was to jump aboard. He wanted nothing more than to go far, far away from the house of Abe.

Life for Ola Grace was not easy. She now was a wife, and

her second born, as she suspected might happen, became Abe's whipping boy. After each beating, Ola Grace would threaten to leave Abe. Her anger would abate when Abe showed a certain amount of remorse, but those periods of peace in the house of Abe were short lived. The razor strap hanging on the kitchen wall was always available. It rarely had a chance to get cold.

The farm on which Abe settled at the time of his first marriage to Clara began to fail. It was not supplying enough income to support Ola Grace and a son who never belonged to him. Abe began to blame Ola Grace for its failure. Crops were poor—his horse could no longer pull the plow. He even tried hitching the Model T to the plow, letting Cecil drive the vehicle while he followed behind, holding onto the plow in an effort to till the soil. It wasn't successful. Abe spent more time digging the rubber tires out of the muddy earth than he did behind the plow.

Two years passed and then news Abe didn't want to hear rang in his ears. Ola Grace was pregnant with their first child. The young mother tried to refrain from becoming pregnant. She couldn't bear the thought of her spouse mistreating any children they might have. Unfortunately, that was not in the plan. The inevitable happened on November 3, 1910, when Francis James VanNatter was born. Abe's seed finally produced a boy.

Abe showed a certain amount of delight over the birth of his first son. At least, he could be of some value for working the farm. That happiness soon faded, however, when after a respite of about two years, Ola Grace had to inform Abe she was pregnant again. On March 19, 1912, Edna Madeline VanNatter was born. This was not pleasing to Abe. His wife had babies and he had to feed them. Thoughts of selling the land plagued him. He was now middle aged and work was scarce. He had never known any other kind of labor except working the soil.

The day the farm was sold marked the beginning of a nomad life for the VanNatter family. The livestock and even the family dog whom Abe loved more than his children were all part of the package that was going on the block.

The sale of the farm created a deep void inside Ola Grace like she had not known since leaving the secure environment of her own family to marry Harry Ellison. She tried to accept the turn of events as God's will, but deep within her own soul, her life was filled with doubt.

Abe purchased an open wagon which he attached to the rear of the Model T. Ola Grace carefully packed their meager possessions into three large trunks. The iron bed that had been a bed for conception from Abe's first child, his three daughters, and now all the children Ola Grace would have was dismantled and loaded onto the wagon. The large kitchen table and six chairs which served as a place to solve many family problems as well as a place for music and communication were carefully placed on the wagon. The large trunks served not only as storage space but also a place to sit whenever the moving family came to a temporary destination. As the Model T and wagon rolled through the open gate leading onto the gravel road, Ola Grace knew there would never be another place she could call home.

MUNCIE, INDIANA, HAD FOUNDRIES, PLACES where scrap metal was recycled and the art of recasting was conducted. For many Hoosiers, these foundries were the only income source for their livelihood. Muncie was also the city that housed the famous Ball Brothers Glass Factory. The canning jars created within these walls were used by every American during the canning season as a source of food harvested from the land during harvest season. Preserving food within Ball Brothers jars was an assurance there would be plenty of eatable food throughout the long winter months. Cellars and pantries were stocked with freshly canned vegetables, including tomatoes. Fruit was turned into jams and jellies.

Abe's entire life survived because of his ability to work the rich land beneath his feet. His farm gone and no other means of support for his growing family, thoughts ran through his mind that perhaps he could get a job with Ball Brothers or one of the foundries, and at least his family would thrive on a regular weekly income.

Muncie was a full day's journey from State Line. It was when the family passed through a suburban town called Yorktown Abe noticed a run-down shack surrounded by plenty of land, a barn, a privy, and a woodshed. Healthy fruit trees and a walnut tree gave the place a quaint setting, although the shack itself appeared to be in much need of repair. There was plenty of vacant land on the property to grow a garden during the planting season and a hand pump on the back porch was certainly a convenience the VanNatters did not have on the farm. This would alleviate toting buckets of water from the cistern several feet from the kitchen door as they had been required to do during the years on the farm. A large hand-printed sign on a post in the front yard facing the road signified the property was "For Rent."

"This might work for us, Oley," Abe said. "Let's see if we can find out who the owner is. I know'd it'll take a little work to git it to where we can live in it, but I think with a little elbow grease we can jes' make do."

The owner of the property lived up the road a short distance from where the shanty was located. Abe found no difficulty locating the landlord. Within minutes, a deal was made and the shack in York Town became the new house of Abe.

When Ola Grace opened the door into their new abode, it was apparent the rats had taken up residency. It had been some time since the place was occupied by another family. The wide, wooden plank floors appeared to have never been washed. Dirty plaster walls covered at one time with ornately designed wallpaper was torn and faded. The former tenants had abandoned a cast-iron cooking range. Although the stove was in need of a good cleaning, Ola Grace was able to get a fire going so she could prepare an evening meal. In the parlor a cast-iron potbellied stove faced the wall. The wall was black from the constant stoking of the fire during the winter months. There were two small bedrooms—one which Cecil would share with his half-brother, Francis. Edna, the baby, would remain in a crib next to the bed Ola Grace and Abe would share in the crowded room off the narrow hallway.

The following morning after arriving in Yorktown, Abe began searching for work. While Abe applied for a job at Ball Brothers and the Foundry, Ola Grace burned sulphur in the bedrooms, the parlor, and the kitchen. She discovered from past experience that this was the most effective method of getting rid of a multitude of varmints, including bedbugs and spiders. By the end of their first week, Abe was hired at the local Foundry. Ola Grace, during that time, scraped the ugly wallpaper from the plaster walls. Clothing and bedding that outlived their usefulness was taken from the rag bag, torn into strips, and woven in rugs. These handmade rugs would be the only floor covering to be placed on the bare floors to cover the cracks in the planks which permitted cold drafts to seep through the floorboards from the frozen earth beneath the house.

While shopping for household staples, the young mother discovered a good buy. Remnants of wallpapers, rolls that had not been completely utilized or sold by the local merchant, lay on a giveaway counter. The kind man refused to take any money. He was only too glad to get rid of the unused wallpaper. Ola Grace carefully cut and pasted the paper then placed it on the plaster walls. Her efforts turned the shack into a clean as well as a colorful dwelling. The windows which had accumulated months or perhaps years of dirt and grime were washed until the faded glass appeared to be almost invisible. Fragmented window blinds were replaced with decorative curtains which Ola Grace cut and sewed from garments no longer wearable by Abe or the children.

It was the end of the harvest and thrashing season when the VanNatter family arrived in Yorktown. This meant fresh straw was available for mattress ticks for each bed. The former tenants also left a large cupboard which, after much scrubbing and a little paint, was transformed into a respectable utility cabinet for the kitchen. There was ample storage space for staples, pots, pans, and dishes. The cupboard even had a hardwood board which slid from a slot in the cabinet's frame. This lent itself for the purpose of rolling fresh dough for biscuits and kneading dough into homemade bread. Ola Grace turned the shack into a livable home for the newcomers to Yorktown.

Abe's job at the local Foundry was indeed a godsend. There was money at the end of each week that gave Abe a sense of security he had not experienced since the days the economy was good and he could support his family by tilling the land. All was well in the house of Abe.

A small Methodist church stood within walking distance from the house. Each Sunday morning, Ola Grace bundled the two infants and Cecil, then made their way to what she always referred to as "The House of God." She had long since reconciled herself to practicing her faith alone. Abe made no pretense as to why he didn't go to church. He liked his privacy and perhaps he felt it would be invaded by church people who found it necessary to convert him to their way of thinking as well as sticking their noses in his business. The church women embraced Ola Grace and her children. For Ola Grace, these women would become her extended family. She had at last felt safety from a world that at an early age dealt her a heavy blow.

It was the end of November when winter blasts of freezing rain turned into heavy snow. Blizzard conditions swept across the prairies like an angry sea ready to devour everything in its path. To keep out the winter's cold, Ola Grace stuffed rags around the windowsills and around the doors separating the inside of the house from the outside. In early December, the young mother was made aware that she was pregnant again. This would be her third child sired by Abe.

It was not an easy pregnancy. Throughout the entire nine months, the tired mother was sick. Having babies only added to the unsettled and unhappy environment within the house of Abe. Abe was convinced women enjoyed being pregnant and any physical complaints were strictly in their minds. The same fears he entertained before he married Ola Grace had come to pass. Within the short years of their wedlock, he had sired two children and now a third. Abe was not a happy man.

Throughout the long winter months, the women from the church gathered at the house of Abe sewing from morning to late afternoon. Diapers were created from flour sacks, and baby dresses were recycled from used clothing, all in preparation for a birth that would take place in late summer. They brought food along with their preschool children, turning the house on the outskirts of Yorktown into a day care center. Throughout the winter, the women worked in harmony humming like a hive of contented bees.

Springtime turned the fruit trees' pastel blossoms into an array of delicate flowers. As spring moved into summer, the delicate blossoms were transformed into branches of heavily laden fruit. The world came alive with new life and new beginnings. The garden in which Cecil diligently toiled brought to the house of Abe an abundance of vegetables. As the church women labored in preparation for Ola Grace's new arrival, they banded together, forming canning parties. Some of the woman preserved the vegetables while some created jams and jellies. Cabbage was shredded and placed in huge crocks, then left to ferment until the crocks turned its contents into everybody's favorite, sauerkraut. There would be no need for any soul to go hungry who lived in Yorktown. Everyone shared and cared.

On August 20, 1914, Ruth Mae VanNatter was born. Much to Abe's chagrin, it was another girl. Abe's bad temper and sulking ways became unbearable.

Nothing Cecil could do pleased him, consequently, the whippings were more frequent. The razor strap was always handy for a stinging belt across the back or on the behind. If the offense was more demanding, it meant a trip to the woodshed for one of Abe's beatings similar to the one he bestowed upon his daughter Helen so many years prior. Each blow Abe doled on the tender body of Cecil Ellison was as if Abe were intending those beatings for Ola Grace. There was no escape. Ola Grace felt trapped. She was in no position to come to the aid of her second born, and now she had conceived three children from Abe's seed.

Cecil was expected to "earn his keep." All outside chores concerning the needs of the household were his responsibility, such as chopping wood and stacking cord after cord in the shed a short distance from the house. In the springtime, he was expected to plow the earth and plant the garden. Abe expected him to toil daily in the cornfields, following long rows of corn rising high above the youngster's head. Stretching his short arms to reach every ear, he would pluck the corn from the stalk then toss it onto the wagon pulled by a team of horses. There was little dialogue between Cecil and Abe. When he was angry, or felt the young teenager was not sharing the workload, Abe's favorite rebuke was "Yer jes' nothin' but a lazy lout and you'll never amount to nothin', not even a hill of beans."

Hours were limited for Cecil in the schoolroom. He did manage to learn his ABCs and a pretense at writing and reading when Abe decided he didn't need any more of Cecil's time away from working the land.

With each pregnancy and each child Ola Grace brought to fruition from Abe's seed, Cecil's bitterness and hatred became more and more an obsession. The abused youngster withdrew from his mom and any association with his stepfather. He only found peace and contentment when he was alone. Night after night he would lay upon his cot listening to the freight train rumbling through Yorktown then passing the back fence of the house of Abe. The mournful whistle seemed to beckon him to come—"Come—Come—hop aboard, Cecil, I'll take you far, far away." The words were like a haunting melody embedded into his entire being. Cecil was 13 years old. He knew the time had come. A time that would remove him from the house of Abe forever.

The cool autumn created a colorful carpet of falling leaves around the trunks of the trees. The chill in the air was a clear indication winter was close at hand. It was on one of those late fall mornings that Cecil made his final decision. He waited until he was certain Abe left the house, then he interrupted his mom's chore of washing dishes. He placed his arm around her shoulder. "Mom—I love ya an awful lot—ya know that, don't ya Mom? I'd take ya away from Abe now if I could and he'd never see ya again. I hate 'im, Mom. I hate 'im! I never hated no one like I hate Abe. He's doin' nothin' fer ya but keepin' ya havin' kids. Every time one of his youngins' is born, I jes' wanna kill it."

Tears welled in the eyes of Ola Grace as Cecil spoke. "I'm leavin' Mom. I'll let ya know somehow jes' where I am. Don't worry. I'll be all right. I can work. Abe seen to it I know'd how to work."

Silent tears flowed freely over the cheeks of Ola Grace as she quietly listened.

She could feel Cecil's rejection from everyone except herself from the moment he took his first breath of life. She wanted to tell Cecil not to go, but, within her tortured soul, she knew she couldn't stop him.

"If I git a job, Mom, I'm gonna come back fer ya and take ya away from that man and his squawlin' kids." Cecil picked up a small bundle of clothing he packed during the night. For one brief moment he held his mother in his arms then placed a tender kiss on her cheek. Releasing his warm em-

brace, Cecil walked toward the kitchen door. "I'll be seein'
ya, Mom—don't worry—I love ya Mom."

Bitter tears turned to sobs as Ola Grace watched through
the kitchen window until Cecil was out of sight. She could
hear the faint whistle of the distant freight train penetrating
the morning fall air. In her mind, she pictured her son hop-
ping onto the moving train and into a boxcar as the train
slowed to almost a halt at the crossing a short distance from
the house of Abe. Somehow, she knew riding the rails would
be Cecil's way of life.

IT WAS AS IF THE moving train knew it was destined to be the
means of escape for the young abused lad as its speed slowed
to almost a complete stop. Noticing an open door to one of
the box cars, Cecil climbed aboard. Settling in a far corner of
the open car, he was certain the way of the tramp, hobo, or
beggar was far better than being subjected to more of Abe's
tortuous beatings. Hatred for his stepfather reached inward
to the very pit of his soul. The freight train and the drafty,
empty boxcar was a magic carpet that would take him far,
far away from the house of Abe.

The steady rhythm of the metal wheels rumbling over
the steel rails caused the youngster's mind to drift into a
deep sleep. He curled his lean body into a fetal position like
a puppy trying to keep warm from his own body heat. For
the first time in his entire life, he felt a freedom he had never
known. Never again would he feel the sting of Abe's razor
strap or beatings from the switch in the woodshed. His tender, immature body bore scars across his back that would
remain embedded in his bare skin for the remainder of his

life. All day and far into the night his body rocked with the motion of the train.

It was as night turned to day that the runaway was awakened by the touch of a hand. He had been dreaming and the gentle touch was as tender as the many times his mother gently stroked his brow. Slowly, he opened his eyes and it was then he realized he was looking into the face of a stranger.

The stranger was tall and thin, probably in his early 30s. As his hand touched Cecil, he spoke. "Well—it looks like I'm gonna have company on this trip. My name's Joe—what's your'n?"

The man's demeanor and the tenderness in his voice reflected a kindness Cecil never thought possible from another human being, especially a man. "I'm Cecil. I jes' run away from my step dad. Couldn't take any more bein' his whippin' post. It seems like he's been beatin' me from the day I was born."

Joe squatted down alongside Cecil. "Well—he was really that bad, was he? I can't blame ya for runnin' away. I did the same thing when my dad beat the hell outta me. Since we're both headed in whatever place this train is takin' us, I might as well make myself comfortable. It's goin' be a quite a spell before the train stops at the next town." Joe stretched out his long legs and leaned against the wall of the boxcar. "Ya know, kid—bein' a hobo or tramp or whatever they wanna call us ain't easy, but when ya ain't got no money and ya wanna be free, I know'd no better way to travel than ridin' the rails. Of course, there'll be lots of days when ya wish ya could jes' git somethin' to eat. I'm headin' fer California myself. It's warm out there, even in the wintertime. I try to go as fer as I can then hop off the train jes' outside the town limits and head fer the nearest house that looks like it might give me a good meal I always offer to work fer' 'em, though. I ain't no beggar. Bein' poor might take away most everythin', but it ain't takin' my pride. Most of the time people are glad to let me do some odd jobs, particularly if they know'd it ain't gonna cost 'em nothin' except somethin' to keep the belly button from touchin' the backbone."

Joe continued. "Say—yer kinda young to be travelin' alone, ain't ya? How old are ya, kid?"

Cecil hung onto every word coming from the stranger's mouth. "I'll be 14 in December, if I live that long."

Joe seemed to ignore Cecil's response to his question. "Ya know, Lad, maybe it's a good thing, if we jes' team up together fer a while and ya learn the ropes and ya learn how to take care of yerself. I'm anxious to get to California before the snow flies. Be glad to have ya come along if you'd like. It does git kinda lonely travelin' by myself."

The hours passed and both travelers dozed off to sleep. As Cecil closed his eyes he realized he found a friend.

"What ya thinkin' about Abe? Ya been mighty quiet lately." The tired mother felt so alone after Cecil left home. She tried to talk to Abe about Cecil, but he refused to discuss the fact his stepson ran away. In fact, he was glad to get rid of him. When Ola Grace attempted to bring up the subject and express her concern about Cecil, Abe would cut her short with a curt remark. "He's old enough, Oley, to fend for himself. Now—quit yer worryin." Abe would then revert into one of his pouting moods and even though Ola Grace willingly let him have his way with her in bed, his incessant sulking failed to diminish.

After supper, the dishes washed and put away, the children tucked into bed, Ola Grace presented Abe with the news she was pregnant. "Abe—it's only been about three years since Ruth was born and here I'm in the family way again!"

Abe's cold stare like daggers flashed from his eyes. He rose from the kitchen table and without making an audible comment left the house. Anger and frustration consumed his entire being. "Good Lord—she's barely gittin' one kid weaned and by golly she's havin' another." The news of another baby on the way sent Abe into a fit of depression much deeper than his cantankerous attitude he had when Cecil left home. The days passed into weeks and there were few words uttered unless something was said that required a response. Night after night, although they shared the same bed, Abe moved as far away from his pregnant wife as the double bed permitted. He arose at the break of dawn, coming into the house only at meal times. It brought back memories of Abe's pouting ways Ola Grace endured when he sent Helen off to the convent. The supper table, breakfast table, and dinner time were void of any conversation.

It was late summer or early fall when Abe decided to break his long silence. "Oley—work ain't been so good around here and I think it's time we ought a think about movin' on—someplace else."

Sadness clouded the tired, expectant mother's face. "I was hopin' we could stay here, Abe. I sure would miss my church folk and Cecil wouldn't know where we went if he tried to come home again." It was obvious to Ola Grace that Abe had given little thought or remorse about the loss of her son. Deep in his soul, she thought he was glad Cecil was gone, and as far as Abe was concerned, he hoped he'd never come back

Abe continued. "I've been thinkin' about Darbyville over in Ohio. It's a short piece across the border and maybe there'll be some work there. They're layin' men off right and left at the foundry. I'll probably be the next one. The rent's almost due again, Oley, and I think we should be on our way before we have to pay fer another month's rent. Winter's comin' and I think it best we git settled before the snow flies."

Ola Grace's belly was beginning to swell. When moving day arrived and with each item she packed in preparation for the move to Darbyville, her heart sank even to a lower ebb. At dawn, Abe pulled the wagon from the lean-to next to the small barn where it had rested since the family's moved to Yorktown. He then connected the weather-beaten wagon to the Model T. When all was loaded onto the wagon and the rooms of the house were empty, Ola Grace closed the door to the house and the friends she made for the last time. Before getting into the passenger seat next to Abe, the sad mother glanced one more time into the rusty mailbox standing at the edge of the gravel road. A single penny postcard lay on the floor of the box. It was from Cecil

> *Hi Mom,*
> *Hope all is okay. I found a good friend. His name is Joe.*
> *He's letting me travel with 'im. We're headed fer Califor-*
> *nia.*
>
> *Will write ya later, Mom. I love ya Mom. I'll write ya*
> *when we reach California.*
> *Cecil*

"Come on Oley! What's holdin' ya up? We gotta git to Darbyville before dark! Ola Grace tucked Cecil's postcard inside her tattered purse, then slowly stepped into the passenger seat next to Abe. When the Model T moved forward, Ola

Grace took one more glance at the shack she patiently turned into a home. They passed the old church that had been her refuge. As the Ford took to the highway, she reached in her purse and withdrew Cecil's postcard. Quietly she read and reread the few words Cecil had written. She could almost feel her son's presence as she gently touched the card, then tucked it again inside her purse.

A rundown clapboard house about a mile from the town of Darbyville attracted Abe's attention. "What about this place, Oley? It says it's fer rent and no place ain't so bad I can't fix it up. Got lots of land around it too, and look at that orchard! This next summer we could pick all the apples, cherries, and peaches we wanted. We might even be able to sell some of the fruit in town. There's even a persimmon tree. Ya know how I like them persimmons."

A small, red barn stood a few hundred feet from the main house. Next to the barn stood the outdoor privy. Another building erected near the barn apparently had been used as a chicken house. Alongside the chicken house was a lean-to which would give Abe's Ford a certain amount of protection against the elements. A covered back porch extended across a goodly portion of the house. On the porch was a rusty pump which obviously hadn't been used for as long as the house had been vacated. A drain, although covered with dirt and grime, permitted the water coming out of the pump to run beyond the edge of the porch onto the ground.

When Ola Grace opened the door into the kitchen, a putrid odor caused her stomach to churn. The inside of the house reeked from stench and filth. The previous tenants apparently had little concern about sharing their accommodations with rats and other varmints. The pregnant mother, already strapped with three babies and with another one on the way, wanted to run—run until she reached the comfort of the little house in Yorktown and the many friends she left behind.

Before Abe began unloading the wagon, Ola Grace placed a sulphur urn in each room. She lit the contents of each container, letting the fumes burn until she was certain no germs or varmints could possibly survive. While the shack, aka, a house, was being fumigated with sulphur fumes, she, Abe, and the children drove into Darbyville to locate the owner of the property. There was no problem getting the landlord's permission for the VanNatter family to move onto the property and into the shack resting on the outskirts of Darbyville, Ohio. Late fall was already beginning to display a tinge of winter. Ola Grace's belly grew larger with each passing day. The task of turning the shack into a home was far beyond the pregnant mother's ability. She missed Yorktown and she longed for her church friends. Even Abe was dissatisfied with the move. There was no work and it seemed as if the entire town was poverty stricken. It must have been in Darbyville that Abe became a junk man. He diligently collected junk for recycling, but even that chore bore little or no fruit. People didn't throw anything away.

Overnight, the fall weather turned into a fierce winter. Blizzards blew across the open plains with icy blasts of cold air and sheets of blinding snow. Ola Grace stuffed rags around the window casings to keep out the snow and the frigid outside temperatures from filtering through the open spaces under the window frames, the plank floors, and the doors leading to the outside. With all her efforts there was little chance of keeping the wintery drafts and below-zero air from entering the shack in Darbyville. A roaring fire in the kitchen range and a roaring fire in the potbellied stove in the parlor was no match for the vicious elements of nature.

Thanksgiving passed. Christmas lost all its reverent meanings and then on January 17, 1917, Elizabeth Melvina VanNatter was born to Ola Grace and Abraham VanNatter. The birth happened during one of the most severe winter storms the Midwesterners had experienced in many years. Snow drifted across the prairie lands like a white, blinding sea, obliterating every fence and fence post for miles around. The heavy blanket of white reached the top of the window-sills. To get to the barn or privy, Abe dug a tunnel under the deep snow to the surrounding buildings. The potbel-lied stove in the parlor and the cast-iron kitchen range were never permitted to cool. Fortunately, shortly after arriving at Darbyville, Abe cut cord after cord of wood and stacked the chopped wood close to the woodshed erected close to the house. He purchased enough kerosene for the lamps to give them light at night and fuel to ignite the wood placed inside the stoves. Fortunately, Ola Grace carefully packed all the canned food she and her good friends in Yorktown prepared the previous summer in Yorktown. The canned food would be the family's only source for survival until there was a break in the weather and an opportunity to move on.

Seldom was a doctor present to assist in the birth of a child. Midwives were scarce. Ola Grace had to depend on Abe to help her deliver their fourth child. Abe always named the newborn. They had to have Biblical names, but where he got the name he bestowed upon the newest addition to the family is still a mystery. He named her Elizabeth Melvina VanNatter. To prove she was born and legitimate, Abe and Ola Grace had to wait until the snow began to melt and they were able to contact a local country doctor who would verify the date of birth of their newborn baby.

Darbyville was far from the Mecca Abe envisioned. Everyone was poor, poor, poor. Nothing was discarded. Abe was ready for another move.

CHAPTER 12

TALL, MAJESTIC BUILDINGS GRACING THE skyline of Chicago were quickly coming into view. Joe rose to his feet then quietly awakened Cecil from his sound sleep. "I think we'd better git off as soon as the train slows, lad. Ya gotta really judge yer timing when ya jump off a movin' train or you'll git hurt or ya could even git killed. The reason I'm tellin' ya we gotta git off here instead of waitin' till we git to the big city is the law and sometimes them city slickers look down on us as beggars and it ain't their notion to share what they got with a tramp. Farmers or country folk are usually more agreeable to us folk and if we offer to do some work fer 'em we can get a good meal. Sometimes they even let us sleep in the barn. It ain't exactly the same as sleepin' in a hotel but the straw is always fresh and it'll keep ya warm."

As Joe spoke the two hobos could feel the engine pulling the endless line of boxcars begin to slow. "Ya gotta watch me carefully, Cecil, when I jump from this boxcar. Do exactly as I do. When ya see me hit the ground ya jump!"

Cecil stood at the edge of the open door to the boxcar. He watched as Joe jumped and began to roll down the embankment. Following his mentor Cecil leaped from the car then felt his body fly through the air. When he hit the ground his body began to roll. When he came to an abrupt stop he opened his eyes. Standing over him was his traveling buddy. "That ain't too bad, Lad. A few more jumps like that and yer gonna have it made."

Cecil's pants were torn, his arms were bruised, and nasty scratches caused by the wild growth of weeds alongside the tracks marred his youthful face. Joe helped Cecil to his feet.

A distance from where the two hobos jumped from the train stood a farmhouse. In some ways it brought back memories of Abe's farm at State Line. Cecil followed behind Joe to a fence separating the train's tracks from a cow pasture. Cows grazed peacefully showing no interest in the two strangers crossing their territory except for a huge, black bull who did exhibit a certain amount of curiosity but made no gesture toward pawing the earth in preparation for an attack.

As the two tramps neared the neatly cared for farmhouse, Joe and Cecil noticed a pleasant looking, middle-aged woman watching them through the kitchen window. Without waiting for them to rap on her door, she partially opened the door then spoke. "Can I help you gentlemen?" she asked.

Joe tipped his tattered hat. "Ma'am—we're hungry. We was wonderin' if ya jes' might have some job you'd like done in payment for a good meal?"

The woman opened the door wider to where she could observe both Joe and Cecil. Looking down at Cecil, who stood just below the first step of the back porch, she spoke. "Is this boy yer son?" she asked.

"No ma'am," Joe quickly replied. "He's jes' might need a bit of protectin' so I asked him to come along with me. Ya see—I'm headin' fer California and I wanna git there before winter sets in. Cecil here is runnin' away from home. His mom's second husband was always givin' him a lickin'. It seems the old man was at his best when he weren't sparin' the rod. Do ya think ya could spare us somethin' to eat? We're mighty hungry, ma'am, and we're sure willin' to work fer ya fer jes' somethin' to fill that empty hole in our belly."

The most callous person could not resist the sincerity behind what Joe was saying. "Well—ya sure seem like two nice fellers. I could use some help around here. My hired hand is sick and I'm jes' not able to take care of this farm since my husband passed away."

Cecil wasted no time getting into the conversation. "Ma'am—I can milk cows and I can slop hogs. I lived on a farm for quite a spell until my old man sold it. There ain't nothin' I cain't do when it comes to workin' on a farm." Cecil's dark eyes pierced the very soul of the kind woman. He could see his mom's eyes in the face of the stranger. He did miss his mom and he would have liked nothing better than to have taken her away from Abe.

"Well—men, my name is Mrs. Thompson. I've lived in this old house since my husband and I were married some 40-odd years ago. I cooked many a dinner for the thrashers and farmhands over the years, but I must admit the work is more than I can handle with only one hired hand to run the place. Why don't ya come in and freshen up a bit while I git ya somethin' to eat. I was able to do the milkin' this mornin', but I'm jes' not up to bringin' the cows in from the pasture this afternoon and milkin' them again. If ya don't mind doin' me a good turn, ya can stay in the barn tonight. After ya git the evenin' milkin' done, I'll fix ya a nice supper."

Joe and Cecil followed the kind woman as she led the way into the kitchen. She took a steaming kettle from the stove then poured boiling water into a porcelain basin.

"Here—Joe—ya and Cecil douse a bit of this on yer face and hands and I think the sandwich I'm goin' to fix ya will taste better."

The day passed quickly. As the sun slowly began to dip below the horizon, Joe and Cecil herded the cows through the gate separating the barn from the pasture. After each cow was thoroughly milked, they brought the buckets of milk to the back porch where they poured it into the separator. The separator was an updated piece of equipment that separated the cream from the milk. Having completed their evening chores, the two hobos joined Mrs. Thompson in the kitchen.

Much time had passed since Mrs. Thompson heard the sound of voices sitting around the kitchen table in her large country kitchen. When the two hobos finished their supper and rose from the table, Mrs. Thompson presented them with another offer. "If ya see the cows are bedded down and if ya see they're put out to pasture in the mornin' after the mornin' milkin', I'd be glad to fix ya a good breakfast before ya git on yer way. Might even pack a little extra fer ya to carry along."

A ladder, nailed to the frame of the barn in front of the cows' stalls, led to the hay mow. It was here the two tramps made their beds on fresh straw recently harvested from the fertile fields. "How peaceful," Cecil thought as he gazed from his bed of straw toward the rafters of the barn. "I wish I could stay here. I could help the nice woman with her farm. The only thing—it jes' ain't far enough away from Abe."

CHAPTER 13

WHEN THE SNOW BEGAN TO melt and new blades of grass peeked through the soggy soil, Abe decided it was time to return to Yorktown. For the first time, Ola Grace was glad her nomad husband made a right decision. She gave little thought as to what kind of house he might rent; she just wanted to return to the place where she had friends and her church. It was as if her God dwelled in that simple white church in Yorktown. When Abe moved the growing family away from her holy sanctuary, she felt as if she were dumped into the pits of hell.

The house in Yorktown had remained vacant since the VanNatters moved on. The warmth and security of the shack Ola Grace turned into a home seemed to reach out and say, "Welcome home, folks, I've been waitin' fer ya." Ola Grace could barely contain her excitement as the Model T came to a halt in front of the house on the outskirts of Yorktown. Abe wasted no time finding the landlord and arranging the necessity of re-renting the property. Hand-woven rag rugs Ola Grace wove during the time they previously lived in Yorktown were quickly spread on the bare floors. The few sticks of furniture were unloaded from the wagon and placed in exactly the same place in the parlor where they rested prior to the move. The cast-iron kitchen range, although never used since their departure, almost sang when wood was loaded into its belly and a roaring fire brought warmth to the kitchen. The house in Yorktown came alive with smiles, laughter, and the humming of familiar tunes. Abe even got out his French harp as they sat down to supper, once again making the rafters ring with music.

Word spread quickly throughout the community that the VanNatters had returned home. The Prodigal Son could not possibly have received a warmer and more generous welcome. Cars, horses and buggies began to arrive, each friendly visitor carrying food. One neighbor donated a couple piglets and some newly hatched chickens. Tears welled in the eyes of Ola Grace as she opened the box in which ten yellow baby chicks were carefully placed. Tenderly she picked each biddy up in the palm of her hand, carefully stroking the tiny creature then gently placing it back into the security of the box. Abe wasn't much for permitting people to offer him charity, but with kind persuasion and being assured he was under no obligation to pay for all the kindness, he accepted the generosity from the church people and the surrounding community. For the first time in many months, harmony reigned in the house of Abe.

With the help of a neighboring farmer, Abe was able to purchase a horse to pull the plow and a cow to provide milk for his growing youngsters. The land was prepared for planting and in time, Abe succeeded in getting rehired at the local foundry. Francis, Abe's first son, was old enough to take over the chores. A regular weekly paycheck from the foundry assured the family of plenty of food on the table. Ola Grace could occasionally buy a piece of store-bought clothing.

Elizabeth was only a few months old when the VanNatters returned to Yorktown. By the following fall of 1917, Ola Grace's remission from being pregnant ended. She was now again in the family way with Abe's fifth child. For the first time since siring babies, Abe did not return to his unsettled ways. On May 25, 1918, Harvey James VanNatter was born.

Chapter 14

CECIL MATURED WELL INTO MANHOOD. No longer was he the innocent 13-year-old who ran away from his stepfather's control on that frosty, late fall morning. While his mother continued to bear Abe's children, he traveled the rails riding from the East Coast to the West Coast and from the north to the south. He was like the planet on which he dwelled, always in constant movement. He was a familiar face to other hobos who gathered around campsites along some railroad track. Night after night he bedded down on the cool earth trying to sleep and always with the realization that dawn would bring more of the same as the day before. There were times the young man was incarcerated, accused of being a vagrant and an undesirable menace to society. He often felt his hands being handcuffed behind his back and a ride in a paddy wagon to the nearest county jail. At least he was assured of warm shelter, a clean bunk where he could lay his tired body, and some food to keep the constant pains of hunger in abeyance.

Although many miles separated mother and son, there was always a bond that brought the vagabond to his mother's side. He seemed to have an innate intuition of knowing Abe's moves, regardless, geographically, where each move might have taken the VanNatter family. Whenever a freight train carrying Ola Grace's rail riding son passed through a town in which Abe set up camp, Cecil had the knack of knowing when the man he detested would be absent from his house and just how long he would be away. Those few precious moments with his mom were the most cherished moments for the young man's life. With each unexpected visit, Abe's seed had produced another child.

Cecil was pleased when he discovered Abe had chosen to move back to Yorktown. He knew the place well. Whenever the train whistled as it passed through the small town, flashbacks of that frosty morn were as vivid in memory as if the realities of that morning were repeated time and time again. He knew exactly the right place to jump from the train. The rusty wire fence behind the house was no barrier as he climbed over the last obstacle to reach his mom's side. There were only two kids when he left home; now his mom had five, none of which were any more important to Cecil than weeds in a garden. Weeds he would pull out and destroy if that were at all possible. He hated everything associated with Abe but he could never desert his mom. He had finally resigned himself to his mother's destiny. She was destined to bear children and live a poverty-stricken life with Abe. He did have one consolation, however, he was assured Abe would never mistreat or brutally beat his mother like the acts of violence bestowed on Ola Grace by his own dad, Harry Ellison.

Ralph Burton Ellison, like Cecil, was now an adult guiding his own ship across the precarious sea of life. The only difference between the two brothers, Ralph had the good fortune of being raised in a safe nest. He would marry, divorce and even join the military which transported him to a faraway country. He would return, however, and plant his roots in San Francisco. Ralph loved the exotic. It was no coincidence his first love was a bronze, black-haired beauty from Mexico. Their relationship flourished into heated passion which culminated into marriage. His world changed. Not only did he discover the restrictions and interference into his private life by the Catholic Church, he soon realized having married a favorite daughter, he also wedded the entire family. The union was doomed from the start. There were no children when the marriage was dissolved, nor was Ralph destined to be a father. Ralph, again, was the sole pilot of his own ship and the master of his own soul.

Cecil's wanderings brought him many times to the City by the Bay. He knew San Francisco well. It was here that he often canvassed the residential sections begging for food in payment for some odd job. A simple token of food was all he ever asked. It was in this affluent city that quite often was responsible for incarcerating him, sending him off to the county jail for what they called "philandering." He often searched for food in the alleys and garbage cans of the haves and the have-nots.

Many times, Cecil's elder brother would plead, "stay with me, Cecil. I'm sure you could find a permanent job that would give you a more fulfilling life." The answer was always the same. "No—Ralph—the rails are the only thing that gives me peace." Then there would be the sound of a distant freight train moving away from the city. He would turn to his brother, accept a simple handshake, then Ralph knew it was time for his wayward sibling to go.

Ralph Ellison, after settling on the West Coast, never saw his mother again. He was faithful, however, in writing letters and sending an occasional photograph. If only he could have known how his mother wanted more. Just the touch of his hand or a gentle kiss would have expressed so much more than pictures or an occasional letter. That empty space created by the sands of time would never be filled.

CHAPTER 15

THE YEARS IN YORKTOWN WERE the happiest years in the life of Ola Grace Jordan VanNatter. She had friends and there was a feeling of permanence. There was always enough food on the table, Abe had full-time employment with the foundry, and even though her social life never extended beyond church activities, Ola Grace was satisfied and felt fulfilled.

As previously mentioned, Abe had an adversity toward any church or religion. Ola Grace never forced the issue of religion with him nor did he deny her the privilege of participating in a world in which he did not care about or wished to be a part. He learned to accept his wife's devotion to her Lord, her saying grace before every meal, and those nighttime prayers before she laid her head on the pillow next to him. Through all the hard times and the good times, there was an unbreakable bond of love between Ola Grace and Abe. He was a good and honest man. Those qualities obliterated all frustrations and thoughts of a different kind of life. She was 39 years old. The years of her marriage to Abe and the bearing of five children had more than fulfilled her and Abe's sexual urges, and she had proven herself as a mother time and time again. Abe could not survive without Ola Grace.

Five years passed since the birth of Harvey. Ola Grace's biological clock began to slow and she was certain her years of child bearing had finally come to an end. It was the beginning of fall, not long after Indian summer subsided and the nights turned into a frosty chill, when Ola Grace realized she had conceived another child. It all happened when the nights were cool and the bodies were warm. Abe for the sixth and last time fertilized Ola Grace's egg with his sperm. Abe's pleasant mood that endured for a five-year period returned to a surly, pouting human being. The wandering man was ready for another change. Before the first snowfall in 1923 Abe was ready to move on. Why he chose the small town in Michigan called Dawaijack is difficult to understand; nevertheless, that small dot that is barely recognizable on any map, a town just across the border into Michigan would become the VanNatter's next stopping off place or temporary destination. It was in a simple wood frame dwelling in a town no one ever heard of that I would grow within my mother's womb. As the days turned into weeks and weeks turned into months my body grew. I was destined to become a living soul and the last offspring of Abraham and Ola Grace Van-Natter.

THE RICKETY WAGON TRANSPORTING THE VanNatters and their personal effects from the farm to Yorktown to Darbyville and back to Yorktown was again hitched to the Model T. Ruth, Elizabeth, and Harvey crowded into the backseat, Dad behind the wheel and Mom beside him in the front seat. Although in their teens, Francis, who like Cecil became Abe's whipping boy, along with his sister Edna decided not to move on with their mother and dad. They were of an age where they were capable of supporting themselves, Francis being 16 years of age and Edna now 14.

My developing body resting safely in my mother's womb rocked with the motion of the car and the sound of the engine. No lullaby could have been more comforting. It sent me off to sleep with thoughts of what life must be on the outside where I would eventually survive in an unknown world. I could hear and I could feel. Dad wasn't much for sugary sweet talk, but sometimes when he and Mom were in bed and the entire world was quiet, he'd put his arm around Mom and I could feel his rough, weatherbeaten hands as they stroked Mom's swollen belly.

Dad worked as a day laborer almost as soon as we arrived in Dawaijack. He didn't earn much money, but the small amount of money he earned managed to pay the rent and put food on the table.

Springtime came and it was planting season. There was never a time I can recall when Dad didn't plant a garden. He depended on the good earth to feed his family. Fortunately, the house they discovered in the tiny Michigan village was blessed with an abundance of land even though the address was considered within the town's limits. Harvey was four, going on five. While Dad walked behind the plow, Harvey followed, letting the freshly plowed moist earth massage his tender bare feet. Where Dad got a goat to pull a plow, I don't know. I just recall Mom and Dad talking about a goat for sale and he thought it was a good idea to buy it.

It was the month of May, on May 25th to be exact, that Harvey had his fifth birthday. Mom loved strawberries. She had more creative ideas as to what could be done with a strawberry than any person I would ever meet. So—Dad planted a goodly portion of the garden with strawberry plants and, like Mom's belly, those plants grew and grew until the right time came for picking. By June, an abundance of red, luscious berries appeared on the vines.

June that year was an exceptionally warm month. It was summertime and by the 24th day of June, I knew it was time to leave the safety of Mom's belly. I was ready to see what the family looked like and if the sound of their voices matched their physical appearance. I somehow knew I was blessed with good and caring brothers and sisters.

Mom knew I was being a bit active, but little did she think I was ready to meet the challenge of the world on the outside. It was strawberry picking time. Mom donned her apron, placed her sun bonnet on her head, then joined Dad in the strawberry patch. She always wore her apron to the garden. She would pick it up by the hem, turning it into a basket to carry vegetables or strawberries into the house. She stooped toward the ground and began the task of picking berries when suddenly she became aware I just wasn't going to wait any longer to be born.

"Dad!—Dad!—my water broke! The baby is coming!" Dad stood only a few feet from Mom when he heard her cry. Ola Grace carefully lowered her body to the ground. Dad dropped his hoe and rushed to Mom's side. Gently he picked her up and carried her toward the house.

Pushing the screen door open, he yelled, "You youngins' git to the neighbors. Mom is sick and Mr. Choapoulus said you could spend the night with them when the baby was bein' born. I gotta git Mom a doctor!"

Mr. Choapoulus saw Dad carrying Mom into the house. Even though my dad had prejudices when it came to foreigners, the neighboring Greek's kindness and know-how was more than accepted. "Abe—ya stay here with Oley. My Francina will take care of the children and I go get doctor."

Dad placed Mom on the old iron bed with its straw mattress that had been the birthing bed for all of Dad's children. He had seen each youngster grow, leave home, and then another one was always ready to take the departed one's place.

Beads of sweat poured from Mom's brow. The pains of labor came rapidly. I could feel myself turn inside my mother's body. I entered a long, narrow canal, my small arms tightly squeezed against my sides. I could hear Dad's voice saying, "Push! Oley! Push! Push harder!"

With each push Mom exerted, I moved downward toward a door that appeared to be closed, but as I moved through the long passageway through the long canal, the door opened. My head rushed through the open door. With one more push from Mom, my 10-pound body touched the straw mattress on the iron bed where Mom lay. Dad was not a novice with the procedure following childbirth. He placed his rough hands around my messy body then, with his teeth, quickly severed the cord that bound me to Mom for nine long months. Dad turned me upside down then gave me a smart slap on the butt to see if I had a voice. It would be the only time in my entire life I would feel a lickin' from my dad's hand. That slap brought out a scream and a flow of tears that could be heard throughout the town of Dawaijack. I was born with a good set of vocal chords and lungs capable of expelling lots of air. Dad scrutinized every inch of my body to see if all the parts were there. He then took me to Mom's side and said, "Well, Oley—at least it ain't another girl."

I won't go into detail how I got my name other than to say Dad wasn't on speaking terms with his daughter Helen's spouse, so he decided I should be named after two other sons-in-law, Loy Kiser and Claude Rainbolt. "We'll call 'im Loy Rainbolt VanNatter," I heard him announce.

It was on the second day of my arrival in this strange world as I lay snuggled against Mom's warm body, I heard the voices of my brother and sisters. They rushed into the room where Mom lay. Harvey stood close to Mom, placing his five-year-old hand on her forehead. "Are ya all right, Mom? I know'd ya was awful sick."

Ola Grace's eyes gazed into the blue eyes of her son Harvey. "I betcha you'd never guess what I got under this cover."

The young boy listened and waited before he spoke. "It sounds like a chicken, Mom. What ya doin' with a chicken under the cover and in bed with ya?"

Mom pushed the covers back, uncovering my head. "Here's yer new brother, kids. You're gonna have ta help me take care of 'im."

Mom had difficulty supplying enough milk for my hungry stomach. She was 40 years old when I was born and, although the children she bore prior to me were healthy, I apparently was considered the weakest of the litter. My physical being was beginning to wane and the entire family worried about my survival.

Dad rarely got excited about anything, except he must have worried about his new son's physical condition. A few short days after my birth, Dad burst into the house. "Oley!— I got a good buy on a goat today. They'll be bringin' her by in the mornin'." Even though he never let on he was concerned about whether I was going to make it, he didn't want to lose his new son. "That goat is gonna give us plenty of milk and ya jes' wait and see, I bet that kid is goin' to snap out of his slump in no time. I heard goat's milk is lots better fer ya than cow's milk." His rapid chatter was nonstop as if he had to sell the whole family in believing he made the right decision when he bought a goat.

"I know'd we can learn that creature to pull a plow. Harvey's big fer his age and even though he's only five, I bet it'll be no time before he can walk right behind that four-legged animal and plow the garden fer plantin'. It'll be good fer him to start learnin' how to earn his keep."

Those words, "earn his keep," were a bad omen for Ola Grace. She heard Abe use those words time and time again when he talked about Cecil. Quietly, she uttered a short prayer. "Please good Lord—don't let Harvey be Abe's whipping boy."

The following morning, a goat was delivered to the house of Abe. Everything Dad predicted about the goat would more than meet everyone's expectations. The animal took to the family and especially Harvey. She never let him out of her sight and would have followed him into the house and would have slept in the same bed if Mom hadn't had specific rules as to what belonged outside and what was allowed in the house.

Harvey named the goat "Nanny." Of course, that wasn't a unique name inasmuch as everyone knew a female goat was always a "nanny." She was a happy creature. She was as capable as any watch dog. When the weather became intolerable, she would take shelter in a small barn erected not many feet from the house. The daily output of milk produced by Nanny caused me to thrive. My cheeks were no longer sunken in my head. My entire body grew plump. Nanny was one of the family.

The goat enjoyed the inconvenience of being harnessed. That was as long as it was Harvey who did the harnessing. She took to pulling the plow as if she knew that lifestyle was what the world expected of her and she wasn't about to be a disappointment.

Dad seldom, if ever, reminisced, but as he watched Harvey take hold of the handlebars on the plow, it was one of the few times he permitted himself to mention Cecil's name. "I recall, Harvey, when Cecil was livin' with us, and he was about yer age, our horse was old and I had an idea that the old Tin Lizzie could do anything, including pulling a plow. Cecil would git behind the steering wheel and I would git behind the plow. We spent more dag burn time diggin' that Ford outta the mud than we did plowin'. Don't know why I didn't think about gittin' a goat then."

There was one problem with Nanny. That was her diet. She found it necessary to consume everything that wasn't nailed down. Nothing ever upset her digestive tract. When Mom hung clothes out to dry, the goat, for some unknown reason, thought Mom was hanging out her favorite desert. It was a constant *en garde* situation; otherwise, the family would have been totally threadbare.

Helen and Mildred continued to live in West Lebanon, Indiana, approximately a day's journey from Dawaijack. The weather was warm and while we could take advantage of the so-called Indian summer, Dad decided it was time the family should take a trip not only on what some people might think of as a vacation, but primarily to show off his latest family addition. I passed the crisis and was fully recovered from the trauma of being born.

One month before I made my entrance into this world, Helen gave birth to a son. Our journey must have occurred at about the time Helen's son began to teethe. Apparently, his fangs grew more rapidly than the rest of his body. Our good Greek neighbor agreed to take care of Nanny during our absence. Dad loaded our entire family into the Model T and we were off to West Lebanon. When we arrived, Mom sat me down on the kitchen table next to Helen and Fatty's new son, Bobby. There was much kissing and hugging since it had been a long time since Dad visited his daughter.

Bobby, who had cut his first teeth, thought he should get into the act of hugging and kissing. The tooth-cutting infant suddenly grabbed my cheek, planting his new teeth deep into my flesh. Needless to say, I must have let out a blood-curdling scream. Helen grabbed her son in one arm and me in the other. To shut me up she placed Bob on one titty and me on the other. Quiet replaced the loud chatter and my sister Helen, within seconds, had two growing infants sucking with great gusto on each titty. It must have been one of the most satisfying meals to come my way since birth. My tiny hands dropped from Helen's breast. Bob released his hold on the other breast and we both drifted off into a baby's dreamland.

We returned to Dawaijack, and it must have been something about that visit with Helen and Mildred that brought about another move by Dad. The town of Muncie, Indiana, drew Dad like a magnet, and it was always in this vicinity that he would settle down, but never in one place long enough to gather any roots.

CHAPTER 16

IT WAS IN THE POOR section of Muncie, Indiana, that my recall becomes most vivid. I was 3 years old. Dad rented a run-down clapboard house surrounded by a weedy yard. In the yard he parked the outdated Model T and the rickety wagon. I can still visualize in my mind's eye the half-dirt and half-gravel road in front of that house. The early morning rains ceased giving way to sunshine and leaving the street in front of our house more mud than gravel.

14th Street was located near a wide boulevard where across the street was a public park. In the park was a huge swimming pool that accommodated children on the shallow end and in the deeper portions people could swim and dive into the deeper water.

Muncie had several parks and at the time when I was a small child, the parks were segregated. A fence separated the park, leaving one side for strictly white people and the other side accommodated the black people.

Lizzie and Harvey got Mom's permission to take me to the swimming pool. Firmly holding onto my brother and sister's hands, we left our house walking along 14th Street to the boulevard, safely crossing the wide street then entering into the world of a carpet of green grass and tall trees. As we neared the man-made body of water and I observed kids splashing in the shallow end of the pool, I released my hands from my brother and sister's hold and made a wild dash toward the swimming pool. I ran as fast as my three-year-old legs could move toward the shallow end of the pool. I jumped in the water like a professional swimmer. When my feet touched bottom, they came in contact with a slippery substance that sent me tumbling head over heels until some kindly soul took pity and managed to stretch out their strong arms and grab ahold of my small body that was totally immersed in water. The good Samaritan kindly handed me to my brother who was much more inclined to give me a slap on the butt than give me sympathy. Pain rushed through my shoulder. "It hurts! It hurts!" I screamed as Harvey wrapped his arms around me. "What did ya do that fer, Loy?" he scolded. "I told ya to wait. Now — look what you went and did."

Harvey tried cradling me in his arms. I screamed, "It hurts! It hurts!" My brother lowered me to the ground. "Some kid pooped in that pool, Harvey. I slipped in it! My arm hurts, my arm hurts!" I screamed. Attempting to create a way to ease my pain, Harvey spoke. "Let's try ridin' piggyback, Loy. Maybe we can do it that way." Climbing onto my brother's back, I placed my good arm around his neck. Harvey carried me until we reached the edge of the park. When we prepared to cross the boulevard, Harvey lowered me to the ground. Before he or Lizzie could take my hand, I broke away, dashing into the street. Within a split second my small body came in contact with a fast moving vehicle. Brakes squealed and tires skidded as a magnificent, black automobile came to an abrupt stop. Not soon enough, however, not until it sent my three-year-old frame spinning downward toward the street's asphalt pavement.

A well-dressed woman driving the car hurriedly exited the driver's side of the car and ran to my rescue. She was panic stricken as she stooped to pick me up then tenderly place me into her arms. The pain was excruciating. My screams became a flood of tears. It wasn't the impact with the car responsible for my pain; it was that first experience in a swimming pool where I slipped and fell in some kid's poop. The cause of my pain was later diagnosed by Mom as a cracked collarbone.

"Where do you children live?" I heard the nice woman say. "I must take you home. The two of you," meaning Lizzie and Harvey, "climb into the backseat and I'll put the child next to me in the front seat. I'll have you home in just a few minutes."

The ride to Shantytown was like riding on a magic carpet. When the long, sleek, black chariot turned onto 14th Street, people rushed out of their houses to see who the prince might be who was entering their territory. When the automobile stopped in front of our house, curiosity took over the entire neighborhood. The commotion brought Dad to the patched screen door. Before the good Samaritan holding me in her arms could reach the front porch, I heard Dad say, "What happened, Lady?"

The woman pushed her way past Dad then gently laid me on the daybed resting against the wall. "Your son dashed in front of my car. It was an accident. I saw the children standing on the curb. I didn't expect this boy to break away from his brother and sister. It happened so quickly. Please let me take your son to the hospital or at least to a doctor and have him examined. He could be seriously injured. I'll be more than glad to pay all the medical expenses."

I can still see the cold, compassionless blue eyes staring at me as the woman spoke. There was no doubt in Dad's mind where the fault lay. Harvey and Elizabeth began speaking at the same time. "Loy fell in the pool, Dad! Some kid pooped in the pool and Loy slipped in it!" Their voices reached a high pitch and the sound of a stranger talking with Dad in the parlor brought Mom out of the kitchen. "What's the matter? What happened?" Seeing me lying on the daybed, she rushed to my side. She knelt down beside the bed and placed her hand on my forehead. "Where do ya hurt, Loy?"

Mom's voice in itself was enough to make me realize all was okay. "My arm hurts Mom—right there." As she touched my shoulder tears flowed like a geyser as they soaked my cheeks.

"Please!—Please!" The stranger pleaded. "Please let me take your son to the doctor. I want to be sure there is no serious injury to this child."

"No ma'am," Dad quickly replied. "It jes' ain't yer fault, Lady. Maybe he'll learn a lesson and watch where he's goin' from now on."

Realizing she had done all she could by offering to have me treated by a professional, she wrote her name on a piece of paper then handed it to Dad. "Please—now if your son does not get better, let me know. You can always reach me at this address."

Mom, Dad, Elizabeth—I always called her "Lizzie," Harvey, and my sister Ruth escorted the kind woman onto the porch. They watched in awe as the woman took her place in the driver's seat of the elegant vehicle then began to move away from our section of town.

Mom was the doctor in our house. She took an old dish rag and with great care to not cause me further pain, she raised my arm then placed it in her homemade sling. Gently she secured the contraption around my neck. She was certain inasmuch as there was no difficulty raising my arm that the arm wasn't broken. "Now, ya jes' lay there, Loy. I'm sure it's gonna be all right," Mom spoke assuredly.

The sound of the engine roaring in the great chariot that had parked in front of our house grew dimmer and dimmer. People who had been standing in the middle of the street observing the traumatic drama unfold returned to their homes except for two active boys tossing a ball to one another in the middle of the graveled road. 14th Street returned to normal.

We must have lived on 14th Street for at least two years before Dad decided it was time to make another move.

CHAPTER 17

DAD WAS NOT A CITY dweller. He related to the earth, always trusting the rich soil to provide for his family and their livelihood. There were few store-bought items gracing the shelves of Mom's kitchen, except for the essential staples required to operate a household. Beyond the purchase of pepper, salt, cornmeal, and flour, everything within the house of Abe was handmade. This included the clothes we wore. Mom could sew. Had it not been for her expertise in recycling worn-out clothes and creating a covering for our backs, the VanNatter family would have indeed been destined to wear rags. As for shoes, if we were lucky, we might get a new pair once a year. Dad would half-sole our shoes until the soles were so thick, it looked as if we were all competing with those unfortunate people born with club feet.

Dad was 67 years old at the time we moved from Shanty Town in Muncie to a little red house situated amid fruit trees and three adjoining gravel pits. One road led to Gaston and the other to Summitville. We always referred to the house as the "house at the crossroads." It would be the final place we would live where our family would remain intact as a family unit.

The house at the crossroads sat on the edge of three large

gravel pits. I don't recall seeing those pits when they were not overflowing with water and fresh fish. The mountainous sand mounds on the banks of the three pits rose high above the height of the house, and in my child's mind were my first impression of what might be a mountain.

I must have been about four years old at the time we moved to the country. There was nothing pretentious about the house at the crossroads. There was no electricity, no convenience of an indoor water supply, and no fancy furnace to supply warmth during the long winter months. Yet, the place would always be home. It would be the final period in my young life that I would share a space with my brother Harvey, my sister Ruth, and my sister Elizabeth. Francis had long been on his own and my sister Edna had married Bennie Hammond, a fellow from Kentucky.

It was at the crossroads that I had an ax placed in my tiny hands and was taught how to chop wood, wood that would keep us warm in the wintertime and wood to burn in the cast-iron, ornate kitchen range for cooking our meals.

It was only a two-bedroom house. Ruth shared a double bed with Elizabeth, whom we called "Lizzie." In the same room on the opposite wall, I shared a bed with my brother Harvey. In the open space between the two beds was a chamber pot, or "slop jar." This proved to be most convenient when the snow was waist high and one needed to shovel snow to get to the privy. After we reached the privy, we had to remove snow from the two-holer seats before urgently answering nature's calling. The second bedroom was shared by Mom and Dad.

Anyone familiar with the Midwest knew the constant threat of storms, tornados, and cyclones. A previous tenant apparently had the foresight to dig into the earth just outside

Mom and Dad's bedroom, creating an underground cave-like structure we always referred to as the "cyclone cellar." The cellar was always cool. Although we never used it as an escape from the winds of a tornado or cyclone, Mom soon discovered it was a great place to store potatoes, apples, and canned vegetables and fruit. Dad built shelving along the sides of the underground structure for the canned goods. The apples and potatoes were placed on the open dirt floor.

In the front yard of the house at the crossroads was a huge, immortal oak tree. That tree was my source of play and exercise. I would climb to its highest branches which rose far above the flat, open prairie lands surrounding our country abode. Harvey, or maybe it was Dad in one of his junk collecting routines, found a large rubber tire. My brother Harvey found a rope. Tying the rubber tire to a rope then securing the rope to one of the branches provided me with a swing. It was here I would play for hours, pushing the tire so high that at times it seemed as if I could easily do a complete circle as it would let me soar upward into the clear blue sky.

Across the road on the northwest corner of the crossroads stood an old dilapidated barn. Accepting the fact that the horseless carriage outdated the horse-drawn vehicle, the buggy was left behind when the former occupants moved on. I soon discovered this old barn and its buggy occupant was my favorite place to play out my childhood fantasies. I would sit in the front seat and pretend I was piloting the hottest horseless carriage in the entire country.

The gravel pits next to the house were always filled to the brim with fresh water. When marine life discovered these man-made pits, I am not certain, but I vividly recall the large carp, which my brother Harvey and I would catch along with fishing for some of the most colorful fish I had ever seen. There were sunfish, bluegills, and bass, and it was not unusual for Mom to prepare a fried fish breakfast with our catch of the day. Crawdads were plentiful and occasionally one might see a water moccasin pushing its way from one side of the pit to the other.

The gravel pits served a multitude of purposes, not only for us but the entire farm community. The white steeple of Zion, a protestant Methodist Church a short distance up the road from our house, often used the pits for Sunday afternoon baptisms. At no time was the steeple of Zion ever out of view. The spiral belfry seemed to touch the closest clouds. The mammoth bronze bell hanging in the church's belfry from the time the building was erected could be heard throughout the entire countryside. It tolled and echoed every Sunday morning, Sunday evening, and even on Wednesday night when people gathered for the midweek prayer meeting. When one in the community completed their earthly journey, the bell would sound. One could almost see the spirit of the departed rise upward toward the heavens. When a loved one, whether a neighbor or member of the family died, their body was gently carried by six pallbearers from the church to the fenced-in land of the dead located directly behind a one-room, red brick schoolhouse adjacent to the cemetery.

Zion was founded on the fundamental teachings of Christianity. There was a great difference, however, in the religion at that time than the present-day hell, fire, and brimstone television evangelists. The preachers standing behind the pulpit at Zion did so because they firmly believed in their message of peace. Money was not their God. Anyone dwelling within the parish of Zion was considered a part of the preacher's flock. When a member was in need of food or clothing, the more fortunate members supplied those needs. No one knowingly would go without food or shelter.

It was an impressive, attractive, picturesque church. I vividly recall the gas lanterns hanging on long chains from the ceiling and the good Reverend arriving at the church before the congregation, taking a long taper and lighting the gauze inside the globe of each propane lantern. By the time the congregation arrived for a Sunday night service, the light from the lanterns projected a glowing warmth through the stained glass windows emitting a warmth which will always be indelibly imprinted in my memory.

Upon entering the church, one would pass through a small vestibule. This was the last place where those among the living would view and pass the final remains of a body whose soul had passed on. From the vestibule, double doors opened into the holy sanctuary. Long rows of solid oak pews brought the flock closer together. An ancient reed pump organ accompanied enthusiastic congregational singing.

Mom made certain each one of her kids received a healthy dose of religion. Every Saturday night was bath night. The old galvanized-steel washtub was placed in the kitchen next to the stove. It was filled with boiling-hot water, and one by one we got our Saturday night purge. "Cleanliness is next to Godliness," Mom would often say. Of course, the routine was a private affair, Mom making certain the kids respected each other's privacy and stayed out of the kitchen. As for me, she would give me a good scrubbing, including several swipes behind the ears and round the nape of the neck.

Each time we visited the House of God, we were expected to wear our best clothes. Even though our clothing was what most people would consider rags, they were all we had and

Mom made certain they were clean. Mom would even put on her only pair of shoes. She had bunions on both feet and shoes only added to the pain, so Mom most of the time went barefooted. Our shoes were half-soled so many times, the nails would pierce through the insole of the shoes. We would literally walk on a bed of sharp nails until we could get home and kick off the shoes and go barefooted.

The church was within walking distance to the house at the crossroads. Whether the weather was sunny, rainy, icy, or snowy, I don't recall Mom ever letting us miss one service at the church. A Mr. and Mrs. Meyers, former school teachers who lived a couple miles down the road from our house, would often stop and offer us a ride to church in their horse and buggy. In the wintertime when the snows fell, they would hitch their horse to a sleigh. We would climb into the sleigh *en masse*. Although the journey was a short one, I shall always have fond memories of those sleigh rides from the crossroads to Zion.

Sunday school was a time when we were thoroughly indoctrinated into the books of the Holy Bible, including the Old and New Testaments. We learned about Abraham, Moses, and Elijah. We could recite Biblical stories to where the lives of those ancients were as real as if all the events were happening on the very ground upon which we walked. When Sunday school ended, we were marched into the Holy sanctuary where another hour was spent singing hymns, listening to prayers, and hearing the preacher present a long-winded sermon about evil lurking on every corner and how the devil was always present to lead us into temptation then capture our very souls. After the hell-raising sermon, the preacher would plead for those who hadn't been saved from the wickedness of the devil to please come to the altar and publicly ask for God's forgiveness. Of course, there was much more to being cleansed than just asking God to forgive you. There was the purification element of baptism. In this church, it was more than just having the preacher drip a few drops of rainwater on your forehead; this church believed in total immersion like that performed by St. John when he baptized Jesus in the River Jordan. The only semblance to the Bible body of water near Zion and the crossroads was the gravel pit. When weather permitted, the congregation gathered on the banks of the gravel pit and with unaccompanied voices, they sang "Shall We Gather at the River?," "Washed in the Blood of the Lamb," "Amazing Grace," and "Leave It There," letting their voices echo over the open prairie like a tidal wave.

It was in those early days of being indoctrinated into religion I began to express myself in song. My high soprano voice would soar above the congregation, i.e., until my brother Harvey's voice began to change and I realized for the first time I sounded like a girl. I would lower my voice down to the level of my brother's sound and there it would stay until my vocal apparatus would change and my male gender was definite and finally identified.

Mom liked to hear me sing and I liked to sing. Harvey and Dad sang too, but somehow, Mom liked the way I sang and would always tell me, "You have such a pretty voice, Loy."

Those Sunday afternoon baptisms at the gravel pit are as vivid today as if they happened yesterday. I can recall the preacher dressed in his black suit, a shirt whose collar was turned backward, wading into the water until it reached his waist. He would then raise his hands to the heavens to bless the congregation and those who chose to take the final step of baptism toward committing themselves as a follower of Christ. His face shone like the sun as the Holy Ghost transformed his being into a modern day John the Baptist.

As each newly redeemed person left the banks of the gravel pit and waded toward the open arms of the preacher, he would grasp their hand. He then would place one arm around the individual's waist, his other hand on their face, ready to close their nostrils. Before the expected dunk materialized, the preacher would then say another prayer. "I now baptize thee in the name of the Father, and the Son, and the Holy Ghost!" He would quickly close the newly saved's nose with his fingers, then without further ado, he pushed the born-again Christian backward over his arm until their body was totally immersed in the gravel pit's water of Zion. Some people came up sputtering, particularly those who forgot to close their mouths. Others, who were well acquainted with the water's depth, would rise from the deep singing and shouting their praises to God.

CHAPTER 18

I SUPPOSE EVERY KID BELIEVES his or her mother is the most beautiful creature God ever created, so when I say my mom's physical attributes were not only beautiful, she had a saintly inner soul. In her youth, she had a perfectly sculptured figure, but six kids by Dad and two by Harry Ellison took its toll. The 20 years she shared Dad's bed and birthing six kids no longer left Ola Grace the slim and petite woman Dad had married. Her teeth were gone and the false dentures hurt. They spent more time in a cup on a shelf than in Mom's mouth. Her feet were constantly sore. Raw and inflamed bunions protruded from both feet. The only time I would see my mother place a pair of shoes on her feet was when she was going to church or for an occasion where she and Dad would drive the old Model T to Muncie.

Dad was 20 years older than Mom. He was 62 years old when I was born. Other than a thinning hairline, his appearance never changed. His skin was wrinkle-free and his body remained as muscular, straight, and firm as it was the day he married Mom. Nor did his behavior become better or worse. He would continue to have long periods of withdrawn anger. His pouting moods left no room for communication. He was like the weather, always changing. There would be periods of storms and black clouds. When his inner tormented mind changed and he was able to break through the dark clouds, Dad was happy and the whole world seemed to be a brighter place.

Mom and Dad loved music. Mom couldn't carry a tune in an oaken bucket, but she still enjoyed raising her off-key voice whenever there was a congregational sing at church or when we would join in song at home. Dad was a passable singer. The only people who would ever hear him, however, were his offspring. He had a light tenor voice with a pleasant timbre. He loved to play the harmonica and during his happy moods, he would play the mouth organ and Harvey would join in on the Jew's harp. If there is anything to inheriting a musical talent, it must have been passed down from Dad. We could all sing, all of us, except Mom.

There was never a respite for Mom from the backbreaking chore of homemaking and taking care of her brood. She never complained. She would go about her daily chores, singing in her off-key manner, scrubbing clothes over a washboard resting in a large galvanized-steel tub or rolling dough for bread on the kitchen table. She never spoke about the hurts that left their permanent scars within her soul. She was always alive as the bright morning sun except when the load became too heavy, then the tears would fall.

Recalling three quarters of a century and those depression years, times must have been very difficult for Mom and Dad. Dad was a proud man. He would never consider asking for charity of any kind. He would find meager jobs that would pay a few dollars each month and with this hard earned money, he paid the rent and put food on our table. Mom patched our clothes so many times we wondered how she could possibly get so much mileage out of rags. She was always searching the rag bag in an effort to find enough material to create shirts and pants for my brother Harvey and myself. Rags that couldn't be salvaged to make more clothing were torn into strips and woven into rag rugs, the only floor coverings we ever knew. Dad was not stingy when it came to driving nails into our half-soled shoes. We could pull nails to the point where many times the sole would depart from the shoe, but that wasn't the case with Dad's handiwork. Nails were pulled and there were always nails to spare.

The only livestock we could boast about at the crossroads were a few laying hens, a couple roosters, and of course, our dog, Jack. He was really Dad's dog, but Jack was part of the family and the only member Dad permitted on his lap for a little extra affection. He was a master jumper. He could leap over the wire fence separating our little house from the gravel road as if there were no fence at all. He didn't have to be concerned about getting hit by a car. If the sound of an engine could be heard coming up or down the road, we would run out to see who it was. Few cars traveled those back roads. Jack was part collie and part something else. He was so much a part of the human race, there were times when he made sounds as if he were actually trying to talk.

When the hens laid their eggs for the purpose of procreation, I recall Mom testing the eggs in water to see if they were fertile. She would then place the eggs back into the nest. The mother hen had an innate intuition as to which eggs were ready to bring forth new life. She would settle down on the eggs Mom placed under her wings and there she would sit until the day a passerby could hear the pecking of a fully developed chick trying to break open the shell, ready to explore the world on the outside. No one dared to disturb the mother hen. No one dared to go near her nest. If I happened to be assigned the chore of gathering eggs that were not fertile, the hen would give a vicious disgruntled warning by ruffling her feathers. If that didn't frighten the intruder, she would leave her nest and make an attack on the trespasser they would long remember. No further communication was needed between a young boy and a setting hen.

It was springtime and the chicks began to hatch. The tiny bills would peck against the wall of the shell until the shell broke open and a fluffy, although a bit wet, yellow chick emerged. I recall so vividly one particular chick that was rejected by the mother hen. Why she abandoned the little fellow was anybody's guess. The mother hen would peck the forlorn piece of fluff until it stood alone, wondering where to seek shelter and protection. I lifted the rejected baby chick from the ground and placed it into the palm of my hand. Gently, I carried it into the house. Mom always had an answer when there was a crisis. She found a small box, just the right size to house the frightened and insecure newborn. She placed some old newspaper in the box along with a canning lid filled with water and a small dish in which she put small amounts of chicken feed, hoping the newborn would make an effort to eat and drink. All was well with the little chick, that is, until I decided my new friend should also be my bed partner. "Loy—I know you love your chicken, but you are not going to sleep with that bird. Now—if you insist on that creature staying in the house, then you put the box next to your bed. That way, you can check on the chick throughout the night."

That first night away from its mother was the beginning of a bonding friendship. That tiny piece of fluff transferred all its love and affection normally given to its mother to me. I was a surrogate mother to a chicken.

I called my friend "Biddy." As the fowl began to mature, I would attempt to encourage the little fellow to join his brother and sisters as they followed the mother hen wherever the mother hen wished to take her brood. All of my friend's siblings would stay close to the mother hen, but when he attempted to join the clan, he was immediately shunned and pushed away. That's when my friend decided I was the one to follow. He would follow me wherever I would walk. We became an inseparable twosome.

I often crossed the road to play in the old barn where the rickety buggy rested. I would take my place in the driver's seat and Biddy would sit next to me in the passenger side. As I pretended I was driving the hottest rod on the road, vibrating my lips to make the sound of a motor, Biddy would beep, beep, beep, as if he were the finest horn ever created for the hottest sports car in the country.

When I would sit in the old rubber tire swing hanging from the branch of the old oak tree, Biddy was on my shoulder, letting the wind rush through his feathers as we soared higher and higher into the sky.

My brother Francis occasionally visited us at the crossroads. I never felt as close to him as I did to Lizzie, Harvey, and Ruth. Of course, that could be due to the fact I was never around him and he wasn't a constant companion as my other three siblings were. It was a Saturday afternoon I shall remember for the rest of my life. As I have stated previously, my chicken was always at my heels. I came into the house on this particular Saturday afternoon and there sat my oldest brother on the davenport holding a turtle. When he saw my chicken, he reached toward the floor and grabbed Biddy. Teasingly, he held my chick in one hand and in the other hand the turtle. He pretended he was going to feed my bird to his turtle. I screamed then ran for the screen door, not realizing my little chicken was right at my heels. I opened the screen door and as it slammed shut, it hit my most valued friend in the head. My chicken lay still on the porch, blood running from his tiny beak. I can recall the tears flooding over my cheeks as I tenderly picked my little friend up and gently caressed it in the palm of my hand. My friend was dead. I was too young to know anything about death. This was my first experience. Mom gave me an old, empty cigar box. Tenderly, I laid my friend inside the box then walked outside where the rubber tire swing hung from the old oak tree. I dug a grave for Biddy, all the time letting the tears run freely. I placed the box with my bird inside in the deep hole, then covered the box with dirt. It would be many months before the pain and loss of my good friend would pass. I know one is supposed to forgive, but to forgive my brother was almost an impossibility.

When Harvey and Lizzie were in school that first year at the crossroads, and it was only Mom and me at home, I had to find ways of amusing myself. The gravel pit was always our source of recreation. It was our swimming hole in the summer and with the use of an abandoned rowboat some former tenant had left floating idly in our private fishing hole, Harvey swam out to the boat and guided it to shore. He made a couple of oars and we would often amuse ourselves floating on the waters of the three pits, fishing for some of the marine life that liked worms.

I was never permitted to go to the gravel pit by myself. Harvey was always with me. I didn't know how to swim so most of my playing in the water took place just sitting in the shallow waters at the edge of the gravel pit. As I mentioned previously, the water was alive with all kinds of creatures including an abundance of crawdads. It was one of those forbidden days when I wandered to the pit and sat on the edge of the water. I removed my pants so they wouldn't get wet. As I sat there, I suddenly felt something grab onto my tiny append-age. I screamed and the louder I cried, the tighter that monster clung to my tiny penis. As I ran toward the house, the creature finally let go of my most precious tool. "Mom! Mom!" I cried as I ran into the house. "I was attacked by a crawdad." Blood was running down my leg. I apparently had left my pants on the shore of the gravel pit.

"Where are your pants, Loy? This wouldn't have hap-pened if you'd listened to us about going to that gravel pit by yourself."

Mom wasn't an over-emotional type when it came to bumps and scrapes her kids were always experiencing. She would smile and sometimes laugh when she didn't think any of our accidents were serious. Gently, Mom began to examine my wound. "It's gonna be all right, Loy. Now, ya jes' hush fer a minute and I'll git the salve. It'll be just as good as new before ya know'd it."

Mom cleaned the pincer marks with her homemade soap, which in itself would kill any germ known to man. Carefully, she rubbed her soothing balm over the still visible wound.

"Put a bandage on it, Mom," I pleaded. Mom saved flour sacks as bandages for such occasions. When the bags were empty of flour, she would wash the sacks then turn them into dish towels. When they were worn beyond usefulness for dry-ing dishes, she sanitarily laundered them and made a special space for them to use as bandages. Mom tore a piece of the cloth into a strip just large enough to wrap around my tiny penis. Not one to be inhibited, as soon as Harvey and Lizzie got off the school bus, I hurriedly dropped my pants to show them my wound. By the following morning, the pincer marks had all but disappeared.

CHAPTER 19

NEW BABIES CAUSED MORE OF a stir among the poor than any other event. A postcard arrived at the crossroads announcing the birth of a little girl. It was my sister Edna and her husband Bennie's first baby. Edna and Bennie lived in Muncie. Bennie wasn't an educated man, but he managed to provide for my sister and now his new daughter. He never liked me much. If he did he failed to communicate or project those feelings in my direction. The rented house he provided for his family, however, was considerably upgraded in comparison to the house of Abe. They had indoor plumbing, electricity and most of all, they had a radio. Before the baby was born, I would often make the trip to Muncie with Mom and Dad. We'd usually spend the night then return to the crossroads the following morning. Bennie worked at the foundry. He was up early in the morning and his first act upon rising was to turn on the radio. I slept on the couch in the parlor. He played the radio at full volume which, of course, would awaken any normal person from a sound sleep. It was always a station that broadcast music from Nashville and the Grand Ole Opry. Without my brother-in-law's awareness, he introduced me to a world of music like I had never been exposed to. The tunes coming through that small tabletop radio made an indelible impression on my mind. I am certain, had a guitar been placed in my hands at that tender age, my musical career would have taken an entirely different route. I loved country and western music. Above everything else in life, I wanted to be a country and western singer.

Mom and Dad were excited about the birth of their first grandchild. The baby had barely time to be washed clean when a fast decision was made to make a trip to Muncie to see the blessed event. Of course, from what they said, I was too young and would have to remain at home with Lizzie, Ruth, and Harvey.

Mom ran out into the yard and grabbed one of her plump chickens that peacefully pecked at the gravel and food spread on the ground. Little beknownst to the chicken, it was living on borrowed time. Before nightfall, that chicken would be plucked of all its feathers, cut up in small pieces, and placed on a platter in the middle of a kitchen table in Muncie.

Mom, as a rule, would grab the chicken, ring its neck until the head departed from the fowl's body, then she would pick off all the feathers, finishing the chore by cutting the creature into small pieces. This time was different. Since it was a distance to travel before reaching Muncie, she grabbed the chicken, tied its legs, then she and Dad would board the open air Model T. She would rest the predestined chicken on her lap and Dad would put his Tin Lizzie into motion.

A short distance from our house, railroad tracks crossed the main road leading to Muncie. There was no signal to alert the Model T of an oncoming train. Dad approached the tracks then proceeded to guide his old Tin Lizzie over the tracks toward the other side. Out of nowhere, a sudden shrill sound of a train whistle shook the Model T and Mom and Dad. The chicken freaked, spread its wings, and took to the air. Mom grabbed for the airborne bird. Dad removed his hands from the steering wheel and reached for the chicken as it flew from Mom's hands and over his head. The man-made horseless vehicle moved forward without guidance. It barely crossed the tracks when the cowcatcher caught the rear bumper of Dad's Tin Lizzie. The vehicle trembled from the impact, then wobbled at a fast rate of speed, zigzagging across an open pasture. Mom and Dad bounced like a couple of rag dolls, their foreheads hitting the windshield. When the vehicle came to a halt, bruised, but not seriously injured, they got out of the battered Ford as the engine gave one single gasp and quit. The chicken dropped from the sky like a lead balloon and lay dead just a few feet from the dying Model T.

"Come on, Lizzie." That was Dad's pet name for his car. "Come on, Sweetheart!" Patiently he turned the crank inserted into the crankshaft. "Come on, Old Girl," he repeated time and time again as if he were talking to a dying animal. It appeared Lizzie understood. One more crank and the engine sputtered and continued to run.

"Oley," Dad said, "I think we'd better fergit about Muncie and go home. I don't think this old girl is gonna make it." Dad's Tin Lizzie did make it to the front yard at the crossroads. As she came to a halt, Dad didn't even have to turn off the ignition. The tired engine quit, never to run again.

It was springtime and the end of the school year was coming to a close. The house at the crossroads was like a magnet during that first year we lived there. It attracted relatives, not only my married sister, but the half sisters from as far away as West Lebanon and Akron, Ohio. The gravel pits served as our own private swimming pool and the surrounding mounds of gravel were like having our own private beach.

The Rainbolts arrived from Akron. Although their off-spring were older than myself, I was, not by choice, an uncle. This title, however, never gave me any respect. In fact, I never gave it much thought as to my relationship to these strangers. While Harvey and I would replace our pants with cutoff overalls at the knees and weighing a ton once our bathing attire was wet, Claude Jr. and Lenora appeared wearing store-bought swimming suits. No one mentioned anything unusual about Claude Jr., not until I brought it to everyone's attention. His tight-fitting swim trunks barely covered his tailbone. I was first to notice a strange looking tail protruding just above the tailbone of my nephew's body. I had never seen a human with a tail. "Where did Junior get that tail, Mom? I don't have a tail like that."

"Be quiet, Loy. You mustn't ask them kind of questions. Everyone's gonna hear ya." No one noticed the tail until I brought it to their attention. Of course, my curiosity and statement didn't go unnoticed.

Urith tried to explain. "It happened when I visited the zoo just before Claude Jr. was born. I stood in front of the lion's cage. The wild beast suddenly lunged toward me, his giant paws almost breakin' through the wire of his cage. I was so frightened. I placed my hand behind my back at exactly the same area where my tailbone is located. I never thought any more about the incident, not until Claude Jr. was born. When he drew his first breath I noticed a fluff of hair growing from exactly the same place where I had placed my hands on my own body. It looked just like the lion's mane.

I passed my sixth birthday on June 24th, 1930. I would begin my first year of schooling at the end of August of that year. That summer was an eventful time for the VanNatter family. It would be the first time Dad would be reunited with his daughter Marie, her husband, and their brood. Marie was Dad's firstborn. It was discovered my unknown half sister lived only a few miles from the crossroads. She had married a man by the name of Walter Wrench and they had two sons. The sons were named Walter Jr. and the youngest one they called "Beanie."

Marie VanNatter Wrench had bright, red, curly hair which she kept cropped close to her round, freckled face. I hadn't seen many silent western movies, but the ones I had seen, the tavern owners, usually women, looked like Marie. She was totally different than anyone else in the family or the other girls Dad had sired by Josephine. There was a brash manner which appeared to be a bit hard, but, one soon discovered under her facade of roughness, there was a kind, gentle, generous, wonderful woman.

I don't recall just how Dad discovered his daughter was living so close to the crossroads. At any rate, on a warm, sunny, Saturday, Marie invited Dad, Mom, and the rest of us to their small farm for a picnic. Marie had set up a long table under a lush looking shade tree. She covered the table with a white, spotless tablecloth and on the table she placed a spread of food like I had never seen. When we arrived in the newer Model T Dad had acquired after Lizzie expired, Marie greeted us as if she had never been missing from the family.

"Now—ya all go and sit down. I have one more thing to bring from the house before we begin eatin'. Loy—you sit there next to yer Mom. Since you and Beanie are the same age, Beanie, you sit there next to Loy."

Everyone took their seats at the long table. Marie asked if anyone wanted to say grace or "Should we jes' git down to the business of eatin'?" Mom offered to say grace and as she uttered the final "Amen," Marie was standing at the head of the table with a large pitcher of ice-cold foaming beer.

"All ya jes' have to taste my homebrew! It ain't gonna do nothin' to ya but make ya feel good. I made it from scratch and I dare say, there ain't no beer in this county that can compare with my concoction."

No one objected as she poured her specialty into a glass set next to each plate. Even the kids were included. The first sip created an impression on my taste buds that has never been duplicated. Not one person sitting at the table refused a second glass. There was a feeling of goodwill and peace around that long picnic table. Dad was ready to sing and play his harmonica. I'm not certain Dad was even aware the beer was an alcoholic beverage. He had a strong aversion to anyone who drank anything stronger than a glass of water. The few sips from his glass of Marie's magic nectar had an effect on Dad that suddenly transformed him into a happy, fun-loving man. He did everything but dance on the table.

When the sun began to set and the day came to an end, it was a new beginning for Dad. He would never again be separated from his firstborn.

My sister Ruth finished her eighth year of schooling. Instead of going into high school, she took a job as a caregiver for an invalid woman. It was not unusual for youngsters to drop out of school. It was much more important for a person to begin supporting themselves and relieve some of the burden placed on parents who had difficulty making ends meet. Ruth was never home much of the time after she quit school. I suppose it was the reason I relied heavily on my brother Harvey and my sister Lizzie to fill the void each family member might create when they left the nest. Dad would leave home at dawn to either labor in the fields or in search of recyclable junk he could gather and eventually turn into cash.

We were poor and never knew the luxury of material plenty. Mom seemed to manage on Dad's meager income, and as long as we could depend on the earth beneath our feet to keep us supplied with food during the summer months and we received our nourishment from the harvest's previous canning season during the winter months, our survival was secure.

Dad was a proud Republican. For him to accept any kind of charity he would always prefer to do without than admit there might not be enough food for our next meal. I fail to recall a time when Mom didn't have a pot of beans cooking in the iron, weathered pot on the wood burning, cast-iron range in the kitchen. The few chickens we had supplied us with eggs, and when the chickens refused to lay, they ended up in a platter for a Sunday dinner. Fruit from the trees were canned, so pie was our usual dessert other than an occasional cake. When Mom baked a cake, all of us kids waited at the kitchen table to lick the mixing bowl when its contents were placed in a pan then placed in the oven to be baked. In the springtime, when an abundance of yellow blossoms crept upward through the green grass, Mom would pick the most tender plants. Dandelion greens were a way of life in our household. I hated them. The only way my palate would accept the bitterness of nature's first sign of spring was to soak the few greens I took on my plate with cider vinegar. There was always lots of cider vinegar. During apple-picking time, apples gathered from the tree in our yard were stored in the cyclone cellar. As the fresh, red apples began to spoil, Mom would juice the apples, can the juice, and then place all the juice contents into Ball Brothers canning jars which were then neatly placed on the shelves in the cyclone cellar. As I recall, they were almost as potent as Marie's homebrew.

Mom had an answer to everything. We never knew or could we afford a professional medical man, so Mom had to be the doctor. Her concoctions were a bit harsh at times. She often made the comment as she held our nose and placed a teaspoon of her nasty creation into our mouths, "If it tastes good, it ain't gonna do ya no good." If the result of her treatment starting with the mouth did not succeed, she had another answer. She was a master enema giver. "If the inside's clean, ya don't hafta worry about the outside," she would say. Mom was a real pro when it came to mixing her ingredients into salves and ointments. One thing was always certain— when it came to fighting germs, something was going to die and there was little doubt Mom was always on the winning end of the battle.

CHAPTER 20

IT WAS AT THE END of August in 1930 I began my first year of schooling. Mr. Erwin, the school bus driver, was always on time as he drove his bus in front of the house at the cross-roads, stopped long enough for each one of us to board, and then we were on our way to Gaston. Sleet, rain, snow, or ice did not prevent our friendly driver from executing his daily, five-days-a-week chore.

He was an unusual man. He knew more about child psychology than anyone I would ever meet, including those who obtained numerous academic degrees. If a child was unruly, he had a knack for settling any dispute without hurting or embarrassing the offender. There was no problem so complicated that Mr. Erwin couldn't solve it. Some kids fell in love with their school teacher. I fell in love with Mr. Erwin. Many times during those tender years, I wondered what it would be like to have a young father like Mr. Erwin. He was kind, gentle, and he would greet us by name each weekday morning. He would deliver us safely to the school in Gaston and at the close of the school day, he never failed to have the bus running and waiting for each youngster to board when the last bell rang signifying another school day had come to an end.

My first grade teacher was a kinky, flaming, curly, red-headed tyrant. She was a small woman whose complexion looked like skimmed milk, and her face was accentuated with red blotches I later learned were called freckles. I couldn't see beneath her long dress, but I'm certain there were undoubtedly freckles on her butt. Mom used to say when a pimple appeared on one of our faces, "It's jes' the devil in ya tryin' to come out." In the eyes of a small child, the devil was sure tryin' to escape from a good many places on the body of Doris Gill.

My first grade of schooling introduced me to a teacher whose mean streak left its mark on every kid who passed through her classroom. Her approach to discipline was never so tame as standing in the corner or sitting on a stool in front of the room. No—at all times, she carried a steel-edged ruler in her hand. Satan's pitchfork couldn't have been more lethal. That instrument was used far more regularly as a weapon to hit small fingers and knuckles that accidentally slipped away from their paper on the child's desk than it was as a pointer to something on the blackboard. In the middle drawer of the teacher's desk, Miss Gill kept a three-hole paddle. This was designed to come down heavy on a kid's butt with the same regularity with which the red headed witch utilized the steel-edged ruler. The paddle was always a matter of double jeopardy. Dad consistently warned, "If any of you youngins' git a lickin' at school, ya can jes' expect another one when ya git home."

My desk was located behind the prettiest girl I had ever seen. She had long, golden, straight hair that fell just below her shoulders. Not only was she pretty, she was smart and most of all she liked me. I never considered myself smart, not like my brother Harvey. I was slow to learn how to use numbers and how to spell. Miss Gill would write numbers on the blackboard. We would copy those numbers on a piece of paper. Once we placed a line at the long column of numbers, we were supposed to add all the numbers together then place a final total under the line. It was the chore of adding each one of those figures and coming up with the right answer which paved the way to my Waterloo. My pretty friend was always right. Knowing I was having difficulty, she would wait until the teacher turned her face toward the blackboard, then she would move slightly to the side of her seat so I could plainly see the answers she had written on her paper.

Doris Gill was like a witch with eyes in the back of her head. She suddenly, literally flew from the blackboard to my friend Lisa's desk. "Lisa!" she screamed. Freckled arms and hands grabbed my little friend by the shoulders, shaking her as a terrier might shake a mouse.

"Get to the front of the room, Lisa!" she shouted. Tears flowed from my friend's eyes. She timidly arose from her desk and moved forward like Joan of Arc being forced to the burning stake. The teacher was right behind her. Reaching the front of the room, Miss Gill reached into the drawer of her desk and withdrew the paddle. She pulled a chair to the center of the room so the entire class could observe her next action. She sat down on the chair, then grabbed Lisa, forcing the child's body across her lap. Pulling the little girl's dress up to her waistline, she revealed Lisa's panties and as she did so her arm holding the paddle rose then descended on the child's buttocks with a stinging blow. The teacher's shrill angry voice rang above the slap of the paddle and Lisa's sobbing. "This'll teach you, Lisa." Another blow struck my friend's bottom. "You'll never, and I mean never, cheat again, do ya hear?"

I wanted to rush to the front of the room and place my arms around my friend's shoulder to help her return to her seat. I should have been the one gittin' the lickin'. Finally Miss Gill released my friend. Lisa tried to muffle her sobs as she sat down at her desk in front of mine. When the recess bell sounded and all the youngsters rushed from the schoolroom out onto the playground, I took Lisa's hand. "It's my fault, Lisa, and I'm sorry. I held my friend's hand until we were called back into the classroom at the end of recess.

Punishment was oftentimes delayed in those early childhood days. Those delayed punishments were more of a threat than an actuality. Not so, with Doris Gill. As I took my seat, the sharp, staccato voice of Miss Gill rang out. "Loy! You will stay after school."

The bell rang for the close of the school day. My classmates filed one by one out of the room and boarded their respective school buses. I was alone. I watched the redheaded vampire draw three lines on the blackboard.

"Come up here to the blackboard, Loy," she ordered. "Now—you will spell and write your name correctly three times within these lines. You will not let the lowercase letters in your name extend above or below the first two lines. The capital letters, like the first letter in your name and the first letter in your last name, will not extend above that top line."

Shaking, I attempted to comply with the teacher's orders. As I stood there, always feeling the presence of the evil spirit behind me, I could hear the school bus revving its engine. I was certain Mr. Erwin was about to leave without me. When the bus began to back away from the parking area, Miss Gill gave me permission to go. Panic stricken, I raced from the schoolroom into the yard. Mr. Erwin saw me. He could see something had gone wrong from the tears streaming down my cheeks as I boarded the bus.

"Why don't ya jes' sit up here next to me, Loy and tell me what happened. Maybe we can fix it." Harvey and Lizzie had already boarded and of course, they were certain I had gotten a lickin' in school. I told Mr. Erwin what happened. "Well, Loy, at least, you know how to write and spell your name."

I still had another semester to go, and of course there was no escape from the clutches of Doris Gill. It was nearing Christmas and there would be a few days away from school and that witch, Miss Gill. Christmas and Santa Claus represented two different things at our house. We soon learned there was no Santa Claus and if there were, he never stopped at the house of Abe.

It was a religious time of year. It was the time, we were taught, Jesus was born and Jesus was God, the creator of all things. He had been born in a manger in a land far, far away all because there was no room for him at the inn. This time of year meant going to church and singing Christmas carols until the same old familiar tunes began to wear a bit thin.

Christmas time in 1930 at the crossroads would be the only Christmas our family would share as a family unit. It wasn't that Dad was a scrooge and disliked Christmas; he celebrated Christmas all year long. If there was anything he had to share, he shared it. For us, to have a roof over our heads and food on the table was the greatest gift of all.

I don't know why Christmas of 1930 was going to be any different than Christmases past, but it was. It was the time of year when cold, wintery air and blinding blizzards covered the earth with a never-ending blanket of snow. Even the water in the gravel pits froze and we could walk across the ice from one side of the pits to the other. It would be my last Christmas before I reached the age of seven and would tag along with Lizzie and Harvey as we boarded the school bus that would take us to the grade school in Gaston. We had never had a Christmas tree from the day I was born. It was Harvey's idea that just he and myself would wander off into the woods and find a small sapling that we could call our first tree. He spoke to Mom about it. The tree was no problem, but as for decorations, we discovered we could bring colored paper home from school and we would create our own tree that would be different than anyone else who could afford the luxury of fancy balls, tinsel, and lights. Mom agreed to pop popcorn which we threaded then draped the tree with popcorn garlands.

The snow was deep, but that didn't hinder Harvey and me leaving the warm house in search of a small tree we could sit on top of the old trunk in the parlor. Harvey was 11 years old at the time, but in my mind's eyes, he was my big brother. We put on our boots and trekked off into the woods to find a tree. I saw a young sapling making its way up through the deep snow. "There it is, Harvey!" I shouted. Harvey handed me the axe and I cut down our first Christmas tree. It was not over three feet tall. It was just the right size to decorate with our homemade paper Christmas ornaments and strings of popcorn.

Lizzie, Harvey, Ruth, and myself sat around the kitchen table for hours creating odd looking ornaments to place on our first Christmas tree. Carefully, we hung the colorful paper trinkets on the sparse branches. Mom, Ruth, and Lizzie strung garlands made of popcorn then draped their creations around the tree. Since we had no electricity, there was no way of lighting the tree. Even without the commercial

customary lights, we all stood back and admired our handiwork. We were in total agreement, it was the most beautiful
tree we would ever have.

We always had sugar in the house and after the tree was
decorated, Mom announced it was time to make and pull
taffy. I don't recall just what the argument was all about between Harvey and myself, but Dad's sudden entrance into the
kitchen and his usual slap across my brother's face brought
the argument to a quick end. My big brother was destined to
be Dad's whipping boy.

As we had always done, regardless of where we lived,
Mom made sure we never missed going to church on Christmas Eve. So it was as we trekked through the crunching
snow toward Zion. The service had already started when
we arrived, and as we approached the lighted church, we
could hear the ancient reed organ playing "Silent Night,"
"Oh Little Town of Bethlehem," and other immortal carols.
As we entered the church and took our place in one of the
pews, the preacher walked to his podium to deliver a short
Christmas message. The congregation followed the sermon
with a community sing. The immortal sounds of Christmas
sung by singers composed of farmers, their wives, and their
offspring formed an unforgettable angelic choir. When the
preacher ended the service with his usual Benediction, we
arose from our seats then followed the congregation as they
boarded their horse and buggies, sleighs, or an automobile
to return to their neighboring farmlands. Snow resumed falling on the quiet earth as we trekked toward the crossroads.
There was something magical about that Christmas. It was
one that is indelibly printed in my memory three quarters of
a century later.

During the night, the winds caused the snow to drift

upon our porch. It was sometime during the nighttime hours a stranger came to our house. On Christmas morning, Dad permitted Harvey to stay in bed instead of demanding he cut wood before breakfast. Dad was the first one to notice a large basket next to the outside door opening into the kitchen. Noiselessly, at sometime during the nighttime hours, a stranger had left a large basket of food including a baked ham. There was an unsigned note attached to the handle of the large basket. The note read, "Just wanted to wish you a Merry Christmas." The stranger in the night supplied our poverty-stricken family with a Christmas dinner like we would never again experience. We were never to know the identity of the good Samaritan who supplied a hungry family with food.

Harvey and I climbed from our warm bed when Mom called and said breakfast was ready. We had to pass the tree to get to the kitchen and to our surprise there were presents under the tree. Mom had secretly woven mittens for each one of us and had placed them at the base of the tree. On the tree top was a tiny 10-cent horn. Mom had bought the horn just for me. Dad had placed some hardtack candies next to the mittens. It was Christmas time at the crossroads.

CHAPTER 21

THE WINTER BEGAN TO SHOW signs of turning into spring. The snow that covered the earth with an ermine white blanket during the long, dark months, now with the onset of rains turned the snow into a slush. At some point in time, Harvey earned enough money during the thrashing season to purchase a secondhand bicycle. He was always in demand for laboring in the fields following behind a thrashing machine and stacking wheat. When corn-shucking time came around, even at his tender age he could easily compete with Dad when it came to shucking corn. The Hannan boys lived on a large farm up the road just past Zion. They were Harvey's buddies. Dad never complained about Harvey's association with the two fellows who were considered ruffians. On Halloween, those boys took great delight in playing Halloween pranks and occasionally Harvey would go along. The most serious prank was to turn over outside privies, much to the victim's chagrin, especially when they chose to make a run for the toilet during the middle of the night only to find it no longer stood where it had prior to their going to bed. Harvey and the Hannon boys were clever. The misdemeanor crime they committed on that night of all nights was never discovered. No victim was ever able to identify the culprits who trespassed upon their land and upset the most important utility where man, woman, and child responded to their biological needs.

It was a wet, slushy morning and a Saturday. We were out of school and for some unknown reason, Dad, before leaving the house to collect recyclable junk, gave orders that none of us kids were to leave the house. It was nasty outside and he didn't want us to get sick. We had no money for doctors.

My brother, who dared to defy Dad's orders, had no intention of changing his prearranged plans. He was going to ride up the road to the Hannon farm. He waited for Dad to leave the house. When the sound of the Model T could no longer be heard, he checked to see if Dad was really out of sight, then he mounted his bike and headed toward the Hannon farm. It wasn't that my brother overstayed his visit at the Hannon farm, the problem lay in the fact that Dad returned home much sooner than expected.

The first words out of Dad's mouth as he opened the kitchen door were, "Where's Harvey?" We knew there was trouble. Dad's face flushed with anger. "I'll give that youngin' a shellackin' he won't forgit when he gits home!"

My sister Ruth happened to be home at the time. She was always a rather flippant, daring soul and in her smart-ass way, she approached Dad with her hands on her hips with the confidence of David when he faced Goliath. "Did ya say yer gonna whip Harvey? You dare, Dad, you just dare, you just dare hit—!" Before another word could escape from her mouth, Dad's fist came through with an upper right, making a direct contact on my sister's pointed chin. She fell backward like a stiff board, her body hitting the bare floor of the kitchen. Blood oozed from her nose and mouth. Before she could gain any composure and rise to her feet, Harvey walked onto the front porch. Dad didn't wait for him to open the door. "Git in the woodshed, Harvey! I'm gonna teach ya a lesson ya ain't gonna fergit for the rest of yer life!"

Frozen in fear, we all stood in the middle of the kitchen as blood-curdling screams filled the wet, cold air. The swishing sound of the switch coming down across Harvey's back filled Mom with terror. Time stood still. It seemed as if it were only yesterday Mom had witnessed the brutal beating of Abe's own daughter. It was a repeat performance of Abe's ire taken out on the youthful body of Harvey. Even her son, Cecil, had not extended further than the ever present razor strap.

We heard the door to the woodshed close. My brother ran from the woodshed into the house. His bare skin revealed stinging red stripes across his back. As Dad followed Harvey into the kitchen, anger in Mom's eyes turned into sharp daggers. She seldom had the courage to confront Dad. On this particular day, his actions stirred her fighting Irish spirit like I never knew could exist in the gentle soul of my mother. Before Dad could close the kitchen door, Mom charged toward Dad like a raging bull ready to crush everything in its way. "Git yer things, Abe, and git out! You jes' hit my youngins' fer the last time!"

Compassionately, Mom moved toward my brother. She put her arms around him. Harvey let the tears flow as he placed his head against Mom's breast. "When he gits outta here, Harvey, I'm gonna see if I can make ya feel better. I'm sorry Dad ain't got no sense when it comes to carin' fer his kids."

Dad didn't bother to pack any of his clothes. He just turned and stomped out of the kitchen and into the Tin Lizzie parked in the front yard. The sound of the old jalopy leaving the yard brought an eerie quietness to the little red house at the crossroads.

Hours passed after Dad's departure. No one knew where he went nor did they care, but Mom was desperate. As she attempted to put a bit of supper on the table, tears of desperation flowed like a waterfall from her eyes. We were destitute and food was scarce. All monies Dad earned recycling junk remained in his pocket. Most of the food stashed away from the previous harvest was almost gone. Mom was always a master at preparing a meal with just a few basic ingredients, usually nothing more elaborate than a little salt, pepper, or sugar. Without these staples to maintain the house at the crossroads, it was difficult to even bake a loaf of bread. Dad was a firm believer in supplying the family with plenty of peanut butter and jars of homemade apple butter, but even those items no longer existed. The contents of the cyclone cellar amounted to a few apples and potatoes on the dirt floor. On the shelves, empty canning jars sat waiting for another canning season.

Mom often took rendered lard and spread it on her homemade bread. She would season the lard with salt and pepper, but now, even that too, was low. Occasionally, she found an eatable apple on the floor of the cellar that was not rotten. This would be added to our lunch box along with lard sandwiches. One of the vivid memories I have of those early childhood years was seeing other youngsters opening their lunch buckets loaded with fresh fruit and sandwiches. Though we had always been taught to not be envious of others' possessions, I must have been the most prominent sinner.

I don't know how we survived during Dad's absence, but somehow after he was no longer part of our family, there developed a pleasant aura over the house of Abe. The preacher often dropped by and he would always bring along enough food until his next visit. As the days, nights, and weeks passed, laughter started to resound throughout the house and Mom's Irish wit and sense of humor let our spirits soar. Mom was always at her best when something she might say would cause people to explode with laughter.

We never knew where Dad had gone when he left the house on that terrible day. He was gone and we didn't care. Somehow, we survived. It was in the early springtime when we gathered around the kitchen table to eat our supper's meager rations, a sound of a Model T could be heard rolling towards the crossroads. As usual, Mom said grace and by the time she said "Amen," we heard the car decrease its speed then pull into our yard. The Ford coughed a couple of times after Dad turned off the ignition. He sat behind the wheel in eerie silence wondering if he dared cross the portals leading into the house. I vividly recall sitting around the table afraid to imbibe in our meager rations as we heard the heavy steps of Dad's hip boots grinding against the gravel we had spread on top the early spring's snow covering the ground.

Saying nothing, he took his seat at the head of the table. Mom rose from her chair, then walked to the cabinet, reached for another plate, and placed it in front of Dad. When she sat down, she folded her hands and offered another prayer. "Thank ya, Lord fer bringin' Papa home. Help him to learn to live in a more gentle way with his family. Amen."

There were no further words spoken as we consumed our food. When the meal came to an end, Ruth, Elizabeth, Harvey and myself cleared the table, washed and dried the supper dishes. Mom and Dad went into the parlor. When the dish chore was completed, and the table reset for our morning meal, Ruth fixed a fresh pot of oatmeal and placed it on top the iron stove where it would simmer and cook throughout the night. We then extinguished the flickering light from the kerosene lamp sitting in the middle of the kitchen table. Without speaking to Dad, we walked through the parlor into the small bedroom my brother, myself and my sisters shared.

Late into the night we could hear Mom and Dad talking. Their conversation never rose much above a whisper. We could hear Dad stoking the fire in the potbellied stove, then the parlor lamp light filtering under our bedroom door was extinguished.

The first chore of the day before breakfast was to chop enough wood to keep the stoves going throughout the day. I had reached the useful age whereby this task was also part of my duties. Harvey wasted no time leaving a warm bed when he awakened. He had learned it was much better to do a job without being told than to wait until Dad entered the room to hit him across the butt with his hip boot. I too climbed from the bed, dressed and was ready to brave the morning chill. The following morning after Dad's return was quiet. Dad had not awakened us nor could we hear him speak on the other side of the closed door. It was after Mom placed all the food on the breakfast table I heard Dad say, "Well, Oley, I got the wood chopped for the day so I guess we can git the youngins' out of bed now. They gotta git ready to go to school."

"Time to git up, kids. Breakfast is on the table." As Mom spoke, we hurriedly arose from our bed. A porcelain basin containing cold water rested on a stand next to the window. Each one of us took our turn dashing cold water on our faces, then en masse we walked into the kitchen. We took our usual places at the table. As we looked at our mother, we noticed the worried look which was always present during Dad's absence had relaxed. There was peace in the house of Abe. There was little doubt, Mom was glad Dad came home.

CHAPTER 22

THE LAST DAY OF SCHOOL was one to long be remembered. When I received my report card and saw that I had been passed onto the second grade, I wanted to stand on a rooftop and shout it to the rest of the world. I was free, free from that tyrant I had as a first grade teacher. She would never again strike my knuckles with her steel-edged ruler or would she ever hit my friend who sat in the desk in front of mine with that lethal paddle that was always present in the teacher's middle drawer of her desk.

I couldn't wait to get home. When Mr. Erwin stopped the bus in front of the house at the crossroads, I leaped from the bus, kicked off my shoes, and yelled, "Mom! Mom! I passed!" I can still feel the fresh grass beneath my bare feet as I ran into the house. I grabbed Mom around the waist. "Mom! I passed. I'm gonna go into the second grade!"

Springtime stirred farmers from their winter's hiatus. The snow melted and the spring rains came. When the rains ceased to fall, even for short periods of time, the people who lived off the land knew it was time for planting. The weather was beginning to feel warm again and new life broke through the rich, Midwestern soil. When the school term ended, all offspring of the farmers could be seen laboring in the fields.

When the work was plentiful, farmers would hire the neighboring farmers' kids to augment the lack of workers. I wasn't old enough to be much help, but Harvey was 12 years old and he had a reputation of being one of the finest workers a farmer could want. That summer of 1931 would separate my brother and me for the first time since I was born.

Charlie Wilson recently married. He had inherited several acres of land from his father and having no children of their own, Charlie and his bride approached Dad, hoping he would be agreeable to permitting Harvey come live with them on a full-time basis. They agreed to see that Harvey went to school and they were most willing to take care of his needs for as long as he resided under their roof.

Mom was not happy with Dad's decision, but in Dad's way of thinking, it meant one less mouth to feed. "Abe, he's much too young to leave home." Dad would quickly reply. "It's time, Oley, to let 'im go. He's 12 years old now, and there just ain't no reason he cain't start earnin' his keep. Now ya jes' can't keep motherin' these kids. They jes' gotta learn how to make it on their own. Them Wilsons are good people and will give Harvey much more than we can give 'im. It ain't like he's goin' to the moon. He'll probably be home every weekend; he jes' won't be sleepin' and eatin' here.

I missed my brother that summer. We always spent a lot of time at the gravel pit fishing, floating around in the old discarded row boat. We had retrieved the boat during the winter and pulled it to shore and anchored it by tying a rope on the boat then securing the rope under a large rock on shore. Even though my brother was no longer there during those long summer days, the gravel pit became my playground. I would often climb onto the boat and let the water's current carry me into the middle of the pit. I never thought of the danger associated with being alone, nor did Mom and Dad. They just presumed I had enough sense to take care, and if necessary, I could always swim toward shore.

Harvey wasn't the only one to leave home that summer. Elizabeth, who by the way, one morning announced at the breakfast table, "No one is to ever call me Elizabeth or Lizzie again. I hate them names. From now on, you all will refer to me as 'Betty.' Of course, we thought she was a bit crazy and even more so when she continued by saying, "I'm not drinkin' coffee again neither. It makes yer hair black." Of course, I never knew my sister when she didn't have black hair. Nevertheless, we all agreed her name from now on would be "Betty."

Betty decided she was going to move to Muncie and stay with my oldest sister, Edna. Ruth eloped with Luther Payne. She was only 17. Over Dad's objections to the relationship, always saying or thinking Luther was a "wop," never permitting the man to enter our house, he did nothing to annul the marriage. Ever since the day Ruth passed her 14th birthday, quit school, and was working for someone else, Luther Payne pursued a relationship with my sister. Now, she was Mrs. Luther Payne.

Each day I would wander off to the gravel pit on a regular basis. I would stare at the clean water. I suppose nowadays, one would call it meditating. It was one particular day, I noticed the rope securing our boat had broken away from the rock and the boat was drifting a few feet offshore. It didn't appear the boat had drifted so far into the deep water that I couldn't retrieve it. I began wading toward the wayward boat until the water reached my waist. As I did so, the boat moved further away and the water became deeper and deeper. My feet no longer touched the sandy bottom. I began to swim. I finally reached the boat and grabbed a hold of the dangling rope. I pulled the boat closer to where I could place my hand on its side, but my hand slipped and I began to sink. How many times I went under, I don't recall, but when my body surfaced after the third or fourth time, I reached for the rope. Gradually I pulled the boat closer so I could grab onto its side. Kicking my feet as fast as they would move, I guided the rowboat closer toward shore. Once reaching shore or the bank of the gravel pit, I tied the wayward boat to the same rock from which it had escaped.

I didn't dare go home—not until my clothing dried. Should Mom or Dad know about the incident, the punishment would have far exceeded the torture of drowning. That secret would remain buried within me for the remaining years of my life.

I was glad when the summer ended. I would occasionally visit my brother at the Wilson's farm and would carry water to the field workers as I rode a small Shetland pony from the main house into the fields. I was too young to know what sex was all about, but Harvey was already seeing the changes taking place within his body. One day he said, "Loy—this girl comes by here almost every day and has practically forced me to screw her." I didn't know what *screw* meant. "You know—fuck her! Now—if you act right, we can take her up in the haymow and we can have a little fun. You just gotta go along and do what I'm tellin' ya."

The girl arrived. She and Harvey were about the same age. It was true, she had a real crush on my brother. He apparently had told her that I was just as horny as he was. Her first statement to me was, "Well—are you as ornery as yer brother?" I quickly replied. Of course, I'm not ornery. I'm a nice boy." Harvey was furious. The girl refused to go to the haymow with him. I saddled onto the Shetland pony and took off for the fields.

My teacher in the second grade was a woman by the name of Miss Bimbow. She was pretty. She was a totally different picture than the months I spent in the first grade with Doris Gill. She dressed in the finest clothing and her hair was marcelled in the most up-to-date fashion. I liked Miss Bimbow. I wanted to please her and I rapidly caught on to her second grade teachings. It was half through the semester when Dad decided we should move on. He wanted to return to West Lebanon. Mom hated the memories of that town, but Dad was the boss. All the kids were gone now, except me. Dad gave no consideration as to my education or the effect the move might have on my learning. I loved the crossroads, the house, the oak tree where I sat many hours swinging in the old rubber tire hanging by a rope tied to one of the tree's heavy branches. Mom loved the crossroads. When the Model T moved away from that memorable place in the country, it also brought an end to our family existence. Ruth was gone, Betty went to live with my sister Edna in Muncie, and Harvey remained with the Wilsons.

CHAPTER 23

MOVING AWAY FROM THE CROSSROADS was not only a traumatic experience for myself but also Mom. I was the only kid left at home and Mom did miss her children. Why Dad decided to move to West Lebanon, I don't know. It was a town that left many unpleasant memories for my mother and at the time of the move Mom's oldest son, Ralph, had already migrated to the West Coast of the United States.

For me, to move at midterm of my schooling was disastrous. A new school in midterm and losing so much time away from a classroom, I soon discovered I had embarked on a sea of confusion. I was not ready to face the challenges of new teachers and their approach to education.

Work wasn't plentiful for Dad on this move. How he managed to find us a place to live and put food on the table is still a mystery. Mom seemed to always have a pot of beans cooking on the stove and as I recall that was our main staple as far as nourishment. Beans and oatmeal.

I was enrolled in school as soon as we settled in West Lebanon. I recall the teacher vividly. She was a strange looking woman, nothing like Miss Bimbow. Her hair was cut short in a boyish bob and she wasn't pretty. It wasn't the fact she wasn't kind like Miss Bimbow, nor was she the tyrant as was Doris Gill, but as I recall, her physical appearance had an adverse effect. When she stood at the head of the classroom all I could see was a woman whose skin had turned to leather. She was more like a wound up robot instead of a human being with abilities to communicate to young minds, particularly mine.

We lived in two different houses in West Lebanon. The first was a two-story house on the outskirts of town. I can only recall that house since our move was at the same time the famous gangster John Dillinger was the celebrity of the day. In my childlike imagination, I envisioned the gangster taking refuge in our house in an effort to find safety from the police.

Our second move was in a house within walking distance to the public school. There were some plusses about the move. Dad's two daughters, Helen and Mildred, both resided in West Lebanon. The elder Ellisons were still alive and continued to live in the old house on Fourth Street. In my mind they were the oldest looking people I had ever seen except for a farm couple by the name of Hickenbottom who lived in a remote part of the country and someone Dad had apparently worked for shucking corn during the harvest season.

For the first time and the last time in my life, Mom decided to visit her mother, Martha Lope Jordan, who lived in Danville, Illinois. I vividly recall Mom's mother. My mom and her mom could have been twins except for the fact Grandma Jordan's face was so wrinkled her head looked as if it was related to a prune. The old woman didn't have the beautiful soft skin and angelic appearance that ingratiated my mother's face. Upon that first meeting I didn't like my grandmother and I don't think she liked me. I could easily understand Mom's lack of excitement when she decided to call on her mother. Mother and daughter had absolutely nothing in common. Nevertheless, although the visit was short, we did go. On our return to West Lebanon, we stopped at State Line where Mom had a brother by the name of Noah. He had twin daughters who were about my age. I don't recall my uncle's wife, but I do recall my uncle. I liked him. He had many of the same qualities with which Mom was endowed.

It was wintertime when we arrived in West Lebanon. The cold, drafty house we lived in wasn't exactly conducive to good health. Within a few weeks after being enrolled in school, I got sick. Very sick, in fact, with a nagging cough and high fevers. Mom kept me bundled as best she could in front of the old potbellied stove, but even that failed to restore me to good health. Of course, I missed school and for all intents and purposes my second grade of schooling never existed. My sister, Helen, happened to drop by the house for a short visit. She took one look at me bundled in blankets and sitting in the rocking chair. "Mama, I'm taking Loy to the doctor. He's very sick!"

Of course, Mom had always been the doctor in our family. But with this disease, her homemade concoctions just didn't improve my sickly condition. "We jes' can't afford a doctor, Helen. I have no money and Abe ain't got no money."

Without any further debate, Helen picked me up, blankets and all, removed me from the chair, then carried me to her car parked in the front yard. Mom followed.

There was only one doctor in the town of Williamsport, the nearest larger town from West Lebanon. Helen parked the car. Without waiting to see if the doctor was in, she picked me up from the backseat and carried me into the doctor's office.

The doctor was in and as he took one look at me, he knew I had contracted the child's disease of whooping cough.

"This lad is very sick," I heard the man say. "He has a very contagious disease. It's a good thing you brought him here today. The authorities must be notified at once. Give him this medicine when you get home and keep him warm. Bring him back in two weeks and we'll see if he's responding to the medication." Helen reached in her purse and withdrew a five dollar bill as payment for the doctor's fee.

When we returned to West Lebanon, I noticed a white sign posted on our front door. The authorities had already been there. It stated the house was under quarantine and no one was permitted to enter the premises other than the immediate family.

For all practical purposes, there was really no need to return to school when I got well. I had lost too much time away from the classroom.

As I stated previously, whenever Dad made a move he was always sure there was plenty of space to plant a garden. The land on which this house was built had plenty of land, including an open lot with nothing but dead grass and a few trees. As in previous abodes, this house had none of the amenities which usually accompanied those residing in a city or town. There was no indoor plumbing or access to running water other than a rusty pump resting just outside the kitchen door. There was no electricity: consequently, our kerosene lamps were our consistent standby for providing light at night.

Dad attempted to keep out the cold icy drafts seeping in the house via the window panes and the outside doors by stuffing rags in the cracks. He would remove ashes each day from the potbellied stove in the parlor and from the kitchen range, carry the ashes outside, and carefully place them around the foundation of the house. He would then place chopped wood in the stoves. He was a master at building fires and within minutes had a roaring fire. Eventually, enough chill was removed from the outside winter air penetrating the cracks in the weatherbeaten house to keep us from freezing to death.

The house within the town limits of West Lebanon was a simple house. It wasn't the most savory place we would dwell or live, but since the day of my birth, we were lucky just to have a place to lay our heads and the warmth of four walls to protect us from the elements. In the many moves we would experience, none raised our standard of living. That required money and money we didn't have. Mom still labored scrubbing plank floors and washing clothes over a scrub board placed in a large steel galvanized tub. We rarely let the fire go out in the kitchen stove. We needed hot water to prime the pump, particularly when the outside temperature dropped below freezing. During those winter months, this was a regular routine. Ashes from the stove were used to bank up against the foundation of the house. This did help alleviate some of the cold seeping through the plank floors. Of course, this had always proved to be effective in most of the houses we lived, but for the house in West Lebanon, it would be my first experience with a house catching on fire. As I sat bundled in front of the stove, I noticed smoke seeping through the plank floors. I called to Mom. "Mom—the house is on fire!"

Fortunately, it was nighttime and Dad was home. Dad had just banked the foundation of the house with ashes from the stoves. He misjudged the hot embers still remaining within the ashes. The hot coals almost immediately ignited the rotted wood of the house resting on the foundation.

Mom and Dad rushed to fill buckets of water from the old rusty pump just outside the kitchen door. Dousing the hot coals with water soon caused the smoke to dissipate and the fire was extinguished.

As the doctor ordered, Helen returned me to the doctor within a couple weeks. Although still ill, the disease was well on its way to leaving my system. Helen bundled me again in warm blankets, then carried me to the car for our return trip to West Lebanon. For the second time in my short existence, my sister had come to my rescue.

The move to West Lebanon and the winter that brought on whooping cough was nothing less than a bad omen of things to come. I should have known there was no possibility of my ever leaving the second grade and graduating to the third. But I hoped. Failing in school was inexcusable, at least in my mind, although it never seemed to bother Dad or Mom. Of course, neither one of them had much education so they really couldn't understand the importance of those early elementary years. My brother Harvey was always smart and by my failing, I felt as if I was totally stupid and couldn't learn.

Springtime brought an end to the cold. The snows melted and green grass pushed its way upward through the slush. Spring was also the time of year when school would be discontinued for the summer months. I was happy and elated to see the semester come to an end. I even found myself whistling as I skipped down the gravel road to our house.

When I entered the house, a strange man was sitting at the kitchen table talking to Mom. Mom attempted to make an introduction, but a cold stare coming from the man's eyes was not one of friendliness. "Loy—this is your brother Cecil." I had only heard about my half brother. I never met him. Instead of saying anything, he stared with an icy stare as if my presence brought back memories of his own early beginning. How Cecil discovered we moved to West Lebanon, no one knows. He wasn't that close to the Ellisons. It had been some time since he had visited Mom. It had to be at least six years. Jumping off the freight train as it was ready to pass through West Lebanon must have sharpened his intuition to know exactly where he could find his mother. It would be the last time I would ever see my half brother. It would also be the last visit Mom would have with her son sired by Harry Ellison. The visit with Mom was probably cut short by my sudden appearance. I hope not. Knowing he wanted to visit with Mom, I ran outside the house. I saw my brother for the final time as he exited the kitchen door and walked toward the center of town. As regular as clockwork, he must have known when the next freight train would pass through West Lebanon. He had moved east and west via the open boxcars since the day he was 13 years old.

Everybody's garden contained a row of corn that spring. Before reaching home, I passed a garden where a row of corn was within my reach. I often grabbed the dried tassel protruding beyond the husk. Without Mom's knowledge, Harvey and I would take corn silk and make our own version of a cigarette. We had seen grown-ups smoke their weed time and time again; consequently, we could see nothing wrong with making our own cigarettes. Of course, when Mom would catch us, she would discipline her two boys in the best way she knew how without mentioning our wayward ways to Dad. This did not deter us however from smoking corn silk.

After stealing just enough corn silk to make a cigarette, I finally reached the vacant lot next to our house where I often sat under a shade tree. I tore a small piece of paper from my notebook, just large enough to wrap around my stolen corn silk and the exact size of a cigarette. The entire act must have been premeditated since I confiscated a couple matches from the match holder hanging on the wall in the kitchen that morning before leaving for school.

I hated West Lebanon. I missed my brother Harvey and Betty. I knew I would certainly fail to pass the second grade. As I sat at the base of the shade tree dwelling in my sea of self-pity, I began to roll the dry fuzzy stuff into the form of a cigarette. I lit the cigarette just like grown-ups and began to puff the lethal fumes into my lungs.

It was one of those warm springs that year and the grass around the area was dry from lack of rain. In previous times, I was always careful to be certain my cigarette was no longer burning before I discarded the butt, but not on this particular day. Taking a final drag on the homemade cigarette, I tossed the butt onto the dry grass just a few feet from where I was sitting. As the butt hit the parched earth, the grass began to burn. I attempted to stomp out the flames, but no sooner would I stifle the fire in one area, flames erupted a few feet away. The vacant lot became a blazing inferno.

Dad was standing in the yard and he saw the smoke rising from the vacant lot. I yelled as I ran toward him. "Dad! Dad! Did ya see that feller drive by and toss a cigarette butt out his car window?"

By the time my words reached Dad's ears, the flames

were lapping at the dried grass near our house. "Start pumping water, Loy, we're gonna halfta put this dang fire out or it's gonna burn up this whole dagburn town!"

It was an unforgivable sin to tell a lie in our house. There were rules laid down in the Holy book and even though Dad cared little about religion there were certain rules he abided by. The rule about bearing false witness was one of them. If those rules were broken while living under his roof, the consequences were always, without fail, a trip to the woodshed and Dad's heavy hand across our butts. Mom, too, had been known to be handy with the switch. The only escape for me as a young lad and the alternative of being skinned alive was to lie.

Mom rushed from the kitchen into the yard. "Oley—grab a bucket!" Dad yelled. I had already begun the chore of pumping water from the rusty old pump as fast as my arms could move up and down. With Mom and Dad alternating the task of tossing buckets of water on the flames, only a wet, charred sea of burned grass remained. When Dad poured the last bucket of water onto the soggy earth, he noticed the cigarette butt on the ground near the tree where I had been sitting. "Yep," Dad spoke as he picked up the remains of my wrongdoing. "I guess Loy's right. Some whippersnapper sure did throw a cigarette out the window of his jalopy. I don't know how I missed him though when he come by our house."

It was the last day of school. One glance at my report card and I knew was destined to repeat the second grade. I don't think Dad ever looked at my report card and I'm not certain Mom paid much attention to whether I was making straight F's or all A's. My school record for that term was all F's. Of course, all the way home the tears rolled down my cheeks. It was probably the first time in my short life I knew the feeling of being a total failure.

After school was dismissed for the summer, Dad was ready to make another move. His Model T practically could drive the distance from West Lebanon to Gaston by itself. Instead of going back to the crossroads, Dad found a brick house on the road to Mathews set amongst a lot of trees and a large swampland. It was a larger house than the one we previously occupied. It was also a time when Betty and Harvey returned home. There are many fond memories of the old brick house in the swamps surrounded by forest. It would be the last and final time my two siblings and myself would share a space within the house of Abe.

I would repeat my second year of schooling in Mathews. Harvey was entering the eighth grade and my sister Betty was now a sophomore in high school. Each morning the school bus stopped in front of our house to take us to school where the elementary and secondary schools were combined.

I don't know why I was so much smarter the second time around in the same grade or if enough education of those second grade subjects by some means of osmosis had forced me to know the answers. At any rate, I was an A student. I actually completed that year without interruptions.

The swamps and the forest behind our house were home for a multitude of wildlife. Harvey discovered he could make money from animal pelts, particularly those of muskrats. The swampland served as a Mecca for setting steel traps that would end the life of some unfortunate creature. How Harvey acquired the steel traps, I don't recall. Nor did I understand why he wanted to earn money by taking the life of another living creature. Nevertheless, before daylight each morning and after the wood was chopped, I would accompany my brother on this gruesome early morning capitalistic venture. He would meticulously visit each trap site. He would carefully release the victim, in most cases deceased, then carry the dead animal back to the house. He removed the pelt from the departed creature's body then carefully prepared the fur to be presented to a dealer who in turn sold the animal's hide to a manufacturer who turned the one-time living creature into a fur coat.

At the end of the school year, I could feel the winds of change in Dad's mind. We were about to be uprooted again. My sister Betty decided not to return to school and since it was the harvest season, my brother Harvey was in demand.

A farmer by the name of Paul Rogers, whose farm was located near Hartford City, approached Dad hoping to have Dad's approval for letting Harvey come and live with his family. Harvey had met the Rogers when he lived with the Wilsons. Paul knew the hard times Dad was having trying to hold a family together, and the Rogers family were all in agreement they would like Harvey to come and live with them at least until he finished his high school years. They would treat him as one of their own. They had a son, but Harvey was more in favor with Paul Rogers than his own son. Paul's mother soon became a second mother to Harvey.

There was no need to fear. Dad would never object to farming out his kids to families that would lend a hand in raising them through their teen years. Much to Mom's unhappiness, Harvey left the house on the road to Mathews to settle in with the Roger family.

Harvey loved the Rogers. They were good people. The family encouraged the young teenager to set his goals and go for it. They offered him a chance for a good education. They wanted him to amount to something more than just a laborer or a farmer. They would have gladly sent my brother on to college. He was college material but that wasn't to be. In my brother's 11th year in school he met a girl. His hormones jumped and the girl he thought he loved was more than ready to relieve those teenage frustrations. Before Harvey could graduate from high school, he married his sweetheart whose name was Edna Grace. To the heartbreak of the Rogers family, Harvey took a job with Warner Gear in Muncie. He would never be more than an ordinary laborer in the workforce of America's mills.

My sister Betty left the shelter of Dad's domain at about the same time as Harvey. She moved into Muncie where she had a pick of boyfriends and could easily find a job that would support her single life. For the second time in my short existence, I was left alone with just Mom and Dad.

CHAPTER 24

MY THIRD GRADE OF SCHOOLING would be in another school, not in Mathews but in Muncie. Why Dad returned to the city, I don' t know except it was probably more profitable to gather junk for recycling than in the smaller towns.

Our next move was a duplex on 14th Street, just a few short blocks from where we lived at the time I was three years old and was hit by a car. This area of Muncie was indeed Shanty-town. It was a duplex house which we shared one-half of the dwelling with a number of tenants who would come and go. There was a narrow driveway where Dad parked the Model T and also separated our side of the duplex from the house next door. Night after night we would see men, always men, park their cars at the curb directly in front of the house of our next-door neighbor. Some men were quite well dressed and some looked a bit seedy. Mom became suspicious. "Abe—I think we're living next to a whorehouse." Mom was right. The madam of the house of disrepute was a mother to a young girl about my age. I must have been nine at that time. I suppose it was a matter of "monkey see—monkey do" that encouraged my new acquaintance to give me my first lesson on the behavior of the birds and bees. By the time I entered the third grade at a school in Muncie, Indiana, I was well indoctrinated into the games people play.

Medicine shows attracted a large, standing crowd. The tents were always pitched in some vacant lot, and the first one that comes to my mind was set up next to the run-down Methodist church located on our street only a few minutes away. The entrepreneurs seemed to realize the suckers who would be most apt to purchase their phony concoctions had to be the poorest people in town. A stage was erected in front of a small tent. To see the real show inside the tent required paying a certain sum of money to enter the tent, but the main purpose of the medicine show was to sell an elixir that was a cure-all for any ailment known to man.

There were no such things as microphones or amplification during the early '30s. The emcee would make his entrance on stage and with a resonant loud voice he proceeded to mesmerize his audience by introducing a sellout crowd to the stars of the show appearing inside the tent. He would then wind up a Victrola and as the music blared out over the standing audience, the featured players made a brief entrance on stage. The women's attire revealed more uncovered flesh than I had seen in all my early years outside my mother's womb. Not only were the women practically naked, they could move their hips in a circular motion which caused my eyeballs to pop out of their sockets. I was too young to be permitted inside the tent to witness the main show; nevertheless, that first medicine show introduced me to the world of "show business."

When the hootchy koochy dancers finished their number and made their exit inside the tent to prepare for the feature performance of the evening, the emcee returned to the stage carrying in his hands a bottle of some strange looking liquid. The slender, greasy haired emcee then proceeded to convince his audience the nectar in the bottle he was holding was a miracle cure for every illness known to man. Reaching into their pockets, the poor audience searched for their last dollar in order to buy a bottle of a miracle cure.

The show going on inside the tent was for "men only." Husbands and boyfriends would hand their bottle of nectar to their wives and girlfriends then line up at the side of the tent waiting to be ushered inside where an X-rated show was about to begin that would probably make the sex industry of today blush.

When Dad was away searching for recyclable junk, the driveway was empty. It was a perfect place to play "medicine show." I convinced my poor urchin playmates to help me erect a stage made of scrap wood I found in the alley back of our house. We found old quilts which had outlived their usefulness. The ragged bed coverings were then stretched over four tall poles until the material touched the ground. This gave us privacy from the outside world. In front of our structure we built a small stage where we could reenact what I had seen at the medicine show. A cigarette-burned hole in the middle of the quilt was large enough to view the happenings on stage as well as seeing any unexpected adult suddenly making an appearance as a means of checking on the kids involved in the world of make believe.

My little friend, the daughter to the 14th Street madam, could do the hoochy koochy dance as well as any of those grown-up women on stage at the medicine show. Mom had given me the name associated with the dancers. If she hadn't I wouldn't have known what "hoochy koochy" meant. In the process of making our medicine show authentic, I mixed

mud and water into a similar consistency resembling the liquid I observed in the medicine man's bottles. My little friend
had access to a number of empty beer bottles. These would
be the containers in which we would place our mixture of
water and mud. We were ready for business.

The show was on. I must have been the emcee, but once
I introduced the girls participating in the main event of the
day, my little friend from the whorehouse and I would make
our exit from the stage then slip under our make-believe tent.
Under the cover of a ragged quilt we began exploring each
other's bodies. I pulled down my pants and my little friend
removed her panties. I saw for the first time the difference
between a boy and a girl. Before that first touch through a
hole in the quilt, I saw Mom heading toward our makeshift
tent. In her hand she carried a stick. If Mom discovered I was
doing something considered a wrongful act, that stick was
used without mercy against the tender skin on my butt.

I jumped to my feet. I pulled my pants up to my waist
and barely had time to place the final button into its proper
place when I heard, "Loy-ee-ee-ee! Whatta ya doin' in there?
Now ya jes' come out this minute or I'm comin' in after ya."

I stuck my head out of the opening in the makeshift tent.
"I ain't doin' nothin' Mom. Jes' playin.'"

"Where's Dora?" Mom questioned. My little friend hurriedly pulled on her panties and her dress down over her
knees as I crawled from inside the tent onto the stage. "She's
in there, Mom." Like nothing had happened, Dora suddenly
appeared fully dressed and as innocent as a newborn babe.
She spoke to Mom. "We ain't doin' nothin' Mrs. VanNatter.
Jes' playin'."

Mom relaxed the threatening stick she held in her hand.
"Well—I think ya jes' better play out here where I can see ya.

Anyway, it's almost suppertime, Loy. Dad will be home soon and I think you'd better come in the house."

Our medicine show play period came to an end. We had to dismantle our makeshift theatre so Dad could pull into the driveway. My show business venture was short lived but never forgotten.

I would often sit on our section of the front porch of the duplex hoping by some stroke of luck my sister Betty would come or my brother Harvey would at least pay us a visit. I somehow knew neither one of them would ever again share a space under Dad's roof. I missed my sister and brother. As I sat there wishing, loud moans and groans could be heard coming from our neighbor's side of the house.

I ran into the house. "Mom! Mom! Something's wrong. The woman next door must be awful sick. She must hurt terrible. What's the matter with her, Mom?"

"Be quiet, Loy. She's waitin' for the stork."

"But—I ain't seen no stork, Mom." I wasn't old enough to know where babies came from or how they were made. I had witnessed our cat having kittens when we lived at the crossroads. I remember yelling for Mom then. "Mom! Mom! Look! Did ya see that tail comin' out of the cat's butt hole?" I observed the entire process up to the time four helpless kittens left their mother's body. Even with that experience I could not associate the same thing happening to people. I still believed a huge bird was responsible for bringing new babies into people's homes.

The woman's groans and moans never seemed to cease. Finally, after many hours, I heard through the walls of our duplex the sound of a slap on bare skin. The baby let out a blood curdling scream. The stork had arrived next door.

Living in the country I often observed new calves after they were born. The newcomer caused so much excitement among the herd of cattle one would have thought each cow was the calf's mother. On the second day after the baby was born, Mom took me to view our newest neighbor. I couldn't believe how ugly the thing they called a baby actually was. It was the first time I had seen a newborn. At least when the cat had kittens at the crossroads they looked like kittens, but this? A baby?

An ancient weatherbeaten Methodist church whose rotting clapboard siding had withstood many years of harsh winters, heavy winds and hot humid summers, served as a haven of hope for the poor people living in Shantytown. Like all churches we encountered since leaving the parish at Zion, the deeply founded Methodist faith was the most prevalent religion in the Midwest. Mom soon became a member of the 14th Street flock. That had one meaning—every Sunday morning, Sunday evening and Wednesday nights would be spent in church. I don't recall much about the church except it was near my mom and dad's friend we always referred to as Grandma Newman. I recall her being old and always smoking a corncob pipe. She was also a guardian for a grandchild who was a bit incapacitated in the brain department. The reason I recall this girl is she was always wanting to play house. Of course, I was invited to play the role of daddy. It was on one of these occasions that Grandma Newman happened to see her granddaughter drop her panties as we played in the shed back of the house. I never saw an old woman move so fast. She was like Doris Gill who could see things from behind, from the sides and in front of her. She seemed to levitate to that shed. I knew there was trouble. I started to run and I ran until I reached home. I was never permitted to see the girl who always wanted to play house again.

The move to Muncie was a trying time for Dad. It was difficult to earn enough money to pay the rent and hope to have enough left over to put food on the table. I entered the third grade when school resumed in August. It was at that time Mom decided to hire herself out as a cleaning woman to supplement our meager existence. It was only a once a week job, but I will always have vivid memories of the big house on the other side of the tracks.

Mom took me with her one day when school was dismissed probably because it was a school holiday.

The house had everything we never had. It had electricity and an electric icebox. When it came time for me to eat my lunch, Mom and I sat down at the kitchen table. She took a couple of peanut butter sandwiches out of a brown bag. As she did so, the woman of the house entered the kitchen. "Would you like a glass of cold milk to help wash down that sandwich, young man?" I didn't dare say I didn't like milk. Blue Gill was the only milk I had ever known. That consisted of all fat being taken from the whole milk, leaving a bluish milky liquid we always called "Blue Gill." I hated it. The kind woman went to the electric icebox and withdrew a large pitcher of milk As she poured the milk into a glass, I knew it wasn't Blue Gill. The richest whole milk ever to pass my lips poured from the pitcher. The glass of cold, whole milk was like a miraculous balm to my stomach. It was a taste that would linger throughout a lifetime.

The big house not only had the convenience of electricity, ice cold milk and plush carpeting that covered the floors, it was also blessed with an indoor toilet that flushed away excretions from our bodies. It even had a radio. For a youngster who had been raised with so little, the lifestyle of the affluent made an indelible impression. That early experience planted a seed.

"Someday, I too, will share in a life of plenty."

CHAPTER 25

ED HARRIS WAS AN AFFLUENT farmer. He owned several acres of land. He had his own generator that provided electricity for the main house as well as the barn and outlying buildings. On one of his acres stood an aged frame house where Ed stored much of his grain for his abundant livestock during the winter months. Dad approached Ed about the possibility of us living there and of course, Ed agreed. It was within walking distance to the crossroads, the gravel pit and Zion. Richard Harris, Ed's youngest son, had been my playmate from the time we both entered the first grade in Gaston. This coincidence made me happy, but not so with Mom. She had been humiliated so many times during her nomad existence with Dad. The idea of moving into a corncrib created another low ebb in my mother's life. The only good to come from the move was a reunification with wives of neighboring farmers who formed a weekly quilting club and of course, there was Zion. Bill Foster was Ed Harris's son-in-law. The Foster farm was only a mile or so up the road from the crossroads, and I had spent many happy moments with Bill, who often took me on his knee and talked to me like a human being. The warmth from the soul of Bill Foster seemed to give my young soul a certain amount of security.

The corncrib consisted of three rooms: a kitchen and a small parlor on the ground floor and one room on the second floor where Mom placed her and Dad's double bed then set my small cot in one corner of the room.

As in all the many moves during my mom's marriage to Dad, Mom went about the backbreaking chore of attempting to turn the corncrib into a home. The shack was surrounded with plenty of room for Dad to stack his collected junk and to plant a garden.

An icy, cold winter followed our move. As I had learned to do when my brother Harvey shared the chores, each morning before dawn I'd go outside, brush the snow off the wood to be chopped, and before breakfast, I had enough chopped wood to keep the fires burning in the kitchen stove and the potbellied stove in the parlor until the following morning.

It was almost like being at the crossroads again. Mr. Erwin still drove the school bus, and each school day morning I could depend on the school bus arriving on time regardless whether the weather be rain, sleet or snow. It was in Gaston where I would enter the fourth grade.

One cold, wet wintery day, the mail brought a letter addressed to Mom. It was from her son Ralph, who still resided in San Francisco. He was good about writing, but never did he journey back to the Midwest to visit his early beginnings. Many months passed since Mom received a note or news from Cecil. Although miles often separated the mother and son, Cecil occasionally would send Mom a postcard. I don't recall Mom ever saying her prayers at night as she knelt beside the bed she shared with Dad and before laying her head on her pillow, she failed to mention Cecil's name. The letter from Ralph reads as follows:

Dear Mom,

With heavy heart and great sadness, I write you this letter. For several years, I pleaded with my only brother Cecil to come live with me in San Francisco. I told him he could stay as long as he liked for however long it might take for him to get a job and stop riding the rails. Cecil was never able to divorce himself from the sound of the metal wheels on freight cars rolling over the steel tracks.

I can only guess how the State of Arizona discovered my location and Cecil's next of kin. He must have kept my address in his pocket at all times. About two years passed since I last heard about my brother. I wasn't aware he was ill. He seemed healthy during our short visit before he decided he wanted to leave for Arizona.

When I was contacted by the authorities, after they discovered my brother's body under a bridge near Phoenix, they said according to the coroner's report, Cecil died from advanced tuberculosis. He had no money and there was no one to claim his body. He was buried in an unmarked grave in a pauper's cemetery somewhere on the outskirts of Phoenix.

I am sorry to bring you this news, Mom. My brother never had much of a chance in life. The short 30 years on this earth must have been a pure torture for Cecil. Maybe, Mom, he is now in a better place. If there is a hell, I am sure Cecil lived in it on this earth.

I love ya, Mom. I often wonder if I'll ever see you again. I sure hope so.

Ever your loving son, Ralph

Mom read and reread Ralph's letter. Tears flooded her tired, worn face. For hours she sat in the rocking chair looking off into space, her inner thoughts flashing back to the time Cecil was born and how he had been rejected by everyone except his mother. Death is final and Mom knew she could never anticipate her second born miraculously appearing on her doorstep.

Traveling evangelists often traveled the countryside. They would receive permission from local farmers to pitch their revival tents in an open pasture. In many cases, the tent was pitched within walking distance to the house we always referred to as the corncrib.

Women preachers were beginning to arrive on the evangelistic scene in the early thirties. Amy McPherson succeeded in stirring up the nation with her "Four Square Gospel" approach. There were other women passing through who claimed to have been anointed by the Great Almighty, all claiming to heal those who were sick just by placing their hands on the ailing one. Either the miraculous healings were preassigned by some quack in the audience or perhaps in some cases the excitement of it all was enough to cause one to get out of a wheelchair and shout his or her praises to God for having been made whole again.

Mom was taken with this stuff. I suppose she was willing to try anything that would give her an inner peace which she so desperately sought. Of course, I was always obligated to tag along when we would walk the dark country roads to a large tent sitting in the middle of a cow pasture. Sawdust was spread over the grass under the canvas rooftop of the tent. A stage or what they referred to as a pulpit was erected and an altar railing was built. The evangelists were high powered salesmen or salespersons. They had a talent for reaching into a man's soul and sending a wave of guilt whether the person was full of sin or whether they were a walking saint. When the preacher was aroused enough to cause the fire and brimstone of hell to come crashing down through the top of the tent, I would tell Mom I had to pee. I would run outside the tent and then I discovered I wasn't alone. Other kids my age had the same idea. So, while those on the inside were being saved, we expended our energies playing tag or hide-and-seek.

It was a Sunday afternoon when we had unexpected visitors. Into our yard came a Model A Ford, and inside were two passengers. One I recognized and the other was a young man I had never seen. My sister Betty and her boyfriend exited the vehicle. When the stranger and my sister entered the house, Betty had to say something to Mom and Dad and she didn't think my ears should hear. I was told to go outside and play.

"Who is this young man, Lizzie?" Mom never adjusted to calling my sister Betty. "Ya ain't introduced us."

My sister looked embarrassed. "This is Bob Lynn, Mom, he's the fellow I've been goin' with."

Mom was never suspicious by nature, but the way my sister was acting, she knew there must be a problem. "I think we'd better go into the parlor," Mom said.

When all had entered the parlor and were certain the door was closed, Betty spoke. "Mom—I'm in trouble. I'm pregnant! I don't know what to do. Bob here, is the father. I cain't say I really love him, Mom. I know'd we shouldn't done what we did, but it happened." Bob Lynn was embarrassed and wanted to run, but he knew the problem had to be brought out in the open. Betty had already missed two periods and there was no doubt about her condition.

Thoughts of the past flooded Mom's mind. When she became pregnant with Harry's child without her consent and raped in a buggy was something she didn't want to happen to her daughter. Above all, to force a marriage without love could be disastrous.

Dad was not aware we had company. He saw the strange car in the yard. Even that could have meant just a friendly neighbor passing by. When he entered the house he noticed the parlor door was shut. "What's goin' on Loy? Why is that door shut?"

"Betty come here with a strange man," I quickly answered. "She said she had somethin' to say and Mom thought they should go in the parlor and sit down. They shut the door cause I wasn't supposed to hear what they're sayin'."

Dad hurried toward the closed door. Without knocking he opened it and all of a sudden the conversation on the other side came to an abrupt end. Mom stared at Dad. "Come in Abe and close the door. We're havin' a conversation and I don't think it's somethin' young ears should hear." It was obvious Mom was upset. When she announced Lizzie was pregnant, Dad coolly turned to Bob Lynn and my sister. "Well—whatta ya gonna do about it? I made a rule in yer growin' up years, when ya make yer bed, ya jes' hafta lay in it."

Mom interrupted Dad from saying anything further. She turned toward Bob. "Do ya love Lizzie, Bob? I don't want you two youngins' doin' somethin' like I did many years ago. I paid a heavy price for what I did. I'd rather have a bastard in our family than to have two people who didn't love each other."

Bob turned to Betty and with great tenderness and sincerity he spoke. "I like ya an awful lot, Betty. In fact, I love you. I just wish you could love me. Will ya marry me Betty? Maybe after we're married you might learn to love me a little bit."

The matter was settled. The next time I would meet Bob Lynn, he would be my brother-in-law.

These were depression years and Bob was working as a grocery clerk with the Kroger food chain. His salary was $15 a week, hardly enough to set up housekeeping. To provide Betty, Bob, and the new baby a safe haven, Bob had to depend on his mother and Dad. The newlyweds moved in with Bob's parents. After the baby was born, the paycheck Bob earned as a grocery clerk and a bit of savings he put away each week, Bob was able to purchase an acre of land on the outskirts of Muncie's city limits. The young, capable groom began the construction of a house on the one acre. When one room was completed, Betty, Bob, and the new baby moved from Bob's parents' home into the one room. Over a short period of time, Bob built another room onto the single room, and by the time a second son was born and the third child being a girl joined the family, the Lynn family owned a three-bedroom house.

My new brother-in-law became a brother to me. The marriage between my sister and the strange man who entered the corn crib, our residence, on that summer day developed into a lasting love that would survive the insecurities of time for well over 50 years.

CHAPTER 26

I DON'T RECALL SPENDING MORE than one winter in the corn-crib. Dad was on the move again. Fortunately, I remained in the same school in Gaston.

Wheeling Junction wasn't really a town. There were a few houses and lots of vacant land located where two roads met each other making a "T." At the "T" in the road there was a small grocery store, a gas station, a feed store and an abandoned one-room schoolhouse. It was a deprived town with lots of poor people just like us, but why Dad chose to move our meager belongings into the schoolhouse, only he could answer that question.

We must have made the move in early spring, since for the first time in my life, I was able to hire myself out to help in the fields and actually earned enough money to buy a used bicycle.

The ancient schoolhouse consisted of an entry vestibule which opened into one large room. Long narrow windows reached from the ceiling down to just above the wide floorboards. In an attempt to separate the open large room into a kitchen, a parlor and a sleeping area, Mom made use of old trunks and boxes which had accompanied the VanNatter family on every move. Fortunately, there were chimneys to connect the pipes of the stoves including a potbellied stove in the entry, another one on one side of the large room, and a chimney for the kitchen range. Somewhere and at sometime, Dad managed to hold onto the stoves including the kitchen range. I don't have fond memories of living in the school-house. In the makeshift parlor Mom created out of nothing stood a potbellied stove, my cot, and Dad's green wicker rocking chair. Dad kept his treasures in a wooden box which he painted red. The box was always padlocked and at no time were we permitted to ever investigate the contents. Dad made it known to each one of us that those were his own per-sonal possessions. During the time I spent with my mother and Dad, I don't recall Dad ever unlocking the mysterious red box.

This abode was another drafty abode, even in the early spring and into the summer months. Even though all the stoves would turn a bright flaming red from the roaring fire burning inside, unless one stood next to the stove, one side of a body would get warm while the side facing the open space remained freezing cold.

Winter arrived in November with an endless series of ice storms and heavy snows. Every tree and every blade

Second grade of school: Gaston, Indiana. Teacher, Mrs. Bimbow.

One room schoolhouse in Wheeling

*The house we lived in at the crossroads and the
gravel pits many years later*

of grass was encased in icy crystals. After an ice storm, the ice-covered branches of the trees would snap and we could hear the loud sound of tree limbs breaking and falling to earth. It was during one of our frequent ice storms that a stranger rapped on the door of the schoolhouse. He was a young man and apparently reached our address via his bicycle. In his hand he carried a yellow envelope. When Mom opened the door, a foreboding cloud covered her face. As she opened the envelope and read the contents, blood drained from her face. "Oh no! It's Mildred!"

The telegram read:

MILDRED KISER BADLY BURNED STOP COME AT ONCE STOP
SIGNED LOY KISER

Dad's favorite of all his children was at death's door. At dawn the following morning after receipt of the telegram, Dad, Mom, and myself crowded into the Model T. I sat on Mom's lap. By the time we reached West Lebanon we were informed that Mildred had passed away. She was only 30 years old. Mildred was the second one in our family to die within a year.

Mildred's demise was a front page story in the *West Lebanon Gazette*.

Flames Claim Young Mother

A heartbreaking tragedy was enacted here about 10:00 o'clock Saturday morning when Mrs. Loy Kiser was so badly burned that she died in Lake View Hospital in Danville about six hours after the accident.

Mr. And Mrs. Kiser had been out to a party Friday evening, getting home late, Saturday morning Loy, who works at Jones Elevator arose and quietly got his own breakfast then went to work leaving the wife and little son still asleep.

About 10:00 o'clock Mrs. Kiser awakened and finding the fire low in the sitting room stove secured, the coal oil can to rekindle it. The stove was placed about three feet from the wall. Mrs. Kiser went between the stove and the wall and began pouring kerosene in the stove from the can. There were live coals in the stove and an explosion followed, the kerosene can in her hands exploding and throwing oil all over her. Mrs. Kiser was wearing a flannelette nightgown and she was immediately enveloped in flames.

Attracted to her cries, the little son, about seven years old, came to his mother's aid and did what he could to try to extinguish the flames. The unfortunate woman rushed screaming from the house and started for the home of Jess Horner, her nearest neighbor. By this time, all her clothing was burned from her except a few strings around her neck. She was so badly burned on almost her entire body and face and head, and had inhaled the flames which hastened her death. She passed away a few hours after arriving at the hospital at Danville.

"It's so dark! It's so dark!" Mildred painfully cried. "Please! Please!" She begged. "Someone pray for me."

Helen, Fatty, Loy Kiser, and their small son, Loy Allen, stood by the stricken woman's bed. Only the small voice of Mildred's seven-year-old son spoke as he touched his mother's unburned hand. "Mommy—I'll pray for you."

The child's prayer was not answered. Mildred lapsed into a coma and within a few hours her spirit passed into the world of the unknown.

A closed, flower-covered casket rested in front of the altar of the Christian Church in West Lebanon, Indiana. The entire town came to pay their respects to Mildred Kiser, the wife of Loy Kiser and their young son, Loy. There was a short eulogy by the minister, then six pallbearers reverently moved the casket from the front of the church to the vestibule. The undertaker opened the coffin so the teary-eyed mourners could take one last look at the grotesque figure lying in the satin-lined box. The body was so badly burned, nothing except Mildred's hands went unscathed by the terrible fire. The morticians attempted to reconstruct the beautiful face of Mildred Kiser with wax, but it was only God who could mold the features of the girl who had been considered the town's most beautiful woman. As the overflowing crowd of mourners tearfully passed the open casket, some gazed at the body while others just said a silent prayer then continued walking toward the exit and the open doors of the church opening onto the street.

Mom, Dad and myself were the last mourners to pass the open casket. Dad, in the eyes of most people, was indestructible. It would be the only time I would see a man of steel bend from the visible emotional strain of loss that accompanies the finality of death. His healthy, ruddy complexion turned an ashen gray. His firm, sturdy body staggered and shuddered like a giant tree ready to fall. Mom grabbed his arm and I took his hand in an effort to steady him. With Dad, there were never tears except the tears weeping bitterly within his very soul.

A misty, cold rain dashed against the faces of the mourners as they boarded their vehicles then formed a funeral cortege to the grave site. The funeral directors erected a tent over the open grave, and a few chairs for the family were carefully placed under a tent for the family members of Mildred VanNatter Kiser. As the last words were spoken and the body of my sister was lowered into the cold ground, the crowd began to disperse. Mom, Dad and myself were the last mourners to leave. Dad glanced one more time at the box containing his youngest child by Josephine as it was slowly lowered into the earth.

As we walked toward the Model T, the rain turned to sleet. Dad did not wait for the weather to clear. We boarded the Model T then began the long journey to Wheeling Junction. The journey was a treacherous one. The sleet turned to ice and soon the earth sparkled like a million diamonds, the road turning into a sea of ice. For Dad to see, he had to open the windshield which was divided into two parts. I sat on Mom's lap. The raining ice guided by the cold wind dashed against our faces. It was well past midnight when we arrived at the one-room schoolhouse at Wheeling Junction. No words were spoken. Dad hurriedly built a fire in the cooking stove and another one in the potbellied stove resting in the small area Mom cordoned off as a parlor. There was no discussion about Mildred's demise. My father never mentioned my sister's name again.

Mildred's death left a great void in the life of Loy Kiser, Sr. As for their seven-year-old son, he went to live with Helen, Fatty, Dorothy, and Bobby. The youngster inherited the fine features of both his father and his mother. He was a happy child and from all outer appearances he adjusted to the loss of his mother, particularly as long as he lived with his Aunt Helen.

Loy Kiser did not remain a widower long. A few months after Mildred's death, he wed another one of the town's beauties by the name of Lois Black. Loy wanted his son returned after the wedding much against the wishes of his new bride. Lois Black Kiser resented the child. Loy Allen was no longer happy, yet he excelled in school. His desire in life was to grow into adulthood and become a lawyer. At the age of eight years, the child was stricken with infantile paralysis. His tiny arms were paralyzed except for a limited use of his right arm.

In spite of all the youngster's adversities, he did complete his elementary years of schooling. He entered high school and although crippled, became the captain of his basketball team. He graduated from high school with honors and had entered into his first year of college when at the age of 18, tragedy struck again. Loy Allen Kiser had gone to an outdoor movie. During the evening hours as he sat watching the picture, the sky opened with a heavy rain.

The air turned cold, consequently, the dampness of the night and Loy Allen Kiser's clothing soaked to his bare skin, he contracted what all thought was just a simple cold. Instead, it was a virus that quickly turned the cold into double pneumonia and the lad with so much to live for passed from this life to the next.

CHAPTER 27

IT WAS NOT UNUSUAL WHEN springtime came and the planting season was at hand, children eight, nine, and ten years of age would carry on their share of work which required tilling the land.

Ruth and Luther rented a farm of several acres near the town of Fairmont, Indiana. It was a typical, picturesque country setting, a rustic dwelling surrounded by large trees and plenty of grass to mow. There was a red barn that housed the horses and the cattle. The cattle were herded into the barn each night for milking, and the horses remained in their stalls during the feeding period. Like most farm houses, there was no indoor plumbing. An outdoor privy stood a few yards from the house. Next to the privy there was a small building they called the chicken coop. The country abounded with wildlife, especially foxes and weasels who often raided the chicken coop during the nighttime hours leaving a path of destruction for us to discover and clean the following morning.

I was elated when it was suggested that as soon as school was dismissed for the summer months, I would spend the summer helping Luther on the farm. We always referred to Luther as "Lute." He was a good man who liked kids and probably the most like Mr. Erwin, the school bus driver at the crossroads. He patiently attempted to introduce me to what farm life was all about. Like Mr. Erwin, Lute seemed to have all the answers for solving any problems a boy my age might encounter.

My sister, on the other hand, was not the easiest person with whom to share space under the same roof. Lute, nevertheless, seemed to rise above her eccentricities, showering her with an abundance of love. I only recall one time during my stay where Lute took a stand against the demands of my controlling sister.

I was happy and felt safe in the home of my sister and her husband, Lute. There was laughter, chores weren't really chores, and their dog, Piney, became my constant friend, always at my heels whether I was in the barn, out in the pasture, or in the fields already plowed for planting.

On this particular day all nature was in perfect harmony. The birds sang, roosters crowed and even the horses and cattle verbally expressed their gratitude for being alive. However, before the morning turned to midday, my friend Piney would save my life.

Before breakfast, I milked the cows, fed the horses, slopped the hogs and threw chicken feed on the ground. When those chores were completed, I turned the cattle out to pasture to graze for the day. After breakfast I returned to the barn. I harnessed a team of horses then guided them to an open field where a large, flat wooden platform structure lay close to the ground. This was designed to break up the clods of earth into small pieces. Once most of the clods of earth were broken down, a piece of farm equipment called a "disk," was pulled over the moist earth to smooth out excess clods. This process signified it was time for planting. The morning wasn't an unusual morning as far as the chores were concerned. Walking behind the horses, we made our way toward the field to be worked. I hitched my team to the drag, then back and forth I stood on the drag as the horses pulled it over the recently plowed earth. There was a certain solitude standing on that drag. I barely tightened the reins I held in my hand as the sun-dried sod began to crumble beneath my feet. My mind would wander letting all my daydreams create visions of a world outside the great prairies. I wondered about life in the big cities such as Chicago and New York. I had heard about mountains, but never saw one. I had never seen the ocean. It was difficult to fathom bodies of water being so vast that one could never see land. As I stood there letting my body move with the rolling of the structure beneath my feet, a large clod of earth threw the drag off balance. My body lurched forward and I was thrown from the drag onto the earth, the drag coming to a stop over my legs and stopping at my waist. My head landed at the hooves of the horse's rear feet. I screamed for help. Piney heard my cry. She tried to alert my sister that something was wrong. When Ruth said, "Be quiet Piney," the dog ran to the barn where Lute was repairing a ladder that rose from the floor of the barn and ascended to the haymow. Lute knew something was wrong. He laid his hammer on the barn floor then rushed into the house. "Ruth!" he shouted. "Piney's tryin' to tell us somethin'. I think we'd better go see what she's tellin' us."

Piney had already begun her trek to the open field where I lay on the ground. She jumped the fences as if they didn't exist. When she reached me she began licking my face and whining as if trying to assure me all was going to be all right The team of horses seemed to be frozen in time. Not once did they attempt to move their hooves which could easily have crushed my skull. Ruth and Lute were behind Piney, and when they reached the field, Lute lifted the drag off my body. Slowly I raised myself to an upright position. I brushed off the dirt from my overalls, then, after determining there were no broken bones, I limped back to the house. Lute remained in the fields to continue breaking up the sun-baked clods of earth.

My sister Ruth was different than the rest of the family, particularly my sisters Betty and Edna. Her personality was totally unlike that of Harvey or myself. I was never around Francis enough to know which genes he inherited. Mom always said, "Ruth's jes' like Grandma Jordan." From what I can recall of Grandma Jordan, I wouldn't call that a compliment.

Before wandering too far from the story of the farm and my sister Ruth, my observation of my sister proved that Mom was absolutely right. She was exactly like the woman I met in Danville.

Lute's finest attribute was patience. He had a philosophy which said, "It is far more important to get along with one's surroundings than to initiate some kind of a conflict." He was an unsurpassed storyteller. His yarns could mesmerize one for hours, especially kids. Everyone loved Luther Payne. Most times he had a real knack for cajoling my sister whenever she was in a bad mood, causing her to smile, then he knew all was okay and the storm cloud had passed.

There was a radical change in the weather during my short stay with Ruth and Lute. Instead of a warm spring, the air turned cold and the rains came. The unceasing rains turned the freshly ploughed earth into huge lakes from the flooding. Luther stored his seed corn in the barn. The husks covering the ears of corn had been removed, but shelling the kernels of corn from the cob was a hands-on experience. It was too cold in the barn to spend hours shelling corn, and my good brother-in-law could see nothing wrong with bringing a large galvanized-steel tub into the kitchen. Lute placed the tub in the middle of the kitchen floor, and while he and myself proceeded to shell the corn, Ruth, who apparently hadn't been aware Lute planned to use her kitchen for a job that was always done in the barn, rushed into the kitchen like an unexpected tornado.

"Luther!" she shrieked. "Git that corn back to the barn where it belongs! You know better than to use my kitchen as a place to shell that corn!"

Lute could say nothing that would calm down my irate sister. The more my good brother-in-law attempted to humor Ruth, the angrier she became. "This ain't gonna hurt yer kitchen, Ruth. It's too cold out there in the barn and this corn has to be shelled. Any mess we make when we're finished, we'll clean it up."

Ruth retorted, "Well, Luther, if you don't take that corn back to the barn where it belongs right now, I'm leavin' ya. Git yer things, Loy, I'm takin' ya home!"

My sister rushed out of the kitchen, slammed the kitchen door and jumped in the car. My happiness for what I had hoped to be for the summer months came to an abrupt end. There was no conversation between Ruth and myself during the drive from Fairmont to Wheeling Junction. Reaching the front door of the old schoolhouse, I hurriedly left the vehicle. Ruth gunned the motor of the car and the back wheels spun so violently against the gravel, the smell of burning rubber filled the air. When Mom opened the door and saw me standing alone, she was certain I must have done something wrong and my actions were the reason for my sister's anger. "I never saw Ruth so mad, Mom. Why would she act that way with Lute? He jes' wanted to git the job done without freezin' to death. We didn't make any dirt in her kitchen, Mom."

Mom listened as I related the event of the morning. When I told her the whole story, she said, "Well, Loy—don't worry about it. I'm sure it's gonna come out in the wash. Ya can mark my word, Ruth will be back home before nightfall."

Luther and Ruth possessed one automobile. Ruth had taken their only means of transportation. They had no telephone, which was not unusual in those times. Morgan, Lute's brother, was a few miles to the north, and it was too far to walk. Luckily, before the afternoon turned into dusk, Morgan stopped by to have a visit with Ruth and Luther. Luther was standing in the yard pondering over what he should do when Morgan drove into the barnyard. "Morgan—ya gotta help me find Ruth. She was awful mad this mornin' when she found Loy and me shellin' corn in her kitchen. She took off in the car and I have no idea jes' where she went. She said she was takin' Loy home, so I presume she at least stopped at Wheeling Junction."

Luther hopped into Morgan's car and within minutes they were driving toward Wheeling and the old schoolhouse. From a small window in the entryway, Mom watched a strange car stopping near the steps leading into our house. Before Lute could reach the front door, Mom opened it.

"Where's Ruth?" The tone of Lute's voice wasn't only angry, it was filled with anxiety and concern.

"Well, Luther, she dropped Loy off here, said nothing and all I heard was wheels spinnin' in the gravel and smellin' the smell of burned rubber. I jes' betcha Luther, she went to Muncie and she's headed right fer Edna's. Now, if you two fellers will come in, we'll sit down and talk about it."

Mom led the way into the portion of the big room we called the parlor. Luther tried to explain what had happened when Mom interrupted. "You gotta go git her, Luther, and you'd better make her know she's not the only one who wears the pants in your family. Ruth has always been like that, always wanting everything her way. She ain't the only chicken sittin' on the roost. She's probably sorry now for the way she acted. Go git her and tell her to git her butt home where it belongs and quit actin' like a jackass."

Muncie wasn't far from Wheeling Junction. When Morgan and Lute pulled into the driveway at my sister's home, the men could see Ruth staring out the window. Before Lute could rap on the door, Ruth had it partially open. "Whatta ya doin' here, Luther? I told ya I was leavin' ya."

Luther pushed his foot against the door, opening it wide enough to move my sister aside. "Git yer things, Ruth—yer comin' home and yer comin' home now. If ya don't do what I'm tellin' ya, then you might as well plan on never comin' home again."

Ruth turned from a feisty cat into a purring kitten. "All right, Luther, I'll be ready in a few minutes."

For well over 50 years, my sister and her husband would remain married. They became parents of four children. Those children produced grandchildren, and then there were great-grandchildren.

Ruth was always considered frail. She would get pregnant and with each pregnancy there was a miscarriage. Death was always imminent. In 1935, Ruth finally delivered a baby girl. She weighed in at 10 pounds. She was the biggest baby I had ever seen. They named her Mildred June.

CHAPTER 28

ANOTHER MOVE WAS IMMINENT. AFTER leaving Ruth and Luther's home, wheat was ready for harvesting. I worked in the fields stacking and tying shock upon shock of wheat as I followed behind the wheat cutter. I earned enough money to buy my first secondhand bicycle.

The harvest time turned the Midwestern landscape from a rich, green carpet of growing wheat into a golden yellow autumn. Everyone worked the fields during harvest time. If a youngster was old enough to hold a rake or ride a horse, he was old enough to be a farmer. It was a time when there was an abundance of food. While the men toiled in the fields, the women prepared a midday meal. The old adage, "It looks like yer cookin' fer a bunch of thrashers," was true. At least 12 hungry men would gather at the kitchen table which had been extended with four extra leaves. The womenfolk saw to it that no plate was ever empty. Every belly was so full, it couldn't contain one more bite of food.

Dad found a bit of vacant land next to a large cornfield off the main road at Wheeling Junction. It was probably a good quarter of a mile from the main road to the site where Dad created a shack which he placed on wheels so when the time came should the owner of the land need the open space, or for some other reason it was necessary to move on, Dad could easily pull his creation behind the old Model T and move to another location. Whatever he constructed was an eyesore to the entire poor community. The corncrib may have housed the season's grain, but at least it resembled a house.

Much to Mom's chagrin, we moved into the shack in early fall. There was one room that sufficed as a parlor and a combination kitchen. Dad then erected an "L" shaped room off the larger room which became Dad and Mom's bedroom. I slept in a small cot in one corner of the so-called parlor.

The winter of 1935 and 1936 was one of the most severe winters to hit the Midwest in many years. Seldom did the temperature warm enough to get above the zero mark. There was snow and more snow, each layer turning to ice. A long, dirt lane from the main road where the school bus left me off at the end of a school day meant I had to traverse the quarter of a mile to our shack. In many ways, this was fortunate, since the shack in which we lived couldn't easily be seen from the main road. Dad had constructed an outdoor privy next to the lean-to where he parked the Model T, but the distance from the main road down the dirt path was too far for me to walk and make it to the outdoor privy when I had to pee. The snow was up to my waist. My ability to keep my bladder in tow had reached its peak; I let the pee go and as it did so, the pee felt warm but my pant legs froze. No amount of starch could have created a stiffer pair of pants.

I don't know how we survived that winter. There were times we were sick and Mom's concoctions didn't work. We couldn't afford a doctor, so Mom would spend hours on her knees at the side of my cot pleading to her God for help.

It was undoubtedly a combination of her prayers and her homemade medicine that eventually broke the high fevers caused by the winter flu.

At the corner of the dirt lane and the main road stood another rundown house. The occupant there was a lonely drunk. He always wanted to strike up a conversation with me as I disembarked from the bus. In my mind, a person who consumed too much alcohol was one to be feared, so I would, in most cases, just ignore the man and keep on walking until I reached the safety of the shack. One day, the man spoke as I passed him by. "Hey Loy! How's yer knob?" Not understanding the connotations of what the man was saying, I just kept on walking. I knew no response to offer the man other than "Mine's fine—how's your'n?"

"Mine's stickin' straight up," he answered without missing a beat. I speeded up my gait toward the shack. I couldn't wait to tell Mom. "Well—Loy, I guess ya said jes' the right thing. Don't git close to that man. Ya come straight home when you git off that school bus. Do ya hear?"

When springtime and summer followed the icy winter, during the tomato picking time, Mom took a job in a canning factory. For the first time in her life, she was earning money. She began to take pride in how she looked. One day Mom was late getting home. When she did arrive, she wasn't Mom. She had been to a beauty parlor. Her hair was cut short, and the hair remaining was nothing but an abundance of curls framing her angelic face.

When Dad faced Mom for the first time after her transformation, he went into a rage. I had never seen my father so angry. He had never in the 20 years they were together laid a hand on my mother, but this time almost brought a final blow across her face. He did much more than wander off into a pouting mood; he was determined to let Mom know he did not approve of her new look.

Long into the night when the light in the kerosene lamp was extinguished, I could hear Dad and Mom arguing. Before dropping off into a deep sleep, the last words I recall my mother saying was, "Abe—I'm leavin' ya and I'm gonna git a divorce." When I awakened the following morning, Mom was gone.

I don't know how Mom was able to go from Wheeling Junction to Muncie, but after a few days passed and Mom was no longer in the shack, Dad decided I was a good age, although a bit young, to farm out to a farmer as he had done with my brother Harvey.

Dad wasted no time in finding a family that would take a good, hard-working 11-year-old into their home. The Smiths were a young couple with a small son who was about five. They had a large farm, many, many acres plus a number of cows, horses, chickens, hogs and whatever livestock one would imagine belonged on a farm.

I knew from the moment Dad dropped me off at the Smith farm and I met Joe Smith, his wife Ellen and their young son, I was headed for disaster. Ellen Smith resented my presence from the start, and all Joe Smith could think about was how much value I had as far as working the fields, milking the cows, and slopping the hogs. I was given a tiny room in the attic of the old farm house, just large enough to accommodate a cot and perhaps a dresser in which to put my meager wardrobe.

Day one would begin the routine I was to follow for as long as I resided in the Smith home. It was at 5:00 a.m. I was told to get out of bed. It was time to milk the cows. The rest of the chores followed including throwing corn on the ground for the chickens. After a quiet breakfast, I let the cows out to pasture, harnessed a team of horses then led them into a recently plowed field. Here I would either hitch a team of horses to a drag, and if the fresh clods of earth were broken, I would hitch them to a disk. The only break would come when it was time to return to the farmhouse for midday dinner then it was back to the field until dusk. At dusk I would unhitch the horses from the disk or drag then bring them back to the barn. I would unharness them and place them in their stalls then give them their share of oats as a token of thanks for a hard day's work. The cows were brought in from pasture. Before I would have dinner or before I could call an end to my long day, I would milk the cows, separate the cream from the milk and finally, tired and worn out, I was permitted to enter the kitchen and sit down for supper. The end of the day arrived and I was more than willing to escape to the small room in the attic and lay my tired, young body down to rest.

I would lie on my cot and think about Cecil, how he had been subjected to so many years of Dad's cruelty and how he finally was old enough to run away from home, hop a freight train and find safety for the first time in his life.

Mom found a job in Muncie caring for an invalid woman who weighed about 300 pounds. She was totally chair-bound and even to relieve herself Mom was obligated to lift this woman from her chair and set her on a portable toilet. The job paid three dollars a week.

Mom filed for divorce almost immediately after her arrival in Muncie. Dad must have received papers indicating such a move on Mom's part and the papers undoubtedly had the address of where Mom was working. At any rate, he hotfooted it to Muncie and to the address where Mom was employed. He begged and pleaded for her to drop her divorce intentions and after much pressure from Dad and discovering where he had farmed me out, Mom conceded. Dad moved in with Mom at her place of employment.

On a Sunday morning Mom and Dad came to visit me at the Smith farm. Apparently Joe had permitted me to sleep in a bit later on that Sunday morning. I vaguely recall Mom coming up to the attic room, gently kissing my brow and handing me a penny. They were on their way to Zion, the country church at the crossroads.

The following Monday morning Joe spoke as he got up from the kitchen table. "Loy—there are seventeen acres that have to be dragged today. If you can get them all done by milkin' time, Ellen and I'll take ya to that dog circus ya heard about." Of course, I was delighted. I looked forward to some kind of reward for my hard work. All day and even through the noonday meal, I remained in the field with my team of horses. I would occasionally take a break so my animals could get a drink of water in the trough near the gate leading into the barnyard. At supper time, Joe helped me milk the cows and I rushed into the house to clean up for my big night on the town of Gaston. We had supper and soon we were on our way to town where a circus tent was pitched. I recall sitting in the front row, and when the show started, my head dropped on my chest and I was sound asleep. I never saw the dog show.

Saturdays were usually a fairly light work day on the farm. I looked forward to some leisure time off after the morning chores were done, but on this particular Saturday, at breakfast, I was informed my day would be spent hoeing weeds in a large garden planted on some land close to the main road. After breakfast, like a good slave I made my way to the garden at the end of the long lane leading from the house to the main highway. Halfheartedly I picked up the hoe and began hoeing weeds. About mid-morning I saw the Smiths heading for the main road, leaving a cloud of dust as they drove past where I was working. I was angry and felt totally used. Thoughts of running away flashed through my mind.

I noticed the bread truck turning in the lane that led to the Smith house. The driver saw me working in the field and he stopped his truck. "Hey, young feller. They're workin' ya kinda hard, ain't they? Don't they ever give you a day off? I have ta go into Hartford City for another load of bread. How about ya comin' with me? I'll git ya back before the Smith's git back. I saw 'em shoppin' over in Hartford City."

I threw down my hoe and ran toward the fence separating the garden from the lane. "Ya bet, fella. I'd be glad to take a break." All the while the driver of the bread truck was yakking during the trip into Hartford City, my mind was thinking about an escape. Thoughts about Cecil flashed through my mind. I knew I was much younger than Cecil. I was only 11 years old, but my young age didn't deter my thinking I might not make it.

We arrived at the dock where the bread man prepared to load his truck. Just as I planned to make my escape, the man returned. I was on my way back to the hell hole and hard work demanded by the Smiths.

It was not a warm reception when the truck pulled up in front of the main house. During my absence the Smiths could readily see I was not in the field doing my job. Ellen met the truck before it came to a complete stop. "Loy, you were told to work in the garden during our absence. I must tell ya we are not happy about ya goin' off with the bread man."

Anger flooded my entire soul. I laid down on the ground and began pounding the earth like a raging bull. "I hate ya! I hate ya! I never git a chance to rest around this place!"

Ellen turned and walked into the house. I eventually calmed down then returned to the garden and began hoeing weeds.

At supper time, after milking all the cows and taking care of the livestock, I entered the house for my evening meal. No one spoke and I didn't speak. I went to bed and eventually must have fallen asleep.

I wasn't told to get out of bed the following morning. In the distance I could hear the sound of Dad's Model T as it turned off the main road onto the lane leading to the house. When Dad arrived, I heard him ask Ellen how I was doing. I heard her answer, "Ya can take yer son home with ya, Abe. He tried to run away yesterday, and we jes' cain't tolerate that kind of behavior."

I hurried and dressed then met Dad at the foot of the stairs. "Come on, Loy. I have a lot to say to ya when we git in the car."

It was the longest ride to Muncie I had ever taken. During the entire journey, Dad threatened me with the house of correction and kept telling me I was no good and would never amount to anything. I had put him and Mom in a bad position and now he had to find a place where we could live.

Mom was surprised when she saw me and it was obvious I caused a real problem. The family who hired Mom for three dollars a week now had the entire family under their roof.

Mom withdrew her filing for divorce. Dad began searching for a place where we could live.

No one was more aware than myself as to how I complicated things for Mom and Dad. Dad was in the middle of a rock and a hard place. My presence at Mom's three-dollar-a-week job including board and room was not acceptable to her employers. They had not intended for their servant's husband to become a part of the package and certainly were not agreeable to adding their wayward son to the household. Dad had to find a place for us to live and a better domicile than the shack at Wheeling Junction.

It was on the road to Summitville Dad discovered an empty four-room house. The crossroads and Zion had once again returned Mom and Dad back to that vicinity. There was lots of land surrounding the house and ample room for tilling the soil and growing food. Other than the house we lived in at the gravel pits and the crossroads, this house would fulfill our needs and give us the comfort like we hadn't enjoyed since the time I was born.

A miraculous change came over Dad. He attended church with Mom every Sunday. He found a fairly good paying job that was steady and even squeezed 25 cents a week out of the money he brought home to give to me as a weekly allowance. Of course, this wasn't just a handout; I was expected to keep the weeds down and get the garden ready for growing food. There was happiness within the house of Abe. Dad even suggested to Mom she take me to Akron to visit the Rainbolts. It was decided we would make the journey before I enrolled in another school, a grade school in Summitville. I would be going into my sixth grade.

There wasn't much attention given to the fact that I had

reached the age of puberty on my 12th birthday. My voice began to change from a high soprano to a crackling baritone as the hormones within me adjusted my body from childhood to the teen years. June 24, 1936, passed. Preparations were made for Mom and me to go to Akron during the first week in August. On July 31, Mom was preparing supper in readiness for Dad's return from work. During the day she had said nothing about feeling ill—not even so much as a headache, but, as she set the table for supper, she spoke. "Loy—I gotta tell ya somethin'. I'm goin' away." I interrupted Mom. "I know Mom, we're going to Akron before I start school."

"No, Loy, where I'm goin' ya cain't go with me."

"Where ya goin', Mom? Is Dad goin' with ya?"

Mom paused for a moment. "Loy—where I'm goin' ya cain't go with me and Dad cain't come along neither. I have to go by myself."

No other words were spoken. I was suddenly overcome with depression. I sat down in Dad's rocking chair. Mom's statements sounded so final. She said nothing about coming back or that I would ever see her again. I would never see or feel her touch for the rest of my life. The foreboding conversation with Mom on that afternoon, the last day of July in 1936, clouded our happiness in the small frame house sitting beside a gravel road leading to Summitville. Dad came home and we all sat down to supper. As darkness overcame the brightness of the sunny day, we prepared to go to bed. I slept in a small room off the kitchen. I could hear Mom saying her nighttime prayers, then all was quiet.

Before another dawn, I heard Mom's voice penetrating the walls of the little frame house. "Dad! Dad!" Those would be her final words. Dad awakened from a sound sleep and I could hear him trying to talk to Mom but she said nothing. I never heard my father pray until that early morning hour of 3:00 a.m. Weeping and uttering a desperate prayer, he knelt beside their bed. "Please God—if there is a God, don't take Oley away from me. Please! Please!" It was the most heart-rending plea I would ever hear from the lips of my father.

Dad came to the room where I lay. Gently he touched me on the shoulder. "Loy—wake up. Mom's awful sick! I gotta git a doctor."

I heard the Model T leave the yard. I lay there on the bed, my body began to shake with fear and uncertainty. "Without Mom—what's gonna happen to me?"

I believe Dad was gone for about an hour. We had no telephone and the nearest phone was at least a mile or more away. Dad apparently awakened our neighboring farmer and asked to use his telephone. When Dad returned another car drove into the yard. It was a doctor. I saw Dad and the doctor walk past my cot and into the bedroom where Mom lay. I can still hear the medical man's words. "She's gone, Mr. VanNatter. There's nothing I can do."

Bitter tears flowed from Dad's eyes. He stood over my small cot and in a broken voice spoke. "Loy—Mom's gone. I hafta git the undertaker."

It was the first day of August, 1936, that Mom took a one-way journey to an unknown world. I was alone in the house. Daybreak was beginning to turn darkness into light. I arose from my bed, dressed, then quietly went into the parlor. The door from the parlor that opened into Mom and Dad's bedroom was closed. Softly, I opened the door. I walked toward the bed where Mom was laying and as I did so, a strange light encompassed her entire body. I had often seen that light when she spoke to her Lord as she knelt in prayer. Peace flooded my mother's face. I couldn't shed tears. I was alone and yet not alone. Mom's spirit was always there.

I turned and left the room as quietly as I entered. I walked through the kitchen, then sat on the steps just outside the screen door. As I sat there, two men arrived. They walked into the room where Mom lay and the last recall I have of that morning was watching the two strange men place Mom's body on a gurney, cover her head and body with a white sheet then place her in a long, black car they called a hearse.

Word spread rapidly throughout the farm community that Mom died. Ruth and Luther were first to arrive, carrying their seven-month-old baby they named Mildred June. After their arrival a host of relatives I had never met as well as all my brothers and sisters pulled their vehicles into the yard at our little house on Summitville Road. Among the mourners was a small woman with whom we were never permitted to associate. She was Dad's sister, Mattie. She arrived with a handsome man I later learned was my Uncle Marion, Dad's youngest brother.

I loved Aunt Matt from the moment our eyes met. How Dad could have harbored such hatred for his only sister was difficult to fathom. "She's married to a nigger and I ain't gonna allow that nigger and my sister to ever be a part of this family." Aunt Matt was no longer married to her black man. He had died many years prior.

Tears flowed freely from people's eyes as they gathered at our humble abode. I couldn't cry. I just wanted to be left alone. I wanted to hold onto the memory of Mom's happy and peaceful face that I had seen before the full light of day.

Before nightfall, the mortician had prepared Mom's body for viewing. I wanted to stay home, but the family insisted I come with them. Entering the mortuary, I noticed a body laying in a cheap pine box. She looked nothing like Mom, yet all who gazed on the corpse said it was. The cold body of the woman lying there was dressed in a garment Mom could never have afforded when she was alive. Her face was painted and her hair coiffured like a mannequin in some department store. Mom never wore makeup. It was like looking at a deserted, freshly painted, empty house. The finality of death and seeing Mom laying in a box caused bitter tears to flood down my cheeks. The peaceful, ethereal light on Mom's face was gone and I was alone.

The following Monday morning, Mom's body was moved from the mortuary in Gaston to Zion. Farmers laid their farm chores aside. Leaving their horses unharnessed, they dressed in their Sunday clothes in order to pay Mom their last respects. There wasn't an empty seat in the country church called Zion.

When the eulogies were said and the service came to a close, Mom's casket was taken from the front of the altar railing of the church to the vestibule. Here mourners took one last glance at the woman always known as Oley. When the last person filed past the casket the coffin was closed and six pallbearers led the procession to the graveyard just a few yards from Zion. Under a huge oak tree, my mother was laid to an everlasting rest.

When Mom died, Dad was 72 years old. Mom was 52. The foreboding of finality at the time Mom attempted to explain to me about her journey was now a reality. I was alone.

*Aunt Mattie, my father's only sister whose only sin
was to marry a black man.*

*Frances Marion VanNatter, World War I hero and veteran, also
acclaimed Lincoln historian. My father's youngest brother.*

Chapter 29

Physically, Dad never changed. He looked the same as he did on the day I was born. He was tall, straight and had muscles that would be the envy of any able-bodied man. There was no bulging fat around his middle most men experience long before they reach the age of 50. Other than his silvery, gray, curly thick hair framing the back and sides of his balding, well-shaped head, he easily could pass for a much younger man.

He handled the crowds well after Mom's funeral. Although it was a Monday and the beginning work day for the farmer, particularly at harvest time, the farmers laid down their hoes long enough to pay their last respects to Mom.

Many of those attending the funeral arrived at our house for a noonday meal. A long picnic table was set up under a shade tree. It was covered with a white, freshly laundered tablecloth then laden with dish after dish of food prepared in someone else's kitchen.

I stayed far away from the chattering mob of tear-stained mourners. I wanted to be alone and wanted no part of the pity uttered from their lips. I hated the day of Mom's funeral. She wanted to be cremated, but the barbaric custom of weeping over the departed one's empty house prevailed.

Had those mourners or Dad observed what I had seen, Mom would have gotten her wish and the memory of her living soul would continue to live within the minds of all those who knew her. I continued to ask myself "Why, why did I have to look at Mom's body in that cheap pine box?" The body no longer resembled the peaceful one I saw taking her final journey into the world of the unknown. Where was the woman who had given birth to eight children, whose hands fed us, kept us clean, and nursed us when we were sick, sewed the clothes we wore and scrubbed bare wood floors until one's reflection was clearly visible?

The handsome middle-aged man who arrived at the funeral with Aunt Matt, Dad's sister, approached me as I stood alone under a tree a short distance from the crowd.

"I'm your Uncle Marion, Loy. I'm your Dad's youngest brother. I'm deeply sorry you lost your mother." There was a warmth about the man which would influence much of my life even though our paths would never cross again. For those few short moments he exuded the kind of spirit I would like to have shared. There was a dignity and kindness about the man who had served in World War I. I looked in his eyes and could see his gentleness coming from the bottom of his heart. He was a war hero and meeting him created a complete understanding as to why he was a leader of men.

While Uncle Marion and I conversed, Aunt Matt interrupted our visit. "I'm yer Aunt Matt, Loy, your Dad's sister. We're all gonna miss yer mom. She was a fine person and a good mother. I regret yer Dad never let me git to know ya." Aunt Matt's eyes reflected embedded pain from Dad's cruel rejection and criticism. Her only sin was to marry a black man who looked white. She bore him a daughter who, fortunately, was more white than black. Long after my aunt's husband passed on, she continued to bear the scars of being married to a "nigger." Even at my tender age, I often recalled the cruel dialogue between family members, people who never knew my aunt's black husband yet felt justified to judge this woman whose wrongdoing only existed in the minds of her peers.

Aunt Matt resembled Dad in physical appearance, but the softness and gentleness was something far removed from Dad's inner being. His prejudices were so deep that even the south couldn't compete with the bitterness my father permitted to fester within his soul.

The crowd dispersed at our little house on Summitville Road. Only the family members remained. The subject of Loy was soon the topic of conversation. "What's gonna happen to Loy? Whose gonna take 'im? He's only 12 and who wants to take a 12-year-old and raise 'im until he can take care of himself?"

"Well—he can stay here with me if he wants to. We'll git along somehow. I know'd it ain't easy to take a youngster his age and raise 'im," Dad interjected.

As Dad spoke a shock wave rolled through every member of the family. Dad's solution recalled memories of how he sent Helen off to the convent. It was as if his every thought before it became words, made a direct contact, always hitting the mark. "Send the kid off to a convent, an orphan's home or even a house of correction. If no one else wants 'im in the family, let someone outside the family take him. He's able to work. He should be good for somethin'."

I wanted to go with my sister Ruth and her husband, Luther, but they made no gesture as to taking me in. Betty and Bob continued to live on Bob's meager earnings as a grocery store clerk. Edna and her husband were already burdened with three children. It was a tall, sandy-haired man who stepped forward. "We'll take 'im." It was Claude Rainbolt. He was all too familiar with Dad's mode of operation in farming his kids out for others to rear.

The following morning at dawn, I left the little house on the road to Summitville. It was the last move and the last home I would ever share with my father.

CHAPTER 30

THE TWO-LANE ROAD ASCENDED FROM the flat lands of the prairies into hill country. I had never seen a hill higher than the mounds of gravel at the gravel pit. Our first lap of the journey came to a halt at a small cabin nestled among trees and tall weeds in the mountainous hills of Southern Indiana. Claude Rainbolt had come a long way since leaving the hill-billy country located on the shores of the Ohio River separating Indiana from Kentucky.

The Rainbolt family originally hailed from Holland. Like many immigrants who had the know-how to live off the land, the families migrated to the Midwest and its rich farm lands.

Josh Rainbolt was born and raised in the same hill country and in the same three-room cabin where he took his bride. It was here he sired two sons and three daughters, Claude, Clyde, Sadie, Emily, and Nellie. The father of the five children was a short, square, stocky, sandy-haired hillbilly who sported a genuine handlebar mustache.

Claude's mother gave the appearance of being tall, but appearance is often deceiving. It was probably due to her high button shoes and floor-length calico dress. Throughout the years, her face remained wrinkle-free and her hair, similar in color to Claude's, revealed no indication of turning gray. Her hair was long and straight. She pulled it tightly to the back of her head then neatly rolled it into a bun. She seldom smiled. Her stoic face could easily have been carved out of stone. Each day she fulfilled her household chores then she would take to one of the rocking chairs in the parlor. Josh Rainbolt would sit in the other rocking chair and should a visitor grace the portal of the Rainbolt cabin, they would either sit on the floor or if a chair was available at the kitchen table, they were permitted to bring that chair into the parlor.

It was prearranged that we would spend one week at the home of Claude Rainbolt's birthplace before traveling to West Lebanon then on to Akron, Ohio. I was more than accustomed to outdoor privies, but the two-holer belonging to the Rainbolts was located some distance from the house. Tall grass and weeds hid the toilet from view. Privies in all the places we lived were some distance from the house, but there was always a well-worn path extending from the house to the privy.

I was deathly afraid of snakes. Wading through the tall grass and weeds as a means to finding the shit house created an inner fear I would never fully abandon. Other hazards arose, far worse than confronting a small, unharmful, garter snake. When I reached the outhouse, giant wasps buzzed around the two-holer toilet seats like nature's helicopters. They erected mud nests in every corner of the airy structure, going so far as to create their mud houses on the underside of the two-holer.

My first trip to the outhouse was my last. I no sooner dropped my pants when I felt a crawling creature investigating my behind. Before I could rise from the seat, I felt the sharp pain initiated by the intruder as he took a bite out of my butt. No one could have paid me to go near that privy again. One could easily pee without being noticed, but as for number two, that had to be put on hold.

Claude's younger brother, Clyde, lived a short distance from the old homestead. He had two children, a girl about my age and a young boy, a couple years younger. Due to a freak of nature, the young boy was born without a tongue. It must have been the second day of our visit, I decided to walk the muddy lane until I reached the run-down cabin belonging to Claude's brother. As I neared the open gate, the tongueless lad ran to greet me. Saliva ran from his open mouth down over his chin. Trying to talk, he grabbed my hand then led me to the simple hut Clyde shared with his wife and children.

Clyde's wife acknowledged my presence, then disappeared into another room. When she returned, she handed me a series of comic books. The characters often seen on the comic page of the newspaper suddenly took on a different look. The cartoons contained unprintable acts of sex performed by macho images like Jack Armstrong, The Lone Ranger, Mutt and Jeff and even little Orphan Annie. If Mom had seen me perusing the pornographic cartoons, she would have washed my mouth out with soap. I was 12 years old and curious; consequently, as I looked at each cartoon, their meanings were indelibly printed in my mind. I handed the books back to Clyde's wife. I knew what I had seen was wrong. Without any comment, I walked into the weedy yard and began the trek back to the Rainbolt homestead. The tongueless child followed me to the road. "Come back—come back. Please—come back," I heard him cry, but my feet never stopped moving. Listening to the child's slob-

bering chatter gushing from his mouth had a nauseating effect.

Before leaving hillbilly country, we visited Claude's sister,
Sadie. It was a house no larger than the one Claude's parents
dwelled in, yet it was within these walls Sadie gave birth
to her two sons and a daughter they named Lenora. Sadie
was married to a "Bowman." All the members of the family, except Lenora, continued to live under the roof covering
a simple hut where each child breathed their first breath of
life.

Why Nellie Rainbolt chose Lenora to be a beneficiary of
her great wealth is an unknown mystery. Nevertheless, Lenora, like Nellie, left the hillbilly country to seek her fortune
in the town of Attica. Like the Vandeventers had taken in
Nellie, Nellie took in her niece. She groomed and educated
Lenora in the same manner in which she had been groomed.
Lenora was sent to the most prestigious Baptist university in
the state. She was permitted to wear only the latest designer
fashions which Nellie chose, and no male was to be a part
of the young girl's life as long as she remained under the
guidance of her rich aunt. It wasn't until Lenora graduated
from college that she liberated herself from the dominance
of Nellie Vandeventer. She was finally free to pursue a life of
her own.

I was eternally grateful for the morning we left the tiny
cabin in the hills of Southern Indiana. We stopped in a small
village where Claude gassed the car for the continuation of
our journey. The station, fortunately, had a rest room and I
could barely wait for the car to come to a halt before I dashed
out of the vehicle and into the more fashionable crapper. It
had been five days and they were the longest days of my life
without relief.

We arrived in West Lebanon and at the home of Helen and Fatty Reynolds. Dorothy, their daughter, prided herself in being quite the intellectual and rightfully so. She was born to be an educator. Even at her tender age she always wanted to play teacher. She, of course, was always the teacher and during that visit, her younger brother Bobbie and myself were the students. It was the day before Claude, Urith, and myself would continue our journey that Dorothy decided to direct her conversation to me. "Loy—Grandmother always spoke about how well you could sing. Why don't you sing for Bobby and me before you go?"

The only songs I was ever exposed to other than church and the occasional visit to Muncie where we would spend overnight at the home of my sister, Edna, were Grand Ole Opry radio broadcasts from Nashville, Tennessee. It was Bennie who turned on the radio and brought the sounds of real music to my ears.

Without announcing what I was going to sing, I let my singing voice escape my lips with "I wonder tonight if my blue eyes—if my blue eyes ever thinks of me."

I knew Mom would have been proud of my rendition. But apparently, my singing voice didn't appeal to Dorothy. "Well—I think ya sing through yer nose." Her comment was destined to be my first rejection as to my ability to sing. I was totally crushed. My singing voice would remain silent for months to come.

CHAPTER 31

"IF YA THINK MUNCIE IS a big town, jes' wait till ya see Akron." Claude spoke as we neared our destination. Claude loved Akron. It was obvious the man from the hills of southern Indiana had found his Mecca. Akron was the city that provided Claude Rainbolt security, freedom, and luxuries beyond his wildest imagination.

The putrid smell of rubber penetrated my nostrils as we approached the rubber tire center of the world. There was no escape from the fumes rising from the giant smokestacks created by Goodyear, Firestone, Goodrich, and the General Tire and Rubber Company. The polluted air emitted from the smokestacks was a personal logo like no other city on our planet.

Goodyear provided Claude Rainbolt and his family a certain amount of security during the pre-depression years as well as the depression years. Building tires was Claude Rainbolt's career and destiny in life.

The Rainbolts lived in a working-class neighborhood on the east side of town. It could never compare with the huge, park-like estates and mansions dotting the west side. On the west side, the Firestones, Seiberlings, and Freitags mingled with the upper class, their rich lifestyles made possible from the sweat and hard labor of those domiciled on the east side of the city.

It was a two-bedroom bungalow situated on the corner of Newton Street and Malacca Street where Claude and Urith would raise their two children. It was a small house, just barely large enough for two people, yet the Rainbolts found enough space to give me a haven under their roof. Urith and Claude shared twin beds in the front bedroom. Lenora was more fortunate; she had her own room in the back bedroom. I was bedded down on a narrow sofa in the living room, or what the house of Abe always referred to as the parlor.

The house had conveniences like I never could imagine. There was indoor running water—hot water just by turning a small spigot jutting out over the sink in the kitchen or the two spigots attached to the end of the tub in the bathroom. Electric lamps were turned on with a push of a button or by pulling a chain attached to the lamp. The floors were covered with soft carpets, so soft one wondered why anyone would even think of wearing shoes inside the house. In the bathroom was a porcelain bathtub large enough to lie in a prone position and be covered from head to toe with warm water. The parlor and dining room were separated by an archway. Oftentimes, Urith would serve as many as eight for a sit-down dinner around the large mahogany table. A telephone and a radio rested on the window seat in the dining room. The radio was rarely turned off except when everyone had gone to bed. The kitchen was fully equipped with an electric stove and an electric icebox that created its own ice. In the basement, a large coal furnace replaced the potbellied stoves. This appliance had the capability of sending heat into every room in the house.

The houses on Malacca Street were constructed closely

together with only a driveway separating each dwelling. No one ever locked their doors and neighbors felt free to come and go into the premises of their neighbors at will. Youngsters played ball in the middle of the street. Urith and Claude had a dog, a pure white Spitz named Peggy. She hated kids, but somehow she became accustomed to my being in her territory so I was accepted. I often joined the kids in the street as we played ball. We never had to worry about losing the ball or knocking it so far we had to run after it, or hitting someone's window and breaking it. Peggy was the best of all ballplayers. She would anticipate the hitter striking the ball and before the guy batting could make it to first base, Peggy retrieved the ball and handed it to the pitcher.

The Hamiltons lived next door. Arthur Hamilton was a quiet, tall, slender man, rather passive, with fair skin and a balding head. His wife, Lily, however, was outgoing and worldly wise, especially for a woman during those years. She smoked cigarettes and would go so far as to have an occasional drink. Right from my first introduction to Lily, I liked her. I soon discovered her to be my source of information, never reneging on an answer for any question I might ask.

Jean Hamilton was the oldest daughter. She was my age, a slender natural blonde and a figure that had all the makings for turning her into a beautiful woman. Marie was the baby. She must have been about five years old at the time I arrived in Akron. She could shed tears that would easily float a battle ship. Just looking at Marie was enough to send the youngster into a crying jag without any provocation.

The friendship between the Rainbolts and the Hamiltons dated back in time before Urith became a born-again Christian. Of course, when Urith decided to change her worldly ways, she had a history of sowing her share of wild oats. She wore high fashion clothing, short dresses that extended far above her knees. She didn't hesitate to add a bit of paint to her face and her hair was smartly marcelled closed to her round face. She loved to dance, roller skate and party. On occasion, I would guess, she even permitted an alcoholic drink to pass her lips. She was more inclined to live within the so-called fast lane than Claude, that is, until the day she was saved and became a member of the Nazarene flock.

The church was fundamental, far more so than the simple Methodist faith Mom exposed our family to. Claude was somewhat like Dad as far as religion was concerned. He was willing to see that Urith got to church, but for participation in any of the church activities himself, he managed to stay free and neutral. Urith often recalled the days when she was, as she put it, a part of the world and its worldly ways. Now that she had given her life to Christ, all those sinful years were washed away by the "blood of the lamb. "She even went so far as to cut Claude off from sexual activity, saying quite openly, "He's jes' too big. I can't handle it." Of course, this sort of advertising created quite a demand from neighborhood women and friends. It was often suspected there were occasions when one neighbor took advantage of this well-hung man inasmuch as her husband only wanted sex for the purpose of procreation.

The Wiggingtons lived across the street. If I had given any mind to the strictness of Urith's born–again faith, there was no comparison to the Wiggingtons. They were Pentecostal and full-blossomed Holy Rollers. Midweek, boisterous prayer meetings were conducted in their home and the sound of unknown tongues echoed up and down Malacca Street, all originating from the open windows of the Wiggington residence.

Eddie Wiggington, although a born-again Christian, had one fault. His love for tobacco far exceeded his interest in speaking in unknown tongues. Occasionally, he slipped into the garage, closed the door, and indulged in a plug of juicy tobacco. When the good book says, "Your sins will surely find you out" was more than true in the case of Eddie. It all happened on a day when Eddie was assured his weakness would not be discovered, he entered his garage, then placed enough tobacco in his mouth to cause his cheeks to bulge. As the brown juice escaped from his mouth and ran over his chin, Mrs. Wiggington caught her husband in the act of committing a cardinal sin.

She was a big woman with jet black, straight hair which she pulled back into a bun. It gave her a kind of missionary look. She was typical of an individual who took their religion seriously and never hesitated to wear the righteous insignia on her shoulder proving her sins were forgiven and her next step from life into the unknown would immediately take her into an eternal heavenly realm. More than once, she caught Eddie in the act of defying God by allowing his body to consume such filthy nectar. She angrily grabbed the nape of Eddie's shirt collar with one hand, practically lifting the sinner man above the floor, ushered him into the parlor, then forced her meek husband to his knees. The louder Mrs. Wiggington prayed for Eddie's deliverance, the more she pounded on his back. Of course, the pressure forced the cud of tobacco to eject from Eddie's brown stained mouth like a rocket. Only when the cleansing was complete and she was satisfied the backslider had thoroughly repented would she permit her penitent husband to rise to his feet The sinner had come home, that is, until the urge for the taste of chewing tobacco overwhelmed his obligation to walk the straight and narrow.

The Anglin family were only a stone's throw from the Rainbolt residence. Mrs. Anglin was Urith's best friend. They shared the same religious beliefs and attended the same church. Urith always referred to her as Sister Anglin, saying she was her sister in Christ. The Anglins had two children, a girl about my age by the name of Mary Frances and a son who was always referred to as "Sonny." I thought Mary Frances Anglin was the most beautiful creature my eyes ever laid eyes on. Of course, my amorous intentions were never reciprocated, so we were no more than school friends.

Ted Anglin was somewhat like Eddie Wiggington, the difference being, Ted had strong leanings toward imbibing in barley corn. This sin, as it was with Eddie, often outweighed his born-again Christian conscience. When Ted's thirst for a drink overcame his desire to be a shining light in God's eyes, he would go on a toot lasting sometimes weeks at a time. He would drink until his body was totally saturated with the devil's brew, then, usually by his own choosing, he would rush to the church's altar to fall on his knees and plead for forgiveness.

Then there was Mrs. Brannon. She lived in a nice house at the end of Malacca Street. Her spouse was a freckle-faced, red-haired Irish fellow who was even more obsessed with the devil's nectar than Ted Anglin. He was not a nice drunk. In fact, he was one of the meanest drunks I had ever seen. I didn't know much about the effects of alcohol, but I soon learned, especially when I noticed the bruises and black eyes on Mrs. Brannon. She was her husband's punching bag.

I liked Mrs. Brannon and always felt sorry for her lot in

life totally under the sadistic spell of an alcoholic husband. She was trapped. Her only recourse was to take her burden to the Lord and learn to live with the bruises on her face and body that gave her a polka-dot look. She was a good barber and the best barber to ever cut my hair. She never mentioned her religion. She was much like Mom in that regard. She accepted her faith as it applied to her personal needs and never tried to convert those around her.

Mrs. Brannon wasn't what one could consider fat, although she did have a stocky stature. She had straight, rather short, jet-black hair—that is, until the day of a severe thunder and lightning storm. She was standing in front of her kitchen sink looking out a window just above the sink when suddenly a bolt of lightning flashed through the open window making a direct hit on my good friend. She fell backward stiffer than a board. When she regained consciousness, her hair was curled in tight ringlets and her black hair turned snowy white.

The Peltons were a young couple and parents of a boy whom Urith faithfully toted to Sunday School and church. Of course, Mr. and Mrs. Pelton I am certain never stepped foot in the Nazarene Church but they had no objection to Urith exposing Bobby, their oldest son, to some sort of religious faith.

Soon after my arrival at the Rainbolt house, Mr. Pelton died, leaving a young widow and two small children. The Peltons were a young family, therefore, upon Mr. Pelton's passing, Mrs. Pelton continued to battle nature's urges for love, commonly known as sex. Boisterous parties soon became the norm. This of course, gave the residents on Malacca Street a certain amount of material to gossip about even though they had not really been privy to see the activities behind the closed doors of our neighbor on the other side of the street.

The elementary school in which I was to enroll into the sixth grade was a good mile or perhaps two miles from the Rainbolt home on Malacca Street. They called the school "Betty Jane." How this educational institution got the name "Betty Jane," I don't know. It was the same school with many of the same teachers that, prior to my arrival, taught Urith and Claude's two offspring, Claude, Jr. and Lenora.

To reach Betty Jane by foot meant treading through an uninhabited area where a small brook separated a clump of trees from an open meadow. A noticeable worn path led to the school's playground. The swift running brook separating the school's meadow and the playground required stepping on stones protruding above the waterline before stepping on dry land. I became so proficient in crossing the stream not a drop of water spilled on my neatly polished shoes.

It was only a few days prior to the opening of the school year that I arrived in Akron and for the first time since I was born, I would have no further interruptions in my education. Urith and Claude, so as not to be embarrassed with the shabbiness of their new charge, took me shopping. By the end of the shopping trip, I was fully equipped with new pants, new shirts, a Sunday suit and any other clothing needed to be presentable on my first day of school at Betty Jane. For the first time in my 12 years, I had the appearance of belonging to the kids on the other side of the tracks.

Entering the classroom on that first day I was greeted with a warm reception. Miss Barr, the teacher, was a bit on the heavy side with coarse, cropped, straight black hair which she wore in a boyish bob. Her teeth were bucked, the two front teeth having a tendency to protrude over her lower lip quite like a rabbit. There was never anything pretentious about this woman. Miss Barr was "what you see, is what you get." Her face was never painted in an effort to cover the blemishes nature had so unkindly bestowed on this wonderful lady. Beauty and kindness radiated from the depth of her very soul. Her goodness obliterated any unsightly physical appearance absorbed by the human eye.

I fell in love with my sixth grade teacher. I could almost hear Mom say, "Remember Loy, beauty is only skin deep, ugliness goes to the bone." Miss Barr loved children. She could have married and had kids of her own, but the rule laid down by the educational system did not encourage female school teachers to marry. For Alice Barr, the children she taught were her children, at least until the close of each school day. Miss Barr would volunteer to take census within her school district so she could enter the home of each one of her students. She wanted to see firsthand the kind of environment her youngsters were exposed to. What kind of parents did they have? Were they receiving proper nourishment, in food as well as proper parental care for a healthy development? I suppose, if there is such a being as a guardian angel, Alice Barr would come the nearest to being that ethereal character, more so, than any educator I would be permitted to encounter during the rest of my life.

Alice Barr was the music teacher for Betty Jane along with other subjects she taught. She succeeded in forming a school orchestra made up of mostly students who could afford to study with private teachers. There were, however, students who were poor and couldn't afford to study or had no access to an instrument on which to practice. I soon discovered, however, a teacher did devote one day a week to teaching those less fortunate hopefuls the art of playing the violin. Her name was Mrs. Harley and she was first violinist with the Akron Symphony. It was Alice Barr who opened that door for me.

I had only attended school a few days when at the end of the day, Miss Barr asked if I would mind staying for a few minutes. She would like to talk with me. This devoted teacher knew she had to find some tool in which to enter into my world. After Mom died, I became somewhat of a recluse, more of an observer than a participator. As a protective measure, I created an invisible curtain which no one was permitted to raise in order to look into my inner consciousness. I didn't want to be touched. Should anyone attempt to inquire about why I remained so quiet, I would shrug my shoulders and respond with "I don't know." I would shudder should anyone attempt to place their hand on me or attempt an embrace. Miss Barr knew she had to find some way to enter my hidden world.

My beloved teacher noticed when I heard music my eyes became brighter and I was far more attentive. When she would sit at the piano and encourage the youngsters to sing, she noticed my mouth remained closed. She observed my interest in watching the other children play their respective musical instruments. "Maybe it's music," she thought. "It just might open the door to his inner consciousness and permit him to have a means of self-expression."

The school room was soon void of all students except myself. Miss Barr remained seated at her desk. Miss Barr pulled up a chair next to her desk then asked me to be seated. "Loy," the kind teacher spoke. "I have asked you to stay so we might have a little chat, just you and me. I've noticed that you seem to enjoy music. Your face lights up when you hear me play the piano or when the other children are working on an orchestra piece. Did you know, I had Claude Rainbolt, Jr., in my classes when he was about your age. He played the violin very well and I had hoped he would go on with his music. I was wondering if perhaps that violin he used to play is still in the Rainbolt home. If it is, I'm sure, if you would like to try, Mrs. Rainbolt would let you borrow Claude Jr.'s violin and then you could take lessons one day a week with Mrs. Harley when she comes to Betty Jane. She gives free lessons. All you would need is a violin."

Miss Barr struck a harmonious note within my soul. I hurried out of the schoolroom, rushed across the meadow, dashed across the brook and finally up the stairs into the house. "Urith! Urith!" I shouted. "Miss Barr said Junior used to play the violin! She said, she bet if he don't play it no more, you'd probably let me borrow it so I could learn. Miss Harley gives lessons fer nothin' once a week at school and it ain't gonna cost nothin'."

Without hesitation, Urith spoke. "I don't see why you can't use that old violin. It's only gatherin' dust in the attic."

I shall always recall that first lesson on the violin. The sound was enough to cause anyone's ears to shudder. In fact, with most individuals, they would put the instrument back in its case and they would never attempt the art of playing the violin again. This was not the case with me. I persisted. I let the bow ride across the open strings of the instrument hour after hour until Urith said, enough is enough. I was exiled to the back bedroom and the only time I was permitted to touch the piano was to let my finger touch the "A" key on the piano so I might tune the instrument. Any time I would attempt to sit on the piano bench to make an effort to place my hand on the keys, Lenora would tell me "This is my piano and you are not to touch it! I will let you at least touch the 'A' key so you can tune your fiddle."

"Loy—ya hafta do somethin' about that terrible sound you're makin'. I can't listen to you and still hear my soap operas. I think you'd better try practicing in the basement where I can't hear any more of that screechin'."

Urith's criticism of my playing did not deter me from my determination to learn how to play the violin. One day, something miraculously happened. Instead of the ear-splitting sound coming out of the violin, a smooth, mellow, warm beauty sounded as the bow gently touched the strings of the instrument. Miss Harley was pleased. She even made me an offer.

"Loy—I am pleased with your progress. I'd like to make a deal with you. If you will mow my yard on Saturdays, I will give you private lessons.

I thought the Rainbolt household would be pleased, but I was mistaken. "Loy—I need you on Saturdays to work around this house. You know, I take in young men's laundry and I have taught you how to run the mango so you can at least do the flat work. I have to earn that extra money since Claude only gives me a small amount each week to cover our groceries." It was true, Urith did spend hour upon hour at the ironing board listening to *Aunt Jamima, Ma Perkins,* and all the other soaps that began at 9:00 a.m. until supper time. She had taught me to help out by ironing sheets, table linens and any other items that could be ironed on the mango.

I would forego my private lessons, but I did not forego my practicing. I was determined to play the violin. I wanted to make music more than anything else in the world. By the end of the semester, I was asked to join the youth orchestra.

I was given second chair in the second violin section. The violin would be my friend through high school and also in college.

It was my second year at Betty Jane on a very cold wintery day that another educator would bring about a big change in my life. I easily passed onto the seventh grade and continued my progress with the violin, but my mouth continued to remain closed when it came to a community sing with the rest of my classmates.

It was on a cold, snowy, icy morning, I noticed a crippled woman making her way from her car and entering the warmth of Betty Jane and the schoolroom where I was sitting. It was Nellie Glover, the superintendent of the school district. The old, gray haired lady was bent over like a question mark. I noticed the effort she was exerting to make her way into the school as she leaned on a wooden cane for support. I later learned this grand lady had been a great concert pianist in her early life until arthritis crippled her body and her hands to where she could no longer play. Now her hands were like fists. Her legs barely moved when she tried to walk. She removed her heavy coat, then placing the scarf she wore around her neck into the pocket of the coat, she laid the coat over a chair in front of the room. "Now — children," the woman spoke as a twinkle in her eye indicated a time had come when we were going to have some fun. "Miss Barr will play a song for each of us to sing." As Miss Barr took her place at the piano, Nellie Glover began walking down the aisle separating the rows of desks. As she stopped at each desk, she would lower her crippled body to where she could hear the sound of each child's voice. As she approached my desk, I was petrified. Would she, like Dorothy, say I sang through my nose?

Nellie Glover bent close to my face and my lips were only making a slight hum. "Come on, young man—I know you can sing louder than that. Come on—let me hear your voice." I exerted a little more sound and she listened. By the end of the song, I was almost in full voice. "My—you do have a beautiful voice. You should always sing."

It was like drinking a good tonic to hear someone say as Mom used to say, "You do have a pretty voice, Loy." Little did I realize that first encounter with the crippled lady would have such an influence in my life in the years ahead. The kind, crippled lady opened another pathway into the world of music. The violin and singing voice would be my savior during the teenage years and far into my early adult life.

CHAPTER 32

URITH TOOK GREAT PRIDE IN her profession as a laundress, seeing the shirts were ironed to perfection as she stood over an ironing board, all the while listening and getting involved with one soap opera after another. When *Stella Dallas* ended, then I knew it was time for supper. The only time the soap operas were placed on the back burner was during the baseball season. I can still recall the sports announcer's voice within my subconscious mind well over a half century later, yelling, "Strike One," "Strike Two," "He's Out!" As far as baseball was concerned, the only players that registered permanently in my mind were Dizzy Dean and Joey Brown.

The radio continued to blare during suppertime, but the evening hours were much more to my liking. There was "The Lux Radio Theatre." Urith's religion forbade me going to movies, so my outlet to the film industry was strictly via the radio. One of my favorite programs was "Gang Busters." This was always at 9:00 p.m. on Wednesday night and if I were lucky, we might get home in time from the prayer meeting so I could tune in to the police sirens coming through the small speaker of the tabletop radio. On Saturday afternoon, as I sat ironing flat work on the mango, Urith would permit me to occasionally listen to the Metropolitan Opera broadcast from New York City. After Miss Glover told me I had a beautiful voice, I wanted to hear every singer who might be sending their golden voice out over the airwaves. I recall Lanny Ross and his "Moonlight and Roses." Occasionally, we would hear Nelson Eddy or Lawrence Tibbett sing "The Road to Mandalay." Then there was Rosa Ponselle, the most beautiful soprano voice that ever penetrated my ears. In those teen years, they were household names. I wanted to sing on the radio.

I continued to improve on the violin. By Christmas time at Betty Jane, Miss Barr announced I was ready to join the school orchestra. I was assigned a chair in the second violin section. Percy Granger's "Country Gardens" was played so many times I could visualize each note as it was written on a sheet of music resting in front of me on the music stand.

Living under the roof of Claude and Urith Rainbolt was a

Betty Jane School Orchestra, Ms. Barr, teacher.

Betty Jane School Police.

period of adjustment. I was a guest and as far as my life was concerned I was really an orphan. I made a special effort to get along, even attending a church I didn't like. It was during those times I realized how deeply entrenched my half sister was in her religion. Sins included in her beliefs were going to the movies, playing cards, and dancing. The women in the church were forbidden to wear makeup and they were not permitted to wear jewelry.

Often, I would stand in front of a movie theatre wishing I could buy a ticket and see a real movie that had sound. All the movies shown during my young life were silent. Sometimes I would get a glance at the silver screen and the moving figures who actually spoke when people purchasing tickets opened the door and entered the theatre. For one brief glance, I would see the silver screen. There was something magic about that split second. Religion or no religion, I was determined when I earned my own money, I was going to the movies.

The Nazarenes were not in the same category as Holy Rollers who managed to get their cookies off by rolling on the floor of their church and speaking in some unknown tongue. The Nazarenes could, however, get fired up about the terrible hell awaiting sinners who were not willing to walk the straight and narrow path of a Christian. The preacher's voice would ring out. "The road to hell is paved and wide, but, the road to heaven is long, rugged and narrow!" When the man of God reached a cooling down point in his sermon, his pleading voice would rise above the sound of the choir's rendering "Just As I Am Without One Plea." "Please—give your heart to the blessed Lord now! Come—walk the narrow path with me." His pleading voice rising over the strains of music coming from the choir was enough to soften the conscience of the most calloused sinner. Those touched by the preacher's words would rise from their seat and tearfully rush to the altar to ask forgiveness for all the sins they thought they committed.

My first Christmas at 375 Malacca Street was the first real Christmas I would experience during the first 12 years of my life. In the Rainbolt house, it was a time for giving, buying presents, hiding presents and trying to find out what a person really wanted. Urith worked full time making candies, baking cookies and all the other goodies associated with the Yule season. If a sweet delicacy could be made with sugar, Urith was a master at turning sweet delicacies into tasty treats that would remain within one's taste buds long after the season passed. There were frequent shopping sprees beginning long before Thanksgiving. Urith, I am certain with monies she earned doing bachelors' laundry, would spend her money to buy gifts and hide them in the back closet of Lenora's bedroom. She would repeatedly ask me what I wanted for Christmas. There was never a time, except the one Christmas at the crossroads, under the roof of the house of Abe, when I could even think about Christmas as a time for giving. What I really wanted was a sled. I knew that was totally outside the realm of possibility. Neighborhood kids had sleds and Akron's share of snow during the winter months was abundant. The streets were hilly and ideal for a fast ride from the top of the hill to the bottom.

I finally expressed my desire to Urith. I recall letting those words escape my lips, knowing, undoubtedly my desire would bring a shock wave across Urith's face. She showed no sign of any emotion nor did she say, "Loy—they are just too expensive. We can't afford to buy you a sled." Unbeknownst to me, Urith and Claude decided to make an attempt at fulfilling my most wanted wish. They decided if they could get a small donation from my sisters, along with the amount of money they would contribute, there was no reason I couldn't have a sled.

Christmas Eve was a time for celebration in the Rainbolt household. It was time for a big feast and after a hearty dinner, we'd gather around the tree. It was present giving and receiving time. The tree was beautiful. I had never seen a tree decorated with varied colored lights, delicate ornaments glistening from the reflection of the lights all shining on the multitude of boxes wrapped in magical colored paper and bright ribbons. There were so many presents piled under the tree, that many extended far into the small living room.

Claude never participated in present giving at Christmas time. He would place a five dollar bill in an envelope and put a name on it for each member of the family. That first Christmas of 1936 was different. Claude decided to go shopping. When all gifts were distributed to each member of the family, there was none for me. My heart sank. There was no sled. My disappointment must have been obvious. I noticed tears welling in Claude's eyes. He rose from his chair then disappeared. I thought Christmas was finished. When Claude did reappear, he carried the most elegant, streamlined sled that would be the envy of every kid in the neighborhood. A large tag tied to the sled's runner read:

From Urith, Claude, Edna, Ruth, and Betty.
Happy Sledding!"

Lenora had long since divorced herself from her mother's church. She was involved in a church on the other side of town that was a bit more liberal than the Nazarenes and a congregation that attracted many young people. Each Christmas Eve, a young man by the name of Norm Simpson would recruit a number of the church's young people to carol in front of the homes of several members of the congregation. The caroling would start at midnight and would continue until 5:00 a.m. Christmas morning. Lenora was one of those singers. The church people were good people and in appreciation for hearing the immortal songs celebrating the yuletide, many would rise from their beds and invite the carolers in for hot chocolate or a bit of food. Of course, the carolers, at 5:00 a.m., deprived from their night's sleep, would spend most of Christmas Day sleeping while other families celebrated Christmas.

The New Year of 1937 arrived and with it came word that Aunt Matt's husband had passed on. None of us knew the man, her second husband being a white man we referred to as Uncle Albert. Nevertheless, it was a call for another trip to Indiana. Funerals and paying last respects to the dead had priority in our family. If at all possible, no relative was excused from attending the final rites and extending their condolences to those family members left behind.

To reach Muncie, Indiana, from Akron, Ohio, was a long and tiring ride. We left at dawn and arrived at the church as the coffin was being taken into the church. The closed casket was wheeled down the center aisle of the church then placed in front of the altar. The undertakers opened the casket, then placed a wreath of flowers at the foot of the deceased. I gazed at the open casket and the man lying in the satin-lined box caused me to wonder what he must have been like when he could talk. He was a good-looking man. As the preacher eulogized the deceased as a faithful husband to Aunt Matt, I noticed small water blisters breaking out on my arms and hands. I would squeeze the blisters and let the residue of the blisters flow across my arms. I then noticed the same blisters were beginning to cover my cheeks and my forehead. I wasn't aware what was happening, except I knew I didn't feel well. My head was hot and apparently my body was becoming more feverish as the minister drudged through the final sermon for Uncle Albert. Unbeknownst to me, I was in the throes of a full-blown childhood disease called chicken pox. No child was exempt from attending funerals of a departed one. As a consequence, I started an epidemic among the offspring of the VanNatter clan. Every child present was suddenly infected with chicken pox. I didn't mention to Urith or Claude I did not feel well when we left Akron. It was only when we followed the coffin from the church, Urith knew something was wrong. My face was beginning to be covered with a polka-dot appearance. I curled my body into a fetal position in the backseat of Claude's Ford and attempted to sleep, but the fever sent me into a fit of illusions and nothing was real. Within hours after our return to Malacca Street, the health inspectors were on our doorstep posting a large white sign on the front door. "Do Not Enter! Chicken Pox!"

Again, during the first few years of my life, my education was put on hold. When Miss Barr heard about my illness, she arranged to have schoolwork brought to the house so I wouldn't lose ground in my pursuit of learning. The chicken pox siege also brought news of Dad courting another woman. He never lost much time, according to his past record, finding another marital partner or mate. He would never consider sleeping with a woman though, without the sanction of marriage. He would seek the services of the nearest Justice of Peace and the union would become binding.

Lily was Dad's fourth wife. No one was knowledgeable as to how Dad met Lily. At the time, The Lonely Hearts Club was a means for finding a mate and it was probably through that organization that Lily became my stepmother.

Lily had an attractive face but her body was the shape of a walrus. I don't know how Dad managed to squeeze behind the steering wheel of the Model T once Lily was seated next to him in the front seat. Dad never took Lily to the house where Mom departed this world. A short distance from where we lived in the corncrib was the Webster farm. The main house on the farm was not a mansion but it was considerably more conducive to living with some dignity and comfort than any roof Dad previously chose to put over our heads.

Mrs. Webster was a recluse. She had no desire to associate with neighboring farmers nor did she want them coming near her property where she contentedly lived with her chickens, goats, a few pigs and a horse. During the time we spent at the crossroads and while living in the corncrib, never at any time do I recall Mrs. Webster ever leaving the confines of her small farm. Gossip circulated throughout the country-side that Mrs. Webster was a witch. Occasionally, one might observe her moving like a roadrunner in her barnyard as she fed her goats, geese, and chickens. I never saw her at any time hitch her horse to the buggy or wagon parked next to the barn. I often walked by the Webster farm as a small child as I made my way to the Herrold's farm where Richard Her-rold was my playmate. As I stood on the gravel road in front of Mrs. Webster's place, the old woman would dart from one point to another then suddenly come to a dead stop. Her ears and eyes seemed to pick up scents and sounds. She was always alert. Her hair was never combed. A pack rat's nest was neat in comparison. The recluse would suddenly notice me standing in front of her place, far enough away where I might make a quick escape. Her cold stare sent shivers of fright through my body. When the woman realized I was no threat to her or her land, she would flash an open grin. Her face revealed missing front teeth. Mrs. Webster's piercing eyes would scan the country road like a buzzard searching for some animal's remains. The female recluse was always called Mrs., yet I often wondered if she ever married. When she passed on, her earthly existence failed to attract people's attention, but the folklore surrounding Mrs. Webster was destined to live on from generation to generation.

When Dad married Lily, there was concern he would re-trieve me from the care of the Rainbolts. This was no threat. Dad was always more than willing to have someone else raise his kids. The Rainbolts spoke of possible adoption. I objected. I already had the middle name "Rainbolt," and I wasn't happy about losing my last name, "VanNatter."

The marriage between Dad and Lily was not a marriage made in heaven. Lily was far from the demure, peaceful soul with which my father's previous wives were endowed. She was not religious; in fact, she was a sinner from the very depth of her human soul. She had the ability to use every four-letter word that would forever disgrace the language of the King. Dad was shocked at Lily's vocabulary. He found it totally disturbing and repulsive. In all his seventy some-odd years, he never permitted the word "damn," to escape his lips. Dad's fourth bride and the trip to the altar of wedded bliss was, to say the least, a bumpy ride. The union would eventually end in the divorce court.

CHAPTER 33

LENORA WAS A SENIOR IN high school when I took up space in the Rainbolt home. Upon graduation from high school, she matriculated in a Beauty College where she studied cosmetology.

I continued to sleep on the sofa in the living room until it was almost time for my graduation from the eighth grade. Then it was on to high school. It was during my eighth year of schooling that I acquired a newspaper route and with the money I received from my first job I was able to purchase my first balloon-tired bicycle. This would be my source of transportation throughout my remaining grade school years and also high school other than occasionally taking advantage of Akron's public transportation system which meant riding the bus. My earnings from my newspaper route not only permitted me to purchase the bicycle but also allowed enough monies left over to pay a meager sum to Urith for giving me a place to live and a roof over my head.

It was during my eighth grade of schooling, another guest arrived on Malacca Street to take advantage of Urith and Claude's hospitality.

Claude and Nellie Rainbolt's niece, Lenora Bowman, arrived from Attica, Indiana. Nellie had taken Lenora into her home in much the same manner she was taken in by the Vandeventer family. She had successfully groomed the young girl to fit in with the elite, sending her to the finest schools and then on to college where she graduated from the country's most prominent Baptist University.

When Lenora arrived in Akron she was accompanied by steamer trunks holding a wardrobe of elegant clothing fit for a queen. There were rich, velvet evening gowns, magnificent silk lounge wear and shoes for every occasion. She wore elegant jewelry. Gems that couldn't be placed on her fingers, in her hair or on her feet, were safely secured in a jewel case.

The new arrival at the Rainbolt residence needless to say only added to the overcrowded conditions in the small bungalow on Malacca Street.

Lenora Rainbolt shared her bed with her cousin Lenora Bowman. I continued to sleep on the couch in the living room. Shortly after Lenora Bowman's arrival, Claude decided he should build me a room in the basement. It wasn't a large room. Claude partitioned a part of the basement with a wall separating the furnace from the walls of the room. It was constructed in a way whereby I could enter my room from a private door that opened onto the driveway or I could take the stairs leading from the main part of the house to the basement. Needless to say I was delighted to finally have my own quarters. It was a chance to be alone and have privacy which had eluded me since leaving my roots in Indiana and moving to Ohio. I had a place where I could practice and study without the annoying drone of soap operas or the monotonous sound of a sports announcer calling each play during the World Series. Claude was as hooked on ball games as Urith was on her soap operas. With Claude, however, I was never certain whether he really liked the sport or just felt it was the macho thing to hear and something he could discuss with his fellow workers. I don't recall him ever going to the stadium to watch a major league game.

Lenora Bowman began searching for employment soon after her arrival. Depression continued to plague the country. Having a college degree did not necessarily guarantee employment.

The Freitags were an affluent family who lived in a large estate on the west side of Akron. They had two children and they were searching for a tutor/governess who was willing to live in and take over the management of their youngsters. Lenora's education fit those requirements and she was soon employed in the Freitag home. She discovered, however, her status was more like a second-story maid picking up after two very spoiled children. Lenora left the employ of the Freitags. She rented an apartment and by chance met a man much older than herself who courted her royally until she became his wife.

At the end of the semester and my last semester of schooling at Betty Jane, my life was about to undergo more changes. To get home after school hours I would cross an open meadow. Running across the meadow was a running brook. I crossed the meadow and the brook so many times during the two years going from Malacca Street to Betty Jane. I would carefully step on the wet rocks protruding above the waterline. I had become so proficient at crossing the brook my shoes never got wet or lost their shine. Unbeknownst to me a black-and-white dog suddenly appeared. The mutt jumped in the water then pushed his way to the other side of the brook. Instead of proceeding to where he thought he was going, he just stood there waiting for me to make that final step from one of the rocks to dry land. As I stepped up on solid ground the dog decided to shake the excess water he collected on his coat, gleefully spraying me with a fully activated shower. The dog then decided he had found a new playmate. I kept telling him to go home but he continued to trot close to my side. We crossed Newton Street and as we reached Malacca Street he bounced upon the open porch as if that was where he lived. When I opened the front door the dog didn't wait for me to go in first. He bounced into the living room. Of course this brought Urith's attention away from listening to her soap operas when she suddenly spied a stray dog trespassing on her domain.

"Hey!" Urith yelled. "Where did that dog come from?" and "Why are you so wet, Loy, ya look like you fell in the river!"

"Can I keep 'im Urith? He followed me home. I don't think he has a home. I'll take good care of 'im and he won't eat much. Maybe I can earn enough money sellin' newspapers that'll keep his belly full."

Malacca Street and the home of Claude and Urith missed their four-legged friend Peggy. Urith loved animals and after the loss of Peggy she began raising Persian cats. They were housed in the basement and even though she turned the felines into pets, it was really a capitalistic venture for my half sister.

I was never much interested in cats. It wasn't that I disliked them, it just wasn't the same as having a dog.

"Well—he's kinda cute," Urith said as she stooped down to the dog's level then picked him up in her arms. As she did so, the dog gently licked her on the cheek At that exact moment, the stray, homeless critter found a home.

Still in control, Urith finally conceded to letting the dog join the family. "Well—I'll let ya keep 'im but remember—if that dog starts gettin' into trouble like chewin' up things or gettin' on the furniture, he goes! Yer gonna hafta keep him in the basement with you. But don't you ever, I mean ever let that dog sleep with ya do ya hear?"

I named my new friend "Toby." He took to Claude immediately and within 24 hours Toby was part of the Rainbolt family. He was never confined to the basement. In fact, I don't think he was ever incarcerated in my room below ground level. He took over the house on Malacca Street as if it had always been his home. At bedtime, we would both take the stairs to the basement and go to my room. He never tried to get on my cot. He was quite content to sleep on the floor close to the cot where I could easily give him a goodnight pat on the head. Toby was more than satisfied with this arrangement, but I wasn't. On our second night as roommates I encouraged the dog to jump onto my cot and snuggle under the blankets next to my body.

All was well until wash day and time for the sheets and pillow cases to be stripped from the beds. Urith began gathering all the soiled linen. When she finished stripping the beds in the two bedrooms upstairs, she made her way to the basement and my room. Pulling the blankets from the bed and glancing at her white sheet under the blanket, her eyes suddenly focused on footprints resembling those of a dog's paws. She screamed!

I was sitting at the mango ironing flat work belonging to her clientele when her sharp voice penetrated the upper floor of the house. "Loy! Git down here! I mean git down here now!"

I knew there was trouble in Rainbolt City. I rushed down the stairs, but before I entered my room Urith met me at the door. In her hands she held a sheet that without a doubt revealed Toby's paw prints.

"Look at that!" she screamed. Her sanctimonious halo began to slip. Her angry voice was loud enough that the entire neighborhood must have been cognizant of my reprimand. "Yer lettin' that dog sleep with ya, ain't ya? I told ya I jes' won't permit it. If ya ever let that dog sleep in yer bed again, he goes! Do ya hear?"

When Urith got mad, which was against her religion, she would refer to it as "righteous indignation." Had Dad been dealing out the punishment though I am certain he would have grabbed my ear and twisted it until I said "uncle."

My little friend seemed to realize there was trouble in Rainbolt City. He stayed next to me during Urith's scolding and seemed to understand the reprimand was as much for him as it was for me. At the end of the day he settled down alongside my bed. I gave him one final pat as a goodnight gesture. When morning came, Toby stretched his head up over the cot until it reached my cheek. He then gave my face a gentle lick. We were ready to begin another day.

CHAPTER 34

THE YEAR WAS 1939 AND I was 14 years old. War clouds gathered over the European continent. Adolph Hitler, Germany's dictator, invaded Poland to the north, threatened Czechoslovakia to the east and with a bit of persuasion joined Mussolini's armies in the south. America wasn't at war at the time I entered my first year of high school. Our good President repeatedly said that no American soldier would again fight on foreign soil.

My bicycle was my main source of transportation. It was fully equipped, including large balloon tires, a bright headlight fastened to the handlebars and a taillight attached to the back fender. The bike also sported a basket fastened to the front fender which not only served for carrying newspapers but other items such as milk or bread when it was necessary to run a quick errand to the local grocery store. Weather was no deterrent for me to ride my bike. It withstood all kinds of weather including rain, sleet, and snow. My red bike was as dependable as the U.S. Postal Service and in most cases, more so. Newspaper deliveries were never late. When I delivered the morning papers, Toby trotted alongside as if this chore was equally his responsibility.

As the war heated up in Europe, for the first time in my

life I learned about people's prejudices. Germans who were American born were suddenly suspect as possible Nazi sympathizers. Russians were to be feared as potential spies. I heard statements criticizing Jews. Christians began placing the blame for the world's mess on those who were not of their faith. Protestants were equally as critical of Catholics and Catholics were critical of Protestants. Compassion and understanding and love for one's fellow man permitted the poison daggers of prejudice to overshadow the true teachings of Christianity. Any item "Made in Japan" was enough to push the button of every laborer who toiled in America's factories.

Claude Rainbolt whom I always respected as a docile man never prejudging another person, at least, not until the news brought an update about the happenings on the European war front. Suddenly, any item marked "Made in Japan" pushed his button. He criticized their ability to copy anything that was "American made." It was true, Japan imports did create havoc within the labor force of America. The Japanese could always sell something cheaper and sometimes better than an American product. I would often hear him say, "I won't buy a damn thing from those slanted-eyed bastards. They're nothin' but slit-eyed copycats." As for Jews, his prejudicial attitude extended to our neighborhood grocer, Abbie Levy.

Abbie owned a little food market on Brooklyn Heights just a couple blocks from the Rainbolt home. I often stopped in at Abbie's store. I might buy a loaf of bread or a quart of milk but most of the time it was just to have a friendly warm conversation with Abbie. He was a fatherly, gentle soul and for me, a young teenager who was no longer a boy and not a man, our chats often overextended the time it would ordinarily take to run a short errand. Claude gave the proclamation, "I don't want anybody in this family to buy one thing from that Jew's store and bring it in this house." Claude seldom took a firm stand on his convictions except when it came to a relationship with a Jew. Abbie was my friend. I couldn't say that to Claude. Instead I would remain quiet and continue to periodically visit Abbie's store.

Akron was well endowed with churches of all types and all different nationalities. Each church practiced their version of Christianity and each church was of the opinion their philosophy was the only way to heaven. Protestants and Jews who did not believe in the Pope, the Virgin Mary and who refused to follow the laws of the Catholic Church were heathens destined to burn in an eternal burning fire. I was taught from early childhood that people were all the same even if they weren't my color or race. Prejudices just didn't exist in my mother's eyes, or if they did she was careful to never prejudge another human being regardless of whether they were black, yellow, red, or white. The part of Akron where I lived was like living in a small town where everyone knew everything their neighbors thought and did, what religion they practiced if any, and if they were foreigners, i.e., Germans or Russians, there were suspicions.

Occasionally, I would walk past an American German home and meet with their young daughter who happened to be in my grade at school. We would cross the open meadow and the babbling brook, never inquiring about each other's heritage. My friend knew I liked music and with her parents' permission they invited me to a Saturday morning German American Club where I heard my first German songs. The members of the club would delight in singing der Vaterland's tunes. I learned to sing "Lorelei," "Glow Worm" and "O Tannenbaum." By rote I learned to pronounce the German words. Those Saturday mornings were a highlight of my life.

A Russian family lived next door to the Germans. They shortened their Russian name to "Nixon." Although their children spoke English with no foreign accent, the stigma of being a Russian was predominant in the eyes of the surrounding neighbors. Mr. and Mrs. Nixon came from the old country and never learned to speak English. They had two grown sons and one daughter, the daughter being a bit younger than myself. She was taught music at home and when she joined other Betty Jane students, it was only natural she play in the orchestra. She often accompanied me when I played the violin and in the final year at Betty Jane I formed my own little orchestra where I took the podium as the conductor. Long after the Akron years, Lillian Nixon would use her Russian birth name, Ludmillla. She would follow me to New York to pursue a singing career.

Being fourteen years of age was a crucial time for me. I began to rebel against Urith's strict religious beliefs. I would occasionally go with Lenora to her church and eventually let it be known I no longer was going to attend the church of Urith's choice. Urith was unhappy with my decision. She finally respected my wishes and I was soon a regular member of the same flock as the one in which Lenora was a member.

Architecturally, it was a pretty church. It had a two-manual pipe organ which happened to be the first pipe organ I ever saw or heard. The sound of the organ filled every crevice of the church. In my mind, it was a real asset toward preparing my ability to tune in to a higher power which everyone referred to as God. There were young people in the church and their hormones were as lively as my own. Although some were a bit older than my tender age they accepted me in their group.

The choir loft was raised just above the pulpit. Beneath the choir loft alongside the center stage where the preacher gave his long-winded sermons a baptismal pool was installed. The pool remained covered except for baptisms. When the pool was uncovered a stairway was clearly visible leading from the pulpit down into the water: The pool was considerably more practical and comfortable than being dunked in the cold waters at the gravel pit. The water was heated as if one were stepping into a warm bath. Of course, the difference being, one was fully clothed when they took their next step toward discarding the sinful ways of the world.

The preacher would climb down the stairs, then step into the water which came up to his waistline. The ceremony was almost identical to the Methodist. There was always a prayer at the beginning of the rite, then each dunkee was individually asked to follow in the preacher's footsteps, i.e., climb down the stairway until their bodies were waist deep. As they did at the gravel pit the preacher carefully placed his arm around the waist of the one to be purified. When the words came forth, "In the name of the Father and the Son and the Holy Ghost I now baptize thee," the preacher quickly placed his hands over the person's nose and without further ado that person was bent over backward until his entire body sank beneath the waters of the baptismal pool. Some would emerge to the surface spitting excess water from their lungs. Then there were those who would come up shouting their Amens and praises to God Almighty, I suppose as a thank you for not drowning during that split-second immersion.

The church also had a ritual of "feet washing." Of course women and men were separated but I recall that rite quite vividly. I think it was supposed to represent humility. I never quite understood the reason. I later learned within the Catholic Church a similar rite extended among the priests.

There were two ordained ministers in this church. A Reverend Dr. Smith and his wife, a Reverend Mrs. Smith. Had the church had no more to offer than these two individuals, I rather doubt I would have accepted to become a member of the flock. Reverend Dr. Smith was a short, stocky fellow who managed to live within a world separate from the congregation he shepherded. He was considered an authority on the Bible's Book of Revelations. His long-winded dry intellectual approach to the mysteries of the last book in the Bible failed to educate me as to the preacher's or the Book of Revelation's intent.

Mrs. Smith was not any more charismatic than her husband. Her occasional sermons failed to do much for cleansing my soul.

The Smiths looked rather sexless. There must have been some contact between the two preachers, however, inasmuch as they brought forth two sons, the elder managing to escape the rigid religious upbringing by leaving the fold and heading to New York in pursuit of a concert pianist career. The second son was somewhat mentally retarded and remained at home.

My interest lay not so much in the dogma of the church but rather the feeling of belonging to a family. It was as if I had acquired a multitude of brothers and sisters who really cared about my welfare. Julius and Hilda Marion, for example. We called Julius J.C. whom we occasionally referred to as Jesus Christ since he was totally obsessed with the teachings of John the Baptist. They took me under their wing and Julius became a father image, one which I never had. He was young enough to understand the tumultuous inner conflicts a teenager is burdened with in the process of making the transition from childhood to manhood. His wife, Hilda, I adored. The Marions had one child, a girl they named Phyllis. When their only daughter married, the Marions sent me train fare to return to Akron from New York to sing for the wedding.

My first teenage crush was the only daughter of the Simpson family. There were three sons. There was Norm, Oscar and a younger brother they called Larry. My infatuation with Mary Evelyn failed to consummate into anything serious, but as for her brother Norm, the eldest, he had all the attributes with which I wished I could be endowed. Women flocked to Norm like a swarm of bees rushing to the side of their Queen. His reputation was well known. He had successfully deflowered more young women within the confines of the church than any other male counterpart. Norm was not only a romantic in the privacy of the backseat of his car, he was a romantic in music.

Oscar, the second born, was entirely different in makeup than his elder brother Norm. Both men inherited the good looks of their father. Instead of being interested in music, although he did have a good, nasal-sounding bass voice, he was considered the intellectual and chose to work in the world of Physics. He graduated from college then married the prettiest girl in the congregation. He became a successful physicist, in later years becoming the vice-president of one of America's most notable corporations.

A tragic accident befell Oscar shortly before his marriage to Imogene Galloway. He was returning Imogene to her home at a rather late evening hour. His car ran out of gas. The car stopped on an unlit country road about one mile from the nearest gas station. Oscar decided he could walk to the station and leave Imogene waiting in the car. When he returned with a container of gas he removed the gas cap then began pouring gasoline from the container into the tank. Out of the darkness bright headlights from another vehicle came rushing at great speed toward Oscar's parked car. The driver of the speeding auto unable to see the man putting gas in his car suddenly hit Oscar sending the young man's body up over the roof of the car. Oscar's leg was mangled so badly amputation was the only alternative in an effort to save his life. There were doubts Oscar would ever walk again. If he did walk, would he be able to walk in time for the wedding? Oscar did walk with the aid of an artificial leg well enough to where he could greet his beautiful bride as she walked down the long aisle toward the altar.

I was asked to play the violin prior to the wedding ceremony. For some reason the church was more inclined to hear me play the fiddle than to hear me sing.

It was summertime and to earn extra money I was hired as a stock boy in downtown Akron's Bond's Clothing Store for Men. The air was hot and humid. The marriage was to take place in an early evening ceremony and there was just enough time for me to leave the clothing store, take the bus to Malacca Street, bathe, dress, and hurriedly make my way to the church.

When I arrived home, the house on Malacca Street was in total disarray. Urith had chosen that particular day to remove all the wallpaper off the walls in preparation for installing new wall coverings. I had to climb over furniture to get to the bathroom. I was nervous. When I picked up my fiddle prior to leaving the house I found it difficult to coordinate my fingers and the action of the bow. My fingers shook as if they were made of Jello. I placed the violin in its case then walked to the bus stop. The ride on the bus gave me time to cool off and relax prior to reaching my destination.

Arriving at the church I went directly to the choir room. I tuned my violin. When I placed the instrument under my chin and prepared to bring the bow down over the strings I had no control. My fingers shook as badly as they had prior to leaving home.

The church began filling to capacity. I made my entrance into the choir loft. The organist began playing the introduction to Schubert's "Ave Maria." She must have repeated the intro to the immortal music at least 10 times before I had the courage to place the fiddle under my chin. When the bow finally made contact with the strings the screeching sound was one of such pain that it was even worse than the first day I was exiled from the living room to the back bedroom on Malacca Street to do my daily practice. Waves of pity rolled in from the seated huge congregation like a tidal wave. When the last strain of music faded into nothing I ran from the pulpit into the choir room. I quickly placed the violin in its case and as I did so I felt the presence of someone standing behind me. It was the preacher's wife. "I want to tell you how beautifully you played, Loy." It was the Reverend Mrs. Smith. Making no comment or bothering to thank her for a compliment not deserved I grabbed the violin and rushed out the back door of the church and onto the street. For seven miles I walked until I reached Malacca Street. How could that woman lie? Thoughts of total disbelief ran through my head. Any respect I had for the preacher's wife totally vanished. Many moons would pass before I would again place the violin under my chin.

The music in the church was controlled by a man named

Clarence Thompson. He never got past the one, two, three, four beat which was firmly ingrained in the man's musical knowledge. Any other beat or change in the musical structure would have been totally foreign to the would-be choral director. His daughter Frances became the church organist when the instrument was installed. She guarded the two-manual organ like a well-trained police dog. No one from that first day of installation was permitted to touch the keys of the organ except Norm Simpson.

As long as I was a member of that church my musical aspirations would never evolve into more than singing in the church choir. Solos were always given to one singer, Arthur Robinson. Art retained his reputation as the fair-haired member and soloist for the choir.

CHAPTER 35

EAST HIGH SCHOOL WAS A considerable distance from Malacca Street. I was able to purchase a weekly pass so I could ride the bus. It was a large school and totally integrated as far as race and nationalities. There was nothing unusual about removing all my clothing next to a black boy in the locker room anymore than it was to sit next to a black person in the classroom. If one were shy when it came to removing one's clothing that shyness was soon disbanded when we were obligated to go swimming. Every male student was obligated to swim in the nude.

It was the fall of 1939 when I entered high school as a freshman. The school was so large and the classes so over-crowded, the approximate 3,000 students were broken up into two sessions—morning and afternoon. My freshman's first semester was designated for afternoon classes. I had no interest in sports so I made no effort to join in either basketball, football, or track activities. East High had a good music program and to get into the orchestra required me to pick up the violin again and audition for the conductor. With reservations, the conductor accepted me but I was seated so far back in the second violin section that any talent I might have went totally unnoticed.

A lively young woman who had more energy than I ever observed being exerted from one human being was in charge of the music program. In today's terms, the petite redhead was really wired. Her name was Miss Payne.

She not only conducted the orchestra, she was also the leader of the Glee Club. I wanted to sing.

Playing in the orchestra was a bore. I never got to play the melody of a number, it was always an occasional note now and then to compliment the first violin section.

It was shortly after entering high school I got the nerve to approach the little ball of fire. "Miss Payne," I chokingly said, "I don't like playing in the orchestra. Could I sing for you? I'd like to be in the Glee Club."

"You know the rules, Loy," Miss Payne said. "No freshman is permitted to join the Glee Club. I would like to hear you sing though."

I don't recall what I sang but when I sang the final note of the piece, Miss Payne uttered the words I wanted to hear. "Well, Loy—that was very good. Let me see what I can do in breaking the rules. We are planning on performing a premier performance of a new work by Aaron Copeland called 'The Second Hurricane.' The work requires not only a very large orchestra which we will have to fill with outside players, it also requires a tremendous chorus. We don't have that many singers in the Glee Club to do this work justice. As with the orchestra we will have to bring in more singers from other schools within the city. Let me see if I can get the powers that be to let you join our group." It was at the next orchestra rehearsal Miss Payne informed me she had permission to let me join the Glee Club.

The production required a lot of hard work and numerous rehearsals outside our regular curricular studies. A huge chorus made up of singers from various high schools throughout the city were placed on risers. The chorus was split into two choruses, one chorus on each side of the stage. In between the two choruses a large orchestra was positioned just below the proscenium stage level.

The musical only had four principal characters. On stage the four characters were placed in chairs similar to seats on an airplane. The story line of the production was set aboard a passenger airliner. Flying high above the earth, the plane was suddenly caught in the eye of a hurricane. The storm was violent. The voices from the chorus of singers using vocal sounds to make the sound of wind rise above the sound of thunder and lightning. The orchestra accented the noise of heavy rain dashing against the windows of the plane. Lightning projected flashes on stage and into the audience. Bouncing like a kite that had broken away from its earthbound string, the fear of death was clearly visible on the faces of the passengers as the musical actors brought the terrifying airborne experience to reality.

The Copeland/Denby and East High School's premier performance of the work topped the charts within Akron's cultural society. Edwin Denby made a special trip to our town to hear the premier performance of the Copeland/ Denby work.

Miss Payne's accomplishment in mounting and conducting the musical spectacle brought her to the attention of Broadway producers. The dynamic educator from East High School resigned her position as Director of Music but she did finish her year's commitment to East High before she was off to the Big Apple.

Honored In Music

Mabel Todd Dies; Teacher Since 1913

Mabel E. Todd, a pioneer in high school music here and at various times called "Akron's most successful woman," is dead at 84.

The beloved teacher and friend of literally hundreds in a career dating back to 1913 died Sunday night at Akron General Hospital. She had been ill at the hospital since Nov. 4.

* * *

FOR 32 YEARS Miss Todd was director of music at various times at South and Central High schools. But the native of Wakeman, O., began her career as a language teacher.

She majored in that subject at Oberlin College, taught it for a while but soon realized her first love was music.

It wasn't long after her switch that her choral groups began winning honors in district and national contests. She directed king-size operettas and organized the first high school orchestra in Akron.

* * *

SHE RETIRED from Akron schools in 1945 at 70 but wasn't ready to let dust collect on her baton. Immediately she opened a private studio and started directing the now disbanded national choir of the YWCA.

Miss Todd also found time to direct the first Mothersingers group here, as well as a chorus for handicapped girls.

She was long active in the Greater Akron Music Association as member and trustee, the Tuesday Musical Club and Akron Symphony Orchestra. Her name also was on the

MISS TODD

roster of Woman's City Club, Altrusa Club and four state and national musical associations.

* * *

MISS TODD continued to make Wakeman her home during most Summers, but her permanent address many years was 112 Hamilton av.

An insight into what type woman she was was given by Beacon Journal Town Crier Kenneth Nichols 10 years ago. He wrote:

"There is only one woman in Akron, that I know about, who is identified by thousands of people with just her first name—and middle initial.

"To these people 'Mabel E.' is all that's needed to identify not only a personality but a career and practically a whole way of life."

Miss Todd leaves a niece, Aletha Todd of Cleveland and a nephew, John Todd of Wakeman.

Services are being arranged by the Long Funeral Home.

My first vocal teacher.

LOY   DOROTHY

Receive Roles In East High Play

The glee club of East high school will present the play, "An Old Kentucky Garden," March 20, 21 and 22 in the school auditorium. Among the players will be Dorothy Decker, 12A and Loy Natter, 10A.

"An Old Kentucky Garden."

Role of Stephen Foster.

CHAPTER 36

As a freshman, I enrolled in classes that would qualify me as possible college candidate material should my grade average remain high enough for acceptance. I didn't know just how I was going onto to college, but up to this point in my life, luck was with me. There were Math classes, Algebra, Geometry, Trigonometry, Chemistry, etc. There were literature courses which delved into ancient classics such as Socrates, Plato, Shakespeare, Dickens, etc.

Classes were large, so hope for any kind of hands on training was impossible. There was no one in the Rainbolt household capable of helping me with an abundance of homework. It was my Algebra class that forced me to make a decision. I would have to switch to a commercial course when I entered my sophomore year. At the end of that first year, the Algebra teacher summoned me to her desk for a consultation. "Loy—I am going to pass you, but only with the understanding you will not take this course again."

The teacher's advice was a wise one. I enrolled in commercial courses when school resumed in September. It provided me with tools whereby I could get a job in an office instead of being forced into the labor movement where I would just be another rubber tire builder or working in warehouses moving boxes or crates from one place to another. I had good legible handwriting. I was fortunate in securing a part-time job with a trucking company where I worked primarily on weekends, posting stacks of bills into large ledgers. The paycheck was adequate enough to abandon my newspaper route and still be able to pay board and room at the Rainbolt house.

As school progressed so did my musical aspirations. A new music teacher was assigned, replacing Miss Payne. Her name was Ruth Meyer. There was a difference, however. Miss Meyer did not have the energetic approach to making music which her predecessor so well displayed. She was a petite lady, with sandy, cropped hair and her claim to music was totally learned in the school of academia. She played the piano quite well and even though her approach to conducting was not exactly up to par with Miss Payne, she managed to draw out of her youngsters a passable sound in music, whether it was singing or playing an instrument.

The yearly operetta during that sophomore year was a musical based on the life of Stephen Foster. It was titled "An Old Kentucky Garden." I auditioned for the role of Stephen Foster. When the final casting was completed, I got the part. Dorothy Decker was East High's leading diva. She won all the female starring roles in the musical productions. There was only one problem. Dorothy was a senior and I was a sophomore. This would be Dorothy's last chance to star in an East High theatrical venture.

The school continued to ride on the crest of the wave from the success of "The Second Hurricane." Long before the production opened, the performances were sold out. The *Akron Beacon Journal* came to the school and interviewed Dorothy Decker and myself. Our pictures appeared in the paper along with an article about two newcomers from Akron who showed great promise for a musical career. It would be a lie to say I wasn't a bit proud. Seeing my name and picture in a newspaper delivered to every home within the City of Akron provided the confidence I needed to believe I could do anything. The success of "An Old Kentucky Garden," snowballed into a multitude of musical activities.

State competitions for singers were being held at Ohio State University in Columbus, Ohio. Most of the competitive performers had been fortunate to study with some of Ohio's finest vocal teachers. All I had to offer was totally natural, just an untrained sound coming from my throat bestowed upon me at birth. I never let the thought enter my mind that I should consider entering the contest. It was Miss Meyer who insisted I give it a try. "I'll drive you to Columbus myself, Loy and I'll also pay for your food and hotel expenses. I feel very strongly that you should not permit this opportunity to pass you by. I do think, however, you need tutoring I am not capable of giving you. I would like to introduce you to a teacher here in Akron by the name of Mabel Todd. She directs and conducts all the musical productions at Central High School. Perhaps Miss Todd can give you some pointers that will enhance your chances of winning at the competition."

It was one remaining week before the competition when Miss Meyer accompanied me to the home of Mabel Todd. Vocal production was Mabel Todd's religion. Each singer who entered into her sanctum had to be willing to accept her discipline and hard work. Each singer was required to sing even if their bodies rebelled and they had one foot in the grave and the other on a banana peel. She believed in a strong, flexible diaphragm muscle that could easily withstand the weight of a 200-pound individual standing on the singer's abdomen. By contracting the diaphragm muscle, the singer would then bounce their colleague up and down turning the singer's body into a living trampoline.

Miss Todd was not an attractive woman. Her stature was small, but her body was like solid iron. Her thinning snow-white hair sometimes appeared with a tint of pink or blue, which often raised suspicions she might be wearing a wig. Her teeth were large and a little bucked which only accentuated the size of her nose. She stood straight. Straighter than most soldiers. The shoulders were always back and down and her stomach muscles pulled in. She had a voice that rang with the brilliance and resonance surpassing the singing voice of most well-trained baritones.

The song I chose to sing for Miss Todd and the song chosen for the competition was written by Bruno Huhn. He had set the classic poem "Invictus" to music. As the great teacher listened, it was as if she were taking personal notes how she could bring out the beauty of my voice to its fullest. When I finished the final note of the song, Miss Meyer rose from the piano bench. Miss Todd sat down at the piano. "Loy, I want you to try these exercises." It was not a long lesson, but it was long enough to secure the sound I wanted to produce at the State competition.

Urith and Claude didn't object to my entering the contest nor did they ask any questions, they just knew the teacher would pick me up after the school day came to an end, drive me to Columbus, pay for my food and hotel accommodations and accepted the fact I was entering some kind of a vocal contest.

We arrived in Columbus about dinner time. When we checked into the hotel, Miss Meyer ordered me to go freshen up a bit then meet her in the lobby. I had never stayed in a hotel or a motel in my entire short life. "We'll have an early dinner, then its off to bed. You must be well rested for your big day tomorrow morning," she said.

The following morning, the butterflies began to churn in my stomach. I was nervous. Miss Meyer and I had breakfast then leisurely walked toward Ohio State campus and the building where the competitions were being conducted. When we entered the building, I could hear singers through the closed doors. I was sure I didn't sound like they did. They were well trained and sounded like they should be in the Metropolitan Opera instead of competing in a vocal contest made up of high school hopefuls. I began to permit doubt to enter my mind. What was I doing there? I wasn't ready for this sort of thing.

My turn came to enter through the large doors into the inner sanctum where a group of judges sat at a long table waiting for their next victim. I had often seen how famous singers walked on stage with great assurance, then take their place in the curve of the piano. I copied every move I could recall from concert artists who visited Akron, Ohio. I might even have placed my hands in a clasped position in front of my body, I don't remember. At any rate, Miss Meyer played the introduction to "Invictus." My voice reacted like a racehorse when the gate was open and I was out to win! My voice was firm and it was obvious I was sending the message of my song directly to the judges' table. I finished the song with "I am the Captain of My Soul." My voice, having taken flight, reverberated throughout the large room. A certain amount of pride flowed in my veins.

It was mid afternoon before the results of the competition were posted. Miss Meyer and I returned to the campus after we checked out of the hotel. As we approached the large bulletin board where the ratings for the contestants were posted, I noticed my name at the top of the list. I won! I had won the State vocal competition.

There was little conversation about my success when I returned to Malacca Street. I hesitated to be overly enthusiastic. The folks at home just took it for granted I had a pretty voice, but as far as a career as a singer, they had difficulty fathoming that. This was not true with Miss Todd or Miss Meyer. Miss Todd wanted to take me as a private student and offered to teach me for nothing. Miss Meyer disagreed. "Miss Todd—I think it's better that Loy find a way to pay for his lessons. He has a part-time job and if he wants to sing then he must pay for the training. I believe, in the long-run, he'll be more grateful for the knowledge you have to offer him."

The lessons were not expensive. I believe Miss Todd agreed to teach me for $1.50 a lesson which, within my limited budget, I could squeeze out that much for one lesson a week. It was certainly much less expensive than the fee Burton Garlinghouse was charging. He had a great reputation as a vocal teacher, but he also had the reputation as being the most expensive. It was $25 for each hour of his time. My work with Mabel Todd progressed nicely. There were opportunities to sing for weddings and funerals, all paid engagements. I had reached the point in my career where I could call myself a professional singer.

As spring approached and the usual citywide May festival was being organized; along with four other young artists, all Akron citizens, I was chosen as one of the featured soloists. Guy Frazier Harrison, a maestro from Eastman School of Music in Rochester, New York, would be conducting the symphony composed of the city's most accomplished instrumentalists. The chosen soloists for the occasion were three singers and one pianist. The singers consisted of a tenor from West Akron, that was the wealthy part of town, and a boy soprano, who to this present day in my memory surpasses any singer I have heard whose voice had not changed. The kid not only was a fine singer, he had a great sense of showmanship. The pianist was a remarkable virtuoso. Her name was Doris Walker. I knew Doris from church. Her parents had purchased a seven-foot grand piano which occupied most of the Walker's living room. They sent Doris to a teacher in Akron who excelled in producing artists that were geared toward being concert pianists. Doris was obligated to practice at least five hours each day and sometimes longer. There was little time for a social life. The piano was her life. Then, of course, there was me and since my repertoire was still quite limited it was a question as to what I was going to sing. Two musical works were chosen. One was an operatic aria from Wagner's "Tannhaeuser," the other was an old English song arranged by Arne entitled "Preach Not Me."

I had not seen or heard about Nellie Glover since grade school. Yet, she was the very person who threw my name into the hat as a possibility for being one of the soloists for the festival. The crippled lady telephoned Miss Meyer. "Please, would you mind bringing the young man to my home? I wish to hear him sing again. I always felt he was quite an unusual talent." Miss Meyer drove me to Miss Glover's simple home on the West side of Akron. The angelic woman welcomed me into her home, offered us a cup of tea, then asked me to sing.

Instead of Miss Meyer playing the accompaniment to Wagner's immortal work, "The Evening Star," Nellie Glover

Akron Ohio Grade 6, 1936.

took her place on the stool in front of an upright piano. I couldn't imagine how the woman could possibly play the accompaniment. Her hands were so crippled, her fingers like claws. I handed my music to Miss Glover. With one hand, she began the accompaniment. It was beautiful. I later learned she had been an accomplished concert pianist prior to her crippling disease of arthritis. My mouth opened and as I finished the last note of the aria, I could see Nellie Glover was pleased. "I told you, Loy, many years ago, you have a beautiful voice. Now—look at you. You must always sing."

My picture along with the other soloists was published in the newspaper. No one at home showed much interest in the fact I had been chosen out of all the young musicians within the City of Akron.

I vividly recall the day when a huge chorus made up of Akron's finest singers and 90 instrumentalists making up a large symphony orchestra gathered at the Akron Armory, a facility that accommodated 3,000 people. As the time drew

Solists for the Akron May Festival.

AERIAL VIEW   MOUNT HERMON SCHOOL   MOUNT HERMON, MASS.

Westminister Choir Summer School.

Dr. Finley Williamson, Northfield, Mass.,
Mt. Herman Prep School.

nigh when I had to catch a bus that would take me to down-town Akron and the Armory, Urith prepared me a dinner of chili and mashed potatoes. I donned my only pair of white trousers, blue serge jacket and white shoes, then noncha-lantly walked the short distance from the house on Malacca Street to the bus stop. I boarded the bus but, before the bus arrived downtown, clouds gathered in the sky and there was little doubt that a heavy rain was about to flood the city with a downpour. The bus stopped in front of O'Neils Department Store. The rains came as I stepped from the bus onto the side-walk. I walked in the rain the distance from O'Neils to the Armory. I was wet. Crowds were already pushing their way into the Armory. I found a quiet place where I could get dry. My clothing dried, but there were mud spots on my white pants and white shoes. I stood in the wings of the stage and within minutes after my arrival the great orchestra opened with an overture. I was the first solo artist to be heard in the evening's program. When the overture was over and the ap-plause died down, I proudly walked onto the stage, climbed some stairs to a podium rising above the orchestra and as the strains of the music began my introduction, my voice reso-nated like a trumpet, carrying my musical contribution to the last balcony of the large auditorium.

It was obvious from the reception and applause from the audience, I had performed well. A neighbor who attended the event offered me a ride home.

The following morning, Akron's leading music critic cri-tiqued the performance of the previous evening. Lenora was first to see my picture and the review. After she completed reading the critic's comments, she said, "If we thought you were that good, we would have gone last night." I believe it was at that point in my development, I decided to keep my dreams and aspirations to myself. I was often invited to sing on the local radio station, but I never again mentioned when or what time I was going to sing. I might passively come home after a broadcast and say, "Did you hear me on the radio this evening?" From experience I learned my aspirations as a singer would remain private and my dreams for the future would remain locked inside until they became a reality.

IT WAS DURING MY SOPHOMORE year that Mable Todd suggested I join her group of students who would be going to summer school presented by Westminister Choir College at the famous boy's prep school, Mount Herman, located in the Berkshire Mountains in Massachusetts. Only those students whose families were considered rich or at least comfortably well off could afford to take part in such a venture. I wanted to go—but I didn't have the money. Mabel Todd was insistent, going so far as to have a private meeting with Urith and Claude. But all was in vain. Mabel never lost faith. "Loy—you are going to summer school and you must believe the money will come so you can take advantage of this opportunity. You will be taught by the best teachers in America including Dr. Finley Williamson who founded the Westminister Choir College."

The seed was planted and I began to nourish the idea. I took on extra employment making ping-pong paddles in a small factory not far from Goodyear Tire and Rubber Company. I saved every penny and each day I visualized my going to summer school. It was one week prior to the time the group was to leave Akron and drive the long journey to Massachusetts, I realized I only had half the money needed to pay the tuition. Miss Todd refused to let doubt gather roots within my mind. "You're going, Loy, even if I must take you myself."

The last week was crucial. It was while shopping with Claude and Urith that Claude brought up the question of my going to school. "You really want to go to that school, don't ya Loy? How much money have you saved?" I said, "Well— I only have half the money, but I'm goin' Claude." Claude waited awhile to respond. "Well—that just ain't enough to git ya there, is it?" I said, "No—but I'm goin'!"

I don't know whether it was Miss Todd's private meeting with my sister and my brother-in-law or whether he wanted to fulfill my wish. At any rate, Claude continued "Well— since you've already saved half the money, I see no reason I cain't give ya the rest. You're goin' to need some new clothes though if ya plan on joinin' them rich kids." The rest of that day was spent shopping for a new wardrobe. My dream to go to summer school was fulfilled.

It was a long drive to Massachusetts and the Berkshires from Akron, Ohio. I remember arriving at the elegant campus and being assigned to a room in the dorm with another chap who prided himself as being a superb singer. Individual teachers were assigned to the students, some were group lessons and others who could afford private tutoring were given private lessons. I grasped onto every word my professor, a tenor by the name of Harold Hedgepath, had to offer. He was undoubtedly the finest singer I ever heard. Dr. Williamson also took private students, but they were so expensive, I knew better than to ask for any kind of help.

A soprano I had often heard in Mable Todd's studio by the name of Gerry Gerraghty arrived at the school in a long limo driven by her aunt. Her mother came along as a chaperone. Gerry was like a magnet. Although our paths had often crossed at Mable's studio in Akron I never was able to speak with her. She was the prettiest Irish lass I had ever seen. Apparently, the same magnetic attraction I felt toward Gerry, she also felt for me. For the entire three weeks, we were inseparable and on Sunday she asked if I would like to go to Mass with her, her mom and her aunt. I'd never been in a Catholic Church. The aunt drove us in the long, black limo to the small town of Greenfield, Massachusetts. People lined up outside the church waiting for the previous Mass to end. There was a box which indicated one must pay to go to church. I was shocked. When we entered the church, and the Mass began, I joined the rest of the congregation as they stood, knelt, crossed themselves, and genuflected. There was no talking in the congregation. For the amount of attendees, it was the quietest church I had ever been in. I didn't understand the Latin, but there was something about the pageantry that made a deep-seated impression. There was a spiritual aura enveloping Gerry as she said her Catholic prayers that left an indelible memory on my mind.

That summer was the beginning of a lasting friendship with the Irish lass from the West side of town.

I had a speech impediment. I knew I could never study with the famous Dr. Williamson. It was like making a direct contact with God. I had difficulty pronouncing the "L" sound when I spoke or sang. Where I got the courage to approach the elderly gentleman one afternoon as I passed his cottage and noticed he was sitting on the front porch gazing at the magnificent surrounding mountains, I don't know. Nevertheless, I stopped in front the man's cottage and actually had enough guts to speak more than just to say, "Good Afternoon."

"Dr. Williamson," I began. "I can't afford to work with you, but I have a problem. I cannot pronounce the 'L' sound." Dr. Williamson spoke. "Come here, young man." I walked closer to the porch. "Let me give you some exercises. Each day at this time, you must come by my cottage and I'll see how much you have improved. But you must practice." The exercises were not difficult, but, with constant practice of learning how to flip my tongue to say the "L" consonant, I was for the first time able to pronounce my name. The elderly gentleman was true to his word. Each day he gave me a private lesson.

The time came to an end when the school closed and we returned to Akron. I continued my association with Gerry, often accompanying her to the convent where we would sing for the nuns. Gerry was a student at the Sacred Heart Academy. Gerry was ready to graduate, then she was going to go on to Westminister Choir College to continue her higher education. I accompanied her to her senior prom. Although I couldn't dance or was forbidden to dance according to Urith's religion, I made an effort. Our lives separated when Gerry went off to school and I never thought our paths would cross again.

CHAPTER 37

WAR RAGED ON THE EUROPEAN continent. Since 1939, Hitler's armies conquered most of the European countries including Norway, Denmark, the Netherlands, Belgium, and France. Hitler's bombers easily flew across the English Channel with the intent of bringing England to her knees by blitzkrieging the towns and cities throughout the United Kingdom. Had it not been for the stamina of the British people, Hitler may have also conquered the entire United Kingdom. Adolph Hitler was well on his way to conquering the world.

America was comparatively safe from enemy attacks. Three thousand miles of ocean separated our land from Hitler's armies and Hitler's Air Force. We had no enemies, not until December 7,1941. There was no hint the Japanese would attack America's outpost of Hawaii. Hours before the infamous attack on American soil, Japanese Government representatives were discussing peace with President Roosevelt in Washington, D.C. While those talks were in progress, the world was shaken to its very core when planes from the Rising Sun brought down a rain of terror and destruction on Hawaii. Bombs fell from the skies over Pearl Harbor destroying much of the United States Naval Fleet. There was little or no resistance from the ground. Many of our prize war ships were sent to the bottom of the sea and thousands of young American men's lives were snuffed out within a few short minutes, seconds, or hours on that fateful morning of December 7, 1941. Those men who were not killed were maimed, young lives totally wasted by the Japanese act of war.

The morning of December 7, 1941, the destruction of Pearl Harbor, was also the beginning of a World War II conflict for Americans that would continue until August 1945. On that day in infamy, President Franklin Delano Roosevelt declared an all-out war with Japan. In the same declaration he declared war on Germany, thus spiraling America into the most devastating conflict of all time. No longer were we isolated from the tyranny of Nazism in the West or the yellow race in the East. Our continent was now vulnerable for mass destruction on par with European countries now conquered by enemy forces. America was not prepared for war. Industries supplying our country with peacetime commodities were rocketed into overnight industries of war. The construction of aircraft for peacetime transportation were now designed to carry bombs of destruction that would rain a fiery hell upon the cities below as they flew over enemy territory. Men who hoped to have their share of the American pie discovered their futures were placed on an indefinite back burner. A time had come for all industry to change from peacetime to a wartime economy.

Overnight, the name of the game, "Uncle Sam Wants You," changed the dreams and hopes of America's finest young men called to offer their lives for the freedom and peace on which the United States was founded. Patriotism was predominant in every American home and lifestyle. Norm Simpson was one of the first men from the church to sign up. He wanted to be a pilot. If Norm flew an airplane like he drove an automobile, there was little doubt he had all the makings of an ace airman. He joined the Air Force. Unfortunately, his dream of being a pilot did not materialize, but as a navigator aboard a bomber he found success. The training periods were of short duration. Norm was shipped overseas to England. Within days after his arrival on British soil, he was assigned a bomber to make a night raid on the enemy's own territory. Reaching the border of Germany, a German fighter plane attacked the American bomber. The plane exploded into a ball of fire. "Missing in action" was the word received by the Simpson family. Was Norm the first casualty to come out of Akron? Many months passed before people on the home front would know whether Norm had died on his first bombing mission or if he became a prisoner of war. There was always hope he might have parachuted to safety.

Draft notices were in the mail. They were sent to all young men, many who were husbands and fathers. No one was exempt. At no time was America so united in her effort to retain our freedoms and our way of life. Housewives whose lives never extended beyond the chores of child rearing, house cleaning, and cooking meals were snapped out of their kitchens and their homes to take their place in jobs previously performed by men.

I was too young in December of 1941. The men who were of draft age at 21 years were the first to be inducted along with men who were in their thirties. 18-year-olds were exempt until the draft age was lowered to those just graduating from high school. Classes at East High School continued to be conducted on a split-session day. At the end of my school day, I too, joined the work forces. I took a job with Goodyear Aircraft working in the cafeteria as a dishwasher. From that position, I moved up to being awarded the title of "second cook." It paid well. I made more money than I had made in my entire life. This did not deter me, however, from continuing to pursue a musical life.

Goodyear Tire and Rubber Company had constructed a marvelous theatre located within the large factory complex which provided sustenance to thousands of workers. It was probably the best facility in Akron for legitimate musicals and plays. The theatre was seldom used. Now that the country was at war, the theatre became a facility for the production of patriotic plays and musicals. A large production was soon mounted on the large stage which incorporated a story line with music. I wanted to be a part of that production. I auditioned and was awarded a couple roles, one of the roles was to play the part of Franklin Delano Roosevelt giving his famous speech via the radio on that day of infamy December 7, 1941. Makeup artists transformed my face into that of the great President. A huge scrim dropped from the fly space high above the theatre's wings until the see-through curtain reached the floor of the magnificent stage. I was positioned at a podium behind the scrim. A transcription recording of the President's speech was played over loud speakers. As the President's voice boomed out over the audience, my lips matched each word, giving the impression I was actually delivering the unforgettable lines.

In another role to which I was assigned I played the part of a soldier of World War I. I would soon be that soldier, except I would be playing the same role 20 years later in real life. The costuming and the setting was a flashback to World War I and as I was about to leave my sweetheart I sang "My Buddy," a popular World War I song.

No other front page stories could replace the news from

overseas. Days of the terrible war passed from days into months and then into a full year. I had met a girl at church I thought I wanted to marry, my hormones were at their peak and marriage seemed to be the only alternative for being relieved. We planned on getting married as soon as I graduated from high school. Wartime marriages to the girls back home was the name of the game. Those unions were consummated just at the time the draftee was to be sent overseas leaving his new bride home alone. In many cases, the young wife became pregnant then gave birth to an absent father's child. The young wife found herself under an obligation to raise her youngster by herself until the war ended and if she were one of the lucky ones, her husband would return to a family he never knew. I was about to become a victim of that vogue. The nearer the time came when Marietta and I would wed, the more uncertain I became as to whether I really loved her. With all the doubts clouding my mind, our relationship began to cool.

I hadn't seen Gerry Gerraghty since the time she asked me to escort her to her high school prom. After the big night, she had enrolled at Westminister Choir College in Princeton, New Jersey, and for all intents and purposes, she was getting on with her life and I was getting on with mine. I was certain since we both lived on opposite sides of the tracks in Akron, Ohio, the chance of any union between us was impossible.

The scene changed two weeks before Uncle Sam notified me that I was wanted. I happened to be shopping in downtown Akron and inadvertently stopped in at Polsky's Department Store. It was at that time the most exclusive store in Akron. The cosmetic counter was just inside the entrance to the store and behind the cosmetic counter was Gerry. The same girl I had dated periodically when I was 14 and the one Urith had politely informed me I had no business going with — a girl who was Catholic and lived on the other side of the tracks.

Gerry was like an apparition standing behind the counter. She was the same kid I often played with during those early teen years but now I found my self looking at a mature woman. She was suddenly transformed into a magnificent specimen of womanhood. She was beautiful. My first glance at Gerry behind the counter convinced me to make a final decision not to marry Marietta. I knew what I wanted.

Gerry's family consisted of Mom, Pop, Gerry, Eugene, Bernice and Mary Katherine Gerraghty. They were a wonderful, fun-loving family with a closeness I never fully experienced in my own family. There was total harmony. The Gerraghtys liked to hear me sing. Pop Gerraghty was a dental technician who operated his own lab in downtown Akron. This was a lucrative business which gave stability to the Gerraghtys, permitting each one of the offspring to pursue their respective careers. Pop Gerraghty was a veteran of World War I. He, more than anyone else, had an understanding as to what lay ahead for me after graduation from high school. He had lost his leg in the first war. Mom Gerraghty was a warm, loving individual whose influence was obvious in the makeup of this wonderful family.

I made a date with Gerry for the following Saturday night. After that date, I immediately broke off my engagement with Marietta. Urith was not happy. "You know, Loy, you have no business dating that rich girl on the West Side of town. First of all, she's Catholic and ya jes' weren't raised to believe in all that pagan stuff. They worship idols and the Bible clearly says, "Thou shall not have other Gods before me." This did not change my feelings for Gerry.

It was mid June of 1943 when I graduated from high school. In less than one week after graduation, I was summoned to the induction center held at the Akron Armory. It was just a pretense of an examination. Hundreds of us lined up in rows. When our names were called, we approached the front of the line. A stern looking military man scrutinized each man as if they were negotiating for a young filly that had been placed on the block. Questions asked were embarrassing. "Do ya like girls, feller?" What a stupid question, I thought. "Of course, I like girls." Did he have an alternative for replacing them? My answer to the man's question was greeted with a cold stare. He must have read in my mind as to what I was thinking. "Take off yer clothes and drop your pants," the man ordered. I had learned from documentary films about Army life, one didn't ask questions, they just did as they were told. I obeyed the officer's command. "Now— feller, bend over and spread yer cheeks apart." Again I did as the man ordered, but thoughts passed through my mind wondering which cheeks he was talking about. Why was a feller's rectum so important for being a good soldier?

At any rate, I passed the so-called physical and was ready to do my part in saving the world from Nazi tyranny as well as being prepared to fight the yellow race.

Within one week following the physical, I was ordered to report to an induction facility in Columbus, Ohio. From Columbus I would be sent to God knows where to learn the art of killing human beings I had never met or would ever know.

I passed my 19th birthday and within a day after the celebration, I arrived at the train depot in downtown Akron. It appeared as if the entire congregation from the church was there to see me off, all except Marietta. I asked her not to come. One would have thought it was a funeral celebration instead of an earthly sending off party. Prayers were raised to the heavens for my safe return. I had no fear, but I guess that must have been youth thinking that perhaps I was immortal. It was never certain any soldier would return. We had been in the war for two years before my induction. Some soldiers had already returned, but they were stretched out in a cheap pine box with an American flag draped over the coffin. No one knew what effects a war would have on the psyche of a young man who was still a teenager. Would I return wiser and kinder toward my fellow man or would I be bitter about life because of my firsthand taste of the ravages of war?

Gerry was at the station when I arrived. During the few short days and few short hours prior to my leaving we cemented a friendship, a bond that was not easily broken. My hand reached for hers. I pulled her toward me until our bodies touched. Would I ever see her again? Gerry promised to write every day even if there would be nothing to write about and I agreed to do the same if it were at all possible. The time for departure was no longer minutes.

Time became seconds and the dim sound of the train's whistle grew louder. Gerry and I moved from inside the depot onto the platform. When the train came to a halt, the conductor called "All Aboard!" Tears welled in Gerry's eyes. I kissed her, probably for the first time since our reunion in the way I wanted to kiss her but never dared. Slowly, I released my embrace, then letting her hand slip from mine, I stepped aboard the train. I took a seat next to the window, my face pressed against the glass. Never during those few short minutes did I permit my eyes to focus away from the girl who lived on the west side of town. The train moved slowly. Like the final curtain of a play, the Akron years came to an end.

June 1943: The Army

CHAPTER 38

"GIVE ME A PACK OF Camels!" I ordered, as I placed 15 cents on the counter at the PX. An unexpected smile broke through the serious expression on the clerk's face. "I hope you don't choke on them things," she said. "Don't you think yer a little young to be puffin on them weeds?"

How did she know this was my first package of cigarettes? I certainly had the build of a man and I didn't look like a child at the age of 19. Memories of my childhood flashed through my mind back to the time Mom caught me smokin' corn silk. "Everyone smoked—why shouldn't I? There must be somethin' to smokin' or people wouldn't do it." I picked up the cigarettes from the counter then turned to exit the PX. It seemed as if my entire life was a matter of "you can't drink, you can't smoke, you can't dance and you can't play cards, ya can't go to the movies, etc., etc., etc." It was the church, that's what it was—them and their insane religious beliefs. I had been thoroughly brainwashed into thinking all the things other people were doing were the works of the devil. I thought about Lenora. Smoking was taboo in the Rainbolt house. She would sneak into the bathroom to light up her Camel or go to the basement. There she would open the furnace door, and blow the smoke from her burning cigarette into the furnace. Of course, neither one of her actions absolved her from the sin she committed. The smell of a Camel moved under the door of the bathroom like a gray cloud and the smell of a cigarette being smoked into an open furnace door rose upward penetrating every vent in the house. Everyone knew Lenora was either in the bathroom or down in the basement. There was no way of hiding her sinful act. When she went out with friends for a pleasant good time, she would come home smelling like a package of cigarettes.

The aroma of a cigarette smelled good whether it was filtered through the vents in the house or from under the bathroom door. If the weed smelled so good, it had to taste even better. There must be some redeeming purpose for smoking a cigarette.

I moved away from the PX toward the open field away from the barracks. Slowly, I broke the cellophane wrapper enclosing my first package of Camels. There they were—20 neatly rolled factory made cigarettes. There was an excitement, almost as exhilarating as seeing and feeling the private parts of a girl for the first time. Relishing the aroma of the tobacco, I lifted the open package to my nostrils. The sweet smell penetrated my nostrils. Slowly, I placed the first cigarette between my lips. Seven years had passed since I heard Mom's voice, "Loy—yer makin' a big mistake. Ya weren't raised like this and you'd better turn back before it's too late." Thoughts ran through my mind creating a perfect picture of the time I almost set the town of West Lebanon on fire. Then there was a mental image of Mom scolding me when she caught me smoking corn silk at the old shack when we lived at Wheeling Junction. "That stuff yer breathin' into yer lungs is pure poison, Loy. I don't want ya to be sick, so please, don't place those filthy things in your mouth."

I reached in my shirt pocket and withdrew a small book of matches which accompanied the package of cigarettes. When the lighted match made a direct contact with the cigarette, I was flooded with guilt. The entire world was suddenly staring in my direction. I took a puff of the store bought weed, then went into a frenzy of coughing. Even though the smoke never penetrated any further than my tonsils, it was as if all air passages to my lungs were closed. I removed the partially smoked cigarette from my mouth and threw it on the ground. I stomped the butt as I would have done to a poisonous insect.

The army and the Red Cross were generous when it came to handing out cigarettes. My supply would always remain in my stash, waiting for the day I could give my supply to people who needed it more than I did.

It was a short stay at the Induction Center in Columbus. It was long enough, however, to be oriented into a new environment On that second morning I joined the ranks waiting at the dispensary for shots. "They're usin' the needle with the propeller, Soldier," I heard a new inductee announce as he left the dispensary. When my turn came to roll up my sleeve and watch the nurse shove the long needle into my arm, I knew what the GI was talking about. The tetanus shot had the kick of a nasty, bad-tempered mule. Following the tetanus shot, there were shots for typhoid, scarlet fever, malaria and probably a few more diseases no longer in my recall.

The next stop after the dispensary was at a building similar to a schoolhouse with old fashioned desks. It was in this room a decision was made to determine a GI's level for reasoning and their ability to follow instructions. A blank notebook was distributed along with examination questions. I thought the test total stupidity. Most of them I never understood so as I had done many times during the school years, I made guesses at the answers. If the test was taken seriously by the examiners, then I most certainly would have been discharged on the grounds of idiocy. The final result, however, proved one thing—I was a good specimen to join the ranks of a foot soldier.

Late afternoon on that first day at the reception center I was assigned to a bunk. As dusk began replacing the daylight, I laid down on the bunk. The shots taken that morning were beginning to take hold. I was sick. Chow time came and chow time went, but I was too ill to care anything about food. Sweat, fever and chills ravaged my body. I must have fallen asleep.

At sometime during that early morning, I was awakened to the sound of a gruff, gravely voice. "Attenshun!" My blurry eyes focused on an officer who undoubtedly hid behind the face of the most evil person I ever encountered. "Git outta that bunk, Soldier! Stand at attention!" I leaped out of the lower bunk and in a half-asleep, half-assed way I raised my body to an upright position and as I did so, I lifted my right hand searching for my eyebrow in a pretense of executing a salute.

"Yer movin' out at 1700 hours today!" No one dared to question as to where we were going. A GI was brainwashed from Day One that the soldier's duty was to execute whatever the commanding officer or noncommissioned officer ordered They were never to question as to a reason or why.

At exactly 1700 hours, a thoroughly disciplined sergeant led the newest group of inductees to a bus. Like sheep being led to slaughter, we boarded the bus and within a short period of time we were marched off the bus into a train depot and onto a waiting train. I must say, the army was considerate enough to occupy the cars that had upper and lower births. At least we could lie down as we rumbled over metal tracks, wondering just where and what direction the train was taking us.

I wasn't the only man who was sick. Each one of us made an attempt to find a berth, whether it was on the bottom or on top was of no consequence. We just wanted to lie down. By the time my head hit the pillow in the upper berth, the fever raging inside sent me into a state of delirium. The typhoid shot had succeeded in raising my body temperature to the boiling point. It was well past midnight when I drifted off into a deep sleep. As dawn raised the curtain of darkness, I realized the fever ravaging my body had passed. My clothing was soaked from perspiration and I was weak. I climbed from the upper berth to the floor of the train and attempted to wend my way to the washroom. From Day One, part of the orientation that a man was to shave each day even though most of our faces were no more than baby fuzz was thoroughly ingrained in our minds. The line to get into the washroom was endless. When my turn came, I entered the small cubical, locked the door, turned on the cold water extending out over the metal sink. I dashed cold water into my eyes, over my head and around my face. I then took a razor from my going away party shaving kit and lightly brushed the razor over my baby face in a pretense of shaving. I then returned to my bunk.

Before I could stretch out on the upper bunk, a loud voice barked from one end of the car. "Rise and shine, men! Hit the deck! We've come to the end of the line!" The train slowed as it pulled into a train station. When the cars came to a halt, I noticed the name of a town posted over the entrance to the depot was called "Macon, Georgia."

"Follow me, Men," I heard the gruff voice of the sergeant announce. Being good soldiers, we followed the sergeant as he led us off the train and onto an army bus. The bus began its journey over strange back roads away from the town until we finally approached an army camp that specialized in training the foot soldier. It was Camp Wheeler. Here I would learn the art of killing. Thoughts ran through my mind. Whether the act would be shooting a gun or stabbing an enemy with a bayonet attached to the end of an M-1, my country was condoning murder!

At the entrance of the camp we passed through a gate into a land of two-story barracks each barrack having its own number. I was assigned to Barracks 3 where I would meet the rest of the platoon with whom I would train for the following six weeks. The building had two floors. Rows of cots rested on each side of the long, narrow room with no more than four feet of open space between each bed. Each cot was stripped of all bedding except for a thin mattress. At the end of each cot was a footlocker. A cot was assigned to each individual on the first floor and those who did not secure a cot on the first floor were sent to the second floor.

A stocky, burly looking officer with two silver bars on each shoulder of his spotlessly pressed uniform entered the barracks. "Atten-shun!" the sergeant CQ called out.

Quickly, each man stood at the end of his cot, bringing his body to an upright perpendicular position. Our bodies stiffened to where we looked like standing corpses and almost as deadly white. The Captain for whom we were all brought to attention, had the most evil face and sadistic grin I would ever encounter. It must have been permanently frozen on his face.

"I'm Captain Gibson. I'm in charge of this battalion and

I'm tellin' ya, no fuckin' man within this battalion will leave here without being the best goddamn fuckin' soldier to come out of this fuckin' U.S. Army. The outcome of this goddamn war depends solely on you—the foot soldier. Now—unless ya want them slanted eyed bastards they call "JAPS" to run this country or if you want that man called Adolph to take over, then our country relies on you to keep our place safe from those bastards. There's no place in this battalion or this platoon for fuckups! There's no place in this man's army for goldbricks or sissies. Whether you smoke or don't smoke, you'll pickup every fuckin' cigarette butt ya see thrown on the fuckin' ground. Yer shoes will shine until ya can see yer fuckin' face in the toe of yer shoe. The buttons on yer dress uniforms will be polished until they look like pure gold. Ya can expect an inspection of this barracks at anytime. Yer bed will be made and there will not be the slightest wrinkle in the sheets or the blankets coverin yer bed. Yer footlocker at the end of your bed and each item goin' into that fuckin' locker belongs to Uncle Sam. From this day until you leave this fuckin' army, everything you have belongs to Uncle Sam, yer underwear, socks, shoes, pants, shirts, tie and hat which you'll wear at all times. Every item you put on yer body whether it be fatigues, or your dress clothes belongs to that great White Father in D.C. No soldier will begin his day without shavin' whether you think ya need it or not! It's time to stiffen that baby fuzz on yer fuckin' faces so you'll begin lookin' like men. Anyone—and I do mean anyone who fucks up in this army will reap the fuckin' consequences."

In all of my short 19 years, I had never heard the word "fuckin'" used, certainly not among the fundamentalists who strived to point the way to heaven.

Like a Nazi goose stepper, the officer turned on his heels

and was ready to exit the barracks. The sergeant yelled, "At-ten-shun!" When the bastard was out of sight, the sergeant in charge of the barracks said, "At ease, men."

I had to go to the bathroom. The latrine was located at the end of the barracks. A visit to this barbaric designed toilet facility was undoubtedly the first step in breaking down any modesty or self-respect a man might have. The urinal was one long trough and the showers were lined against a wall with no partitions for privacy. The commode arrangement was as close as the old two-holers we had in the outhouse, although at that time two people never sat on the two-holers in the outside privies at the same time. We would soon become educated in how to operate in the field or on the battle lines by digging trenches for the purpose of evacuating our body wastes.

I returned to my place at the end of my cot as the sergeant was ordering the men to fall in line and march over to the supply house. Here we were issued work fatigues and a knapsack. Next came our uniforms, including summer khakis, shirts, tie, a woolen uniform complete with hat and an overcoat. We were then fitted with the most comfortable shoes that ever graced my feet. We were issued boots and special leggins. As a final touch, we were given our socks and underwear, all in the color of brown. Once we acquired our GI clothing, we were taken to another section of the depot where they issued us our bedding. This included a couple sheets, a couple blankets, a pillow and a pillow case.

After the issuance of our GI clothing, we were ordered to fall in again. We marched back to the barracks. Upon our return, the sergeant took an inventory of each item that had been issued to each man. A large box was presented to each soldier and in that box we were to place all our civilian clothing in preparation for shipping it home. Those items would be our last contact with a civilian past until the war came to an end.

The sergeant stood at the end of the barracks as each GI began the task of making his bed. I would dare say, there were few men who ever made their own bed. This was obvious when the sergeant inspected each cot and ordered the man to remake his bed over and over again. I vividly recall an inspecting officer visiting our barracks. He had white gloves, and his gloved hands would touch the windowsills. If there was one speck of dust on the white gloves, all the men in the barracks were punished and would be grounded for an entire weekend. All trips to Macon were off. All GIs looked forward to leaving the base, especially when someone of the opposite sex patiently waited at the bus station hoping for a night on the town.

The mess hall was not far from our barracks. It was noontime and time for chow. The chow was typical food we would receive with regularity during the weeks we would spend at Camp Wheeler. It was mostly freeze dried foods, a new invention which consisted of dried eggs, potatoes and most vegetables. To say the least, although the food was edible one would never refer to it as home cooking.

Not much time was allotted for chow. Once the GI finished eating the mess the cook so generously piled on our plates, we were ready for the next phase of military service

Always marching in line, we returned to our barracks and ordered to don our fatigues. When we were dressed, then it was on the double as we again lined up in formation to march to another part of the camp for issuance of our weapons. We were given two guns, one an M-1 rifle and the other a carbine, which we soon discovered was far from ac-

The photo above and those on the next page were taken at Camp Wheeler, Georgia.

curate when it came to hitting the target. Accompanying the M-1 was a bayonet. This was a sword-like weapon which we soon learned to affix to our M-1 for use in hand-to-hand combat.

It was at the end of the long first day at Camp Wheeler and we still had one more stop. We were taken to an office where each man was issued a set of dog tags. The dog tags were small metal objects held on a chain which was then

Army buddies: Futch, VanNatter, Humphry, Westmore.

secured around the GI's neck. Each tag was engraved with the soldier's serial number, mine being 35231727. Each individual number was so deeply engraved into every GI's brain it would remain there until the day he died. Should he be captured during combat he was informed to never give any information other than the serial number etched on his dog tags. If the GI happened to be killed and placed in a cheap pine box his dog tags would identify him as a soldier who died in the line of duty.

At 9 o'clock, the bugle sounded taps and the last order of the day was executed by the sergeant. "I don't want to catch any of you men with yer hands underneath the blankets." As the sergeant walked toward his room at the end of the barracks , he flipped a light switch. The lights were out.

CHAPTER 39

"HUP - TWO, THREE, FOUR - hup - two, three, four—git in step soldier! Bring them shoulders back and down!" The sergeant stood at the side of the marching platoon far enough so he could observe each soldier's feet, making certain each GI was in step with the rest of his comrades. I soon learned, march, march, march, must have been designed to prepare the foot soldier for the long walks he would encounter in the field of battle. The sergeant assigned a tall Texan fellow by the name of Mosher as our platoon leader. It was his responsibility to see each man was present at roll call. He was also responsible for having the men in his platoon prepared for inspections. The only respite the GI would have from this chicken shit routine was on Sunday morning. We could either sleep in or we could go to church.

Reveille sounded at 5:00 a.m. Before the bugler sounded the last note, each GI hit the deck, rushed to the latrine for a quick pee, shave then rushed outside to stand in formation. After roll call, it was to the mess hall for our morning meal. After chow, it was off to the jungles of Georgia to play war games. Noontime was the best time of the day. It not only meant we would be fed again, but it was time for mail call. I was one of the lucky ones.

Gerry had kept her word. There was a letter for every day I had been away. I received more mail than anyone. Expressions on the faces of some of the fellows changed from anticipation to anxiety. Many of the guys were married. Some had children so young, there was a strong possibility the men's offspring would never remember their father. There were men who soon experienced total desertion by their spouses. Some wives had a lover by the time her husband gave up his civilian existence to don the uniform of Uncle Sam's army. Our second day at Camp Wheeler introduced us to hand-to-hand combat.

In an open field a framework of steel bars was set up and from that framework hung sandbags simulating an enemy's body.

"Men!" The officer's voice rang out over the open field and we all came to attention. "At ease, men. Men—I want ya all to take a good look at them sandbags. I want each and every one of you to visualize those sandbags turning into one of those slanted-eyed bastards that you're probably goin' to face when you leave here. Those small slits they call eyes are staring into your eyes. You're facin' the enemy! It is your duty to act first, whether you're confronted with another foreign soldier, women or children, they're yer enemies and yer attack on them fuckers has to be certain one less Jap will never see the light of a new day. I'm gonna show ya how to protect yerself when you're faced with one of them bastards.

"Now—remove yer bayonet from yer knapsack. Take yer bayonet and attach it to yer M-1 rifle, like this." The officer proceeded to show us the correct way to attach the lethal weapon to our gun. "Now—I want ya to imagine you're gettin' ready to run a 100-yard dash on a football field. You rush forward toward the Jap, show yer teeth like a mad dog growling with a low guttural sound that'll pierce the ears of yer enemy. Direct that bayonet on the end of yer gun right through the bastard's gut."

Just the thought of hand fighting and stabbing another person to death was far beyond my comprehension. To take another life, regardless of whether their skin was black, yellow or even the life of any enemy was an unforgivable sin. I wanted to run.

"Come on there Private! Keep that bayonet right in front of you and run like hell until the blade sends a hole through that son-of-a-bitch from his belly button until it comes out his ass hole! You'd better learn to run like hell toward that bastard and growl like a goddamn mad animal that's cornered because that's exactly what you'll be doin' when you come face to face with them fuckers."

I made another feeble attempt to obey the officer's orders. I prayed each day and each night I would never be in the situation where this part of the war would be forever embedded in my memory. I was not alone. Soldiers sleeping next to me and men who shared the same barracks were men who came from an upbringing that taught them right from wrong. Killing was not a disease the young men in my barracks could cope with physically or emotionally. The entrance into the hell for which we were being trained would leave an emotional mark on our lives that would never heal.

Following the bayonet exercise on how to kill with a bayonet came training in Karate. I was never much good at physical strength in an effort to wrestle an opponent to the ground and I was certainly wasn't cut out for Karate. We were told to face our opponent.

My opponent was a tall, husky, Italian draftee from Philadelphia. I later learned the guy was a street kid and in most cases a leader in a gang. When the instructor announced "action!" I felt my opponent's huge, hairy arm around my neck. The pressure the fellow put against my Adam's apple and windpipe sent me into a world of dizziness, then blackness as my body crumpled to the ground. The burly guy reached down in an effort to help me to my feet. "I'm sorry, partner," he said. "My attack on you was a flashback to the days when I had to protect myself on the streets of Philly. It's always been me or the other guy and the other guy had to be first to go down." He held out his hand. "Come on, let's be friends. If we're sent off to some fuckin' jungle, I might be able to get that bastard of an enemy and save yer life." The olive skinned, muscular soldier helped me to my feet. I had acquired a buddy.

Basic training was intense and endless. Each day consisted of military maneuvers simulating battlefield conditions. There were all-night marches where we marched in formation from 7 o'clock until 6 o'clock the following morning. There were cold nights spent bivouacking in snake-infested fields, sleeping in pup tents and evacuating body wastes into a long trench referred to as a latrine. Before leaving a vacant field, we policed the campground, picking up every cigarette butt or piece of garbage that might have been carelessly thrown on the ground during the night. Nights and days not spent playing war games in the open fields of Georgia, were spent on the rifle range or going through what they called the infiltration course. The rifle range, strangely enough I found rather relaxing inasmuch as shooting my M-1 was something I excelled in. By the end of the training period, I was awarded my first medal, a medal for marksmanship.

Somehow the rifle range brought back memories of the

crossroads when Harvey and I placed tin cans on a fence. Where we managed to come into possession of a BB gun, I don't know, at any rate, we would pull the trigger and make a direct hit on the cans, sending the cans flying off the fence onto the other side. I felt sorry for city kids. Most had never been outside the City of New York or in other cities many had never been off their city block. None, unless they were part of a gang, had held a gun in their hands and now they were called upon to shoot to kill. Killing was the name of the game.

Next to me on the rifle range was a Jewish soldier from New York City. He was far more interested in talking about Broadway and the theatre than learning the army's requirement for firing a gun. A target was placed at the end of the range. Behind the target a deep pit was dug and each GI had to take his turn in the pit to count the scores. The two GIs laid low in the deep pit while the bullets hit the target then passed over their heads. If the riflemen missed the target or were so completely off center, a pair of white female bloomers was raised from the pit. These bloomers were known as Maggie's drawers. I excelled in this particular exercise, but not so with my Jewish comrade. Each time he fired his M-1, the gun jumped from his shoulder, smashing him in the face, usually the nose or the mouth. The poor guy looked like a war zone when the exercise wound down and we headed back to the barracks. The fellow's mouth, nose, chin and eyes gushed blood. He looked like a freshly butchered piece of meat.

Our basic training accelerated and was now into its second week. When we were drafted, it was announced our boot camp training would be a six-week period, then we would be scheduled for overseas duty. I managed to cope with most of the training, but not so with the Infiltration Course. This was set up in a swampy area where we were obligated to crawl through mud, over tree stumps and logs, and under barbed wire. At no time were we permitted to allow our rifle to touch the muddy course. While we crawled on our bellies, six officers sat on a platform raised about 36 inches above our heads. Each gentleman of the army was holding an automatic weapon which they fired over our heads, sometimes letting the bullets come as close as 24 inches. This exercise was called "actual combat conditions." Should the soldier rise above the three foot or 24 inches as he crawled over the muddy earth, he no longer had to worry about the war.

To say I wasn't scared would be a downright lie. My lifestyle never was an athletic one and crawling through barbed wire over logs or through mud holes did little as far as fitting into the life I was accustomed. I wasn't aware of anyone being near as each breath of life pushed me under the barrage of bullets, not until I felt a strong hand shoving my butt into the ground. I realized then, I had company on this trip through hell. It was Sergeant Olson, our NCO in charge of our barracks. He was the familiar voice that could be heard throughout the camp as he commanded his men to "fall in," "parade rest," and "at ease." His voice, as he approached my rear end, changed to a voice of compassion. He knew I was frightened. "I'm only tryin' to save yer life, VanNatter. Ya can git killed before ya git out of this fuckin' country if ya don't keep yer ass down!" I felt his heavy hand give my rear end a hard shove.

I survived the infiltration course. The army being fully aware no soldier could possibly go through an exercise like that afternoon on the Infiltration Course and return to the barracks with a clean rifle. Up until the bugle sounded and the lights were out, my comrades cleaned, cleaned and cleaned again the weapon that would be their savior in war.

It was seldom our barracks and platoon failed to pass inspection, therefore, we were entitled to weekend passes. I had acquired two buddies from the South, one from Atlanta, Georgia, and the other from Savannah. The two guys whose last names were Humphrey and Futch were two GI's that would follow me overseas and we would meet again in London. Futch was a gentle soul. From all indications, his upbringing had taught him compassion and kindness. Humphrey was different. On a weekend pass, I discovered he had a sadistic nature, particularly in his dealings with women. Another chap joined our trio by the name of Wetmore. The four of us formed a brotherly bond. We boarded a bus parked at the entrance of the base which transported us to the center of the town of Macon. Humphrey and Futch knew exactly where to find the nearest watering hole where there were girls, girls, and more girls all ready and willing to have a fling with a GI. I was a virgin and I am certain my buddy Wetmore was probably one also. We had never tasted the joys of opening the pearly gates of the fairer sex. I watched other GIs having no compunction about grabbing onto any girl, then leaving the watering hole to fulfill their sexual urges. The army, as far as I was concerned had done a good job orienting me to the consequences about premarital sex and particularly sex with a gal who was accustomed to having several bed partners. Humphrey and Futch quickly grabbed their conquest for the evening, leaving Wetmore and myself wondering if they would return with a good dose of clap or something worse. The following morning after our weekend escapades, the army wasted no time calling for an inspection. One they referred to as "Short-arm Inspection."

Sergeant Olson stood at the end of the barracks. "Okay, men—git yer clothes off and stand at attention. I mean—all yer clothes soldier! The Doc's comin' here to see if any of you men got a good dose of clap last night."

Totally naked, we stood in front of our footlockers. The men on the second floor descended the stairs to join the men on the first floor. Only one GI found it impossible to follow the sergeant's command to strip his body free of all clothing. He was Private Shafer. The young man was somewhat effeminate, in fact his body was shaped more like a woman than a man. How he got in Uncle Sam's army had to be a mistake. At any rate, he was part of our platoon and he made every effort to act as masculine and macho as the rest of us.

As each man stood in front of his respective footlocker, his exposed penis hanging soft and loosely waiting for the inspecting doctor's arrival. Private Shafer finally obtained enough courage to appear. He entered the barracks on the first floor dressed in a sexy, silk robe. Cat whistles rocked the rafters of the barracks. Blushing and totally embarrassed, Shafer disrobed then took his place beside one of the GIs.

"Atten-shun!" the sergeant's voice rang out The inspecting officer was ready to have a good look at every man's most valued appendage. "At ease, men," he ordered. The cocky, stern looking Captain began his parade up and down each side of the barracks. "Skin it back soldier and milk it down," he shouted. If there was the slightest discharge from the GI's penis, he was ordered to the dispensary for immediate attention.

I stood next to the Italian street kid with the hairy arms. His penis was apropos to the rest of his physique, meaning it far outweighed the GIs who were considered the usual size. He was endowed with the ugliest looking penis with a foreskin covering its head to where he found it difficult to comply with the Captain's command. The man had never heard of personal hygiene. When he did manage to push the foreskin away from the head of the penis, the organ looked like it was wrapped in cream cheese.

I thought the officer as well as the GI onlookers were going to vomit. The officer turned toward Sergeant Olson. "Sergeant—take this man to the shower and give him a GI bath." The man followed the sergeant to the latrine and the shower. On the way the noncommissioned officer picked up a scrub brush that had been used the previous night to clean the barracks floor. When the cleansing process was completed, the GI returned to stand in front of his footlocker. "Now!"—the officer ordered. "Skin it back and milk it down. That's better. I never want to come into this barracks again and see such personal filth." At the issuance of his final statement, we immediately came to attention and saluted the officer as he made his exit from the barracks.

I thought little about making music during those few weeks at Camp Wheeler. My upbringing had instilled in me the necessity of always attending church on Sunday. The first Sunday at Camp Wheeler, I made my way to the chapel. When I entered the one and only chapel that served the spiritual needs of GIs whether they be Protestant, Catholic or Jewish, I was astonished at the sound of the organ and the magnificent music originating from the choir loft.

The chaplain was a Baptist from Texas by the name of Captain Rankin. He was what we called a "hard shelled Baptist." In my prejudiced mind, he was to be avoided as much as a Priest or a Jewish Rabbi.

The soldier playing the organ was none other than Private Shafer, the same chap from the second floor of the barracks who appeared for short-arm inspection in a sexy silk robe. Unbeknownst to me, he had been assigned the job as organist and he did know how to play the organ. He made that simple two-manual box in the choir loft sound like a cathedral pipe organ. I wanted to sing. Of course, Shafer had already been tabbed as a bit queer. To be seen with him was cause for other GIs to stare in my direction and wonder about me. Nevertheless, I got up enough courage to ask Shafer for an audition. If I recall, I think I sang "The Holy City," and Shafer made the organ sound like a symphony. He liked my singing and asked if I would consider singing the same song in church the following Sunday morning.

Inasmuch as I had been washed in the blood of the lamb so many times since Mom died, I probably gave the most enthusiastic interpretation to the familiar sacred musical piece with more zest than any other living singer. News traveled fast after that Sunday morning. The camp had a singer in their midst. The following morning after my rendition, I was summoned to the commanding officer's headquarters. When I arrived, I was ushered into the inner sanctum and stood before a full Colonel. I immediately came to attention and waited for the man with an eagle decorating each shoulder of his uniform to speak.

"At ease, Private. Please be seated." I took a seat in one of the plush chairs in front of the Colonel's desk. "I heard you sing in church yesterday morning. I was very impressed and would like to make you an offer. We have on base a fine concert pianist by the name of Gilbert Miller. He's from Chicago and prior to being inducted, he toured extensively throughout the United States. In fact, I think he played at Carnegie Hall at one time. It entered my mind, as I heard you sing, that perhaps you two men would make a good team. How would you like to give a concert for the Waves who are stationed in Milledgeville?"

"I would like nothing better, sir," I responded.

"Well I can easily arrange for you and Private Miller to be relieved from duty to practice. Let's get this show on the road."

I raised myself out of the chair, stood at attention bringing my right hand up over my right eyebrow. "Thank you, sir," I replied. I turned on my heels and started walking toward the door. "Hold on, Soldier. You've got one week to get a concert together. I'll be driving to the concert and I expect the two of you to ride with me."

Gilbert Miller lived up to his reputation. He made the piano sound like a full orchestra, even though the instrument on the base wasn't exactly a Steinway Grand. I don't recall the number of hours we spent rehearsing, but when the big night arrived, Gil and myself were ready.

The campus at the University of Milledgeville was no longer occupied by young female intellectuals working toward a college degree. It was now a major training facility for women who chose a military life with Uncle Sam's Navy. It was a beautiful campus where the grounds were manicured to perfection amongst the mossy trees of the south. The theatre on campus was a performer's delight. Some of the world's greatest artists had performed on its stage. Now that stage was going to belong to me and Gilbert Miller.

There was a feeling of exhilaration as I walked from the wings of the theatre to center stage. A sea of blue uniforms and white caps filled the theatre to capacity. When two GIs appeared in their simple undecorated brown uniforms, a cheer and applause shook the rafters of the building. The applause and cat whistles were comparable to GI audiences where well-known sex objects appeared on stage.

When Gil and I performed our last number on the program, we hurried off stage toward our assigned dressing rooms. Waves were already backstage seeking an autograph. I felt like a star and my ego was taking flight. How I wished my good teacher, Mable Todd, could have been there that night.

I was invited several times to come to Milledgeville after that concert. I would sing for one of the local churches and in turn be entertained with a noonday dinner at one of the old plantations.

I had met many people from the South throughout my young life, but never really knew them. I knew little about the Civil War other than the fact the main issue as to why the war was fought was slavery. Milledgeville is a historical town. It played a major role in the war between the north and the south. As a village, its beauty surpassed anything I had ever seen. The tree-lined streets dripped with a lush mossy-like substance contributing to the cool shade from the hot Georgia sun. Large plantation mansions surrounded by a landscaped carpet of green and colorful flowers seemed to reverse time one hundred years.

It was a memorable Sunday, after singing in the local church, I was invited to a plantation home on the outskirts of Milledgeville. As I rode along the countryside, I felt like I was in some kind of a time machine. When the car in which I was riding turned into a long driveway leading to the mansion at the end of the road, I can still visualize the black servants as they greeted me when I stepped up the stairs onto the veranda then entered the spacious home.

The entry encompassed a wide reception room. To the left of the reception room, I noticed the dining room with the crystal, sparkling chandeliers hanging over a large table. The dining table was elegantly dressed in the finest table linens. It was laden with the finest china, silver and crystal that only people of great wealth could afford. As the black servants poured water over the ice in the finest paper thin crystal goblets, a musical, tinkling sound echoed throughout the room. There was a place card with my name neatly printed in front of a place setting. I was given the honorary position at the table, sitting next to my hostess, an old lady whom I later learned was well over 100 years old. She was a woman who had reached the end of the century. Her hands and face were nothing more than thin, wrinkled skin covering a body that had once belonged to a striking, young, beautiful woman. She was the last remaining citizen of Milledgeville who had survived the Civil War. Had my hostess shown any animosity toward a Yankee sitting to her right, the grand old dame had perfected etiquette to the nth degree. I learned a lot about the Civil War on that memorable day. While black servants carried steaming food from the kitchen and placed each delectable dish on the dining room table my friend spoke.

"You know, young man, it was in this very house my mammy and me hid General Lee in the attic while the Yankees diligently searched for him. Not a day passed, the Yankees failed to come to my door trying to find the General. The one place they did not look was in the attic. Had they done so, our good General would have become a prisoner of the Yankees. There is a trapdoor in the ceiling. Only the family knew where the break was in the ceiling. When the Yanks would go away, my mammy would take a long broom handle and rap on the trapdoor. The General, in turn would release the latch holding the door in place, and a narrow stairway would unfold till it reached the floor. Once a person ascended the stairway, they could easily pull the stairway up after them. Every day, my mammy and me carried food to the good General. We were careful to see he had plenty of water. Of course, we would ring a special bell that would alert the General we had prepared his sustenance for the day. We also supplied him with plenty of water for bathin'. In all those months, though, he never gave a thought as to shavin' his long beard. It was not until the day the war between the north and the south ended did the General leave his secret hiding place. I can still feel the kiss of gratitude as he pressed a kiss on my lips and a kiss on Mammy's cheeks as he bid us that memorable farewell."

CHAPTER 40

INSTEAD OF THE ORIGINALLY PLANNED six weeks of basic training we got a reprieve and the training period was extended
into ten weeks. Day after day we made our way to the open
fields of Georgia simulating battlefield conditions. I had a
deathly fear of snakes and the open fields and tall weeds
seemed like a likely place for snakes to conceal themselves
from intruders into their territory. On one of the exercises, in
fact, it was toward the last field maneuver that would wrap
up the basic training exercise, along with three other fellows,
I was assigned the duty of leading the platoon into battle.
The army referred to us as the BAR team.

The weapons were heavy. They were long, heavy metal
cylinder-type weapons which we carried over our shoulder.
As I previously mentioned I had a deathly fear of snakes.
Wading through the tall grass I inadvertently let my eyes
wander toward the ground instead of keeping up with the
other three GIs carrying the same kind of weapon I was
holding over my shoulder. When my eyes, at some point in
time, left their focus on the ground and looked at what lay
ahead. The platoon was practically out of sight. I couldn't
possibly make it to the front. I had to do something. Someone laid down a smoke screen and the first word flashing

through my mind was "Gas!" I shouted "Gas! Gas!" As if they were obeying an order from the Captain, all the men immediately took their gas masks from their knapsack and secured them on their face. As they did so I rushed through the white cloud of smoke and took my place with the other three members of the BAR team.

The leader was angry. Had he not been a decent guy and also one with a sense of humor, I probably would have ended up in the brig for attempting to go AWOL. When the smoke dissipated, the sadistic Captain who maintained some distance from the platoon so he could observe how each man behaved under combat conditions proudly paraded toward his fighting group of soldiers. His voice echoed across the field. As he spoke, I could see a slight smile on the face of the BAR leader. "Men!—I'm proud of you. That exercise was done so well, I wouldn't be afraid to lead any one of you into battle."

Like a Nazi goose stepper, the Captain turned on his heels then headed toward a waiting Jeep. Sergeant Olson's voice gave an order, "Fall in, men! Forward!—March!

I must have inadvertently let my hands touch some poison ivy. When we returned to the barracks my hands were red and swollen. I would run hot water on them and although it eased the pain temporarily the poison continued to spread.

Our barracks was beginning to thin out. Each day, many of my comrades were missing. They were shipped out to some unknown destination. We had always assumed we were being trained for fighting in the Pacific and our platoon would remain intact. The final days of training brought deep emotional reactions. War games were rapidly turning into reality.

No GI was born to be a killer. In spite of our brain washing we could always identify the GI who couldn't adjust to the life of a soldier. One fellow was a sensitive fellow by the name of Lippincot, a sibling from the famous publishing firm. Night after night he could be seen sitting on a stool in the latrine saturated with booze. Other GI's would attempt to sympathize with the guy but all they succeeded in doing was to make the chap more anti-social. "I'm getting' out of this fuckin' army. They're not gonna send me to some hell hole on this planet." His eyes were blurry and his speech thick. He was one of the few rich kids who had parents influential enough to make his life easier. With their political connections, the young chap could have been placed behind a desk and destined to never leave the shores of the United States. What happened to Lippincott? I don't know. Was he one of those guys who was mowed down on the beaches of Normandy?

Once a man was inducted into the army it was not a simple matter to obtain a discharge. If the situation was odd enough, the only recourse a determined GI would have for getting dismissed from military duty would be on the grounds of a Section 8 or a Medical Discharge. Alcohol addiction was not considered grounds for a Section 8. Only a few cots away from mine was another chap who hated the army. He too, was determined to end his stint with Uncle Sam. He began urinating in his bed every night.

A foul smelling odor began permeating the barracks. It was during our weekly inspection of the barracks, an officer stood next to the bed pisser. He detected the foul odor originating from the GI's cot. The officer's hands moved quickly. He ripped the bedding from the cot and then the man's secret was discovered.

We stood at attention in front of our footlockers. "At ease, men!" The officer then stood in front of the suspect GI. "Ya know and I know, Soldier, this man's army cannot tolerate a man pissin' in his bed. If this is yer way of gittin' out of this man's goddamn army, I know and you know you made yer point. "Now—git yer ass over to the dispensary."

The poison ivy covering my hands continued to ravage my skin. Daily I went to the dispensary. During that time, more GIs from my original platoon were shipped out. I was the last one to go. By November of 1943, the hands cleared up enough to permit me a short furlough back to Akron, Ohio.

I boarded the train in Macon and as memories of Camp Wheeler the training ground for the foot soldier began to fade, I wondered many times about those men in the barracks. They were a great group of America's finest. Were they shipped to the Atlantic side of the war? Or, were they using their hand-to-hand combat weapons on some Godforsaken, unknown island in the Pacific?

CHAPTER 41

THE SHORT FURLOUGH AND MY departure from Akron a few days later lacked all the fanfare I experienced when I left the city in June and was drafted into Uncle Sam's army. Army orders preceded my arrival home. "You are to report to Fort Meade, Maryland, no later than November 15th, 1943." Inasmuch as Gerry was away at school and she would have been my only incentive for spending the short furlough in Akron, I was actually looking forward to moving on at the government's expense.

It was an overnight journey to Fort Meade, Maryland. I arrived at the downtown Akron depot in plenty of time to catch the all-night train ride to an army camp that lacked even less amenities for comfort than Camp Wheeler, Georgia. Wet, cold weather or the fact I belonged to Uncle Sam is unknown, in either case, Fort Meade served to fulfill a prediction of things to come. The drab surroundings of Fort Meade proved to be nothing more than a holding tank for hundreds of men whose cots were lined next to the walls of the long barracks. I let my body collapse on one of the vacant cots and must have fallen asleep. The bugle sounded at 5:00 a.m.

GIs hit the deck and prepared to stand in the freezing

rain to answer "here," as the roll call was called. We were then separated into platoons. As in basic training we then marched in formation to the mess hall where we were permitted to have breakfast before returning to our barracks to fulfill our assigned chicken shit routines.

Of all the qualified candidates to be selected as a temporary noncommissioned officer no one was a more unlikely candidate than myself. I was never asked if I wanted to be an acting sergeant. I was simply told. "You will accept the responsibility." There was no increase in my monthly paycheck—there was no advantage other than being in the position of ordering those men under my jurisdiction to perform chicken shit duties. These included KP, scrubbing barrack floors, making sure when the soldier was upright the bedding on his cot was wrinkle free. It was a waiting game. There would be daily dispensary calls where we were given more shots and more physical examinations. Like a good soldier I sewed the three stripes on the sleeve of my Eisenhower jacket as well as on the sleeve of my fatigues. I was careful not to sew the stripes too firmly. I knew as soon as the orders came to ship out and we were ordered onto the deck of a ship the stripes would be removed. Those stripes would be ripped from my sleeves and like Cinderella, I would be returned to the lowly status of a private.

It was Thanksgiving Day. GIs lined up at the mess hall. Metal mess kits banged in the wind as we waited for the doors to open hoping the previous diners, i.e., top brass and visiting dignitaries, were kind enough to leave enough turkey on Thanksgiving Day for the ordinary foot soldier.

We weren't permitted to associate or rub shoulders with the gentlemen of the army. Top brass, visiting senators and congressmen might object to some of the complaints the GIs might have. The GI was nothing more than a lowly animal responsible for turning the ugly war into a glorifying experience for those who reached the status of an army gentleman.

Metal mess kits banged in the wind on this cold, wet miserable day as we stood outside the mess hall waiting for the previously decorated chow hall to be stripped of its fineries of tablecloths and cloth napkins. When the door finally opened we held out our mess kits toward the Mess Sergeant who in turn slopped food onto our government issue mess kits.

First came the mashed potatoes sans peelings. Gravy was poured over the mashed potatoes. If we were lucky, a piece of what was at one time a turkey was added. A dab of yams was added, then for dessert a canned peach was tossed on top of the entire, unsightly slop. The food was as cold and unappetizing as the weather outside.

There were no passes during the three weeks spent at Fort Meade, Maryland. During those three weeks we marched, we policed the area, that is, picking up cigarette butts from the ground. We cleaned latrines and polished shoes and buttons. There was never any time allotted for doing nothing.

The day before shipping out, another physical examination was in order. It entailed another look at our rectums, the doctor pushing his finger into our testicles to see if any man might have a hernia, or, if there happened to be some shot we had not already been given, a needle was always present to be inserted into our arm. Then shipping-out day arrived.

The shadowy vision of the wet, misty morning our platoon loaded onto a train continues to remain within my memory as clearly as if it happened yesterday. Where we were going was anybody's guess. After what seemed to be many hours and daytime turned into night, the troop train slowed as we pulled into Manhattan's Pennsylvania Station. Like sheep, we were then herded onto a waiting army truck whose canvas siding around the bed of the truck was so tightly closed no one could see in and no one could see out. When the truck pulled into another army camp somewhere in upper Manhattan, we were informed we had reached Camp Shanks.

Camp Shanks was more depressing and dismal than Fort Meade. Since it was our last stop, one might even consider it a death house where we would wait for our fate to be consummated. We were herded into a room lined with double bunks that were only a few inches apart. Morale was low and the top brass did nothing to lift the spirits of those carefully chosen as Uncle Sam's perfect male specimens for what he thought would make a good soldier. We were confined to the barracks like a group of caged animals. The only time permitted to leave the area of our bunk was at chow time, then it was back to the barracks, go to the latrine, stand roll call and with nothing to do while waiting for further orders we collapsed on our army cots.

It seemed to be the middle of the night when a loud demanding voice shouted, "Rise and shine, Soldiers—we're shipping out!" In unison, each man hit the deck. The adrenalin in each man came alive with anticipation. This was for real!

I don't recall just how many army trucks made up the cortege that would travel the streets of Manhattan under the cover of darkness, but I was in one of those trucks. Heavy side canvases covered the bed of the truck, blocking out a view of Manhattan's skyline. The only time I was cognizant of our possible location was when we reached the lower end of Manhattan Island and stopped at a pier where a mammoth ocean liner's image broke through the morning fog and darkness. It was the Queen Elizabeth I, the largest seagoing vessel the British had to offer. In peacetime, she was Queen of the sea. Now her colors were as drab as the uniforms of the 3,000 GIs who were herded aboard.

All the elegant refinery was stripped from the ship's interior, including the luxurious staterooms. The dining room with its tinkling crystal wine goblets and brilliant, delicate china along with the magnificent crystal chandeliers were no more. Lush carpeting was removed from the decks and the winding stairways, leaving nothing more than bare wooden stairs and bare decks. Walls were removed to make room for thousands of hammock-like bunks hung from the ceiling to the floor. Private bathrooms became ordinary latrines utilized by whomever was first to make it to the toilet.

Our knapsacks and mess kits were our constant companions. Passing through a buffet line was always the same. The server gave us food like he was slopping hogs. When we left our sleeping area we would reserve our spot on the ship by placing our dufflebag on our bunks. The only attribute during that three-thousand-mile voyage was the army no longer subjected us to their chicken shit routines.

The morning of our departure an eerie quiet engulfed the ocean liner as tugboats slowly ushered the Queen through the still, calm waters of New York harbor, leaving behind the blacked out skyline of New York City. There was not even a glimpse of the Statue of Liberty. Once the ship reached international waters, the great engines of the Queen began to grind. We had reached the point of no return. Great ocean swells rocked the boat like a cork bobbing up and down on top of the waters of one's favorite fishing hole. Feet that had at one time been firmly planted on the ground, were now in a state of being airborne unless one happened to be near a column or bannister to give one enough support to defy the laws of gravity. In the mess hall or dining room, mess kits crashed off the wooden tables onto the carpetless floor with a crashing sound as a warning of things to come.

German U-boats along with Japanese submarines roamed the ocean like hungry sharks seeking to attack any moving object riding the swells of the open sea. To avoid being attacked, the great ship never sailed in a straight line. For the next 11 days, it zigzagged over the Atlantic's troubled waters. Few men ventured from their bunks. No one was permitted to go on deck. Sea sickness was rampant. To climb from one's bunk onto the floor of the ship was not conducive to a good appetite even if we chose to make our way to the dining room. Holding onto the staircase railing in an attempt to reach the dining room located on the upper deck was enough to force one back to his bunk. Each attempt to place a foot on the ascending stairway caused the stomach to churn in waves comparable to the sea beneath us.

I don't know how many American soldiers the great ship ferried from the shores of America to the European shores before the group of men I was with were herded aboard. There were many. The ship was never torpedoed or attacked from the air or from the ever present adversaries searching the seas under the turbulent waters of the Atlantic. Our ten-day wartime voyage ended on the morning of December 24, 1943.

A ghostly quietness surrounded the ship in the early morning of our arrival in a foreign land. The comforting sound of the great engines were quiet and the ship no longer rolled with the great swells of the Atlantic. I made my way to top deck. For the first time in 10 days, I was awed at the sight of a land where the mountains met the sea. In the distance was a small village. I was told it was an ancient Scottish town they called "Grennoch." As the troops left the ship, we were boarded onto a waiting train. Throughout the day the train would carry us from Grennoch, Scotland to England. At no time during the long journey would we see the light of day. Everything was in total darkness. Not even the light from a match or cigarette lighter was permissible. Villages and large cities passed unnoticed. Darkness was a way of life.

Had these rules been betrayed, residences, factories and offices were subject to being erased from the face of the earth. Hitler's bombers continued their paths of destruction throughout the British Isles as they had done since the infamous attack on the British empire which began in 1939.

Throughout the day and far into the night, the troop train rolled over the tracks from Scotland to somewhere in England. It was well past midnight when the train came to a halt at the English village of Litchfield. Fatigued from the long journey, each GI secured their backpacks over their shoulders, picked up their dufflebags which contained only the bare necessities for survival, disembarked from the train then boarded an enclosed army truck. Our destination—the King's Guardsmen barracks located a few miles from the town of Litchfield. Any amenities the barracks may have had prior to our arrival were sadly lacking. The buildings were cold and dismal. Double bunks lined both sides of the long open rooms. I succeeded in getting an upper bunk This bunk had only a light blanket to ward off the cold. I stretched out on the bunk and began my journey into a dreamworld that would remove me from the army and the air war that ravaged the British Isles.

"Okay—Soldier—rise and shine!" A rough hand slapped

my behind as the gruff voice echoed in my ear. "You're it, Soldier, you're gonna spend the day on KP."

Only two hours had passed from the time I laid down on the bunk. It was 5:00 a.m., Christmas morning. Half awake I staggered toward the latrine, dashed some cold water on my face then resigned to my fate I headed toward the mess hall and into the kitchen where a mountain of dirty pots and pans awaited my arrival. My morale was low, I don't recall the Mess Sergeant being so generous as to offer me a cup of coffee. That didn't bother me since I wasn't a coffee drinker, but I could have used a substantial breakfast before hitting the detail of the day. We continued to eat from our mess kits. Fortunately, as the GIs lined up for breakfast, their mess kits filled, they would dine on the menu of the day and when they finished their meal they took their metal kits to a large vat of boiling water where their only eating utensils were sterilized. I seldom permitted myself the luxury of succumbing to self-pity, but on Christmas day, 1943, I felt it was totally warranted. I hated Uncle Sam's army!

I wasn't relieved of the KP detail until 10:00 p.m. Christmas night. Turkey had been served with all the trimmings during the day, but when I sat down on one of the long benches to delve into my Christmas dinner, the sergeant quickly informed me the turkey was all gone.

"How about a pork chop?" I felt like a stray dog coming to someone's back door for a scrap of food. The Mess Sergeant tossed a half-cooked pork chop onto my mess kit. He then decorated the piece of meat with a spoonful of cold mashed potatoes. I gulped the unsavory food like I was hungry. I began to have the same hatred for the army as the Lippincott kid. I was ready to find some way to git outta this goddamn army.

The barracks in Litchfield served as a facility to house a pool of men who would replace GIs killed or mangled on the battle fronts of North Africa or Sicily. GIs were as dispensable as left-over food tossed to swine or thrown into the garbage. The supply of GIs was limitless. The Replacement Depot in Litchfield was true to its name. We were there to replace the maimed and the dead ones, slaughtered under the name of God and freedom.

Horror stories circulating throughout the King's Barracks were rampant. In most cases the rumors were true. An American Colonel by the name of Colonel Killian had been assigned to the post as Commanding Officer. Hitler's henchmen would have had difficulty running a close second to this sadistic creature. His kicks in life were solely geared toward how much suffering and pain he could inflict on another human being, which happened to be those men who, by a freak of some insane planning ended up at the King's Barracks in Litchfield, England. Colonel Killian's legacy was that of a man who was highly educated in the art of making a person's life miserable, actually going so far as to cause the loss of human life.

The year of 1943 was rapidly coming to an end. There were two GIs imprisoned in the Guard House who had originally served in North Africa or Sicily. Fright caused the men to flee the scene of battle. They knew their lives were in jeopardy when they walked away from their campsite. This did not deter the two men from trying to escape the fiery inferno on the front lines. Freedom was short. Both men were captured and their reward was to be sent back to England where they would await trial. Desertion was cause under military law for one to face the firing squad. Colonel Killian had other ideas. Without compassion or mercy he interrogated the two frightened soldiers. As he exited the Guard House, he ordered two military policemen to go into the men's cells and beat each one of the soldiers until they were more than willing to go back to the front lines. "I want ya to whip those sissies until they'll beg to be sent back to the fuckin' front. What in hell do them two wimps think this war is all about?"

The Military Police obeyed the Colonel's command. With no provocation the young American GIs were crucified as the police proceeded to beat each man with a long leather whip and with their fists. The men fell unconscious to the floor. With one final gesture, one of the MPs kicked a downed soldier in the side of his head. Both soldiers were dead. The MPs had completed their mission.

The rumors about the deaths of the two GIs rolled through the barracks like a tidal wave. Revenge was in everyone's mind, particularly two paratroopers who managed to get a pass into Litchfield. They sat at a pub drinking until the pub closed for the night then they began their long trek back to the barracks along a dark country road. Alcohol had flowed like water into their bodies and their minds and their bodies were numb with overindulgence.

The only automobiles on the road were property of the military. Bright headlights sent a piercing beam of light down the country road. Like aircraft caught in the search lights protecting London, the two GIs were spotted walking along the road. The driver of the car brought his vehicle to a halt then offered the GIs a ride back to the base. It was a command car so often seen roaming around the base at the King's Barracks. When the driver of the vehicle rolled down the driver's side window, a gruff voice spoke. "Wanna ride, Soldiers? Ya guys are kinda late for curfew." It was the voice of Colonel Killian. The Colonel unlocked the back door to the vehicle and the two GIs took their place in the backseat. Before the officer could put the car in gear and resume the journey back to the base, one GI placed a choke hold around the Colonel's neck. The other soldier quickly opened the driver's door to the car then pulled the officer out of the car and to the ground. "Ya fuckin' bastard—ya son-of-a-bitch." The soldiers' voices rang like a shot from a gun through the still night air. Blow after blow they struck the head of the Commanding Officer. "This is just a small taste of what you did to our buddies, sir." The Colonel lost consciousness.

The paratroopers picked the limp body of the Colonel up from the graveled road then placed his bloody body in the backseat of the command car. One of the GIs took over the steering wheel while the other watched guard over the hostage in the backseat. When the command car reached the guard gate, the MP stood at attention. Signaling to the MP their Commanding Officer had had too much to drink, the command car was permitted to proceed.

The driver brought the car to a stop in front of the Commanding Officer's quarters. No effort was extended in an attempt to see the officer was safely ensconced within his own domain. Leaving the Command car parked in front of the Colonel's residence, the men returned to their barracks.

The Colonel recovered. He resumed his duties as Commanding Officer. The incident of that weekend did not phase his sadistic practices, and there was never a word mentioned about the two paratroopers who had unmercifully beaten the man. The Colonel made no gesture toward prosecuting the men. It would be several weeks hence while working with classified documents at the headquarters in London, I read the story about Colonel Killian confirming all the rumors that circulated throughout the King's Barracks.

There was an investigation. Unfortunately, the matter was treated lightly. Colonel Killian was returned to the United States, reprimanded and fined a sum of $500. In further documents I read where he was reinstated as Commanding Officer of the Replacement Depot in Litchfield, England.

No prison routine flaunted on a convicted felon could possibly have been more degrading or demoralizing than the time I spent at Litchfield. From the break of a new day into the evening hours, there were marches, policing the area, KP and when a slight break seemed imminent for the GI, the Commanding Officer ordered each man to the gas chamber to test various types of poison gases. Sometimes, these events would take place as many as three or four times during the day. The procedure involved entering the gas chamber wearing gas masks. Once inside the chamber, we were obligated to remove the mask, get a good whiff of the poisonous room-filled vapors, then replace our mask before leaving the chamber. An examination was then conducted whereby the GI was obligated to identify all the various types of gases their nostrils were exposed to.

During the time spent at the King's Barricks in Litchfield, England, music took a backseat. I only recall one evening where outside artists came to entertain at the camp and that was Scotland's beloved Harry Lauder and Irving Berlin. I had always gone to church on Sunday morning and didn't deviate from that routine as the weeks passed in the dismal surroundings of Litchfield. I never got to sing nor did I feel like singing. The GI who played the organ, however, needed my services. Not to sing—but to pump the bellows in the back of the antique organ while he demonstrated his expertise on the ivories by playing a Bach Fugue.

My time was running out. I knew it was only a matter of

days before I would be shipped out probably to North Africa or Sicily. I dreaded that moment and knew there must be a way I could bypass that experience of fighting a real war with a gun and a bayonet.

I knew how to operate a typewriter and had even taken shorthand in high school. There was a personnel office on the base and with enough courage under my belt, I wandered into a Quonset hut temporarily set up to handle all personnel problems in the camp. An efficient, masculine WAC guarded the door. "What can I do for you, Soldier?" The female soldier eyed me suspiciously. "I understand sir," — although I was addressing a person of female gender, "they need good secretaries in London."

"Are you a secretary?" she questioned in a rather doubtful response.

"Of course," I quickly responded. "Why do you think the army sent me to a special Clerk School while in basic training?"

"Can you take shorthand? Gregg Shorthand that is. None of this Pitman stuff."

"Of course," I quickly responded. I had taken shorthand in high school and like my Algebra class, the teacher said she would pass me providing I didn't take the class again, at least not in her class. I also knew 120 words a minute was the requirement for securing any kind of an office job as a secretary. "I can run a typewriter, too," I quickly added. I'm a whiz at runnin' a typewriter."

Without suggesting my skills be tested, a pleased look flashed across the WAC's face. "Well — they are looking for experienced and efficient secretaries at Eisenhower's headquarters in London. It's called ETOUSA. Have you ever been to London, Soldier?"

"No—I always wanted to go though."

"Well Soldier," she continued. "This is your lucky day. Get your dufflebag packed. You're leaving on the afternoon train."

London, England: Air Blitz by the German Luftwaffle, 1943

CHAPTER 42

A LIGHT, MISTY RAIN BRUSHED against my face as I exited Victoria Station then stepped onto the streets of London. Heavy clouds descended from the heavens like a soft protective blanket, the only deterrent against Hitler's Luftwaffe's devastating bombs falling on the English capital.

Blitzed London was in battledress. Her historic buildings were sandbagged, her art treasures removed to safety, her shop windows boarded-in as a protection from the blast rather than to hide the fact there was little on display or for sale. Her streets were dustier. It was no accident that nothing was so well sign-posted as in peacetime. All night it was difficult to find one's way owing to the blacked-out office buildings, residences and shops. Formerly London's West End was ablaze with multicolored lights. Now—everything was hidden for dusk meant "lights out" except for a few indispensable hooded traffic lights and air-raid shelter indicators.

I hailed a taxi and within minutes was transported to my assigned billet on Green Street which was only one block from Grosvenor Square. It was a delightful room. Prior to the war the townhouse where my room was located must have been some person or person's city home. The only source of heat was a small gas heater which required inserting a shilling in the slot on its side. I soon discovered that one shilling barely took the chill off the room. Another shilling had to be deposited to bring a little more than an hour of warmth. The room was situated on the third floor.

Those who dwelled in the heart of the city or the Mayfair District sought refuge from the incessant bombings outside the City of London. Their elegant townhouses, like the great ocean liner "Queen Elizabeth I" were transformed into a source for billeting the American soldiers. It would not be until after the war ended, England's "IN" crowd and citizens of the more affluent society could again enjoy the luxurious comfort of city living.

The advent of the war and the first German blitz over the English capital changed the face of the Mayfair District of London. The era of gaiety; eat, drink, and be merry; tails, white ties, and luxurious evening gowns was put on an indefinite hold.

Green Street was a short block located between Park Lane and Grosvenor Square. Park Lane overlooked Hyde Park and tall pretentious looking apartment buildings lined the avenue. It was obvious these dwellings were designed for the rich similar to Park Avenue in New York City.

The sedate buildings at Grosvenor Square retained the same elegance as they had for decades. It was in these picturesque buildings the American army housed ETOUSA headquarters. This was the home for American military policy makers. It was a workday home for top military brass from four-star generals to the lowly private who labored at the lowest rung of the military ladder.

It was chow time when I arrived in London. I discovered where the mess hall was located and like all chow lines I stood in line behind my fellow soldiers. There was a difference however, I no longer needed to have food slopped onto my mess kit. There were real plates and real glasses and cups. Even the desert was served in a separate ceramic dish.

After I finished my evening meal, I decided to stroll down Green Street toward Park Lane. I turned right on Park Lane and it was then I noticed Marble Arch, the entrance into Hyde Park. Directly across from Marble Arch was a hotel, a cinema and a Lyon's Tea Room and also a Penny Arcade. Also near Marble Arch was another building that had been taken over by the Red Cross. This was called "Rainbow Corners." Rainbow Corners was a place where GIs could dance to the sound of big bands, sit and relax at the bar and often there were special musical concerts.

The night was still young when I took my evening stroll. I noticed the cinema was featuring an Alice Faye movie called "The Gang's All Here." I purchased a ticket and just presumed I would enter the theatre and take a seat. Not so—an usher met me at the door then guided me toward an empty seat about halfway down the aisle of the theatre. I thanked the lady, but that is not what she wanted. She held out her hand for a tip.

I was seated next to an English girl whom I never met and would never meet again so there was no need, to strike up a conversation, not until halfway through the movie, the sound stopped and a huge sign flashed across the screen. "Alert." Then I heard the wailing of the air raid sirens. I moved closer to the girl then got up enough courage to ask her if the Jerries had arrived yet. All she did was point her finger to the ceiling of the theatre.

The sound of bombs exploding soon rocked the theatre causing it to react in pain like an ocean liner who is confronting an unusual storm on the open sea. As the bombs fell, it seemed as if the walls of the entire theatre moved and all air was sucked out of the auditorium. The guns in Hyde Park exploded and after about 25 minutes, the raid seemed to come to an end. The steady sound of the "All Clear" brought a sense of relief to those watching the movie.

When the words "The End" flashed across the screen, I quickly rose from my seat and exited the theatre. The smell of smoke was choking as I left the theatre and wandered onto the street. Flames from the fires caused by the bombing lit up the skies of London. Searchlights circled the sky, revealing giant balloons attached to steel cables flying high above Great Britain's capital.

I watched in awe as an enemy flyer jumped from his burning aircraft and parachuted toward the ground. Like a fly caught in a spider's web, the ray of light scanning the skies, focused on the young pilot. The British guns had successfully made a direct hit on one of Hitler's Luftwaffe planes. When the German flyer reached the ground he was immediately captured. He would never see his homeland again, not until the war came to an end.

The fires lingered and the smell of sickening smoke-filled air made breathing a bit difficult. Reaching my room, I removed my clothing then let my body stretch out on the comfortable bed wondering what the next day would bring and just how I was going to get along with the full Colonel to whom I had been assigned as a private secretary. At 3:00 a.m. I was awakened by the sound of the air raid siren. The Jerries were back for the second time since my arrival in London. I was frightened. My body shook with fear. I could hear the bombs exploding nearby and with each explosion thoughts flooded my mind of being buried alive in a pile of rubble should the Jerries make a direct hit on Green Street and the place I was about to call home.

The raid must have lasted a good 25 minutes before the "All Clear" sounded and I drifted off to sleep. At 5:00 a.m., I heard the sound of a bugle. I must have been dreaming I was in the barracks at Camp Wheeler. It wasn't a dream. I heard noises coming from the middle of Green Street. I gazed out my window and saw soldiers streaming out of billets, lining up in formation in preparation for a new day's inspection and roll call. I dressed quickly, ran down the stairs and onto the street arriving just in time for roll call and the morning inspection.

The dress code for all men under General Lee's command meant neatness at all times. Buttons were to shine like gold nuggets, shoes were to be polished with a mirror-like finish and our dress uniforms, now our everyday work clothes, must have the appearance of cleanliness and be wrinkle free as if they had just returned from the dry cleaners. Our battledress often referred to as "fatigues," would only be worn when we were assigned house cleaning chores.

The inspecting officer paraded back and forth like a stuck up bantey rooster carefully scrutinizing each man's appearance. If there was any sign of an overnight growth of beard, the man was reprimanded. If his hair was too long he was ordered to go to a barber and God help the soldier if his shoes did not shine or there was a wrinkle in his coat or trousers. It was the same chicken shit GIs endured during basic training and what I had endured at the Replacement Depot in Litchfield. Would it never end?

There were certain perks associated with my transfer to Eisenhower's headquarters. The best perk included the number of hours one was obligated to work. A civilian job could not have been better. Our hours were from 9:00 to 5:00. No overtime. Other than an occasional after-hours assignment, the GIs time was his own. I had the idea that being sent to London instead of shouldering a gun in some God forsaken hole in North Africa or Sicily I had escaped the war. Not true. The twice a night and sometimes three bombings never ceased. We could almost set our watches to the exact times the Jerries would reach the shores of England and begin their devastating raids over the British Isles.

Like a good soldier, I reported to the Colonel's private office at the exact time. A cold, uninviting stare from a giant of a man sitting behind a huge desk greeted me. I removed my overcoat, quickly placed it on the clothes rack. Before I could sit down at my desk I was summoned by the Colonel to take dictation. "Get your pad Private, we have work to do." Trying to give an impression of being a professional, I picked up my steno pad, then rushed to the inner sanctum where the Colonel sat in his big leather chair, his hands resting on his pretentious executive desk.

The man began dictating before I could take my seat. Hurriedly, I scribbled shorthand forms which were to be readable once I returned to my desk and the typewriter. Unfortunately, I tried to force my mind to recall everything the Colonel dictated. When I returned to my desk, I couldn't remember one word the man said and when I attempted to read my notes, they were like a foreign language, one that I had never seen nor heard.

When the day came to an end, there was little doubt the chemistry between the Colonel and myself would not consummate into a marriage made in heaven. I was fired. I was certain my next stop would be that of a foot soldier on the front lines in North Africa or Sicily.

The Colonel did fire me, but instead of sending me back to Litchfield, I was told to report to G-2 which happened to be the intelligence section of the headquarters where all top secret documents and confidential documents were carefully guarded. It was another secretarial position and I was assigned as an assistant to a WAC who happened to be the private stenographer for the Officer in Charge, a Captain Cochran. I was never certain as to the WAC's name, but she was a warm human being from Idaho and immediately we were on a first name basis. "Private, I want you to call me Libby. That's what all my friends call me."

Carefully, she began indoctrinating me as to what the job entailed then she politely took me into the boss' office. Captain Cochran sat leisurely puffing away on his pipe which was always his constant companion. Libby made a quick introduction then left me alone with the Captain. "Private," he said. "Let's see what you can do as a stenographer. Libby gets a bit over loaded at times and she needs help. Hopefully, you're going to be just what we're looking for." With my steno pad always in hand, I sat down in front of the Captain's desk. He began a rather lengthy dictation and I quickly tried to write out the Gregg Shorthand forms on my pad. When the session came to an end, I rushed out of the office, still hoping I could retain in my memory everything the Captain dictated. I attempted to read my notes, but, as before on my first day of being employed at the headquarters, I discovered I didn't recognize one symbol. I called Libby to my desk. I showed her my notes and when I told her I couldn't read them, she remarked, "Loy these are very good. I don't understand why you can't read them." Libby stood behind my shoulder and as my fingers glided over the keys of the typewriter she translated my notes to perfection. "I'll make a deal with you, Loy. You're a much better typist than myself so why don't you take the dictation when the Captain calls, and I'll translate your shorthand for you while you do the typing."

It was a good arrangement. Libby then discovered there was an opening in the Adjutant General's Office and encouraged me to take it.

After my one day as private secretary to the Colonel, I discovered, at the end of the day, there was a note on my bed. "VanNatter—you are being transferred across the street to Number 8 Green Street. Prepare to move immediately.

At Number 8 Green Street I shared a large room on the third floor with eleven GIs all sleeping in double bunks which took up a goodly portion of the room.

Number 8 Green Street was a three-story townhouse similar to the one I billeted in for one night but where I had a private room. On the lefthand side of the stairway leading to the third floor was a small cubicle which served as a bathroom. That room was equipped with a toilet and one large bathtub. One latrine serving 12 men could be very disconcerting at times, particularly when nature called and the one and only facility was occupied.

The men who shared the quarters on the third floor were an amiable group of men. They came from different parts of the U.S. and each man had his own ethnic background. Some of the men came from large American cities, others from small villages and there were those transplanted from the land where they worked as farmers. Some came from large families, others came from being the only son. Many of the men were married. One chap was the father of so many children, the only respite his wife had from getting pregnant was to send her spouse off to war where he could no longer hang his pants on her bed post.

Mail call was the highlight of the day. News from home was the only event during the day which managed to lift and maintain a healthy morale for each American soldier. Gerry never wavered from her promise to write everyday. By the time I settled in at Number 8 Green Street, the mail room orderly presented me with a large packet of letters. Most of them from Gerry.

I opted for the top bunk at No. 8 Green Street. On the bottom bunk was a blond fellow. I don't recall where he was from, or even his name, but I soon learned he had been a professional actor before Uncle Sam took over his life. He was a shy, slightly built fellow with blue eyes. I hadn't given much thought to music or show business since arriving on the European war scene. When my bunk buddy learned I was a singer, the world of make-believe juices began stirring in my soul. The army was doing a production of Thorton Wilder's *Our Town*. The cast was made up of GIs except for the female leads, which were transported from across the ocean. All the women had at one time or another played on Broadway, consequently, they were seasoned performers.

My bunk buddy would go to the theatre each evening, then upon his return he would talk about the rehearsal. He was playing the featured role of the "drunken organist." John Sweet starred as the narrator. The production was being presented at the Haymarket Theatre near Piccadilly Circus. I wanted to be a part of that production. My evenings were free to do whatever I chose, provided I was in bed by curfew time and bed check.

The show was cast. There were no parts, at least I didn't think there were until one night after rehearsal my bunk partner returned to the billet. "Hey Van—can ya play the organ?" Up to this point in time I was always referred to as "Van," never by my first name, Loy.

"Sure—I can play the organ," I quickly responded. I had taken a few lessons in Akron and although I never got a chance to practice on the church organ I did get permission to rehearse on the organ located in the Masonic Temple.

"I think I can get you into the production, Van. I'm playing the part of a drunken man who plays the organ. There is a phony organ on stage. It's just part of the set, but in the wings at the theatre is a real organ. If you'd like to try out for the spot, I'll talk to the director tomorrow night."

My friend was good at his word. "I spoke to the director, Van. He wants to hear you play. He said, 'if this kid plays as well as you think he can, then he's got the job. There's not much time before we open.' Oh, by the way, Van, the director is from Cleveland, Ohio. Since that's next door to Akron, you should hit it off."

The two-manual organ was far enough offstage, the audience was never aware as to where the sound was coming from. The small, two-manual organ was a toy in comparison to the one at the Lutheran Church in Akron. Why I lugged a few pieces of music from Akron all the way to London, I never quite understood except I had sung a number of songs in the concert at Milledgeville, Georgia. Handel's "Largo," was one of those pieces of music I transported from the U.S.

I sat down on the organ bench backstage. I turned on the light above the music rack then placed my music in a pretense of showing my expertise as an organist. The stops on the organ were preset so it wasn't necessary to orchestrate Handel's "Largo." My fingers moved over the ivories like a pro.

"Hey there, Private. That's good! You can really tickle those ivories. If you want the job, ya got it! Be here for rehearsal tonight. We'll be rehearsing every night until we open." The director's words sent me into orbit. I was going to be on stage with real, professional actors even though I was out of sight in the wings.

The play opened to a sold out audience. If I recall, I think even the Royal family were sitting in their box seat just above the stage. When the cue was given for the music to begin my fingers reached for the keys. As the lights dimmed so did the light over the music rack on the organ. I couldn't see the keys and I couldn't see the music. Whatever I played was not Handel's "Largo."

When the final curtain fell, the director wasted no time getting back stage. "Private—you're fired! You said you could play that goddamn organ. What the hell were you doing on those fuckin' keys?"

I was devastated. I walked dejectedly back to the billet feeling like a total failure. My bunk buddy was a compassionate fellow. He knew the hurt I was feeling.

"I spoke to the director, Van and asked him to give you another chance. He said the best he could do was to permit you to carry an umbrella at the cemetery scene."

The offer was more than I hoped for. Each evening I shared the dressing room with other actors and like a real pro, I applied grease paint to my face as if my part was one of the featured roles in Thorton Wilder's "Our Town."

CHAPTER 43

EACH NIGHT AND EARLY MORNING since my arrival in the English capital air raids were as regular as clockwork. Eight o'clock in the evening, midnight and three a.m. I marveled at the GIs' non-concern for their safety who shared my room at No. 8 Green Street. Their prevailing attitude was, "if the bomb makes a direct hit, so what—we no longer have to worry about tomorrow or the war." Either my psyche had not adjusted to that point of view or I was smarter than the rest of the men. At any rate, when the wailing siren sounded, I leaped from my bunk, grabbed my pants and headed for the basement.

It was during the three in the morning raid when I was stopped cold as I made my way down the stairs toward the basement. It was undoubtedly one of the most destructive raids over London since my arrival and it successfully targeted some of the most crucial areas of the city. There was a direct hit on General Montgomery's headquarters located only a few short blocks from Green Street. Incendiary bombs fell on top of buildings and as soon as they hit the solid surface of a roof they immediately began burning, rapidly pushing their flaming devastation from the rooftop to the floors below. The bombs were approximately 12 to 14 inches in length, but their capability of making firewood out of the buildings in which they came in contact was a reality.

I had reached the second floor landing when I was suddenly confronted with the noncommissioned officer in charge of quarters. "Where do ya think yer goin' Soldier? Hold it right there!"

"I'm goin' to the basement, sir."

"Well, Private—you'd better think again. I'm ordering you to stand by that fire bucket. If one of them fuckin' incendiaries reaches this floor, I want you to put the goddamn thing out before it burns the billet down."

I stopped long enough to make a quick response to the corporal in charge. "You go to hell, sir." Without wasting another second, I continued rushing down the long staircase until I reached the safety of the basement.

When the usual morning inspection arrived and all the men from the billet rushed to stand formation in the middle of Green Street, I was ordered to report to the commanding officer. Weighted down with anxiety and apprehension, I entered the reception room of his office. I tapped lightly on his door. A gruff voice on the other side of the door responded with a "Come in!" He was a second lieutenant sitting behind a desk. I immediately came to attention and stood as stiff as an early morning erection. "At ease, Private. I understand you committed a very serious offense during the raid this morning. We just can't let your actions go unnoticed. At no time, Soldier, will you show the disrespect to a superior as you displayed in this morning's early hours. Your actions were no less than that of a traitor. Should I so desire, I could make a case for a court-martial. Shirking your duty to save your own butt could cause you to be placed before a firing squad.

"To show that I'm not one of them chicken-shit officers, I am not going to report this matter to the judge advocate. Instead, when you've completed your daytime duties at the headquarters, you will spend every evening polishing fire buckets from the first floor of yer billet to the top floor. You'll rub those fuckin' fire buckets with steel wool until they shine like a new baby's ass. You are grounded for the next two weeks, Soldier, and confined to your billet during your off duty hours. Dismissed, Private."

Our Town had closed, and since I was fairly new in the largest city in the world, I hadn't encountered much of a social life. At the end of each day, I returned to the billet, donned my fatigues, then sat on the stairs of each landing polishing fire buckets until I could see my reflection in the galvanized steel pails. This time alone gave me a lot of time for reflection. I thought about home and Gerry. I wasn't cut out for a military life, yet it chose me; I didn't enlist. Self-pity set in. I wondered what it would be like to be married, have a home of my own, have kids, and settle into a life of what most people thought was normal. I thought about the fellows I trained with at Camp Wheeler. It was certain that those guys in my platoon were sent to the Pacific. Our entire basic training as a foot soldier was geared toward a war with Japs, not the Germans.

It was during the final moments and the end of my punishment when one night, while permitting the steel wool to grind its way into my flesh, I heard voices coming through the main door downstairs. "Hey, Van! Where in hell are ya? We jes' found out you're in London and we're here to pay ya a visit." It was the familiar voices of Humphrey and Futch.

As the two fellows approached the landing where I was putting the finishing touches on a fire bucket, we grabbed each other like long lost brothers. "We're sure lucky Van. When we got home for a short furlough, the orders were there. We were to report to Fort Meade in Maryland. When we arrived in London, we were assigned to General Montgomery's headquarters. We think we lucked out better than you. At least, we got our own rooms. Those times sleepin' with a room full of GIs and smellin' all those farts are over."

"Boy, that was one fuckin' raid the other morning. Futch still ain't over it. Futch, why don't ya tell Van about it. You really know what this damn war is all about."

Futch took over the conversation. "That was the most horrible night of my life, Van." The air raid siren sounded and I hurriedly dressed, opened the door from my room onto a long corridor and stairway that made getting up on the roof easier. The fellow who had a room next door preceded me up the stairs. We were supposed to throw off the incendiary bombs as they struck the roof and before they ignited. I followed my buddy up the stairs and as he opened the door to step out onto the roof one of those fuckin' incendiaries struck my buddy in the back, carving out a hole from the guy's shoulder blades down to the crack in his ass. He was dead! Dead! Can you believe it! Only seconds before we were kidding about tossing the bastards onto the street below." Futch's voice began to quiver. "I picked the poor bastard up, blood and all. I put him over my shoulder then carried him down the stairs to his room. I laid his bloody body on the bed, then called the CQ to get the medics. The medics came. Their actions were as routine as going to chow. They placed the body in a plastic bag, then wrote, 'Killed in Action,' on the outside of the bag."

I was glad to see my buddies again. We managed to rendezvous at Marble Arch each evening, play a few games at the Penny Arcade, then return to our respective billets. I was invited several times to come and see my Southern buddies' billets. They were within walking distance. There was no such thing as riding public transportation due to the constant bombings and threats of air raids. I was always a bit hesitant to wander far from Green Street for fear I would be caught in an unexpected raid. The tube, or subway, was the only public transportation. It was also the safest place to be in case of a raid. To get to Montgomery's headquarters was not difficult.

Futch was located on the first floor of a town house similar to where I lived, except each GI had his own room. "Come in, Van. Glad to see ya." It was a comfortable room with a fireplace and a window over the bed in which Futch slept. My eyes wandered around the room. On the fireplace mantle my buddy had placed an incendiary bomb. "What in hell, Futch, is that thing doin' there? Didn't they ever tell ya they can explode any time, even if you think they're dead?"

Futch chuckled. "Well—Van—last night when the Jerries came over they must have intended to make a direct hit on me. That son-of-a-bitch came crashing through the window and landed on my bed. I sleep with the window open so no glass was broken. I jumped outta bed then waited for the thing to start burnin', but it didn't do nothin'. I was thinkin' the Jerries sent me that piece of shit as a souvenir—so, I placed it on the mantle.

Meeting with Humphry and Futch was the beginning of a social life for me. There was no one I could relate to in the office and I was beginning to feel a bit lonely in London town. There were times we would go to Rainbow Corners, enjoy some entertainment, have a cup of tea, and sometimes do a little dancing with some of the English girls who came to Rainbow Corners to meet.

A concert was being given by a group called "The GI Glee Club." It was made up of GIs, including officers and enlisted men. I went to the concert and was more than impressed with the sound. I later learned they had sung all over England, broadcast several programs over BBC, and even though their daytime chores were executed as the army required, the men would gather at night for rehearsals.

The leader of the Glee Club was a little German fellow by the name of Heinz Arnold. To this day, I don't know how he managed to get into the American army. If I were to describe Heinz's physical stature, the nearest I could come would be to say he had the stance of Charlie Chaplin. He was short, with a good head of wavy, light brown hair. When he walked, his right foot and his left foot pointed in opposite directions.

Heinz gained considerable recognition in the music world, first as an organist, playing Sunday afternoon organ recitals at Westminister Abbey. When he was inducted into the army, the chaplain wasted no time conscripting Heinz as his assistant.

Colonel Brown was the officer in charge of the G-2 Section. He loved music and with his help, Heinz was able to get access to the best singers the army had to offer to compose a Glee Club, which, by the time I came on the scene, was very well established.

After the concert at Rainbow Corners, I got up enough courage to approach Heinz. "I would like to hear you sing, Van. I think we could use another voice in our group." At that time, I could sing the high baritone parts as well as singing second tenor, so after Heinz heard me sing, I was given a formal invitation to join the group.

Colonel Paul K. Brown watched over each man in the Glee Club like a guardian angel. He booked us in various churches throughout London and into neighboring villages. He arranged numerous broadcasts over the BBC for the English public and gave me my first opportunity to sing as a soloist on a direct broadcast back to the United States.

The dark, drab, cold, foggy, winter months began to subside, and as the days grew longer, more people ventured onto the streets. Street singers strolled along Green Street with their hurdy-gurdys on Sunday morning, rushing to pick up a few shillings as GIs tossed coins from the windows of their respective billets.

As the weather warmed, people took advantage of the spring-like weather to stroll through Hyde Park. I found myself renting a row boat on Saturdays, and I would row around the small lake located amidst statues of Peter Pan, the Pied Piper, and other mythical bronze statues placed throughout the park. Hyde Park was full of action. On Sunday mornings, those so inclined readily took their place on a soap box and expounded their points of view religiously and politically. There was always an audience.

Heinz Arnold knew London. He had opened doors into the arty group in London's West End and the Mayfair society. One of those friends was an English woman who shared ownership of a manor in Craven Hill Gardens. I was first introduced to this kind woman as Miss Grimsley, but when I was accepted into the artistic circle, she would always be referred to as "Grims." Maggie Teyte was a world renown singer who specialized in French art songs. She and Grims had purchased the manor as joint partners. However, Maggie managed to escape the incessant bombings of London by coming to the United States to continue her international career.

Grims was a wealthy woman. She loved creative people, artists of all kinds, writers, painters, musicians—and once included into her circle, her three-story mansion became a home away from home. It was a fully staffed house. I don't recall how many servants, including a cook, she managed to sustain during those war years, but after once being a guest at Grims' Craven Hill Gardens home, they could always look forward to the creme-de-la-creme treatment.

It may have been Grims who encouraged me to contact the Royal Academy of Music and take advantage of some vocal study. Whenever I would sing at one of Grims's soirees, she would say, "Now, Van, I want to hear you sing 'Ave Maria.'" I had only learned Schubert's immortal song in Latin. Grims listened, then when the last note was sung, she spoke. "Van, that was beautiful. That German singer by the name of Richard Tauber is taking this country by storm, when it should be you the English people should be hearing. I don't even like the timbre of his voice."

I did contact the Royal Academy of Music. The head vocal instructor at the Academy was a man by the name of Dr. Arnold Smith. He had a private studio in Kensington Gardens, and fortunately, the subway made a stop within a block of the great maestro's home.

It was a rose-covered cottage. He called his home "Carlind Cottage," because it was a place where Caruso lived when he was in London, and the great singer Jenny Lind often resided there. Dr. Smith increased the size of the house by adding a huge studio onto the small cottage. The studio easily housed a seven- or eight-foot concert grand piano, as well as a harpsichord.

I made an appointment to sing for the famous vocal specialist. When I arrived, I knew immediately I was in the presence of a great teacher. I soon learned that singers from all over the world would seek his tutelage whenever they visited London. I was still a teenager; consequently, anyone over 30 seemed old. Dr. Smith took his place at the piano almost as soon as I arrived. I handed him a piece of music, and with the expertise of a virtuoso, he played the introduction to my song. When I finished singing, he spoke. "Well, Mr. VanNatter, you do have a beautiful instrument. I would like to work with you while you are stationed in London." That first introduction was the beginning of my studies abroad. Twice-a-week, I would board the tube and head for Kensington Gardens.

EASTER OF 1944 ARRIVED IN early April. I was due for some furlough time, or at least a couple days pass so I could get away from the headquarters and visit some of the outlying areas. Gerry had relatives whom she had never met living in an ancient Roman walled-in village called Chester. I had made a promise. If and when I reached the British Isles, I would most certainly find a way of visiting the Gerraghty clan. I sent Tom Gerraghty a short note expressing my desire to pay them a visit. Almost immediately, upon receipt of my note, I had a message saying how delighted they would be if I could visit their home and at least spend one night.

Although I was scheduled to sing some excerpts from the "Messiah" on Easter morning, I managed to get a pass that would permit me to spend Thursday and Good Friday in Chester.

I boarded the train at Victoria Station. As it moved toward the outskirts of London and into the countryside, I marveled at the beautifully manicured gardens and the country manors owned by Britain's upper class. The war seemingly had little or no effect on the grandeur of the luxurious lifestyle of the rich land owners. For the first time since arriving on British soil I found peace. As the train moved farther and farther away from London, the incessant bombings were a thing of the past. The days were longer now; consequently, the Jerries discontinued their 8 o'clock evening bombings, restricting their unwanted visits to midnight and 3:00 a.m.

When the train reached Chester, I disembarked into a medieval world I had only read about in history books. The Eastgate of Chester was the principle entrance to the city. Its famous archway was erected in 1769. This replaced the narrow medieval gateway flanked by octagonal towers. When the gateway was no longer, remains of its Roman predecessors were found incorporated in the ancient stonework.

To the north of Eastgate, I had a fantastic view of the Cathedral and its monastic buildings. On the right near the steps leading down to Frodsham Street, the lower courses of the Roman Wall and the foundations of a thirteenth-century drum tower could be seen just outside the present wall.

Two thousand years had passed since the Romans chose as the site for a fortress a low stone hill at the head of the estuary of the River Dee, which they named Deva. This was the beginning of what is now known as the City of Chester. The village continues to stand as the oldest remaining Roman-walled city in England. The River Dee flows through the heart of the city, and during the thirteenth and fourteenth centuries, Chester enjoyed the status as one of the most flourishing shipping ports in the country. It would have been a cosmopolitan city with ships from the Baltic, Ireland, France, Spain, Portugal, and the Low Countries entering the harbor, but at the end of the medieval period, the gradual silting up of the river began to interfere with traffic to the harbor. Several attempts were made to preserve the navigation, but this was to no avail.

The Irish side of Gerry's family were poor. I couldn't help but recall my own beginnings as I observed their humble lifestyle.

One person stood on the platform as the train slowly came to a stop at the depot in Chester. She was a tall, fiery red, curly haired, slender woman standing alone, letting her eyes scan the train's cars. Few soldiers visited Chester. When I exited the train, I was greeted as if two old friends were meeting for the first time after a long absence.

The luxury of an automobile was rare for most English people. The only means of transportation was either by foot or an occasional taxi. In Chester, I knew that if I were to see the village, I would have to walk. Margaret Gerraghty suggested a tour of the village, but only if I were not too tired after the journey from London. "Our village is not a large one and we are well within walking distance to where my family live."

As we chatted away, I learned much about the history once associated with this bustling port. As we crossed the last bridge, and before arriving at Margaret Gerraghty's home, she pointed out the iron shackles welded to the railings on either side of the bridge. "Loy, you will notice the iron shackles welded to the railings. Many years ago, it was the custom to confine criminals to the bridge whereby they were on constant display. There was no such place as a jailhouse to house the dregs of society. The unfortunate felons would remain shackled to the railings until the day death freed them from those tortuous practices.

"The Romans gave Chester its street plan; the visitor who

walks today along the four main streets within the walls is following the lines laid down by the Roman engineers almost two thousand years ago. Even the smaller streets and lanes, like the one on which we live, perpetuated the memory of vanished features of a village that was once a significant Roman fortress."

We crossed the bridge and Margaret Gerraghty guided our footsteps onto a narrow, cobblestone street. The houses were joined together, forming a continuous row of ancient brick dwellings. As we approached Foregate Street, people opened their doors, curiously seeing who the stranger might be who was a guest of the Gerraghtys. Housewives peeked through their lace curtains, and children stopped playing on the cobblestone street to get a good look at the visiting Yank.

It was a small house in which the Gerraghtys resided, yet it was a roof over the heads of Tom Gerraghty, his wife, Margaret, Tom's elderly mother, and their five-year-old daughter, Shawn. A wood burning stove stood in the corner of the combination parlor and kitchen. There was only one bedroom, and I wondered how the Gerraghtys planned to bed me down for the night They had an answer. I would sleep on the cot placed against the wall separating the parlor from the kitchen.

My overnight visit in the home of Tom Gerraghty was like a day in Brigadoon—a mythical village that could only become a part of this world for one day every one thousand years.

Tom Gerraghty worked in the coal mines in Wales. When Tom arrived home, his face and hands still black from digging coal from beneath the earth, he gave me a warm welcome while his elderly mother poured boiling water into a porcelain basin placed near the stove. When Tom made his transformation from a coal miner to a member of the white race, we all sat down at the small dinner table, toasting each other with a pint of ale. Food was scarce during war time in England. I know this family used much of their allotted rations just to entertain me for one night. This did not deter us from joining in song, in laughter, and absorbing the Irish wit and fun. Time passed quickly.

It was Holy Week, and the Gerraghtys were devout Catholics. They followed the laws laid down by the church religiously, beginning with Lent and the six weeks prior to Easter Sunday. It was a time of confessions and atonements.

On Good Friday, I walked with Margaret Gerraghty to the cathedral. The majestic Catholic Church in Chester stood on the same land century upon century. It was probably one of the finest examples of Gothic architecture in Europe. I marveled at the Catholics' loyalty to their faith and how beautifully this was displayed as I reverently entered the cathedral. Not even the shuffling of feet could be heard as the faithful stood facing the seven icons, each icon representing a specific phase of Jesus of Nazareth's final journey to the cross.

The Chester Cathedral and its gothic structure towered above the city. Upon leaving the church, Margaret suggested we take another route to the train station. "You know, Loy, our town is located right on the edge of Wales. It's only a few minutes' walk to the small bridge spanning a narrow portion of the River Dee. We can walk across the bridge, if you would like, and then you can say you have been not only in England and Scotland, but also in Wales."

Stepping into Wales, I wanted to keep going. There was so much to see and learn. Unfortunately, time was of the essence and I had to return to London. I never saw the Gerraghty family again. Although the post–war years finally erased the pain and suffering of the British people, I did, many years later, make a return visit to London. On that visit we rented a car and drove north toward Chester, stopping at Stratford on the Avon for a short visit, then driving through a thick, unyielding fog to Chester. It hadn't changed much in 20-some odd years. I attempted to find the unforgettable Irish family who had befriended me during the war. It was to no avail.

Chapter 44

IT WAS LATE IN THE evening when I arrived back at my billet in London. Heinz had volunteered the Glee Club's services to perform the Easter section of Handel's "Messiah." We often performed at the small chapel near Grovesnor Square. While I was in Chester, Heinz discovered a WAC who could sing. She was a soprano and was capable of singing the female soprano solo parts. I was given a chance to sing the baritone arias. She was not an attractive girl, but during rehearsal there did seem to be an admiration of each other's talents.

The church was already filled to capacity as we climbed the narrow winding stairway to the choir loft. Every top brass in all of ETOUSA, including generals, colonels, captains, lieutenants, and even a few lowly privates, had found room in a pew to hear the Easter service. Needless to say, I was nervous. The soprano and I, as soloists, took our places in front of the Glee Club, and even though I didn't want to come across as antisocial, I didn't encourage a conversation with any of the Glee Club members or with the soprano who happened to be my colleague. This was not the case with the soprano who happened to be engaged for this one performance.

The soprano was to render her rendition of the immortal soprano arias first. I don't know what happened to the homely, petite canary, but when she began her aria, "I Know My Redeemer Liveth," her voice soared into the upper range, higher and higher, until the notes she sang were no longer a part of Handel's masterpiece: It was as if she undertook the chore of rewriting the "Messiah."

When the WAC took her seat next to me after the final note, she began nudging me in the side and whispering; "How did I do? Was I good? Do you think they liked my singing?" I became more irritated and agitated by the second. I still had to perform. Just as I stood to render the first baritone aria, I turned toward the yakity yaky WAC, looked her straight in the eye, and whispered, "Do you really want to know, or are you seeking a compliment? If you expect a compliment, you are not going to get it. You sang so sharp, I was beginning to wonder exactly what key you were singing in before you brought the aria to an end!"

Heinz had already started the introduction to my big number. Having expressed my viewpoint to the WAC's performance, I let my voice soar and ring throughout the small chapel. As I sang, the top brass turned in their pew and let their eyes wander upward toward the choir loft.

When I sat down, I was well aware I had pushed a sour button with my criticism of the WAC's performance. Coldly, she turned to me and in almost a loud voice spoke. "Private— you will never sing with me again!"

The WAC's rebuttal to my critique was true. I would never sing with her again. For the remaining months I was in London, I continued to sing with the Glee Club, but the prima donna WAC was never again engaged to perform with the Glee Club.

The days were long, and the weather showed signs of

spring as there was more sunshine. The flowers, dormant from a dark winter, broke forth and bloomed as the balmy air of spring replaced the dark, gloomy days of winter. There were fewer air raids by the Jerries, however, during the short period of darkness between midnight and dawn, the Luftwaffe continued to make their nightly visits.

On Mother's Day, 1944, the Glee Club was invited to broadcast a special Mother's Day program back to the United States via the Mutual Network. The program was also aired over BBC. Heinz asked me to sing a special Mother's Day song. The Irish were known for their songs about mothers. There was "Mother McCree," and another one called, "For My Mother." That was the one I chose to sing. It was a tribute to mothers everywhere.

The setting for the broadcast and the performance was hardly the picture of a luxurious studio or a radio station environment. Our setting was located in an open airfield, in the midst of bombers and fighter planes that were fueled and ready to take to the air at a moment's notice. The bombers resembled giant birds earthbound for a short moment prior to taking flight across the English Channel to deliver fire and devastation upon the enemy. The spring rains waterlogged the muddy ground beneath our feet. A light, misty rain dampened our faces. Instead of the luxury of a pipe organ, Heinz Arnold carried a small reed organ housed in a suitcase—the kind used to bring a sense of churchiness to the soldiers in the field and those who served on the front lines. The broadcast was a big break for me. Not only was my voice heard throughout Great Britain, Gerry and her colleagues at Westminister Choir College in Princeton, New Jersey, gathered around their radio to hear the soldier, her soldier, whose dozens and dozens of letters and plans for the future remained protected from anyone knowing our thoughts even though we were separated by many miles.

Congratulations came from the top brass, including General Pleas B. Rogers. The broadcast was so successful, the Glee Club and myself were invited by General Lee to give a command performance concert for England's General Montgomery.

General Lee was billeted in a luxurious manor not far from Grovesnor Square. The General's house had four floors, perhaps five, should one include the basement which housed the kitchen and the kitchen staff.

When we arrived at General Lee's London home, we were greeted by a first lieutenant who served as General Lee's doorman. He ushered us through a marble lobby into a waiting elevator. The elevator operator was a second lieutenant. When we reached the second floor, the door opened, and we stepped out onto a large marble landing. Through an open archway, we could see a large dining table where 12 men sat, each one bearing the features of World War II's most celebrated military leaders.

When the main entrée was served and consumed, General Lee rose from his seat at the head of the table and announced our presence as we stood in the open archway. I carefully observed each man as we stood, wondering why the world's most distinguished brass would choose to gather in one place where one German bomb could turn the building and everyone in it to dust should there be a direct hit.

After each song, the 12 men politely applauded, including General Montgomery. I looked at the familiar face whom I never met personally and had only seen his photograph in the newspaper. He seemed pompous and snobbish, as if he would have to take a bath should his arm accidentally brush against an enlisted man or lowly officer.

When the concert came to an end, General Lee, whom I had met previously, rose from his seat, walked behind the officers sitting at the table, then stood directly in front of us to congratulate us on such a fine performance. He also extended General Montgomery's congratulations. This confirmed my impression of General Montgomery. He apparently felt it beneath his dignity to congratulate each one of us himself.

"I'm sure you men haven't tasted ice cream in a very long time." The general continued speaking after his congratulations. "The servants in the basement have arranged to give you a treat. Thank you again, men." We all stood at attention, then quietly left the inner sanctum of the most favored military leaders of the century.

Two tables, previously appointed by General Lee, were neatly placed to the side of the large kitchen. The general was right—it had been a long time since we had tasted real American ice cream.

I learned early in the game, being a soldier, one just didn't ask why—you just obeyed any order given by a superior. So it was, shortly after the concert for General Montgomery, that I arrived at No. 8 Green Street and noticed an order laying on my top bunk. "VanNatter—you are being moved immediately to the St. James Hotel." It was mid-May, and there was a lull in the nightly air raids. There was the luxury of actually sleeping from bedtime to dawn without being awakened by the wailing sound of the air raid sirens. The weather had changed from the damp, wet, usual English weather to a balmy summer breeze. The St. James Hotel was located at the foot of Green Park overlooking Buckingham Palace. With my move to a private room, I was also given the rank of private first class, one step above the role of a private.

My new quarters were located on the first floor of the old hotel, not far from the front desk. I tossed my dufflebag onto the floor, then stretched out on a real bed, the first I had encountered in the army except for the weekends I spent at Grims in Graven Hill Gardens. It was at the end of my workday and I was tired. Letting my eyes close for a few moments of sleep, the hotel was suddenly rocked by the sound of what I thought was an airplane in trouble. The vibration of the aircraft shook the entire foundation of the hotel. The noise stopped, and then there was a terrible explosion. It was the first unmanned rocket, a flying bomb, to be launched from the shores of France, programmed to land in Great Britain and on the British capital. It was called a V-1.

The explosion caused by this newest weapon of war created by the Nazis was the beginning of a 24-hour barrage of unmanned rockets. When the weather was clear, one could look upward to the sky and easily see the instrument of death. One was never certain where the unmanned bomb would fall. Once the sound of the engine stopped, an eerie quietness filled the atmosphere. The flying bomb then dived toward earth like a falcon in search of its prey. Defying the heavy fogs that rolled in from the sea, the Germans had invented an unmanned weapon that could fly in all kinds of weather. Each day and each hour an increasing number of V-1s were launched from the shores of France. During those times, one could only hear the frightening sound, and if we were lucky, we might escape being another casualty, providing the flying bomb passed the vicinity where no one was standing, only to bring down its devastation of fire on another part of the city.

The war was taking a different turn. The V-1s and V-2s would plague the Allied Forces and the British people until war's end. Psychologically, the V-1 was more frightening than the nightly raids by the Luftwaffe. There was no escape from these missiles. No one knew when the rocket's engines would no longer sound, nor did they know where the flying bomb was going to fall. Frequent London fogs increased the attacks. Horror stories circulated throughout the British Empire. The unmanned military weapon for which there was no defense began to take its toll.

In my new quarters, I no longer had to stand in the middle of Green Street for early morning inspection. It was a much longer walk to Grosvenor Square than the few short steps from Green Street to the headquarters. Often, when I would wend my way through dense fog, I could hear the sound of a V-1 in the distance, and within seconds it sounded as if the bomb was right over my head. I would dash into a doorway, hoping and praying the monster in the sky would pass and allow me one more day of time on earth.

I recall one incident that could not have brought me closer to the front lines of battle. It was a foggy morning and 12 GIs prepared to board an army vehicle parked in front of their billet. The truck was to transport the men to their respective jobs. As the last man boarded the truck, the unmistakable sound of a V-1 rocked the cloudy sky. It couldn't be seen, only heard. The motor stopped. The men, believing the danger had passed, settled in for their ride to their respective jobs. The danger did not pass. The man-made missile seemed programmed to circle over the area where the GIs were billeted. Like a falling star, the missile fell from the sky making a direct hit on the truck carrying 12 of America's finest men to their deaths. There were no survivors. Nothing remained of the young soldiers' bodies except a few dog tags scattered on the pavement and the sidewalk in front of their quarters.

The civilian population was equally vulnerable to V-1 attacks. Like the GIs, the unmanned rockets quickly became a way of life. When the sound of death from the skies filled the air, attempts were made to find shelter, but there was no place to hide.

I remember well the morning a group of civilians waited in line outside a fish market. When the proprietor arrived to unlock the doors to his establishment, the unmistakable sound of a V-1 filled the sky. The market was located in the suburbs of London near an elementary school. The sky was clear on this particular morning, and all eyes of the people waiting in line gazed upward. The missile was clearly visible. It passed over the people waiting to be admitted to the fish market, and from all indications it appeared as if the rocket was destined to land at a nearby elementary school. Instead, the V-1 made a complete circle. It returned and made a direct dive where it blew all the people into oblivion who had hoped to purchase their main meal of the day. The angel of death successfully claimed the lives of each one of those civilians. No one escaped the reaper.

On June 6th, a day that will forever remain in my memory, I prepared to walk to the headquarters. This day was different. Instead of V-1s, wave after wave of bombers filled the sky, all flying toward the coast of Normandy where earlier that morning the Americans and the Allies launched the bloodiest battle of the entire war. The day had come for the invasion of the Continent itself.

I was indeed fortunate on that day in January of 1944, when I found my way to the personnel office and with enough confidence bluffed my way into a job at ETOUSA in London. I would have undoubtedly been one of the soldiers loaded onto an LCT craft and quite possibly have met my end as I tried to make it to shore at Omaha Beach.

We could only surmise the horrible events taking place on that rare sunny day of June 6th. American bombers and the RAF filled the sky over London like flocks of gigantic birds. When the LCT crafts reached the shallow waters of the beach, soldiers jumped into the water hoping to make it to shore, but they were mowed down like a wheat cutter cuts row upon row of wheat. Crimson blood splashed against the shores of Omaha and Utah Beaches. Lifeless, bloody bodies floated in the cold English Channel waters until a strong swell would toss the deceased men upon the sandy beaches of Normandy.

Every soldier, whether nestled in the confines of the English capital, or one of those who successfully touched the sandy beach of France, learned to live each moment as if it were their last. It was the beginning of the road to Paris, where every village must be reclaimed and freed from the tyranny of Nazism and Adolph Hitler's Aryan Race.

Balmy summer evenings in London brought out young lovers to Hyde Park. I had no interest in dating when I joined the army. My thoughts were always about Gerry, and I felt strongly about being loyal, although nothing was cemented as to whether she would marry while I was gone or would she wait for me. I learned much from the lovers laying on the green in Hyde Park. There was no shame nor modesty. Each couple was totally oblivious to others as they performed their passionate love trysts. Should one need an education in human sexual behavior, the soft, green grass of Hyde Park was the perfect place for observation and participation.

Grims continued to occupy my free time with her parties. Even though I was grateful for her hospitality and generosity, I was beginning to feel like I was in a fishbowl among the Mayfair crowd. Craven Hill Gardens was a place that reiterated the old adage, "eat, drink, and be merry, for tomorrow you may die." Heinz had already secured his place in Grims' bed. I often spent the night at Grims manor. The following morning after an evening of partying, I would awaken to the sound of someone entering my room. She was a pretty little maid and one I hadn't seen during the many visits at Grims' manor house. She greeted me with a warm good morning, then proceeded to open the blackouts so I could welcome one of the few bright sunny days in merry ole England. She chatted away with her cockney accent, dashing around my room like a dancing butterfly. Certain I was totally awake, a tray of food she had left in the hallway suddenly appeared, which the young maid placed on my lap as I lay in bed. She gently fluffed the pillows under my head, then placed the tray in a position where I could easily consume a typical English breakfast. Her name was Ada. She made my hormones jump and I finally had the courage before the young lass left my room to say, "When is your day off, Ada? How would you like to have dinner with me, then perhaps we could go dancing or maybe to a movie?"

"My day off is Thursday, sir," she replied. "I'd like very much to go out with you, but I don't think Miss Grimsley would approve."

"Well," I said, "why don't we make this our own little secret?" I was surprised at my boldness. "Miss Grimsley expects me at a dinner party on Thursday, but perhaps I will tell her I'll be working late and cannot attend the dinner. I know we can't be seen together in this house, but perhaps on Thursday evening you could meet me at Marble Arch at, say, 6:00 p.m.

"Remember, Ada, you mustn't tell a soul. This is our secret!"

As planned, I met Ada on the following Thursday at 6:00 p.m. We went to a small restaurant near Hyde Park, after which we strolled through the park, watching lovers stretched out on the cool grass. The thought of lying down on the grass surpassed the idea of going to a movie. I placed my arms around Ada, then gently lowered her to the ground. It was my first time to make love to a girl.

It was well past midnight when I walked Ada back to Craven Hill Gardens. She entered by way of the servant's entrance, and I moseyed back to my quarters at the hotel.

The following weekend, Grims again extended an invitation to Craven Hill Gardens. I secured a weekend pass and as I had done previously, went to my assigned room in the house of Grims. Not a word was mentioned about my tryst with Ada. When my breakfast tray arrived the following morning, I was informed, not by Ada, but another servant, that Miss Grimsley wished to see me in the drawing room.

I quickly dressed then made my way to the drawing room. Grims sat like a queen at the long library table as I entered the room. It was not the usual cheery, musical-sounding greeting to which I had been accustomed. Without hesitating, Grims spoke. "Van—in England we do not associate socially with people who are not in our class. I do not consider one of my kitchen maids to be in my class or yours. You not only insulted me by your absence last Thursday evening, but also that of my guests when you chose to spend an evening with someone far beneath your social status in lieu of my invitation to dinner. I wish to continue our friendship, but don't ever let an incident like this happen again, particularly in my house and with my servants. All right, Van, you must excuse me, I have work to do."

I resented the scolding. I felt Ada was more in my class than the snobs with whom I was constantly being bombarded. I let the incident pass and my friendship with Grims continued. I would spend many weekends and furloughs at Craven Hill Gardens, even when the war came to an end and I would leave France for a few days in England. I would never, however, see Ada again.

Liberation Day in Paris, August 1944

CHAPTER 45

TROOPS LEFT DAILY FOR THE continent, replacing men who either lost their lives or were casualties of war in their quest to liberate France. Once the Allied soldiers established a beachhead on the coast of Normandy, they moved quickly through the countryside and villages, liberating the French people from the tyranny and occupation of Nazism. By August 1944, the south of France was totally liberated at the cost of 2,500 American lives during the first week of fighting. Now, soldiers coming from the north were rapidly closing in on the French capital.

The unceasing buzz bomb attacks were beginning to take their toll. I wanted to leave London and was willing to volunteer for front line duty, providing my commanding officer was willing to release me from my duties at headquarters. Colonel Brown was always my ace in the hole. It was after a Glee Club rehearsal that I approached the officer and expressed my desire to move on.

"Are you certain you really want to go, Van? We'll all be going over soon, but we have to wait until we are more assured the way is clear for us to set up our headquarters in Paris. There is a forward echelon group leaving London at the end of this week. If you are determined to leave London now, I can arrange for you to join the six officers and six enlisted men who are slated to prepare the headquarters in advance of our arrival after the liberation of Paris. You would be the 13th man traveling with the group. You would be transferred to the command of General Pleas B. Rogers. He is in charge of Seine Section. This means you would no longer be a part of Eisenhower's headquarters."

I met General Rogers many times during the months of active duty in London. He had written congratulatory letters in appreciation for my participation in the music scene and had even awarded me a Certificate of Merit. Although I knew better than to volunteer for anything in the army, in this particular case I accepted the challenge to join the 12 men who would be leaving London at the end of the week.

It was the 22nd day of August 1944. The forward echelon group weathered the rain and the fog for a journey to South Hampton. The incessant pouring rain and heavy, watersoaked clouds did nothing to lift the morale of the men riding in an army truck on their way to England's seacoast. Air raid sirens wailed unceasingly as we rode through the streets of London, then through the suburbs and countryside. We finally reached the outskirts of South Hampton and the English Channel. No one was certain as to where we were going. We only knew we would be crossing the channel. We were also aware we could expect to come face to face with an even more hostile world than the buzz bomb attack imposed on the people in the British Isles.

There was little or no conversation among the 13 men chosen for this adventure. Everyone was deep in thought, wondering if we would live long enough to tell others about the tragedies of war. As we motored along the quiet countryside, while listening to the rain beat against the canvas tarp covering the army vehicle, I began to have second thoughts about my willingness to volunteer for this mission.

The truck came to a stop at an army base on the outskirts of the city of South Hampton. We pulled into an all black camp, whose only protection from the elements was tents. I was assigned to a pup tent. An army cot was placed on a muddy, dirt floor. During the night I could see water rising from the opening of the tent until it passed my cot and out the other end of the tent like a fast moving river.

We arrived at the camp just in time for evening chow. I always had sympathy for the black man who was suddenly thrown into a sea of white people. This picture was totally reversed. The all white forward echelon group was indeed the minority.

We lined up for chow along with the black GIs who were assigned to this God-forsaken camp on a more or less permanent basis. A long table covered with a canvas canopy was our mess hall. There was an array of pots and pans on the table, and at the end of the table rested a galvanized steel tub of boiling hot water. This, of course, was to sterilize our aluminum eating utensils before placing them back into our knapsack until the next meal. A black mess sergeant stood on the opposite side of the table and doled out generous portions of food onto each mess kit.

In this camp there was no segregation. The blacks rubbed elbows with whites, and regardless of whether the officer was decorated with one bar or happened to have four stars on each shoulder, it was a time when rank had little or no consideration.

Spam must have had a good year in 1944. On the long chow table the mess sergeant stood behind the largest chunk of spam I had ever seen outside a can. For each man the mess sergeant sliced a slab of the man-made meat as large as a T-boned steak. He then generously slapped the slab of meat onto each soldier's mess kit. Just looking at the spam was enough to turn one's stomach, but when the potatoes and the thick, unappetizing gravy was added to the slop, it was enough to make one vomit. To top off the meal, the sergeant threw canned peaches on top of the gravy and mashed potatoes. I had observed hogs being served with more dignity.

Sometime during the nighttime hours the rains stopped. At daybreak, the sky was clear and the air was warm. As the sun rose over the Eastern horizon, one could even see a touch of blue interspersed with white floating clouds, instead of the heavy rain clouds that had drenched the British Isles for days and weeks. Our black hosts treated us with their version of powdered eggs along with a glass of canned orange juice and some hash. As soon as we consumed our morning meal, we were ordered to board the truck.

It was a remote beach not far from the black camp where we would touch land one more time before crossing a dangerous and oftentimes violent Channel. Anchored at the water's edge was an LCT boat with its mouth open like an eager crocodile preparing to swallow whomever entered its mouth. I had often seen newsreel movies of this type of boat as it was used during the invasion of many Pacific Islands. There were newsreels of the invasion on D-Day showing soldiers being mowed down like sticks as they attempted to jump from the LCT boat into the cold waters of the English Channel. We were fortunate on this particular day. The sea was not angry; it was like highly polished glass. We boarded the strange-looking vessel, and the mouth of the floating vessel closed. The sound of the engine begin to grind, and we set sail across unpredictable waters.

The only ripples in the water were those made by the wake of our small boat. Land mines floated like jellyfish on top of the water. One wrong move by the navigating officer would have been certain death for 13 men assigned to this forward front echelon unit. Minefields were within arm's reach of each man as we stood upright, side by side inside this shallow craft.

As the coast of France came into view, we could see the silhouetted figure of General Rodgers waiting for us, standing on a high cliff overlooking Omaha Beach. Like those men on June 6, 1944, when the mouth of the boat opened, we were ordered to disembark into the waist deep waters and wade to shore. Although time should have washed away the blood-soaked sands, there continued to be residue of young American blood making an indelible red stain on the sandy beach. As each man successfully climbed the steep cliff and reached the point where the general stood, the kind officer firmly grasped each man's hand.

Before boarding the waiting army truck, the general gave us our orders. "Men, we had originally planned on going directly into Paris free of our weapons, but the picture now is very bleak. We are entering into a battle zone where only God knows what we can expect. I am issuing you your weapons so you will be prepared should we come into close contact with our enemy." The general handed me a pistol. He might as well have handed me a broomstick. I had no idea how to shoot a pistol. I had only fired carbines and M1s. "General," I tried to speak, "General, I don't know how to shoot a pistol." The General stared at me in disbelief. Well, Soldier, if you can't shoot a goddamn pistol, trade it for a carbine. I don't have time, nor do we have time, to even discuss the matter. We gotta get goin' men!"

From Omaha Beach to Le Mans was a long, tedious ride. Le Mans would be our first rest stop before continuing our journey into the darkened "City of Light." The streets of Le Mans were void of`all traffic. Only one vehicle dared to travel the road leading to Paris and that was an army truck with 13 men, a general, and a driver. Hours passed and darkness began to overshadow the daylight.

It was well past midnight when we reached the outskirts of Paris. Exploding bombs, Molotov cocktails, and gunfire rocked our truck as we sped down the wide boulevards. Our journey came to an end when the truck quickly turned into a small courtyard off Rue Rivoli. It was a small hotel. I later learned it was called the Hotel Louvre since its location abutted the world-famous Paris museum.

All of us had to use latrine facilities, but I was the first to ask for relief. The general granted my request while the other men lined up in formation to be assigned their specific time for guard duty, which meant guarding the military truck in which we were safely transported into Paris.

The hotel was a quaint place to spend the night. With only candle light, the concierge led me to a room, but did not tell me "WC" meant water closet or toilet. She placed the candle on a table, then lit another candle to light her way as she returned to her desk in the lobby. My room was delightful, with French doors, covered, of course, with blackout curtains. A strange looking commode was installed near the bed. Not understanding that the French refer to a toilet as a WC or water closet, I just presumed the oval-shaped porcelain bowl was a French toilet I proceeded to urinate in the bowl, then searched for a place to flush my body fluid into the sewage system of Paris. I turned a tap and water spewed forth, almost to the point of spraying me in the face.

When I turned the tap to an off position, my golden stream slowly moved out of sight into a hidden, underground, foreign sewer.

Quickly, I returned to the courtyard and took my place in formation. The general completed his assignments for guard duty, then addressed the rest of the men. "You men who have not been assigned a two-hour watch over the truck can go to bed now." The general turned toward me. "VanNatter, I am assigning you and Sergeant Harris the detail of standing guard at my office. You will stand at my door for two hour intervals. I expect you, Sergeant Harris, to stand guard beginning at 7:00 a.m. this morning."

I returned to the assigned room where I had taken advantage of what the French called a *bidet* and laid down on the comfortable bed. I blew out the candle, and in the darkness I crawled into bed. I slept like an undisturbed baby. There were no more air raid sirens, or the sound of V-1s, or bombs exploding. Even the gunfire we heard driving through the city to our stopping off point was quiet. If it did continue, we were not aware of the war of fire in this section of Paris.

A rap on the door at 6:00 a.m. told me it was time to get up. I crawled out of bed then staggered toward the blackout curtains. When I opened the heavy drapes, rays of warm sunshine poured through the glass in the French doors that opened onto a private garden of neatly trimmed grass and tall trees shading a well-appointed patio. Potted blossoming plants were neatly placed on the walkway leading from my room into this unexpected Garden of Eden. For a few brief moments, the war had come to an end.

I glanced at my watch. It was 6:30 a.m. Quickly, I shaved in cold water, brushed my teeth, combed my hair, then dressed in my battle fatigues, including the leggins around

my ankles, then picked up my carbine. I was ready for whatever lay ahead during my first day in the French capital.

General Rogers' quarters were on the second floor of the
hotel. Before opening my K-ration, the army's version of
breakfast, I climbed the flight of stairs to the second floor.
Sergeant Harris was standing guard at the door opening into
the general's quarters. I said my usual "good morning" to
the sergeant, then leaned my carbine against the wall next
to the general's door. With two hours to spare before I was
obligated to fulfill my time as guard, I proceeded down the
stairs without my gun toward the lobby of the hotel.

Loud voices filtered through the thick, double-glass doors
that opened into the hotel lobby. During the early morning
hours, the natives apparently discovered the Americans had
arrived. En masse they pushed their way into the courtyard.
Like being packed within a can of sardines, they forced their
bodies against the glass doors that opened into the hotel
lobby. I don't know what happened to the solider who was
on guard duty next to the truck, but within a split-second the
glass doors crashed open and suddenly the natives ran amok
and began rushing toward me. I was suddenly airborne. My
body was picked up by the mob and I was carried out of the
lobby into the courtyard. High above the crowd I rode on
the hands of the mob. They carried me onto Rue Rivoli like
a conquering hero. Farther and farther away from the hotel
the mob's voices shouted "Viva American! Viva American!"
They handed me a bottle of wine, hoping I would take a swig
and join in toasting the liberation of Paris. The crowd began to sing their version of the "Star Spangled Banner," then
with great gusto, "The Marseille." It appeared as if Paris was
finally freed from the Nazis. I don't recall how many blocks
I was carried above the crowds before I was finally lowered

to the street. Unexpected gunfire suddenly brought the gala celebration to a rapid halt. German soldiers hiding from the American liberators had found their way to the rooftops and began firing at the celebrating crowds below. I saw bodies fall to the ground and in the street as the Red Cross ambulances rushed to pick up the injured and the dead. German tanks appeared, their lethal turret guns blasting at any and all moving living things as the monstrous war machines rolled down the middle of the boulevard. It was impossible for the Red Cross ambulances and paramedics to efficiently come to the aid of the wounded or the slain. I watched in disbelief as I took shelter behind one of the large pillars lining the sidewalk near the Tuillieres Gardens. I had no defense. I could only bring to mind the battlefield exercises in basic training. "Hit the ground, VanNatter! Hit the ground!" "They won't kill me—I can sing!" Those stupid thoughts ran through my mind. I managed to crawl on my belly toward where I thought the hotel was located without being seen by the enemy. Somehow during the melee, I managed to reach the hotel, or what I thought was the hotel. When the shooting started, the hotel management quickly pulled down a solid steel shutter that covered the large plate glass windows and doors opening into the lobby of the hotel. I hurriedly ran into an alley to an open door that I thought might be the back entrance to the hotel. Without hesitation I entered the open door into a dark room. A massive group of natives had also chosen the open door and the dark room in an attempt to escape the rain of fire hitting the boulevards. Hot, smelly bodies were crammed together as they attempted to escape from this unexpected final stand by the Bosch.

When they spotted my presence, they screamed, "Vousette Americain? Americain!" Their hands and arms surrounded my entire body. "Souvenir, síl vous plaît!" They screamed as they grabbed at my battle fatigues. I noticed a stairway. I pushed my way through the crowds, hoping to find some way to get to the upper floors of the hotel. I reached what appeared to be a stairway and as I looked up from the darkened basement room, I saw Sergeant Harris standing at the top of the stairs. "Where in hell have you been, VanNatter? Are you so goddamn stupid ya don't know a war is goin' on? We gotta git outta here and the general wants us out now! Oh, by the way, here's your gun. It might come in handy before we git out of this part of town!"

I took the gun and feeling more like a soldier instead of a stupid idiot, I slung the carbine over my shoulder and rushed from the lobby into the courtyard where most of the men had already boarded an army truck. Sergeant Harris and myself were the last to board. Thinking we were ready to take off, one of the officers yelled, "Hey—I left my helmet in the hotel! I gotta git that helmet! They'll blow my god-damn head off!" The officer jumped from the truck and ran into the hotel. Within seconds he retrieved his helmet, then quickly jumped aboard. Like a bat out of hell, the driver of the truck placed the vehicle into gear, revved the motor, then took off fast enough to fly, filling the air with the smell of burning rubber.

The truck turned onto Boulevard Haussmann. The sound of gunfire began to ebb and we came to a stop in front of the Ambassador Hotel. In peacetime, this was probably one of the most elegant hotels in an exclusive part of Paris. I was assigned a room on the top floor. Of course, there was no electricity, consequently, there was no elevator. I climbed the four flights of stairs to my assigned room. It was a mag-nificent room with a view of Paris and the boulevards that one only sees on a picture postcard. The room was complete with a modern bathroom, a real toilet, a large bathtub, and all the amenities one associates with a complete experience in luxury. I turned on the hot water tap, but the water never reached a temperature above freezing. My ideas of a bath were soon disbanded. The room on the top floor was a typical French design. The hotel's roof curved over the side of the building, resembling icing on a cake. The magnificent picture window presented me with an unforgettable view of Paris, with its wide boulevards and the Tour Eiffel. No one moved on the streets below. The sidewalk cafés were devoid of customers. There was no automobile traffic on the streets. The only vehicles moving on the wide boulevards of Paris were those belonging to the U.S. or British army.

Our K-rations were confiscated and given to the chef at the hotel. At chow time, I discovered for the first time what was meant by French cuisine. The chef turned our K-rations of freeze-dried nothings into a dinner beyond the realm of imagination.

I returned to my room after dinner. I inadvertently failed to close the blackouts before letting my tired body fall asleep. There was a rap on the door. "VanNatter, you will stand guard at 5:00 am." At least it will be daylight, I thought, as I drifted off into a deep sleep.

At midnight, a loud, steady "All Clear," instead of the wailing sound of the air raid "Alert," penetrated the Parisian air; a sound I was quite familiar with during those months in London. When I opened my eyes, I could see flares dropping from the sky, lighting up the city like the noon-day sun. As the flares dropped, I heard the sound of bombs and guns. Hitler was making one more attempt to recapture Paris. German Migs dived from the sky until they reached tree-top level, then began strafing everything that moved. I wondered about the fellow standing guard next to the truck in front of the hotel. Was he able to find shelter from the barrage of bullets? I lay in bed shaking like a frightened puppy.

The raid passed and I wondered if the Krauts would return before my 5:00 a.m. guard duty. I was wide awake when the CQ ordered me out of bed at 5:00 a.m.

I don't recall having breakfast before relieving the soldier guarding the truck. He apparently survived the night raid. I placed my gun over my shoulder in a guard position and took my place in front of the hotel where the army truck remained unscathed from the night's attacks.

Dawn was beginning to turn night into day. I looked upward toward the hills of Montmartre and out of the morning, misty fog, a white cathedral with a magnificent dome rose above the low clouds. It brought back childhood memories, pictures Mom had shown me in a book depicting somebody's image of heaven. I was mesmerized by the vision piercing through the early morning clouds. The magnificent edifice was a symbol of protection for the entire city.

Only one lonely, inebriated soul dared to walk on the sidewalk past the Ambassador Hotel. Closer and closer he came to where I was standing. We were told that should anyone approach the truck, we were to say, "Allez," meaning "go" in French. "Allez! Allez!," I yelled, but apparently the drunk did not understand French with a Midwestern accent. He continued to stagger toward me. I brought my rifle down from my shoulder in a threatening manner, ready to shoot if necessary. I pointed the gun at the man's head. The man's eyes were blurry from the effects of alcohol. His face made a direct contact with my face with a watery, inebriated stare. He said nothing. He turned, then continued his staggering gait along Boulevard Haussmann. I heard the man's voice for the first time when he staggered into a lamppost. "Oh, pardonnez-moi, monsieur." He slowly backed away from the lamppost then unsteadily wove his way from side-to-side down the sidewalk, attempting to make some progress as to where he thought he was going.

When my two-hour duty came to an end, I returned to my room. There were orders lying on my bed. "Private, you will be moving immediately to the Commodore Hotel. This hotel is for officers only."

Moving was nothing new. I placed my personal effects in the dufflebag. I wasn't surprised about the move. To mix the lowly enlisted men with the army's brass was indeed a no-no. I wasn't surprised my moment of luxury lasted only one night. I hadn't taken much out of my dufflebag except for a few toilet articles and a washcloth which I used earlier that morning to give myself a French bath.

The Commodore Hotel was only a few feet from the Ambassador. I walked only a short distance when a gentleman stopped me. He was French but he spoke English quite well. "I would like to speak with you, Monsieur," he said. "I want to thank you for getting the Bosch out of our city. My name is Monsieur Kravatz and I am Jewish. Here is my address. When Paris becomes safe again, I would like you to come to my home for dinner with me, my wife, and my young son."

I thanked the kind gentleman, then gave little thought to the encounter. I settled into what I knew would be temporary quarters. Once ensconced, at least for a few days, I was then ordered to meet with the 12 men with whom I had traveled with from England to France at an old bank building across from the famous Paris Opera House at Place de Opera. This building was chosen as our future headquarters for the Seine Section Command.

Upon entering the building, it was obvious the Bosch had hurriedly abandoned the building. We entered the building with extreme caution. We were quite aware the Germans were masters at creating booby traps in the most unsuspecting places. One could open a desk drawer and the entire desk might explode. One might open a closet door and discover a bomb had been carefully hidden to where it would detonate when the touch of a hand was placed on the doorknob.

On our second day of post–liberation, we discovered the bank building to be a treasure chest for collecting German souvenirs, but only when we were certain all danger of booby traps had passed. There were propaganda booklets and newspapers. There were Nazi insignias which at one time had been a part of a German soldier's uniform.

Those early days following the liberation left much work to be done. We spent days searching for German soldiers who remained in the city long after the Nazis surrendered Paris to the Allies. Sniping was prevalent for many, many weeks post–Liberation Day.

Each day brought an onslaught of German soldiers, dressed in their camouflaged dress uniforms, who had sought refuge amidst the thick, tree-lined foliage lining the boulevards of Paris. There were elderly men, much too old to be fighting a war, who were arrested and brought in for interrogation. They were stripped naked, then given a prisoner-of-war uniform before being shipped to the German POW camp on the outskirts of Paris. It was not unusual to find each one of these men to be walking arsenals. I had never seen so many weapons planted on individuals still fighting for "der Vaterland."

Although the city was supposedly liberated, Paris was not a safe city. For days, weeks, and months, sniping continued throughout the city. We remained in battledress during this entire period of time.

Monsieur Kravatz did not forget his offer for me to come to dinner. Once settled at the headquarters, the gentleman appeared at my office. "Monsieur," he said, "I would like for you to come to dinner this Wednesday night if you are available. My wife and my son are anxious to meet you." That Wednesday evening would be the beginning of a standing engagement with the Kravatz family.

It was a long walk to the Left Bank and to the area near the Bastille. The city was dark, and every doorway was a potential hideaway for harboring a sniper waiting to send a bullet through a wandering GI.

I reached the address Monsieur Kravatz had given me. It appeared to be an old tenement building. I began the long climb of stairs in the dark since there was no electricity and the only light the Parisians had was from candles. The French people were permitted to have enough gas only to prepare one meal a day, and it was this one meal my new Jewish friends wished to share with me. Monsieur Kravatz's young wife was a delight, as was the young son. We sat around the long table discussing the war until late evening. I guess I was too young to realize the dangers that lurked on the darkened streets and in the doorways as I traversed from the Left Bank to the Right Bank. My evening with the Kravatzes was well worth the risk. As I departed, my friends insisted on extending a standing invitation that I was to have dinner with them every Wednesday evening until I would someday return to my homeland.

*Nazi souvenirs collected on Liberation Day as we prepared
headquarters, August 24, 1944.*

CHAPTER 46

GISELE RACINSKY WAS ONE OF the first civilians to be hired by civilian personnel to work for the Americans at the headquarters located in the old bank building across from the famous Paris Opera House. She was assigned to me as my assistant. I can still visualize her appearance as her fashionable shoes, with the solid, thick wooden soles, resounded on the carpetless floor on the first day my new assistant entered my office. Her heavy Persian Lamb coat and her neatly coiffured hair, piled in curls on top her head, gave her the appearance of being much taller than she actually was. The girl's infectious laughter seemed to brighten the entire world and was like a constant ray of sunshine even on the often cloudy, cold Parisian days.

Little did I realize my first introduction to my assistant would be the beginning of a lasting friendship long after the world conflict came to an end and our world was at peace. Only an unexpected death many years later would bring about a finality to a friendship that was born on that September day in 1944.

* * *

Gisele returned to Paris after many months hiding from the Nazis with her father in a small cabin deep in the forest of the Pyrenees Mountains. Gisele and I decided that each Sunday afternoon would be reserved for the two of us to meet and explore Paris. During those weekend rendezvous, I learned about Gisele, the war, and the father she protected. Gisele's father was a Russian Jew. The story of Maurice Racinsky, his marriage to a beautiful French aristocrat and his two daughters began long before Gisele and her sister Francine were born.

During the Bolshevik Revolution, thousands of Russians, particularly those with great wealth, began a slow and treacherous migration from their native land to other countries that might offer them a safe sanctuary from the brutal, barbaric conflict raging throughout their native land. The mass exodus from Russia were people from an elite society who could not accept nor would they accept the new socialist regime sweeping their country. The wealth of Russia at the time of the Bolshevik Revolution had been controlled by the upper class. The conflict between the very poor and the very rich gave cause for igniting an uprising among the downtrodden people of Russia that brought about a revolution that would have a lasting impact on the entire world. The revolution was vicious and bloody. Killings and brutalities of those who had, versus those who had nothing, forced a mass exodus of Russia's elite. Many migrated to China. Others found their way to the United States, and many found refuge and safety in other countries throughout the continent of Europe.

Maurice Racinsky was one of those elite society members where money and the luxury money could buy was plentiful. He was a young man at the time of the uprising. With government control of Russia by the people instead of the czar, it was imperative that thousands of Russia's upper class, whose wealth was accumulated from the backs of the laboring working peons, must exile themselves from their homeland to avoid the consequences which would strip them of their riches, luxurious lifestyles, and could possibly result in their deaths. Instead of following the flow of thousands to other lands such as China or the United States, the Jewish handsome young man migrated to France and to Paris. Hidden on his person and within his luggage were priceless gems, which fortunately were not detected as he crossed many borders of numerous European countries before he reached France.

It was in Paris that the young Russian would begin his trade as a master merchant, buying and selling diamonds and pearls.

He was a good-looking, virile young man, but he was a Jew. Being Jewish was a stigma and not easily acceptable within the upper-crust society. The Russian immigrant was obligated to tactfully infiltrate into a society belonging to the richest of the rich if he wished to establish a successful business.

Marcella Plechette was a young, vivacious, French mademoiselle whose beginnings were deeply rooted within the aristocratic segment of French society. She became known for her physical beauty as well as her artistic bent, which attracted the famous crystal sculptor, Lalique. Maturing into a fully blossomed young woman, Lalique invited the young woman to work with him in his studio as he created his immortal works of art. Marcella was given the position of signing Lalique's name on each piece of crystal created by the famous artist, prior to the work of art being sent to the marketplace and sold to only those who could afford the price of the great artist's creation.

Marcella was born into wealth and into the French aristocracy. Working as an assistant to Lalique was quite acceptable to the family, but the day a young Russian immigrant by the name of Maurice Racinsky entered Lalique's studio, the lives and future for the young French woman and the Russian vender of precious jewels were destined to change.

Marcella was impressed not only by the handsome physical appearance of the Russian lad, but she loved his wit, his kindness, his tenderness and his generosity. The French lass was reared under the auspices of a strict Catholic upbringing; Maurice was Jewish, a religion not exactly compatible with the Catholic Church. Nevertheless, against all objections from her peers and her family, Marcella was determined to wed Maurice Racinsky. She was excommunicated from the church and her family, as well as the aristocratic society into which she was born.

Maurice and Marcella found a roomy apartment on Rue Maubeuge, located near the foothills that ascended upward toward the artist's paradise of Montmartre. It was in this apartment that the young wife would become a partner to her husband in the business of selling not only the precious gems Maurice brought from Russia, but also the importation of precious gems and pearls from other countries throughout the world.

Before the end of their first year of marriage, Marcella gave birth to the couple's first child, a daughter they named Gisele. When Gisele was two years of age, Marcella discovered she was pregnant for the second time. This new addition to the Racinsky family brought forth another daughter whom they named Francine. The two daughters would bring to completion the family of Maurice Racinsky. Although the seed of Maurice was that of Jewish blood, as each child was born,

Marcella, although not in favor with the Catholic Church, would rush to the local parish priest, who in turn baptized Gisele and Francine. This action removed the Jewish stigma bestowed upon them by their father, Maurice Racinsky.

The daughters of Marcella and Maurice Racinsky were equally beautiful. Gisele had the black hair and fair skin of her father. Francine was blonde. Her features were more in keeping with the porcelain-like features of her mother Marcella.

The Racinsky family was happy. All was peaceful and prosperous until war clouds gathered over the European continent. Although both girls were baptized and confirmed as Catholics, half-Jewish blood flowed in their veins.

Germany's tyrannical military might moved like a giant earthmover through Poland, Czechoslovakia, Holland, Norway, Belgium, and finally France. By the time the German army reached the borders of France there was little or no resistance. Nazi forces soon controlled the French capital.

Conquering France, Hitler, as he had done in all the conquered countries, continued his ethnic purge of all Jews. The annihilation of the Hebrew race became front page news throughout the world, yet the free peoples of the world turned their backs on the realities occurring in a world that was no longer safe from the evil, tyrannical forces sweeping across Europe. The devastating air blitzkrieg that brought fire and destruction to the people of Britain, and the unexpected air attack from the East that destroyed much of America's naval fleet in Hawaii, was cause for the leaders of the free world to launch a worldwide conflict against Hitler and his forces. It was the beginning of World War II, probably the most heinous of wars in the history of mankind.

Many people in Paris were of Jewish origin. The French

people were no exception when the Nazi regime decided to rid the country of this ethnic group of citizens. Families were separated and torn apart as they were loaded into boxcars and sent to Hitler's Vaterland, either to work as slaves or—should individuals, men, women, and children have nothing to offer in the slave work force—they were herded en masse to what was referred to as "the showers." Poison gas instead of water flowed from the shower heads. From the showers the dead bodies were then moved to massive crematoriums where they were turned into ashes, or in some cases buried in mass graves. Hitler's domination over mankind was determined to eliminate all Jews inhabiting the continent of Europe and the world.

The terrible and most heinous atrocities committed by the madman and his henchmen were not totally brought to light until an unconditional surrender of Hitler's rampage came to an end and the world was once again at peace.

Gisele was a young teenager at the time the Nazis invaded her country. The Jewish purge was dominant in the minds of the French people, and the young French lass was more than aware of the dangers her family faced. She knew it was only a matter of time before the Germans would come and arrest her father. Each day many of her friends disappeared and it was assumed they had succumbed to being loaded onto a boxcar and shipped to Hitler's Vaterland as slaves.

Although the two daughters were baptized Catholic, they were predominantly Jewish blood. Many of their close friends were Jews. Their father was a merchant, and being a merchant, his world was surrounded by others who in many cases were also Jews. Like thousands of Jewish families, the Racinsky family could also be uprooted from their homeland, sent to a concentration camp or labor camp, and in time be just another statistic whose final journey would end in the gas chamber.

Labor camps and gas chambers were not hidden secrets within the French society, particularly, in the Jewish society. Long before the United States declared war on Germany, the Swedish Red Cross detected and knew about the horrible atrocities being committed behind the Iron Cross of Germany. America knew, but did nothing to bring the slaughter of humanity to a halt.

Gisele attended Mass faithfully. She wanted to help, and with the help of the parish priest she was able to obtain the names of Catholic families who would be agreeable to taking Jewish children into their homes. Gisele manufactured false identification for a number of Jewish children, changing their birth certificates from that of a Jew to that of a baptized Catholic. How many the young Frenchwoman saved from extinction with her acts of bravery, I don't know. As she completed a different identification and birth certificate for each child, she found a home that would most graciously accept the youngster as their own. Many of those children would never see their natural mother or father again.

One year prior to the Allies freeing the French people from the Nazis, trouble began brewing within the Racinsky household. The Racinskys continued to live in their spacious apartment at 36 Rue Maubeuge. From their dining room window, the family could gaze out onto Rue Maubeuge and see the SS Troopers parading in front of their apartment house. There was a great foreboding fear in the hearts of each member of the Racinsky family, especially Gisele. She was certain, unless a plan was created for an escape, that her father and she would be arrested. They, too, would be another number to join the hundreds of Jews daily crammed into a boxcar for the fateful journey to Hitler's Vaterland.

It was wintertime, and before France's liberation, at dawn, that Gisele was awakened to the sound of feet scuffling against the marble floors at the entry to 36 Rue Maubeuge. She could hear the men speaking. Quickly, she rose from her bed. She rushed into the room where her father and mother were sleeping. She reached out to shake her father from a deep sleep. "Papa! Papa!" she whispered." We must go! The Bosch are here! They are in the hall and soon they will be coming up the stairs and rapping on our door!"

Maurice responded to Gisele's plea. Quickly he dressed, then leaned over the bed to give his wife a final farewell kiss. "Come Papa!—We have no time!"

Gisele grabbed her heavy Persian Lamb coat, her father quickly placing a warm cashmere overcoat over his shoulders. The two frightened Parisians hurried into the kitchen. Making no audible sounds, they raised the window which opened onto a fire escape. Quietly, father and daughter climbed through the window and rushed down the long, iron stairway to the ground undetected.

Marcella Racinsky reached for her dressing gown then walked the long corridor to the entry door opening into the Racinsky apartment. Just as she approached the door, the SS troopers broke the door from its hinges and it came crashing to the floor. Facing her intruders like a cornered tigress, Marcella angrily spoke in French and if there was any question about her anger, she could also converse in German. "Who are you looking for?" she screamed as she confronted the four uniformed officers.

In fluent French, an SS trooper said, "We have reason to believe Madame, you have a Jew living here and we have come to make an arrest. Where is he? You know, only too well, the punishment one can expect for harboring a Jew!"

Marcella screamed. "I don't know what you're talking about. You've awakened me from my sleep, you've broken down my door, and now you are accusing me of harboring a Jew. There is no Jew living here. Go ahead! Search the place. You will find nothing!"

The four officers began their search. They opened closet doors and even uncovered the head of sleeping Francine, who lay shivering from fright as she lay in her bed. An officer pulled the blanket away from the young girl's face. Deciding she didn't look like a Jewess, the men prepared to leave the premises. On their way out, their eyes focused on a large safe in a room the Racinskys used as an office.

"Open that safe, Madame!" the trooper ordered.

Marcella quickly retorted. "No!—If you wish to open the safe you must do it yourself. I do not recall the combination."

A cold stare of disbelief stared into the eyes of Marcella Racinsky. The officer turned abruptly on his heels then exited through the broken down door. When the shuffling of German boots reached the ground floor and they made their exit from 36 Rue Maubeurge, Marcella walked from the long hallway into the kitchen. The window was open. She knew then her husband and daughter had made their escape.

GISELE AND HER FATHER, MAURICE Racinsky, began their long walk to St. Lazarre Station. Like an animal trying to escape its predator, they darted into darkened doorways each time the sound of a motorcycle or stomping boots could be heard echoing upon the cobblestone streets.

The night of terror seemed to have no end as they moved swiftly from Rue Maubeuge to St. Lazarre Station. Gisele purchased two train tickets to Port La Douane, a place of refuge where the family often vacationed. It was a seaport village. Long before the war and the Nazi occupation of their beloved France, Hotel Les Cygnes served as a favorite Shangri-la for the Racinsky family. It was in this small hotel that Gisele and her younger sister were conceived.

"Hurry, Monsieur et Mademoiselle," the train master said as he motioned to the two fugitives to get aboard. The train was beginning to slowly move away from the platform. Gisele and her father hurriedly climbed aboard, saying nothing to the train master other than "Merci Monsieur." There were no eyes of suspicion directed toward daughter and father as they made their way down the long, outside corridor in search for an empty compartment. The escaping Parisians wanted a place to themselves. Near the end of the train's last car was an empty compartment. Gisele and her father seated themselves on the long bench-like seat, then snuggled together, feeling safe for the first time since they were so rudely awakened in the early hours of the morning. Gisele gently placed her Persian Lamb coat around her father and herself. Only dawn would awaken them from their restful sleep.

The train stopped at small villages just long enough to let more travelers aboard. No one made a gesture of disturbing the privacy of the two fugitives. The countryside looked so peaceful. The cattle and horses grazed in the green pastures. Deep in thought, father and daughter wondered if the terrible war had bypassed the countryside where people continued to live in peace.

Throughout the daylight hours, the train rolled over the

metal tracks, taking Gisele and her father farther and farther away from the City of Paris. Daylight turned into darkness and the conductor announced, "Port de Douane." There
were no waiting passengers to board the train, nor were there
people anticipating the arrival of relatives or friends. The
train's platform was totally void of people. Gisele and Maurice quickly disembarked, then began the long walk over the
cobblestone streets toward the Hotel Les Cygnes. An occasional sound of an SS trooper's motorcycle could cause the
two fugitives to dart into a darkened doorway.

As they approached the inn, an elderly concierge could
see the unexpected visitors through the leaded picture window of the lobby. He was no longer the youthful man Maurice and Gisele remembered. Like so many, age advanced
rapidly for those who hoped to survive the Allemande's evil
occupation of their land.

Cautiously, Gisele and her father entered the hotel. "Monsieur et Mademoiselle, you arrive early this year." The concierge continued, "May I inquire as to why you have chosen
the wintertime in which to pay us a visit?"

Maurice, always cautious of a listening ear, quietly related how the Germans came to their apartment in Paris in
the middle of the night and how his daughter helped them
escape.

"You cannot stay here, Monsieur. If you register, the
Bosch will most certainly arrest you. I do have a plan that
might help you. But, first, let me find a room which will be
least suspect should the Bosch come tonight to check the registrar."

The elderly concierge, bent over with rheumatism and
age, led the two Parisians to the second floor, then out onto
a small veranda where a flight of stairs led to an attic room.

Quietly, the inn keeper removed a key from his pocket and unlocked the door opening into a small room. He then lit a candle resting on a table beside the bed. A gas jet stood on the floor in front of the bed. The concierge reached in his pocket for a match, then ignited the gas heater. Within minutes the room was warm. Seeing his guests were safely ensconced, the concierge prepared to leave the room. "Monsieur et Mademoiselle, you must not leave this room, not even to use the water closet on the second floor. If you need to use the toilet facilities, then use the chamber pot that is under the bed. In the morning you must prepare yourself for a long journey. I will do everything I can to help you escape the Bosch, but now you must rest. I will awaken you when I think it is safe for me to return and bring you some food."

Gisele and her father lay on the bed. Their deep sleep was disturbed when the sound of a gruff German officer's voice noisily echoed from the ground floor and lobby to the hidden room in the attic where the two sought sanctuary. Gisele was first to be awakened. She could hear the guttural sounds as the officer and the concierge spoke.

"Monsieur," the officer asked in a polite manner, "have you seen an older man and a teenage girl pass this way. We have reason to believe they left Paris early this morning in an attempt to avoid being arrested. You would certainly recognize them since they are Jewish. As you might be aware, Monsieur, Der Fuhrer is attempting to rid France of all Jews."

The concierge was fluent in French and in German. Keeping his composure, he spoke to the SS officer in German. "Herr Commandant, people do not come to the inn as readily as they have in the past. The war has made travel impossible. I have had no new people register at this hotel for some time. Herr Commandant, I know the rules. All passports must be left in my possession and the registrar must be in order when my books are inspected at midnight. If you like, Herr Commandant, you may look at the registrar. Perhaps you would like to search the rooms on the second floor."

Frightened, Gisele shook her father. Papa! Papa! The Bosch are here! They are interrogating the concierge. I heard him ask our friend if two Jews came to the hotel this evening. What are we going to do, Papa?"

Gently, Maurice placed his protective arm around his daughter: "Remain quiet, ma cheri. It is going to be all right. Our friend will not betray us."

The German officer left the inn satisfied the concierge told him the truth. The inn keeper hurried to the attic room. Lightly he rapped on the door. Maurice rose from the bed, then stood in front of the door, "Who is it?" he asked in a muted voice.

"It's Monsieur Defarge," the voice on the other side replied. Maurice quickly opened the door. When the inn keeper entered the room, he closed the door, locking it with the key. "Monsieur et Mademoiselle, you must leave here before daylight. The Bosch were here and they suspect that two fugitives who left Paris on the early morning train are now in Port de Douane. Maybe I can help you."

"I have a dear friend who has a cabin high in the mountains whom I believe will give you a safe place to stay. The Allies are making rapid headway in freeing our people from the Boscsh, and the French underground are also doing their part to bring this terrible war to an end. It should not be many more months before this human misery will cease. It's a long climb up the mountainside. As you reach higher elevations you will undoubtedly be confronted with snow. I will prepare some food for you for your long journey and will also give you a letter as an introduction to my good friend, Monsieur de Jordan. As you near the cabin you will see a cave. I would suggest you try to make it to the cave before darkness sets in at the close of day. There you can bed yourselves down for the night, then perhaps you can reach Monsieur de Jordan's cabin in the morning. The cave is easily visible, so please follow my directions carefully."

The concierge removed a piece of paper from his tattered coat. On the paper he drew a crude looking map showing a way to escape the village without being detected, as well as landmarks to look for as the fugitives searched for the cave.

Before the first sign of daylight, Gisele and her father left the security of the inn. A heavy fog rolled in from the sea, covering the entire village as the two fugitives stepped onto the street. Quietly they walked, always on the alert. The Bosch continued to sleep. The blanket of fog presented them with a protective covering. When they reached the edge of the village, they began a long climb up the mountainside. The higher their feet carried them the trees seemed to reach out with an arm of encouragement. Snow began to fall from the leaded sky, covering the ground already white from a previous storm. The only sound heard was the treading of their cold feet on top of the winter's snow. It was a world of silence. Neither daughter nor father spoke. An occasional jackrabbit crossed their path, or a deer dashed in front of them in search of food. The creatures of the forest would glance at the two intruders on their land, then move on through the deepening snow for a sign of vegetation that would alleviate their hunger.

Throughout the day, father and daughter trudged their way up the mountainside. Dusk began to settle in over the cold, wintery land. Farther and farther the fugitives moved upward. When it appeared darkness would bring their journey to a halt, Gisele spied the opening into the haven promised by the concierge. "Papa! Papa! There's the cave, Papa! I see the cave! It's exactly at the place Monsieur Defarge told us and the one he has drawn on this map."

The entrance to the cave was small. The fugitives could only enter by lying flat on their stomachs, then crawling through the tiny opening leading into a large, underground room. From the opening into the cave, enough daylight penetrated the darkened haven to see someone else had preceded them. They had left a stash of sticks and brush to build a fire. Maurice quickly built a fire and as the warmth from the fire replaced the cold outside, Gisele unveiled the food Monsieur Defarge had so kindly prepared. For the first time since their departure from Paris, there was a sense of security and safety. Gisele and her father quickly ate the food. Their hunger subsided, they lay on the ground in front of the burning embers. Sleep was most welcome for their tired minds and bodies. All was at peace.

Barking dogs awakened Maurice. It was the dawn of another day. He crawled from his resting place next to his daughter into the daylight. A tall man stood at the opening of the cave. Maurice steadied his body in an upright position as he faced the stranger. "Bonjour Monsieur!" Cautiously, Monsieur de Jordan moved toward the dark-haired, bearded man. "What can I do for you, Monsieur? Who are you? It's much too cold now to be in the forest. My name is de Jordan, Monsieur. What is your name?"

Maurice Racinsky quickly announced his name, then reached in his pocket and withdrew the handwritten note from Monsieur Defarge. He handed the note to Monsieur de Jordan. As the man quickly read the note, Gisele crawled from the cave, then stood next to her father. "This is my daughter, Gisele, Monsieur. We need a place to stay. The Bosch are searching for us this very moment because I am a Jew and my daughter is guilty of forging birth certificates for many Jewish children, then placing them in Christian homes so they would not be sent to some labor camp or, as we all are aware, be taken to their untimely deaths in a gas chamber.

Without waiting for all the circumstances which had driven this man and his daughter from their home in Paris to the bitter cold of the forest, he spoke. "Come now; I'm sure you're very cold and hungry. We will discuss your situation after we have some food and you are given some warm clothing."

Gisele and her father followed the kind man to a rather spacious cabin not far from the cave.

Once inside the cabin, Monsieur de Jordan spoke. "I will prepare you some food. Please remove your clothing and I'll find something warm and dry for you to put on. Sit down there next to the fire. After you have eaten a good breakfast, I will show you to a room which will be your home until this terrible war comes to an end. There are two beds in the room and a radio where you can hear all the latest news. The Bosch seldom come this far into the forest, so I am quite certain you'll be safe. However, you must not at any time attempt to locate your family in Paris. Any action in that regard would only alert the Bosch, and they might begin searching these forests for you and perhaps others who have sought refuge on this mountain.

The kind good Samaritan had not failed his friend, Monsieur Defarge. The elderly innkeeper at Port de Douane had successfully prevented the two fugitives from being arrested and probably annihilated. Monsieur Defarge's voice seemed to speak reassuringly, "My friend, Monsieur de Jordan will give you refuge and a place to stay where you will be safe and warm until war no longer exists in our land and the rest of the world."

It was a warm, sunny day in August 1944 when the radio newscaster announced the liberation of Paris. Gisele and her father did not have to walk down the mountainside. Monsieur de Jordan gave his two winter guests a ride to Port de Douane. They entered the Les Cygnes this time with no fear and no need to hide. Within two hours after their arrival, they bid farewell to Monsieur de Jordan and Monsieur Defarge. The train arrived, and without fear, Maurice and Gisele boarded the same train on which they made their escape. The ex-fugitives were on their way home to Paris.

After the war: Loy, Toot Sweet, Gisele, and Walt Treadway.

Girls, girls, girls!

The Racinsky family.

A Sunday afternoon along the shore of the Seine.

CHAPTER 47

NOT ALL FRENCH PEOPLE WERE pleased to see their liberators. Artists, writers, singers, actors and even prostitutes often collaborated and prospered during the German occupation of France. Chavalier was an actor and a personality with a high reputation, not only in France but in Hollywood. During the occupation of France he never ceased entertaining the German occupational forces, nor was he ever charged with being a collaborator and penalized for his participation when the war finally came to an end. Germain Lubin, however, was a different story. She was a world famous Wagnerian soprano who gained international fame on the Wagnerian stage. When the Nazis took over France, many of her friends were Germans and devoted fans to the famous singer that reverted back to the time she starred in many of Richard Wagner's immortal operas at the Festspielhaus in Bayreuth, Germany. When the German forces marched into Paris, she often guested many of the soldiers in her home.

The Metropolitan Opera in New York City made several attempts to bring the great singer to the United States when Kirsten Flagstad, the leading Metropolitan Wagnerian soprano, decided to return to Norway to be with her husband at the beginning of the war. Hitler refused to give the great singer a permit or visa to leave France during the occupation. Lubin's career continued to flourish in Europe as one of the world's greatest Wagnerian artists until the war came to an end. It was at a time when those who collaborated with the enemy were punished. Germain Lubin's punishment was that she would never again be permitted to sing in France or appear on the operatic stage.

Prostitutes who flourished under the German occupation and had even participated in Hitler's baby factories remained loyal to the Third Reich. When the American soldiers arrived in Paris, they often catered the brothels, and in many cases they made a date with death. It was not unusual for a soldier to proposition a lady of the night, accompany her to what he thought was her place of business, and prepare the preliminaries for the sexual act. Then, when the girl was lying beneath his naked body in preparation for sexual satisfaction, she quietly reached under the pillow, withdrew a sharp knife, and plunged it into the back of the unsuspecting soldier. For the American soldier it was instantaneous death. The prostitute would leave his bloody body in the room, then depart from the premises. The concierge would discover the body. She would notify the prefecture de police, who in turn would notify the military. In turn, the military would contact the family back home with a statement that the young American soldier was killed while in the line of duty.

The weather was beginning to turn from an Indian summer to a cold, wet fall. Gisele and I continued our Sunday rendezvous. Vendors stood on the street corners roasting chestnuts. I would often buy a bag of the warm, freshly roasted chestnuts, then we would sit in a nearby park, grasping the warmth from the chestnuts in our hands before placing them in our mouths. It was during one of our Sunday afternoon tête a têtes that Gisele invited me to her home on Rue Maubeuge. For the first time since arriving in Paris I would meet her mother, father, and sister Francine.

Being invited as a guest in a French home was a rarity. I learned the French were more inclined to meet at a café than having a guest in their home. My first experience with the Jewish tailor was an exception.

I arrived at 36 Rue Maubeuge at the appointed time. Memories of Gisele's accounting of the night the Gestapo climbed those same flight of stairs in an effort to arrest she and her father flashed through my mind. Reaching the second floor, I crossed the wide hallway to the massive entry door opening into the Racinsky apartment. I rang the bell and when the door opened, the most extraordinarily beautiful woman answered the door. "You must be Van." She spoke in broken English. I soon discovered only Gisele and her sister Francine could speak my language. "Entre' Monsieur," she said in French as she warmly took my hand, then ushered me down a long hallway toward the parlor where Maurice Racinsky sat with his two daughters.

Maurice Racinsky face revealed an unforgettable gentleness. His black hair framed his tender face. He sported a fully grown beard, which only accentuated the man's handsome features. When all formalities were concluded, we moved from the salon into the dining room.

The table setting was a work of art. The finest china and crystal goblets were placed on a spotless white table covering. Silver and china glistened from the light of the candelabra resting in the center of the table. A number of dishes were properly placed for each item to be served and consumed during the dinner hour. The formality was much different than with the poorer family—the Jewish tailor with whom I had a standing Wednesday night dinner engagement,

Dialogue during the dinner hour was spoken in French, and as Monsieur Racinsky poured the wine, which he diluted with water, Gisele and Francine made an effort to interpret the ceaseless French dialogue into English for my benefit. Dinner wine was scarce and I noticed that not only did Papa Racinsky dilute the precious nectar, but Monsieur Kravataz also found it necessary to water the wine, hoping to make the supply last a bit longer.

When the final dinner course was served, Marcella Racinsky placed a small liqueur glass before each one of us sitting at the tables. She opened a bottle of liqueur, then poured the contents into each tiny glass to the brim that was placed at the side of each table setting. It was a drink the French people called "Calvados."

At the Terminus Hotel I had observed American GIs tip the bottle to their lips and drink the over 100 percent alcohol as if they were drinking a bottle of beer. I attempted to follow my peers and as I did so the room went blank. Like a blind man, my fingers touched the wall of the wide corridor as I gingerly attempted to find my way back to my assigned room. When I reached the room I lay on the bed. It was a matter of a few hours before my eyesight returned and I was able to rise from the bed and stand erect. Nevertheless, so as not to embarrass my hostess, I managed to let the strong alcoholic after-dinner drink enter my mouth. On its way down I could feel the burning sensation as it reached my stomach. I lifted my glass, then joined in with a "votre sante'."

From that first day of liberation I quickly complied with the custom of kissing each other on the cheek upon a first greeting, then again when it was time to say goodbye or goodnight. I graciously thanked my hostess and host for a pleasant evening then proceeded to gently kiss Gisele and Francine on the cheek. I then kissed Gisele's mother. As I prepared to leave, Gisele stopped me. "No, no, Van, you cannot leave until you kiss Papa!"

My skin, which was a pale white due to little exposure to the sun either in England or since my arrival in France, turned a beet red. I'd never kissed a man, not even my own father. Maurice Racinsky quietly sat at the head of the table waiting for my next move. I took a deep breath, then with all the courage I could muster, I let my body bend low enough to come face to face with Maurice Racinsky. Quickly, I let my lips touch the bearded man's cheek.

That memorable evening at the home of Maurice Racinsky was the beginning of many dinners and many parties — 36 Rue Maubeuge became a home away from home.

Chapter 48

Hotel Terminus was not a luxury hotel. Although each soldier assigned to Seine Section was given his own room and a bed in which to sleep, it was soon decided by the top brass that that arrangement was much too luxurious for the lowly GI. We were on the move again. This time, it was to an abandoned department store, formerly known as "Magazin Dufayel." This was not only to be our permanent billeting facility, but it was also a transient stopping off place for GIs scheduled to go to the front line of battle.

The building had two floors. Double bunks were lined up against the walls of the first and second floor. Only one latrine accommodated the men on the first floor and one latrine on the second floor. We were issued burlap mattress ticks, and in one corner of the room were large stacks of straw. Sleeping on straw was nothing new in my young life. As a child, a tick filled with straw was the only bed we knew. However, our ticks were not made of a porous burlap where the straw could easily come in direct contact with our bodies.

I shall always recall that first night in our new quarters. It was the beginning of a very complicated life. On the lower bunk next to mine, a GI spoke. "Hey, Soldier. I've got a problem. I don't know why I did it, but I did it; now I have to make a decision and hopefully it's goin' to be the right one. I got this six-week old puppy I found on the street when I arrived in Paris." He reached under his army blanket and brought forth an adorable bundle of black fur. "I'm headed for the front tomorrow mornin'. I can't take this dog with me. I was wonderin' if you'd take my dog?"

He handed the puppy to me. When I cuddled the pup next to my body, I was stuck. There was no backing down. I placed the pup beside my bunk thinking the lower bunk was practically on the floor and the animal would know I was within its reach. The dog had other ideas. She began screaming and it wasn't until I reached down and put the pup under my blanket that she became quiet. Even before I was asleep, the four-legged creature began to snore.

The following morning, I took the dog with me to the office. That morning was probably the beginning of a lasting friendship with Gisele. She found my new charge a home, but only until the weekend, then I was obligated to take care of my own mutt. I became a weekend father to an English spaniel that Gisele and I named "Toot Sweet."

A GI, a blond-haired chap by the name of Percy Hampton, a Canadian, was assigned to an upper bunk on the second floor of the Magazin Dufayel. He was given the job of working with me, wading through mountains of military papers. How Hamp got into the American army, I don't know, nevertheless we bonded as buddies. At that time the lower bunk under Hamp had not been assigned, so I made my move from the first floor to the second floor of the billet. This was an advantage. We were given a locker in which to hang our clothes and keep our personal effects, but we were never permitted to lock the lockers. Hamp was not pleased to sleep on straw, nor was I. We went nosing around the ancient department store the former German army used as a warehouse. We came upon a mound of raw silk they used to make parachutes. The idea of a silk mattress passed through Hamp's mind at the same time it flashed through mine. "We'll create a silk mattress by filling the burlap tick with raw silk."

Our first night on our beds of silk was pure heaven. By morning, the shape of our bodies was deeply and perfectly molded in our luxurious silk-filled mattresses. There was one problem: the soft, silk cloud we envisioned turned overnight into stone.

The morale of those men billeted in this former German warehouse was low. It was so demoralizing that many GIs chose to stay in a hotel and pay for a night's sleep rather than sleep on top of a wooden bunk at the Magazin Dufayel. Many bunks remained empty, and soon there were orders announcing that bed check would be taken twice a night— one at 8 p.m. and again at midnight. If the soldier had not returned to the billet by midnight, he was considered AWOL and that could lead to serious consequences.

Hotel rooms were cheap, even something a private first class could afford. Hamp and I took advantage of our raw silk mattresses, which took on the shape of our bodies. Each morning we carefully pulled the blankets tightly over the burlap tick, making the most perfectly made bed in the barracks. Before taking off for our hotel rooms, we would return to the billet, let the blankets fall in an exact replica of our sleeping bodies, cover our pillow, then it was off to the nearest hotel in Pigalle. So as not to push our luck to its fullest extent, there were some nights we would sleep at the Magazin Dufayel.

Hamp was worldly and much more sophisticated than myself. He soon conquered the affection of a young female teenager by the name of Renee Chopin. Not only was the girl pretty, she came from an affluent French family. Of course, one didn't have to know Hamp for a long period of time before he or she realized the young Canadian could smell money.

The family of Rene' took to Hamp. He did have charm and after a fashion could speak a little French They invited my bunk buddy to dinner several times a week and practically accepted him as a possible son-in-law. It was at one of the dinners that Hamp mentioned his buddy in the army was an American singer. Monsieur Chopin's ears pricked up like a rabbit deciding he should run. He, himself, was the leading bass with the Paris Opera. Anyone who sang with the Paris Opera was a superstar, and even though I had a certain amount of envy, I was also totally impressed with their talent. A morning after one of Hamp's trysts with Rene' and a good dinner at the Chopin's, Hamp arrived at the office full of excitement. He strolled over to my desk. "Hey Van, I had dinner with the Chopin's last night. I discovered he is with the Paris Opera and one of their leading bass singers. I told him all about you and he wants to hear you sing." Hamp had only heard me say I was a singer. He never heard me.

The following Thursday, my buddy and I walked the dark streets of Paris to an elegant section of the city and the pretentious apartment building in which the Chopin's resided.

Monsieur Chopin was a distinguished looking man, rather tall, with silvery gray hair. When the dinner hour came to a close, he ushered us into the salon. Madame Chopin sat down on the piano bench, then placed her hands on the keyboard of the grand piano. Monsieur Chopin was going to sing for us. It would be an aria from a French opera written by Gounod entitled "Faust." When the man reached the last note of the aria, we all joined in applause.

Before he sat down, he asked if I might consider singing for his guests. I agreed and as I had in the past, I sang Richard Wagner's "Der Abendstern," from Tannhaueser.

"Monsieur, you sing very well." Our host continued. "I have a dear friend who is head of the vocal department at the Paris Conservatoire. I think he should hear you. I will be happy to make an introduction. I will arrange a meeting for you this coming week. My friend's name is Monsieur Pierre Paulet."

Hamp and I had to return to the Magazin Dufayel before bedcheck. It was a long walk from the Chopin apartment, but though the evening was still young, we decided to stop at a small café for a glass of wine. We entered the café next to the picture window overlooking the boulevard. People were more inclined now to promenade the sidewalks than they did prior to the first few weeks post–liberation. I paid little attention to the patrons sitting in the café. As Hamp and I conversed a well dressed man sitting near our table eyed us suspiciously, then withdrew from his side pocket a gun. I paid little attention to the man as we entered the café and certainly was not aware that a gun was being pointed toward the back of my head. A gendarme happened to be passing by the outside of the café. By chance he glanced through the window and could easily see Hamp and me sitting at the small table having a glass of wine. His sharp eyes also focused on the well dressed man who sat only a short distance from where we sat. The gendarme spotted the man removing the gun from the side pocket of his coat. The police officer rushed into the café and like an attacking tiger, he grabbed the man's arm, causing the would-be shooter to drop his deadly weapon. When the officer questioned the gunman, he did not speak French. German was his native tongue. The man was quickly handcuffed and taken away by the police. I had escaped by a hair's breath of being another soldier killed in the line of duty.

Hamp's French was more fluent than the few words I spoke or had learned. It was on our long walk back to the Magazin Dufayel that Hamp suggested we both get some private tutoring to learn the French language. Near the headquarters was a small school called "Le Carpentier." To fill our evening hours with something constructive and useful, we enrolled in the school with the sole purpose of learning how to converse with the French people. Even though I spent much of my free time with Gisele, she only chose to speak English and made no effort to help me learn to speak her native tongue. There were only two students in the class—Hamp and myself. The professor was an elderly man. He was definitely a stereotype as to how I thought a professor should look and act. He was a little man with a full head of gray hair and a well-groomed goatee gracing his handsome, dignified, chiseled face. Within a few lessons I learned to speak a limited French where I could easily find my way around Paris. The man's ability to teach the French language was soon to be our loss. We arrived at the school one evening at our usual time and found the room to the classroom locked. It was then we discovered that our kind professor, at some time during the evening hours, suddenly died. I never bothered to seriously learn to speak French after that. I would pick up words here and there and manage to converse in a fractured way, but to fully comprehend and speak fluently would never again be a part of my learning.

Monsieur Chopin, as promised, did arrange an audition for me at the Paris Conservatoire. I had no idea how 1was going to pay for the lessons should I decide to study. Monsieur Paulet did appear to be impressed after I finished my audition number. He wanted me to study with him as a private student, and when I inquired as to how much my lessons were going to cost, his reply was, "Monsieur, I am not going to charge you. After all you have done for our country, to give you lessons is the least I can do to repay you." He then began to search through a stack of music and finally discovered an aria from an ancient French opera. "I think this would be a good piece of music for you," he said as he sat down at the piano and began to play the introduction. It was a lyrical tune and the professor was correct. The tune did compliment the timbre of my voice. "For our next lesson," he said, as he handed me the music, "I would like for you to have this piece memorized." It was settled. I had been accepted as a student. "You must come every week at least twice for lessons," he said, as I prepared to bid the kind man a goodnight.

Monsieur Paulet was a rather large man, especially since most Frenchmen are small in stature. He played the piano well, however, but when the man demonstrated his idea of "how to sing," doubts were created as to whether this man was the right teacher for me. By the third or fourth lesson, I knew his technique for singing was doing more harm than good. I was, however, introduced to a French repertoire I would never have known had I not met Monsieur Paulet.

Heinz Arnold and Colonel Brown successfully recruited the former members of the GI Glee Club. Concert dates and radio broadcasts via Paris Radio were becoming more and more frequent, which, of course, left little free time for any other activities: During my absence from the group, Heinz acquired the talents of a baritone from Tennessee by the name of Walter Treadway. He wasn't handsome, but he could sing—he could sing like I wanted to sing but didn't know how. Walt was skinny. His hair, like my own, was beginning to get a bit thin, particularly around the crown. His face resembled more the face of a prizefighter than a singer. Walt was assigned as the Protestant chaplain's assistant, the Chaplain being a dyed-in-the-wool Baptist from Texas, the same religion as Captain Rankin at Camp Wheeler, Georgia. The job provided Walt with consistent transportation. He always had access to the chaplain's jeep. Walt never had to walk.

We had a mutual admiration going. He liked my singing and I liked his. We became good friends. In fact, over a period of time, my friendship with Walt overshadowed my association with Hamp. We would double-date occasionally, with me always choosing to be with Gisele. Gisele introduced Walt to a girl by the name of Claude, and we became a foursome. Hamp met a more worldly wise mademoiselle by the name of Muriel. Occasionally, the six of us would go out together, but most of the time it would be Walt, Claude, Gisele, and myself. It was during those free time get-togethers that I really bonded with Gisele. She had taken me to her home on Rue Maubeuge many times, and the Racinsky family soon became my family. I would share dinner with them an average of once a week. This, of course, was always a relief from the slop the army continued to serve the GIs stationed in Paris.

The GI Glee Club was in demand. The places we were asked to perform soon took precedence over any extra activities in which I might choose to become involved. We sang in various churches, including Notre Dame cathedral and the Madeleine. When we performed at Notre Dame, instead of being heard in concert from the choir loft situated high above the huge sanctuary, we were asked to take our place on the grand altar of the great cathedral. Here we had an unobstructed view of the magnificent edifice and the famous rose-stained glass window situated just above the magnificent five manual pipe organ.

I had no understanding of the Catholic Mass, yet I was mesmerized by the pageantry and beauty. I had sung many Latin liturgical pieces, but they were always learned by rote.

I recall vividly the theatrical effect of the long procession, led by the cardinal leading the altar boys, and the assisting priests as they carried a large gold container, supposedly housing the relics of Ste. Teresa's body. The golden receptacle was reverently placed on the altar and would remain there until the Benediction and the Mass came to a close.

We were often invited to sing Sunday evening vespers at the famous Madeleine church located at Place Vendome. I sincerely believe we eventually sang in almost every Catholic Church in Paris other than the famous Sacre Coeur. I wanted to sing in that church, but it was never to happen.

Walt was visiting Rainbow Corners one day and happened to notice an announcement posted on a bulletin board. It was placed there by a famous singer who had reigned at the Metropolitan Opera as one of the company's leading divas during the golden age of opera that starred such notables as Enrico Caruso, Rosa Ponselle, Geraldine Farrar, Challiapin, Lucrezia Bori, and many others. The announcement invited any American GI who wished to sing an opportunity to study the art of singing with Raymonde Delanouis. Walt answered the call and had already taken one lesson before telling me about his find.

He invited me to go with him for his second lesson. Needless to say, I was totally mesmerized with the petite songstress, the beauty in her voice, and the ease with which she demonstrated her techniques to Walt. I wanted to study with Madame Delanouis.

After Walt's lesson, she invited me to sing for her. Of course, in that time of my life, I had no fear of singing for anyone who would listen. But the idea of having to pay for my lessons was another story. I recently had been promoted to corporal,which did add a bit more money to my monthly paycheck, but not enough to warrant even one lesson a week.

Gisele came to my rescue. "Van," she said, "you get one carton of cigarettes a week. Let me sell them for you and that will give you the money you need to take lessons."

Even though the army and the Red Cross were most generous for supplying soldiers with cigarettes, I never really acquired the habit. I agreed to supply Gisele with cigarettes and in turn for each carton I would receive $20. This would pay for four lessons each week.

Raymonde Delanouis lived on the Left Bank at 15 Rue Vanneau. It was probably the most elite section of Paris where the nouveau riche were excluded. Only old French wealth could afford to live on Rue Vanneau. It was a large apartment on the sixth floor. The apartment overlooked the garden and mansion of France's French premier, the famous World War I veteran, General Petain. Of course, since the liberation, a new premier was elected, so now it belonged to General Charles DeGaulle.

Petain, like the famous warrior of earlier times, was exiled in disgrace to an isolated island. He was accused of not resisting the German's invading armies and was therefore considered a traitor to his country.

Turning left from St. Germain Boulevard, the streets became more narrow. Rows of apartment dwellings were joined together, and the only way one would know where they were going was by observing the street number above a narrow door opening from the sidewalk into a courtyard. The apartments looked more like a movie background set. Each building had its own concierge. At 15 Rue Vanneau, the concierge resided in a small building in the middle of a cobblestone courtyard. Here the guardian of the apartments had an unobstructed view of anyone entering the premises.

When a caller or visitor rang the bell located under the number of the address on the sidewalk entrance, they entered into a large cobblestone courtyard. The concierge carefully scrutinized and interrogated each person before they were permitted to enter the door where a spiral flight of stairs would take the visitors to the upper floors of the building. Apparently, Walt and I passed the scrutiny of the bird-like eyes of the concierge.

The famous singer's apartment encompassed the entire sixth floor of the building.

When we arrived, daylight was fast fading into darkness, and the only light in the studio came from a number of burning candles resting on the piano and the fireplace

Madame Delanouis was not French; she was Belgian. She learned her craft at the famous Brussels Conservatory of Music. As she progressed in her career, she would tour in concert and opera in the cities of Austria, Germany, Italy, and France. Her concert repertoire included the great masterpieces of Schubert, Brahms, Schumann, and, of course, a wealth of French art songs.

Upon our arrival she immediately asked me to sing. Although her piano playing never extended beyond playing with one hand, she apparently thought I had a certain amount of talent. She accepted me as her student. Our first introduction was the beginning of a lasting respect and friendship between the great singer and myself. She insisted I plan on taking a lesson every day if at all possible, and sometimes those lessons would last for three hours. The more time I spent with the singer, our relationship that developed was not only between student and teacher, but we became devoted friends. I began to learn about the life of the great singer.

Still attractive, Raymonde Delanouis must have been a real beauty during her active years as an opera diva. She was petite, pretty, and undoubtedly attracted the eye of any eligible bachelor. So it was just before World War I that a high ranking French army officer by the name of Thomas Delanouis won the favors of the Belgian chanteuse.

At the time of the couple's meeting and many love trysts, war clouds gathered over the European continent. The couple married and a bond was cemented for an entire lifetime. World War I was quickly turning into a bloody conflict. No one was safe and Monsieur Delanouis was concerned about his wife's welfare. He had to find some way of getting her out of Paris and out of France. Raymonde resisted. She did not wish to leave France nor did she wish to leave her husband.

The managing director of the Metropolitan Opera, Galli-Gassetti, happened to be in Paris at the time the military conflict was on the verge of being thrust into a world war. Whether Thomas paid the famous impresario for the privilege of letting his wife sing for him, which was often the case during those early years at the Metropolitan, I have no way of knowing. I do know an audition was arranged. "I sang so badly," Raymonde said as she related the aftermath of her audition. Purposely, she had thoroughly made up her mind that she would not leave France. As she sang the last cadenza of her audition aria, the great impresario motioned Raymonde to come to a small table where he sat listening to his new find. There was no question about her signing a contract for her first season at the Metropolitan Opera in New York City. Rehearsals for the opera season were already in progress. Raymonde Delanouis was to become the youngest member of the notable cast of great warblers.

The young singer was welcomed with open arms by the greatest singers the world has ever known, Geraldine Fararr became a lifelong friend. Caruso gave her a new technique in breathing, and when Chaliapin sang the role of "Boris Goudinoff," he always insisted Raymonde be cast in the role of "Fedora." Wilfred Pelletier was not only an opera pianist, he eventually became one of the Met's most prominent conductors. He and his wife Rose Bampton became close friends, a friendship that would last a lifetime.

When the young singer arrived in New York and the Metropolitan Opera, a Dr. Dubrosky and his wife insisted the new diva come live with them. They resided in a prestigious, large apartment on Central Park West overlooking Central Park. For the entire opera season, Raymonde would make this address her home. She could spend hours at the grand piano learning new repertoire and would never be disturbed or interrupted.

I was fascinated with Madame Delanouis's past career. She was not an old woman at the time we met, but the war had interrupted her career. Other than occasional concerts within the city of Paris, she seldom ventured outside the city. It would be long after the war came to an end that she would return during the summer months to her beloved Venice, Italy.

I loved her stories about the golden years of opera at the Metropolitan. It was as though I were actually living through that remarkable time. The world's greatest tenors were mesmerized by the talent and the beauty endowed upon this young Belgian mezzo soprano.

Enrico Caruso was known for being a lady's man and soon made his advances known to the singer. Of course, they never went far, Raymonde's love remained in France and her loyalty to Thomas would never falter during their entire lifetime. She often said of Chaliapin that she loved him on stage, but offstage he was an uncouth beast. John McCormack, the world-renown Irish tenor inherited all the wit of Ireland. He could always keep her laughing. She would tell me occasionally about his sex life, and how he found it absolutely impossible to sing after he made love. Consequently, Monsieur McCormack's sex life must have gone wanting all during the opera season since he was highly in demand.

Raymonde Delanouis—Metropolitan Opera Diva, 1911-1927,
Loy VanNatter—World War II veteran who studied with her in
Paris 1944-1946

Madame Raymonde Delanouis had not corresponded with her friends at the Metropolitan since the time the Germans occupied her homeland. An idea came to mind. Supposing, Madame, you write to your friends at the Metropolitan, and I will send your letters through my APO address. In turn, they can write back to you in the same manner, and I shall bring their correspondence with me when I have my lessons. The idea worked. Little did I realize that what I was doing would eventually open doors that would have forever remained closed had I not been an instrument for her corresponding with her devoted friends and colleagues at the Metropolitan.

CHAPTER 49

THE WAR IN EUROPE AND the war in the Pacific continued to rage. It appeared as if there would never be an end. At times, the Allies were convinced the Germans were being forced back to their homeland, but that was only an illusion.

Sniping by the few remaining Germans hiding in Paris became less and less. Instead of battle fatigues, leggins, and helmets, we donned our Eisenhower jacket, shirt, and tie. We no longer carried our weapons and for all intents and purposes, those stationed in the headquarters fulfilled our nine-to-five duties similar to what we would do when we returned to the civilian world.

I continued my lessons on a daily basis with Madame Delanouis. Colonel Brown had a knack for securing engagements for the Glee Glub, which occupied much of our free time. The only hitch in the overseas experience was the place and conditions in which we were obligated to be housed.

Returning to the Magazin Dufayel at the end of our working day was dismal. Winter was setting in and the place was cold. Of course, that wasn't unusual, inasmuch as no one within the city of Paris had any kind of heat to keep them warm. In normal times, Paris' central heating system was never turned on until October 21st, but the war had taken its toll on all luxuries often taken for granted.

A portion of the open space on the second floor of the billet was partitioned from the sleeping quarters and turned into what was referred to as a Day Room. When off duty, a GI could use this part of the billet for reading or listening to a small portable radio.

Large, undraped windows of the Day Room permitted one to gaze directly into the bordello across the street. The windows of the whorehouse were also undraped. To most GIs raised in a puritanical upbringing, looking from an undraped window of the Day Room into the undraped window of the bordello provided the innocent ones a thorough education in human sexuality. The onlooker was provided all the positions known to man that would thoroughly indoctrinate one on how to have sex, leaving both participating parties totally exhausted and satisfied.

It was a cold and wet November. On Thanksgiving Day, the Glee Club was engaged to perform at the George V Hotel for a non-denominational Thanksgiving Day service.

Thanksgiving Day was considerably different than the ones celebrated in the past. The usual turkey dinner with all the trimmings was served onto a metal mess kit, instead of the luxury of fine china and the home-cooked meals most families enjoyed on the home front.

My digestive system was beginning to rebel against the army chow diet, and it was shortly after the day to give thanks that I began daily visits to the dispensary.

Gisele, Toot Sweet, and myself had a standing rendezvous on Saturdays and Sundays to meet. We would walk in the park or perhaps take in a museum or church. Gisele was instrumental in getting her sister, Francine, a job at the headquarters, and it was soon after her employment that she met a young warrant officer by the name of Mr. Simmons. It was unfortunate for Francine that her mother and father discouraged the relationship between the American and herself. It would be many years, and after the war came to an end, when all our war time friends had married, but to different spouses, that in remembering the war years and the U.S. Army headquarters in Paris the French girls would reminisce during our frequent visits to Paris after the war. The association with the American GIs by the French girls would prove to be the happiest period of their entire lives.

December 1944 was a cold and bitter month. It was my first anniversary on foreign soil, and living conditions in the military and billeting at the Magazin Dufayel never improved. My little dog Toot Sweet continued to be shifted from one French home to another, and the war placed the Allied forces on the defensive instead of the offensive. The German army succeeded in a counterattack, arriving in Luxembourg and becoming an immediate threat to all communication zone installations in the forward area. The 3619th Quartermaster Trucking company was given the mission of moving a portion of the 101st Airborne Division to Bastogne on December 10th. This company was expected to return to Paris the following day, but the situation made it impossible to release the trucks as planned, and it became necessary for the officers and the enlisted men of the company to become a part of the combat element of an airborne battalion, even though they were not familiar with combat conditions. The setback for the Allies turned into one of the bloodiest battles of the war. It would always be known as "The Battle of the Bulge." On a daily basis, Der Fuhrer would make a claim that he would be back in Paris by Christmas. It was the highest moment of expectations for the German army and the lowest morale point for the American and Allied troops in the war against Germany.

News of German atrocities flowed into the French capital. One hundred American soldiers were lined up by German officers and shot in retaliation and retribution. American officers ordered one hundred German soldiers to be killed in the same manner. Casualties could not be replaced with troops from the states quickly enough to compensate for the number of soldiers being slaughtered and wounded. The situation was so volatile that men were taken from behind the lines operations including headquarters personnel. These men were sent to the front lines of battle, even though many had never shouldered a gun since basic training. Those pulled from their cushy jobs at the headquarters were in many cases mere cannon fodder for the German armies to mow down as a farmer would cut through a field of wheat.

The possibility of being shipped out became a reality. I was trained as an infantryman and had received a marksman medal while in basic training at Camp Wheeler, Georgia. For six intensive weeks, I was taught the art of killing and almost brainwashed into thinking it was okay as long as those bastards I killed were either Japs or Krauts.

It became a political game at headquarters as to who would be chosen to participate as a combat soldier instead of a pencil pusher. Soldiers assigned to plush office duties were now subject to being called at any moment. It became a matter of political maneuvering. Enlisted men made daily visits to the dispensary in the hopes of finding a doctor who would declare them unfit for combat duty.

Hamp, Mosher, Becker, and myself were assigned the detail of preparing the Seine Section Headquarters for total destruction at a minute's notice. For several evenings, our life centered around sorting through confidential documents, securing them in a safe place, then waiting for what we thought was going to be the inevitable.

One fateful morning, a coworker and myself were called into the commanding officer's office. We stood at attention as we stood before the pipe-smoking captain. "At ease, Men." The man behind the desk continued speaking. "I need two volunteers. You two men are trained for combat, most of my staff are not. If you are willing to volunteer, I believe I can arrange for you to receive an officer's commission as a second lieutenant."

I knew the officer was lying. No way would this simple captain have the authority to automatically award an officer's commission to a lowly GI. The chap standing beside me spoke. "Sir, I'll go." I remained quiet. I returned to my desk and my coworker left the office. He was never heard from nor seen again.

I often mentioned my fears to my friend Colonel Brown. His only response was to walk away. Little did I know at the time that it was the good colonel who decided who would be the chosen one to face the German army.

My morale slipped to its lowest ebb. Whether it was the turn of events, the deplorable living conditions, or the food the army dished out, I don't know. I began to feel very ill. Food I consumed either turned to diarrhea or vomiting after each meal. There were numerous visits to the dispensary and finally it was decided I should be hospitalized.

The hospital was located on the outskirts of Paris. Day after day my French friends and GI buddies would arrive at the hospital, all concerned about my condition. Since there was no public transportation, the French people would walk a great distance from homes to spend a few moments with me at the hospital. I shall always cherish that memory of their devotion, love, and friendship.

There was no privacy in a military hospital. Beds were lined against the wall with just enough space for a nurse or attendant to give a shot or clean up a mess. In the center of the large room was another row of beds separated by about the same amount of space. Throughout the night moans and groans echoed throughout the ward,

I recall a black soldier brought into the hospital in the middle of the night and placed in one of the center row of beds. He appeared to be in excruciating pain. His abdomen was distended far beyond anything I had seen on a man. No pregnant woman could have a more distended stomach unless she was due to deliver a newborn. I noticed when dawn broke through the soiled windows that the black man was gone. I presume he died in the middle of the night.

In the next bed to where the black soldier apparently expired, lay a young Russian. He could speak no English. His neck was so severely swollen and the swelling extended to his shoulder blades. I began to ask questions. The poor man could speak no English, and I was never privy to know how he managed to get into Allied hands.

The story of the man was related to me by one of the nurses. Apparently, the Wehrmacht had invaded the village in which the Russian lad lived with his mother, father, and sister. The German army invaded the village. The soldiers began slaughtering all the inhabitants and when they were convinced they had completed their heinous crime, they proceeded to set fires to each house in the village until there was nothing left but ashes: The young Russian lad witnessed the soldiers shooting his mother, father, and sister. In an effort to escape the carnage, he crawled inside the fireplace and pushed his way upward into the chimney. When it appeared nothing but death reigned over the village, he slid from the chimney down to the base of the fireplace. Laying before him were the charred bodies of his mother, father, and sister. He was frightened. He managed to find his way into a nearby forest, thinking he could find a safe place to hide. Within hours, his freedom was taken away when a German soldier captured him. The young Russian was not interned in a concentration or labor camp, but was taken to a laboratory where he became a subject for experimentation. The scientists cut into his throat and neck.

Throughout the night the sound of the man choking broke the dark silence in the ward. He managed to leave his bed and stand, thinking he could get more air as he gasped and choked. The night nurse arrived on the scene, but instead of calling a doctor, she proceeded to pound the ill man across the back, saying, "Well now, what's wrong with you?" I must have fallen asleep. When the light of early dawn broke through the soiled windows of the ward, I noticed the Russian's bed was empty. Like the black soldier, he undoubtedly expired sometime during the darkness of the night.

The tests the hospital flaunted on my ailing body were far more uncomfortable and tortuous than I anticipated. For the purpose of X-raying my digestive system, a nurse arrived at the side of my bed holding a cup which contained a pint of blueish, almost purple liquid. "Drink this soldier," was the only thing I heard the woman say. As I placed the contents of the cup to my mouth and took one swallow, my stomach churned. I rushed to the latrine at the far end of the ward. The nurse followed me and stood outside the door. I vomited like I had never thrown up in my entire life.

When I opened the door to exit the latrine, the nurse stood there with a sardonic look on her face. Well, Soldier, I guess you'll just have to try again. This has to stay down. It's the only way they can take pictures of your gut. Within minutes, the nurse was back with another pint of the purple poison. "Nurse," I said, "I'll have to take this in the latrine. I know it will just come up again." She followed me, but since the latrine was about the only private room in the hospital, I immediately went to the commode, poured the stuff down the toilet, flushed it, then greeted the same nurse as she waited outside the door. "Well, did it stay down, Soldier? If it didn't, we've got more." I wiped my mouth and with a convincing pretense and said, "Yes, ma'am, it stayed down."

I was finally released from the hospital and returned to active duty. There was little or no sign of life on the streets of Paris. People were cold and they were frightened. The war was bloody. GIs and Allied soldiers were being slaughtered faster than the supply of men could replace those killed or wounded. My days, too, were numbered. I knew eventually that I would be sent to the front. Hamp, knowing what my commanding officer offered me, said, "Gee, Van, if you can get a commission, I'll volunteer to go to the front." There was no convincing him that the officer was lying. Hamp volunteered and it would the last time I would hear from my Canadian buddy until the war in Europe finally came to an end.

It was 1944, New Year's Eve and prior to Hamp leaving Paris to prepare himself for that commission the commanding officer supposedly offered. Hamp and I decided to celebrate at the Lido, an elegant nightclub on the Champs Elysees near the Arc de Triomphe. Hamp met a couple of girls, both strangers to us, and without informing me invited them to join us at the club. We had exactly $25 between us. Champagne was $16 a bottle and we splurged. With the nine remaining dollars, we ordered four slices of cake. The champagne was quickly consumed. Hamp excused himself to go to the latrine and in an effort to avoid an order for another bottle of champagne, I asked the girl I happened to be paired with to dance. This left the girl Hamp had chosen sitting alone at our table. She was a brazen and impulsive young woman and she wanted more champagne. Next to our table sat a lieutenant and his girl friend. Nonchalantly, Hamp's choice for the evening moved toward the lieutenant's table. Without asking, she reached for the open bottle of champagne resting on the officer's table. "Do you mind?" she asked as she replenished her glass with the lieutenant's champagne. It was the lieutenant's girl friend who responded. "Yes, as a matter of fact, I do mind." She reached in the officer's side pocket and withdrew a pistol. She raised the gun into the air and fired one shot above the crowd. There was panic. Leaving the girl I was dancing with standing alone in the middle of the dance floor, I took off like a striped-ass monkey toward a sign that said "Sortie." When I reached the outside of the club, Hamp was leaning against a lamp post.

I never quite forgave Hamp for placing me in that situation. Whatever happened to the two girls we had picked up and left stranded at the club I never asked, nor did I return to the club to find out.

When we left the club, 1945 had arrived. Instead of returning to the Magazin Dufayel, we decided to go to our separate rooms at a hotel we often used as an escape from the discomfort of the ex-German warehouse. When Hamp reached his room, there was a pair of women's shoes outside his door. As he opened the door, he interrupted a GI and a young woman in the throes of sexual passion. The concierge had rented his room for a couple hours during Hamp's absence. She quickly assigned Hamp another room. The following morning there was a knock on my door. It was a young Polish girl whom I was well aware had spent the night with the GI that had taken over Hamp's room and now she wanted to get in bed with me. This was quickly refused. I never saw the Polish girl again. I hurriedly dressed, then made my way back to the Magazin Dufayel.

Hamp left Paris for the frontline of battle the following week. What happened to my buddy would remain a mystery. Was he just another GI to die in the line of duty or did he survive? Several months would elapse before our paths would cross again.

Even though the citizens of Paris continued to be without electricity or light to their homes, restaurants, and nightclubs, the opera and theatre were excluded from the rationing and business was good. Even the brothels were able to thrive. The lightless streets of Pigalle brought out prostitutes hustling GIs with their promises to zig zig and suk suk. On every street corner a girl waited her chance to cash in by selling her sexual favors to GIs on leave from the front lines. Prostitution was legal in Paris, but it was only in the brothels that doctors regularly physically checked the women for any sign of venereal disease. Battle-fatigued GIs furloughed to the city invariably headed for the nearest brothel or took advantage of being promiscuous with one or more of the street corner girls. Gonorrhea and syphilis became rampant. I considered myself fortunate. I had been well educated during basic training about the dangers of sex, so refrained from giving into my youthful burning hormones that wanted to say yes but insisted on saying no.

The Battle of the Bulge was the turning point in the war. Patton was brought in from North Africa along with his tank squadrons to flaunt his military genius. Within days after his arrival, the Patton forces successfully pushed the Germans back toward their Vaterland. Allied bombers filled the skies over Germany raining death and destruction down upon the German people. The air attacks far exceeded that which the Nazis flaunted upon the British during their unforgettable blitz.

Gradually, my fears of being shipped to the front lines subsided and the Glee Club concerts continued to be fulfilled uninterrupted.

My work with Madame Delanouis progressed nicely. I learned a number of songs, German Lieder and French art songs such as Faure, DeParc and Debussy, but my good teacher never permitted me to sing with a piano accompaniment, not until every single measure of the music was counted to perfection. My good teacher would repeatedly say, "Van—when you count out the music and have learned all the notes, you will then be ready to put your voice with the piano." My teacher was right. One evening I arrived for my usual lesson. There was an attractive lady sitting in the salon. "Van—tonight you will sing for the first time with the piano. I have invited Madame Laurettete to accompany you." As my voice began to interpret the music for which I had been well schooled, I realized the wisdom of my good teacher. The accompaniment to songs by Brahms, Schumann and Debussy were suddenly brought to life, leaving me with the confidence knowing I had learned my lessons well.

Before leaving my teacher's apartment that evening, Madame Delanouis spoke. "You are ready now, Van. I wish to have you give a concert here in my home." It would be my first full solo concert engagement in Paris.

The guest list included not only the elite of Paris, but some of France's most accomplished singers. One of those singers was the famous Germain Lubin, recognized as one of the greatest Wagnerian sopranos in the entire world and who reigned on the same pedestal as Kirsten Flagstad. I later learned she often sought the expertise of Raymonde Delanouis and they became devoted friends.

Germain Lubin was one of the first guests to arrive at my concert to be performed in Madame Delanouis' salon. The salon setting, the candle light and the distinguished guests seemed to regress back in time to the period of Mozart, Chopin, and Schubert. The great singer was a beautiful woman whose smooth, creamy complexion accented her magnificent face. Her large frame was typical of a Wagnerian singer. Her speaking voice was warm and rich with the same timbre of voice that so adeptly suited the roles of "Isolde" and "Brunhilde." When all the guests arrived and were comfortably seated in a formal salon off the studio, dressed in my military uniform, buttons shining like the diamonds bedecked on the hands and around the necks of my hostess' distinguished ladies, and the gentlemen dressed in formal tuxedo attire, I took my place in the curve of the grand piano. I had indeed come a long way from those high school days in Akron, the May Festival and the State competition. Deep within, I knew Mable Toad would have been proud. Although nervous, I sang, probably better than I had sung in my entire life.

CHAPTER 50

MARCH OF 1945 ROARED INTO the French capital like a lion but the breezes were considerably warmer than they had been during the months of January and February. There were positive signs the war might be coming to an end, at least on the European front. Each passing day revealed more and more French people taking to the streets to stroll along the wide boulevards and enjoy the ever popular sidewalk cafés.

Our headquarters moved from Place de la Opera to an office building on Avenue Kleber near the Arc de Triomphe.

It must have been a weekend I had custody of my little dog, Toot Sweet that I decided to take her with me to one of my lessons. As we reached the sixth floor landing at 15 Rue Vanneau, I placed my hand on the doorbell. When the door opened, it was not the reception I anticipated. "You cannot bring that dog in here!" Madame Delanouis screamed. "Leave her down there in the courtyard." Holding my little ball of fur safely in my arms, I turned and walked down the six flights of stairs to the courtyard below. I tried to explain to Toot Sweet she wasn't welcome in the famous singer's home and with each descending step I attempted to beg my petit chien to be very quiet. I sat her down on the cobblestones, then returned to the studio on the sixth floor. I could see my forlorn little pooch from the studio window. She looked so alone in that great big courtyard. I began my vocalizes and the sound of my voice filtered through the closed apartment window. Those sounds ignited a howl from the courtyard that carried all the way to the opera house. I looked down toward my little friend and I could see her mouth wide open, hitting notes that were never within my vocal range.

Madame Delanouis let her hands come down heavy on the ivories. "Merde!" she screamed. Go down there and get that damn dog!" I had never seen my teacher so angry. I hurried out of the apartment and down the six flights of stairs to the courtyard. I picked up Toot Sweet, then returned to the apartment on the sixth floor. " You should sell that damn dog. With the money you could get for that animal, you could give a concert in Paris at Salle Gaveau."

"Sell my dog?" I couldn't believe anyone would ever think of such an evil thing.

How dare this woman suggest getting rid of my dog? It would have been as sinful as selling my own child. I did not sell Toot Sweet, and I did not give a concert at Salle Gaveau.

It was shortly after our office moved from Place de Opera to Avenue Kleber, another secretary was added to my correspondence staff. I don't recall the girl's last name, but her first name I shall always remember. Her name was Adrian. She was a native Hollander and one of the most efficient civilian employees I had the good fortune to work with since coming to Paris other than my good friend Gisele. Between the two girls, I knew the work would be completed. There were two other French girls on the staff, but they spent more time flirting with the opposite sex than typing the voluminous correspondence demanded from each workday. One of the girls was star struck. Most of her day was spent applying makeup and studying her face in a mirror. I learned very quickly after her employment and after she was assigned to my staff, her one ambition in life was to be a film star. It was certain she never injured her long fingernails on the typewriter keys, since she rarely touched them.

Adrian was a strange woman. I attributed much of this strangeness to the fact she wasn't French. There was an aloofness about her, yet she spoke an impeccable French and her English was almost accent free. Her one dream was to study medicine at the University in Paris and become a doctor. I happened to express a desire to learn to speak French. Gisele, although we were together many hours during the day and many times during the evening and always on the weekends, always wanted to speak English. Adrian heard me express my interest in learning French. "I'll help you, Van. You could come to my apartment for dinner this coming week and we shall begin your lessons."

I agreed to make the time and of course Madame Delanouis was delighted I was finally going to learn to speak the French language.

It was during the course of that first French lesson, I learned about Adrian. She actually could have been the perfect spy. In my department, I was dealing with highly confidential documents. But something kept me from reporting Adrian's story to the authorities. I liked the girl and even though it may have been my duty to pass the information on to the proper authorities with what I learned on that evening of our first French lesson, I saw no value in it. The war with the Germans was almost at its end.

Adrian's story began when the Germans took over Holland. It was during the occupation, the young Dutch girl fell in love with an SS trooper. She continued her relationship with the officer during the entire occupation of Holland and was highly ridiculed and persecuted by her own people. This did not deter her loyalty to the man she loved. When Allies moved into Holland, she and her German soldier managed to escape into Germany. There was an attempt to get to Berlin, but during the long, arduous journey, Adrian's lover was killed as she watched a Russian soldier grab the SS trooper and shoot him in the head.

Adrian had to find a way to escape. A stroke of luck flowed in her direction. With her fluent knowledge of English and French, she quickly made herself known to the conquering Americans. With careful manipulation and planning, the Dutch girl succeeded in reaching the French capital.

I don't know what she gave as a resume when she entered and applied for a job with the Civilian Personnel Office; I do know she was immediately hired to join my staff to work in the adjutant general's office.

I kept Adrian's secret. I knew to tell Gisele about Adrian's background would have been a fatal blow. Adrian did enroll at the University and she did study medicine. All during the remainder of her employment with the headquarters, her evenings were spent studying and taking classes. She didn't dare return to her homeland, not even after receiving her Doctorate. In Holland, like many other countries, any girl who collaborated with the Nazis had all their hair shaved from their head and was then paraded through the streets as a traitor to their country. Adrian's actions would be considered treason and could easily have ended in death. I was to never know if Adrian ever returned to her homeland.

An unpredictable, digestive and intestinal problem returned and again and again. I was hospitalized in an army hospital on the outskirts of Paris. As the disease had taken its toll in December of 1944, the bout this time was even more severe. There were numerous dispensary visits. The doctors would say, "You're just drinking too much of that cheap French wine, Soldier." Of course, that was far from the truth. I wasn't a drinker—not beer, not hard liquor and not wine.

I took my place in the admission line along with several other GIs waiting admittance. Lying on the cold flagstone floor lay a handsome German soldier, still dressed in his camouflage fatigues. He was severely wounded, yet, no nurse or doctor came to the young man's aid—not until each American GI was admitted and placed in a bed. He was much sicker than myself and many of the other GIs. In my compassionate mind, the man deserved medical attention. To the present day, I often wonder about that young man. Was he ever laid upon a bed or did he ever receive medical attention? Did he die like the other two men, one an American black soldier and the other a Russian?

Numerous tests, similar to the ones I previously experienced, were again repeated. I was placed on a bland diet, which was actually as tasteless and unpalatable as the daily diet at the mess hall There were numerous x-rays and again a nurse would awaken me from a sound sleep, holding the pint of purple liquid in her hand then ordering me to drink. The bitter potion did not stay down except when I poured the contents down the commode. This was my secret.

I don't know what the tests revealed as to my physical condition, but word reached the headquarters I had some rare disease and they were thinking about sending me back to the states for treatment. Visitors arrived on a daily basis, walking the long distance from their homes in central Paris to the outskirts of the city. The Glee Club often visited the army hospital in Paris to entertain the bedridden soldiers. As

I lay there, I suddenly felt the presence of 11 men standing at the foot of my bed. They began to sing and it sounded good. I climbed out of bed and began singing with them. The following morning, I was not shipped home; I was ordered to return to duty.

My friend Gisele had an excuse for another party — a welcome home party. She had given me so many send-off parties when it appeared certain I would be sent to the battle front, which of course, luckily for me, didn't happen.

The spring rains of April 1945 brought the dawn of a new beginning. It was the wind up for the most devastating war ever to be fought on the European soil. Berlin was a pile of rubble. People lived in bombed out shelters and even rats were not wasted when it came to fulfilling human hunger. It was a true springtime in Paris and at last there was hope toward going home for the American GI.

On April 13, headlines covered the front page of the army's only newspaper, "The Stars and Stripes."

"Franklin Delano Roosevelt is Dead!" Our Commander in Chief had survived only three months after taking the oath of office as a third-term President of the United States. I was too young to vote, even though I had already served the majority of my military life overseas. I was shocked, however, to hear Republican GIs so willing to criticize the man no longer with us, a man who was the savior for many Americans during those desperate depression years. I was one of those Americans. We were poor and the legacy our President gave to people like me gave us a chance for a better life.

Harry S. Truman took over the reins from our departed President. Like his predecessor the man who owned a retail store selling hats in Independence, Missouri, too, would survive as a man whose desire was to serve the people and the underprivileged.

Less than a month would pass after the death of our President; the news the world long awaited blared across every newspaper headline. It was May 3, 1945.

HITLER DEAD!

DER FUHRER FELL AT GP, AND ADMIRAL DOENITZ

TAKES OVER HELM

Of course, the article continued with statements from Doenitz that the war would continue. Next to the story announcing the death of Adolph Hitler, in small captions, the article quoted Winston Churchill:

"PEACE IS AT HAND"

After the death of Hitler, the Americans and the Russians advanced quickly throughout the dictator's homeland and the shattered bombed out German Capitol of Berlin. The Russians were first to arrive in the Eastern Section of Germany, including Berlin. The Western Allies met the Russians halfway and began the task of occupying what was referred to as West Germany."

The French press were first to announce the capitulation of Germany. It happened on the morning of May 7. I had not seen the papers until I reached the office and noticed Gisele had placed a copy of "The Figaro" on my desk. The blazing headlines on the front page announced the news the entire world long awaited.

CAPITULATION SANS CONDITIONS! —
UNCONDITIONAL SURRENDER.

On the newspaper's front page Gisele had written a note.

Today, 7 May I know you are on your way back home soon and that boy will not come back. I feel very sad, but then I feel wonderfully happy. God bless you and Gerry.
Your French Friend, Gisele

The war did come to an end in Europe but for the American soldier, the war was not over. Heavy fighting continued in the Pacific and many soldiers who fought on European soil were immediately shipped from the Port of Marseille to somewhere in the Pacific. Percy Hampton was one of those soldiers. I never expected to see or hear from my Canadian friend again. It was VE Day and the phone on my desk rang. It was Hamp. "Hey Van! I'm in Marseille. I didn't get that commission that son-of-a-bitch promised—I'm still a Corporal. They're getting ready to ship me out to some goddamned hole in the Pacific! Ya gotta help me, Van! Maybe you can do something. See if you can pull some strings and get me back to Paris."

"I don't know what I can do, Hamp. I'll try." I hung up the phone and called my Commanding officer. "Sir—you remember Percy Hampton, don't you? Well—I just heard from him. He's in Marseille and he sounded a bit panicky. He wants to come back to Paris. Do ya think there's a chance for gittin' him back?"

The officer reached for the phone and within a few minutes it was arranged for Hamp to be returned to the headquarters in Paris.

For the first-time since the war began, lights were turned on in Paris. The Metros were running—people danced in the streets and speeches and more speeches were orated from the stages of the most prestigious theatres in Paris. Gisele and I wanted to be alone. We walked quietly along the Champs Elysees then sat on a bench under a mammoth chestnut tree relishing every moment we would have together before I would return home.

It was early afternoon when we noticed a Jeep making its way through the throngs of people crowding onto Champs Elysees Boulevard. Behind the wheel was the familiar face of our friend Walt Treadway. "Hey, Van!" he yelled in his rich baritone voice. "I've been lookin' all over for ya. They want you and the rest of the boys to sing at the Olympia right away. Glenn Miller's orchestra's playin'. It ain't everyday ya git a chance to sing with Glenn Miller's Band! You and Gisele hop in. I think we can get there before all the top brass finish their long speeches."

Gisele and I hopped in the Jeep and Walt put the car into gear, honking his horn all the way in an attempt to clear the street of celebrating Parisians so we could make it to the Olympia Theatre at the Trocadero for the VE celebration.

The streets of Paris were not the only places crowded with people who suddenly came out of hiding from the long months and years of war. At the theatre mobs pushed their way into the lobby of the theatre. Walt, Gisele and myself entered by the way of the stage door. Brigadier Generals to Four Star Generals were seated central stage. Walt and I arrived just in time as the Glee Club prepared to walk from the wings of the theatre out onto the stage to contribute to the celebrations. The band struck up the intro to the "Star Spangled Banner," then the "Marseille" and ended with "God Save the Queen." The capacity audience rose from their seats and the singing voices of thousands echoed from the rafters of the theatre.

The full Glenn Miller orchestra filled the orchestra pit. The only one missing was Glenn Miller himself. His orchestra had contributed so much to the morale of GI Joe. Glenn Miller disappeared over the North Atlantic, never to be seen again, but the spirit of the great American musician would prevail and would live in the hearts of the GI and the men who carried on the harmonious sounds created by America's great musical legend.

As dusk preceded nightfall, for the first time since I arrived in Paris, the City of Light was no longer in darkness. The famous fountains were no longer silent and dry. They raised their sprays of rushing water toward the heavens like a soaring spirit who was no longer bound to earth's ravages of war. Church bells rang from the great cathedrals and a perpetual 24-hour Peace Mass was instigated at the magnificent Sacre Couer overlooking the City of Paris. From the Place de la Concorde to the Arc de Triomphe people paraded en masse leaving little room between bodies. Prayers, tears and laughter circulated throughout every city and town in America as well as Europe. The day finally came when "There were Blue Birds over the White Cliffs of Dover."

Gisele and I stood on the terrace of the great Sacre Coeur Cathedral, looking out over the huddle of roofs, reaching to the horizon and into uncertain fringes of the countryside. We watched in awe as the lights of Paris sparkled like falling stars coming to earth to light the way of peace. The dreaded fears of war for all people in Europe had finally come to an end.

CHAPTER 51

IT WAS AN OVERNIGHT TURN about face for the military brass toward the ordinary GI Joe. Instead of a mess hall where food was served on metal mess kits, the army either leased or purchased a real restaurant. For those men stationed in Paris, we were suddenly eating in a first class eating establishment. Maybe, it wasn't the finest Limoge china, but it was a far cry from the world of clanging mess kits and boiling hot water at the end of the line in which to clean our eating utensils. We didn't even have to wash our plates. We were encouraged to invite guests to dinner from time to time. It would be the first time since Liberation Day or since I arrived on the European continent that the food was edible. But the army went even further.

They set up a PX where one could get all the real ice cream he wanted and all the beer he wished to drink. It was real American beer. The French beer had an undesirable taste. A soldier had to be desperate for a bottle of beer to drink it.

I continued my lessons with Madame Delanouis on a daily basis. She would often mention the name of her former husband, Thomas Delanouis, and thoughts were ever constant in her mind as to whether the only man she ever loved survived the war.

Thomas Delanouis was anti-Jewish. He was a German collaborator. His anti-Semitic columns accompanied with his photograph appeared daily in France's leading newspapers. He had long since divorced the famous singer and remarried a much younger woman, who bore him his first and only child. Although Raymonde's separation and divorce from her husband was not a pleasant experience, she was always available as the closest confidant to her ex-husband. She had accepted his new wife. Many times, she warned Thomas he must leave Paris. The Allies were certain to invade and re-capture Paris from the Germans. If and when that happened, his life and the life of his wife and baby were at stake. Word circulated from the French Underground that any collabo-rator with the enemy would be severely punished. Thomas Delanouis met that criteria.

Thomas refused to listen. He loved Paris and he was not anxious to leave his beloved city. He refused to heed the warn-ing of the approaching Allied Forces. Nationwide broadcasts pleaded with the French people to stay off the highways. Anyone traveling in a vehicle or walking along open roads or highways would be strafed by planes that could fly as low as the tree tops spraying bullets of death to those who dared to walk or drive along the highways and defy the warning. No one would be spared nor would they survive.

Thomas was in the process of writing his daily column for the newspaper at the same time the warning was broadcast over the air waves. He rushed home to his wife and infant son. The family was soon ensconced inside an automobile and the treacherous journey began.

Moving swiftly through the streets of Paris, Thomas guided his automobile onto the open road. The roaring sound of approaching aircraft rocked the sky. As the Allies promised, American bombers dropped their bombs and fighter planes dived from the sky to treetop level, pinpointing their deadly attack on all moving targets.

The Delanouis automobile was struck with a spray of bullets. Thomas' wife and baby were killed instantly and the writer was critically wounded. The paramedics reached the site of the riddled car only to find there was no hope for the mother and child. Thomas was still alive. He was rushed to a nearby hospital. Although critically injured, when the hospital staff left his bedside, he retrieved his civilian clothing and escaped without being seen.

Against all odds, Thomas Delanouis successfully reached the Swiss border. He managed to cross into Switzerland undetected and it was here he would seek asylum. Fortunately, he carried enough francs on his person which permitted him to take the train from the Swiss border to Zurich. With enough money to sustain a simple lifestyle, he immediately sought medical care. Upon his release from the doctor who cared for his wounds, Thomas found a room in a small pension located on the outskirts of Zurich. He changed his identity, but seldom left the confines of his chosen prison.

Thomas Delanouis was a wanted fugitive and a traitor to his country. There was no contact between the writer and his former spouse. This all changed on V.E. Day. The French Government demanded the Swiss Government extradite all collaborators who sought refuge in Switzerland and Thomas Delanouis was one of those most wanted.

It was a warm sunny morning and the writer leisurely finished his morning coffee while he perused the newspaper. There was a rap on the door. Thinking it was the concierge, Thomas opened the door. Two Swiss policemen greeted him.

"Monsieur," the one gentleman spoke. "You are Thomas Delanouis and not Monsieur Lusanne du Lac, is that correct?" Thomas attempted to deny his identity, but it was to no avail."Monsieur, we must take you to the Prefecture de Police immediately. We have been informed by the French Government officials that you are on their most wanted list of fugitives as a traitor to your country. We are quite aware that you came to our country in an effort to avoid the punishment that is undoubtedly in store for you. You must leave Zurich at once."

The two policemen refused the writer permission to gather his personal effects. Thomas was ushered immediately onto a police wagon parked just outside the pension. Within minutes, the famous writer was being interrogated by the Justice of the Court.

Thomas Delanouis, whose days of glory had previously protected him, knew his fate was sealed. "We can no longer give you asylum, Monsieur. You must leave our country at once. You will be ushered by these two arresting officers to the Banhoff where they will accompany you to the border. When you reach your homeland, you are on your own. May God have mercy on your soul."

The arresting officers handcuffed the fugitive then remained on the train with their charge. As the fugitive neared the border of France, the handcuffs were removed. Thomas excusing himself so he might use the lavatory, managed to escape the watchful eyes of the guards. As the train slowed and before it came to a complete stop at the line of demarcation, Thomas jumped from the moving train to the ground. Unnoticed by the French border guards, the writer began his long journey on foot, hoping to reach Paris without being detected by the French police. Well aware of the fate and severe punishment he would receive for being a traitor and a collaborator, he carefully maneuvered his steps as he passed through small villages so as not to arouse suspicion as to his identity. His life could end under the blade of the guillotine or he could spend the rest of his natural life in a dark, dirty, prison cell where he seldom would see the light of a new day. Once he reached Paris, he knew his fate lay in the hands of his accusers and the courts.

Many days and many nights passed before he reached the outskirts of his beloved City of Paris. He walked along the Seine until he reached the Left Bank of the divided city. He began searching the address of the apartment he had once shared with his ex-wife. It was an address he had once shared with Raymonde so many years prior. Raymonde no longer lived there. He questioned the concierge. Not detecting the identity of the man to whom she was speaking, the middle-aged concierge gave the writer the singer's new address.

Always with caution and aware his every move was being watched, the desperate man carefully maneuvered his steps until he reached No. 15 Rue Vanneau. No longer the proud military officer and distinguished writer who had gained national respect during his day in the sun, his shaking hand reached for the buzzer that would open the street door into an unfamiliar courtyard.

"Bonjour, Monsieur—may I help you?"

The weak voice of a shriveled shell of a man and one of complete submission spoke. "Oui, Madame. Perhaps you can. I am looking for a Madame Delanouis. I was told she now lives at this address." The concierge carefully scrutinized the man dressed in ragged clothing and a face that had gone unshaven for many days. There was no resemblance to the distinguished face that had been familiar to thousands when his photo appeared with his daily column published in many of France's leading newspapers.

The concierge spoke. "Monsieur, may I announce as to whom is calling upon Madame Delanouis?" Thomas quickly responded. "No, Madame—please tell me on which etage is Madame's apartment. I know she will see me.

Hesitantly, the concierge told the strange man where Raymonde was located.

"She is on 6 etage, Monsieur: You must be very careful, the stairs are narrow and steep. You will have to find your way in the dark. Are you certain, Monsieur, you do not wish me to announce your presence?"

Without responding, the disheveled man moved slowly away from the concierge's window. He took the few short steps leading into the dark entry hall and the narrow, winding stairway leading to the apartments on each floor. His body racked with excruciating pain and his breath short, he slowly climbed the darkened spiral stairway until he reached the top floor.

The bathroom window of Madame Delanouis' apartment was open. It faced the courtyard and the sound of the voices echoing from the courtyard interrupted Raymonde's morning toilet. The resonant timbre of a man's voice, although weakened, left no doubt the famous writer had survived the war and had come back into her life. Her heart seemed to stop beating. She had long reconciled herself to the fact the man whom she always loved was killed on the same day death took his young wife and son. Tears welled in her eyes as she listened to the echo of heavy, tired feet come closer to her door. She took one last glance into the mirror to see that her hair was properly combed, hoping before the man could ring her doorbell she might regain her composure. Slowly, she walked the long hallway leading to the entry door of her apartment. She placed her eye over the tiny eyeglass embedded in the heavy, solid wooden door. Her eyes filled with tears as she watched the man, aged beyond his years, reach for the doorbell that would announce his presence.

Tears turned to sobs as she opened the door. A long, close embrace and kisses replaced the spoken word. "Don't speak, Thomas—please! We will talk after you have some food." Silently, Raymonde ushered the unexpected visitor into the studio. When he was seated, he spoke. "Raymonde, ma cheri, I cannot stay here. It will cause you much pain and trouble. I know the police have watched my every move. Why they did not arrest me at the border, I have no way of knowing. I do know, however, when I again step onto the street, I will be taken into custody. If I might stay here for the remaining part of this day and tonight, I will leave tomorrow morning."

Raymonde hurriedly prepared some food for Thomas. While he was consuming the first meal he had eaten since leaving Switzerland, Raymonde prepared the writer a warm bath. She took his soiled clothing and through out the rest of the daytime hours and far into the night, she laundered his shirt, underwear and socks and mended the torn material in his suit. Gently, she helped her ex-husband's tired body into the small bedroom adjacent to the parlor.

I arrived late afternoon for my lesson. Raymonde's champagne personality had gone flat. Her face revealed a sadness I had never observed. She sat down at the piano ready to begin my usual vocal exercises, but instead of permitting her hands to strike the keys, she spoke. "Van, would you mind returning tomorrow? I have just received an unexpected guest and I wish to spend as much time with my friend as I can since he will be leaving tomorrow morning."

I knew better than to ask any questions. It was obviously a personal problem only my good teacher could solve. Quietly, I left the apartment and began the long walk back to the Magazin Dufayel.

The morning light filtered through the window facing Rue Vanneau. Raymonde was awakened to the sound of running water in the lavatory. Thomas, clean shaven and bathed, donned his freshly laundered clothing. He placed his worn cravat around the collar of his spotlessly laundered shirt. With courage and dignity recaptured, his trademark in years past, Thomas Delanouis was ready to face his day of reckoning.

Raymonde sat next to Thomas on the sofa in the salon. Quietly, they sipped their morning coffee and then after a few quiet moments, Thomas spoke. "I will leave you shortly, ma cheri. I know when I step onto Rue Vanneau, my fate is sealed." Gently, he took Raymonde into his arms. Many years had passed since the warm embrace of this man had comforted the great singer as it did at that moment. Gently he kissed her, then, before parting, he spoke. "I have always loved you, ma cheri." Thomas stood and with one farewell kiss and embrace, he turned toward the door opening onto the stairway landing. Raymonde listened to each footstep as it descended the stairs. Quietly she walked to the large leaded window in the salon that opened outward onto Rue Vanneau. Tears flowed freely as she observed the gendarmes order Thomas into the waiting police wagon. The price for being a traitor and a collaborator with the enemy must be paid. Thomas Delanouis was sentenced to spend the rest of his natural life in a dungeoness prison far from the gay Paree he always loved.

The evening after Thomas Delanouis' arrest was not a night for singing. My beloved teacher and mentor greeted me at the door of her apartment then returned to the Charles V sofa in the studio. Her eyes were red from weeping. She wanted to talk and I had gained her confidence to where she wanted to confide in me regarding the events of the past 24 hours.

Tears flowed freely when she related the death of Thomas' young wife and their infant son. She explained how he escaped into Switzerland successfully able to evade the Allied armies moving toward Paris.

"Thomas was in the next room when you came yesterday for your lesson, Van. I could not tell you about his arrival. Now, I must find some way to help him. It was very dangerous for him to return to Paris. The police could have arrested me for permitting him to stay here for only a few hours. I must find some way to help him."

I wanted to comfort my friend and teacher. I reached into my pocket and withdrew some chocolate and a package of cigarettes. "Here, Madame. I'm sorry for you and I'm sorry for Thomas. This isn't much to give you now, but, when I return tomorrow, I can bring something more."

Not a day passed that Raymonde failed to trek the long journey to the dirty, gray walls of the prison on the outskirts of Paris. By evening, she would return to her apartment and when I arrived for my lesson, the great singer would tell me how the famous writer was adjusting to incarceration. Madame Delanouis had money. She invested her earnings well. This permitted the singer a comfortable lifestyle and it was only the war that caused the life of plenty to change to a life of few luxuries. With her financial assets, the singer was able to retain the finest legal professionals money could buy. This, however, proved to be futile. There were no loopholes whereby the convicted traitor and collaborator could be freed. Thomas Delanouis was destined to remain incarcerated for many, many years, long after the war's end before he would once again smell the fresh air of freedom.

The famous writer must have served the next 20 some odd years of his life in the prison on the outskirts of Paris. He was released, but only when it was certain he would have only a few remaining years of life. The love of Raymonde and Thomas survived those few years. Their relationship became one again. Before the end and the time of Thomas' death, the couple would make their yearly visits to their beloved Venice, the land surrounded by water where the saga of Thomas and Raymonde began.

CHAPTER 52

It was on May 5, 1945 Europe was liberated from the tyranny of Nazism. June and July passed and at the beginning of August, Gisele informed me she would join her family for their usual month of August vacation in the south of France. I was lost without my friend. The entire month seemed like an eternity.

It was, however, a history-making month. The war continued to rage throughout the Pacific, took the lives of thousands of American GIs and there was little hope the Japanese would surrender.

New weapons of war were constantly being developed. One of the most dreaded was the potential atom bomb, created based on the calculations Albert Einstein passed on to the Government of the United States. He had given them the formula for splitting the atom and as a result the most horrifying weapon of war of all time was developed.

Harry S Truman had only been the military's Commander in Chief for approximately four months when he made the decision to end the war by exploding the atom bomb over two Japanese cities, Nagasaki and Hiroshima. It was a day to live in infamy. The entire population of both cities was either vaporized from the enormous heat emitted from the explosions or they were permanently scarred by the terrible man-made weapon of war. The Japanese who survived tried to reach the rivers and the ocean to find relief from the horrendous pain suffered from the two bombs. It was after the second bomb exploded that Japan's leaders were brought to their knees and gave an unconditional surrender. The war in the Pacific had come to an end.

The world was finally at peace. Still the army made no gesture toward sending those stationed in Paris back to their homeland. Work in the headquarters was constant. Charles DeGaulle was the man of the hour. He never hesitated to mingle with crowds in the large cities and small villages. Everywhere the war hero passed, thousands of French people thronged just to get a glimpse of their beloved General. He played a big part in freeing the French people from the tyrannical forces of evil.

Each day as the Government of France became more stable, the more anxious I became to go home. I knew I must do something with Toot Sweet. I knew it was just a matter of time before I, too, would return home, yet, that day never came. I attempted to be transferred from the army to the Air Transport Command, but my commanding officer refused to release me. I had met several men in the Air Force, some pilots, and knew they flew quite often from Orly Field to England. That's where I found an answer for Toot Sweet. I saw no reason she could not go to England should Grims be willing to keep her until the time came for me to return to the states. The answer to the letter I wrote to Grims was positive. "Of course, Van I would be delighted to have Toot Sweet. Do you think you can bring her into England without the usual quarantine?"

"No," I answered. I wasn't sure I could bypass the British customs, but I thought it was worth a try. I contacted an air force buddy. He was leaving for England very soon. He agreed to smuggle Toot Sweet into England and onto British soil.

The morning the pilot prepared to fly from Orly Field to London, Walt drove Toot Sweet and me to the airport. The airman was true to his word. He reached for my little dog, snuggled her under his jacket and boarded the plane. Toot Sweet and the pilot were the only passengers. Reaching London, the pilot hid my dog inside his jacket. The dog seemed to realize her fate was at stake. Not a sound or movement did the tiny creature make as the pilot denied having anything to declare when questioned by the Customs officers. Within an hour after landing in England, Toot Sweet was safely ensconced in a three-story mansion at Craven Hill Gardens.

I heard from Grims on a weekly basis saying Toot Sweet had adjusted well to the life of a Londoner. But—one day a letter arrived stating my dog was very ill. "Please, Van, try to come to London soon," she pleaded.

I was eligible for furlough, yet each time I requested that much time away from duty, it was denied. I could only hope my commanding officer would give me an extra day so I could find medical help for Toot Sweet. I lucked out. I was given that extra day.

Pilots consistently flew across the Channel as often as I might take the Metro from the Champs Elysee' to Place de la Concord. One of my buddies was flying to England on the weekend. "Sure, I can fly you over to see your dog," he said. Just meet me at Orly Field on Thursday morning.

Thursday morning, as I prepared to leave Paris, the clouds opened and rain fell like a cloudburst over the City of Paris including Orly Field. It was the heaviest rainfall I experienced since arriving on the European Continent. Walt agreed to drive me in the Chaplain's jeep to the airport. When we arrived, I noticed a huge military plane in the field several feet from the shack that protected people from the elements. I watched through a small window opening out onto an air strip. A couple of men moved quickly darting from the right wing to the left wing in the process of putting fuel inside the tanks. A voice came over the loud speaker. Come on, Sergeant, we gotta git goin'." I was the only NCO standing there and I knew it had to be me.

The plane I was about to board had served to transport paratroopers over enemy territory. When I entered the man-made flying machine, instead of seats, a row of bucket seats lined each side of the plane. I chose to take the closest bucket to the cockpit. Nervously, I strapped a belt around my waist.

"How many times have you flown, Sergeant?" The pilot turned to speak just before he revved the plane for takeoff. "Never, sir. This is my first time."

The pilot turned his eyes away from mine. Slowly, we began to move onto the runway. I wondered how the man could see where he was taking the plane; the rain was coming down in sheets of water. "Do you like music, Sergeant?"

"Sure do," I quickly replied.

"I hope you like classical music. The London Symphony's broadcasting from London. Sir Thomas Beecham's conducting." He handed me headphones that covered both my ears.

The drone of the engines were deadened as the symphonic beauty of Beethoven's Fifth subdued the sound of the whirling propellers. I could feel the vibrations as the plane moved over the muddy runway. The plane shook as the rutted ground beneath us caused the wheels of the plane to bounce. Like a miracle, it was as if a great hand reached under the wings of the plane and lifted us away from the soggy ground below. Higher and higher we climbed through the heavy clouds until the darkness of the gray sky disappeared and we were transported into fluffy white billows of a goose down softness. The sun was shining. As we approached the shores of England, I could see the white caps topping the ocean swells as the plane neared the emerald green earth of the British Isles.

"Look over there to your left, Sergeant. There's the white cliffs of Dover—the cliffs that made a song famous.

England from the air looked like a precious jewel. For miles, we could see the manicured gardens surrounding the great estates of Lords and Ladies as well as small farms dotting the countryside. As we approached London, we could easily see the Houses of Parliament, Big Ben and Westminster Abbey. From the air, I observed the famous landmarks I had often visited during that final air blitz of England.

As we began to descend and the airstrip came into view, the earth seemed to turn upside down as the plane tilted to the side and we circled above Heathrow Airport. Lower and lower we descended until the plane seemed to stop in mid-air, then slowly, we approached the runway, touching the ground with the ease of a giant bird. I thanked my friend for the ride and his kindness in helping me overcome the fear of flying.

I boarded a bus at the airport that would take me above ground to Trafalgar Square.

Having ridden the underground for many months prior to leaving for the continent, I had no difficulty taking the tube from Piccadilly for the short journey to Marble Arch.

London was different now. When I stepped off the escalator into daylight and into the usual London fog, I recalled the frightening moments when air raid sirens were not silent as they were at this moment. Bombed out areas between Marble Arch and the Hamilton House at Craven Hill Gardens had already been rebuilt. It was a different London than I had known in early 1944.

Toot Sweet was very ill. "Van, you must take her to the doctor." Grims' watery eyes were proof she had learned to love my little wartime waif as much as I did. "I don't think she is going to make it, Van. There's a veterinarian not far from here. I shall telephone him and let him know you are coming."

Throughout the night, I nursed the dog that had just passed her first birthday. She barely responded to my caress. Her eyes watered and her nose ran from the raging fever within the once-beautiful, silky black-haired creature's fragile body.

The following morning, we walked the short distance to the vet's hospital. He was a good, kind, and gentle man who exuded great compassion and tenderness for my little dog. He examined my sick friend, and then with no provocation asked, "Where has this dog been?" I told him about the soldier who was on his way to engage in battle. He asked me to care for his dog. I explained how she survived against all the adversities in an effort to live.

"You know, Sergeant, it is against the law to bring an animal into our country without their first being quarantined. You could be in serious trouble with the British government. The problem now, however, is far greater than threats from the authorities. Your friend has distemper. There is no cure and it is always fatal. It would be best for you and your dog if you would permit me to put her to sleep. It won't hurt. She will be relieved of all her pain and suffering and be at total peace. You may watch, if you'd like as I give her an injection."

The doctor seemed to communicate with my friend. He gently patted Toot Sweet then whispered something in her ear. Toot Sweet walked with the vet as if she were walking next to a dear friend.

I stood from where I was sitting in the doctor's office. I took one more glance at my little war time waif. When she was no longer in sight, I opened the door onto the street and with a heavy heart walked toward the Hamilton House and Craven Hill Gardens. No one seemed to care as the tears flowed freely from my eyes.

CHAPTER 53

THE FRAGRANCE OF CHESTNUTS ROASTING over open fires on street corners permeated the Parisian September autumn air. Gisele returned from her month long vacation in the south of France. I was glad to see my good friend. We had been an inseparable twosome from the first day she entered the office at Place de la Opera. Her absence from Paris during the entire month of August was almost intolerable. I hadn't realized how lonely Paris might be without my dear friend. Gisele looked wonderful. It was obvious the vacation at Les Cygnes had served her well. The warm sun of the Riviera and the daily relaxation lying on the sun-baked beach of the Cote-de-sur, had changed her cream-like complexion into a golden brown.

The war was over and the fall of 1945 initiated the Parisian's social season. It would be the first time for many French people, long before Liberation Day, they could once again enjoy the fall festivities. Gisele gave parties at Rue Maubeuge and I was the only American invited to the gatherings. My friendship with Gisele grew more securely bonded each day, but it was a friendship that would never consummate into anything more than a pure, platonic relationship. She would never have permitted me to break my bond with Gerry on the other side of the ocean.

I had, for many months been the tool enabling my good friend and teacher to correspond with her many colleagues at the Metropolitan Opera. Her home in Paris had always been, during the pre-war years, a stopping off place for great singers, conductors and musicians, including Rose Bampton, Wilfred Pelletier, Rosa Ponselle, Salcedo, Geraldine Farrar, Lily Pons, and many others. I faithfully would deliver to her the letters, unopened, as they arrived in my name at my APO in Paris. By permitting my good teacher to be in contact with her friends, it proved to be a door that would open for me a world far beyond my expectations. An entre' into the world of the Metropolitan Opera.

Going home was becoming an obsession. Thanksgiving of 1945 passed. The Glee Club remained intact and we continued singing concerts and Sunday evening vespers in various churches throughout Paris. I could still recall the good Colonel saying to me when peace came to Europe, "Van— are you still worried?" He was more than aware of my concern about being sent to the front lines of battle. In fact, I had always suspected he crossed me out of the potential ones to go every time my name was submitted.

In December of 1945, I again approached my commanding officer about going home. I had ample points which made me eligible for discharge, but his answer was always the same. "No, Sergeant. We need you here." I asked about a furlough. Anything other than a weekend pass was denied. I had saved some money. I planned on purchasing a ring for Gerry, but instead, I went to the officer and asked if it were possible to have some free time to go skiing at St. Moritz in Switzerland with Hamp. I had never skied, but Hamp and I often went ice skating at a rink in Paris. Hamp's ability to glide effortlessly over the ice was astounding. I had skated, but always on a frozen pond at a neighborhood park in Akron, Ohio. Observing the complete control my buddy exuded on ice more than convinced me he undoubtedly was just as accomplished as a skier.

"I'll teach you to ski, Van. There's nothing to it."

When I approached the commanding officer with the idea, again his answer turned into a flat "No."

My inner spirit began to rebel. Some way, somehow, I would find a way to escape Uncle Sam's fuckin' army.

My good friend Libby, the WAC from Idaho, was chosen as the first American girl to be married in Paris after the war. She had been going with a sergeant for most of our tenure in the French Capitol and now Shaparelli had agreed to pay all the expenses of a grand wedding at Notre Dame for Libby and her sergeant fiance. She asked me to sing for the occasion. I had sung at Notre Dame previously during one of our GI concerts, but this time I stood alone.

As my voice delivered the immortal strains of Schubert's "Ave Maria," it was like a parting memory for all the months I had lived in Paris.

I heard rumors that if a GI got a job in Paris or in Europe and had enough points to be discharged, the army was obligated to let the soldier go. During a lunch break, I happened to pass the War Shipping Administration's office. I still don't know what led me to walk in that direction. I noticed a well dressed man who looked like an American coming down a short flight of stairs leading onto the street. "Sir, can you tell me who the personnel director is for possible employment with the War Shipping Administration?"

"Well," the man spoke softly, "you're talking to him. May I help you?"

I wasted no time telling the man exactly what I wanted. "Sir, if I got an Honorable Discharge from the army here in Paris, would you give me a job?"

The man hesitated, then spoke. "Why don't you come to my office and we'll talk about it." I followed the man into his office. He began speaking as he took his seat in the big leather chair placed behind his desk. "Well, what did you say your name was?"

I repeated my name. "Well, I do need some help here. What have your duties been at the headquarters while serving in the Armed Forces?"

I gave the man a rundown as to what my activities had been since being sent overseas. "Well, sure Sergeant. I'll give you a job. It would mean, however, you would have to remain in Paris for quite an indefinite period of time. Probably, long after all the troops have returned home."

There was a period of silence. The man's statement was not what I wanted to hear. "I want to go home, Sir. I spent almost a year in London and another two years in Paris. The war is over and I want to get on with my life."

"I have an idea." As the man spoke he reached inside the side drawer of his desk and withdrew a piece of paper. "I don't know whether this will work, but, it might be worth a try. Would you be interested in joining the Merchant Marines? I think they might sign you up for one trip and that would get you back to New York. You'd be paid for the trip. A friend of mine headquartered in LeHarve might be able to fix you up. His name is Michael Renner. Come back tomorrow about this time and I'll have a letter of recommendation and an introduction for you."

The good man, whose name is totally gone from my memory, had planted a seed. I had every intention of following through with his suggestion. It would mean getting a Friday off so I could make it to LeHarve and still be back in time for work on Monday. Should the Merchant Marines accept me, they would be hiring me in Europe even though my ultimate goal was a one-way trip to the United States.

I was excited about the prospects of going home. It had never been done before, at least not to my knowledge, where a soldier succeeded in outsmarting the army. There was a chap whose name was Gordon who worked for Colonel Brown in G-2. Gordon had never seen his son who was born after he was drafted into the army. I knew he wanted to go home, so when I approached him with the information I received from the War Shipping Administration, his response was, "Let's do it! I can get an extended pass and I have a buddy who works for the American Embassy who has no trouble getting away. He has access to a command car and I'm sure he will be glad to take us to LeHarve. Van — this is the best fuckin' idea that's come my way since I got into this fuckin' army."

Only Gisele and Hamp knew my plan. Gordon had no difficulty in getting full cooperation from Vincent at the American Embassy. He wanted to go home as badly as we did. Fortunately, my commanding officer permitted me to have an extended three-day pass. At dawn, on January 8, 1946, Gordon and I met our third party, Vincent, on a street corner not far from the a Magazin Dufayel. A command car reserved for top-ranking military officers and dignitaries pulled up to the curb. We were on our way to Le Harve and the first step toward getting out of the army and hopefully, home.

Vincent was from Cleveland, Ohio. I don't know how the man managed to land the cushy job at the Embassy, but Gordon was right—he wanted to go home. Like he was chauffeuring a couple VIPs, Vincent sped through the traffic-free streets of Paris. We soon left the city behind and were on the main highway to LeHarve. Mile after mile, we casually rolled through the countryside of Normandy and quaint provincial French villages. At about 11:45 a.m. the bombed-out skyline of LeHarve appeared in the distance.

We pulled in front of an unpretentious building near the Pier. It was the main Headquarters for the Merchant Marines. Vincent quickly parked the vehicle and the three of us rushed into the building, climbed a flight of stairs and there we saw Mr. Renner's name on the door of an office. The sign posted on the entry door was good news: It said, "Overt," which in English means "Open." We had made it in time. In France, at noon, all French people immediately leave their place of business for a two-hour lunch break. The entire world could disintegrate, yet nothing would break the routine the French established long before their involvement in wars. The time was 11:59 when all three of us stood before an attractive French girl sitting at a desk on the other side of a swinging Dutch door.

"Is Mr. Renner in?" I breathlessly asked. "We must see him immediately. We have driven all the way from Paris, hoping he will give us a letter of employment as Merchant Marines. We all have enough points for discharge and we don't want to wait any longer for the army to get us back to where it all began."

"I'm so sorry, Messieurs. Mr. Renner left the office just a few minutes ago and I don't expect him to return till Monday morning." As she spoke, the receptionist was busily preparing to leave for her lunch. The office would not reopen until 2 p.m. As she escorted all three of us from her office and prepared to post the "Ferme" sign over the door, she spoke.

"Sometimes, gentlemen, Mr. Renner does return for a short period of time in the afternoon, even though he plans to be away for the entire weekend. Why don't you take a chance and come back at four o'clock. If he does come in, I'll make certain he is aware of your visit and that you desperately need to see him."

The morale of three GIs fell to its lowest ebb. We walked away from the Merchant Marine Headquarters, thinking the entire trip had been in vain. We walked to the nearest bar. All shops were closed and even if they had been open, there was little or nothing to purchase. We seated ourselves at a table in a far, dark corner of the pub. We ordered a large pitcher of French beer and even though my dislike for French beer was obvious, Vincent poured the contents of the pitcher into each one of our glasses. Time seemed to stand still. Sipping the woody-tasting beverage, we reminisced about the good times as well as the bad times. Gordon spoke freely about his wife and about his young son, whom he had never seen. It was the Draft Board that caused the two lovers to make a decision to marry. They had been high school sweethearts and by the time Gordon left for his basic training, his wife was pregnant. When his wife was ready to deliver his first child, Gordon had already been sent overseas. That was three years ago.

I knew little about Vincent's background and he offered very little as to his pre-war experience. He just wanted to return to Cleveland. He never mentioned having a girl waiting for him. Gordon and I just assumed he came from an affluent family and that was one of the reasons he ended up in a cushy job at the Embassy in Paris.

As for me, I dreamed about Gerry every night, every hour and every day since the day we parted on that day in June of 1943 at the train station in Akron, Ohio. The daily letters and the packages chuck full of love arrived on a regular basis, and this kept the flame alive for the feelings I had for the girl who lived on the other side of the tracks in Akron.

At 3:30 p.m., we rushed back to the Merchant Marines' headquarters. A man followed us as we entered the building. As we prepared to enter the office at the top of the stairs, the man spoke. "May I help you fellows?" he politely asked.

"We're lookin' for a Mr. Renner," I said.

"Well, I'm Renner," he replied "What can I do for you?"

I reached into my pocket and withdrew the letter from the personnel director at the War Shipping Administration. I handed it to Mr. Renner. The four of us entered the office.

Without hesitation, Mr. Renner handed the letter to his secretary. "Type up a letter of employment for these men, each one of them." Turning toward us, he continued speaking. "Sure, fellers, I'll give you all a job for one trip and you'll get paid for goin'. Glad to have you aboard. I have a troop ship headin' for the states in five days."

It was well past midnight when we reached the outskirts of Paris. Vincent dropped Gordon and me off in front of the Magazin Dufayel. In the dark, I quietly climbed the stairs to the second floor, removed my clothing then crawled into the lower bunk without disturbing Hamp, who was asleep on the top bunk. My good news about going home would wait until chow the next morning.

On Saturday morning, I broke the news to Hamp. "I'm

goin' home, Hamp! Only two more days and I'll be out of this fuckin' army."

Two more days remained before I was due to return to my desk at the headquarters. After chow, I bid adieu to Hamp then walked down the hill from Pigalle to 36 Rue Maubeuge. I had to tell Gisele the good news. I would be on my way home within a few hours.

On Monday morning, Gordon, Vincent and I met at the Separation Center. We were first in line to start the machinery that would free us from a regimented life. Only Providence knew whether our plan of escape from the clutches of the military would work, not until we held a piece of paper in our hand which clearly stated: "Honorable Discharge."

As we waited at the front door of the Separation Center, approximately 500 men lined up behind us. Each man and each woman had their own story. GIs had married French girls and decided to remain in France. Others had taken jobs in Paris which would delay their return to the United States. No one would have dared to do the unthinkable as Gordon, Vince and I had done.

The mustering-out process was similar to the day we were drafted into the army.

The physical examination was nothing more than "Bend over, Soldier and spread your cheeks apart." The examining officer took a quick glance at our rectums and the crack in our butts." Okay, fellows, you can go!" There must have also been an X-ray taken of our lungs at that time. On the discharge papers nothing was mentioned about my hospitalizations, but it did mention a tuberculosis scar on my lower left lobe. This, however, did not deter my getting out of the army.

Expecting Vincent to follow us, Gordon and I moved forward to the next station where we would finally be handed our Honorable Discharge. We heard the officer stop Vincent. Sir, your records indicate you should stick around for a while. You seem to have a health problem, Soldier." Vincent seemed perfectly healthy to me. I wondered if by some fluke, the army had mistakenly handed the wrong physical examination results to Vincent instead of to me. I had been guilty of many dispensary visits and a couple hospitalizations.

Gordon and I stood at attention as we faced the Major. A phone call interrupted his job of handing out Honorable Discharges. As he spoke on the phone, we listened and the news we were hearing from one side of the conversation was not good. From what we could gather from the Major's side of the dialogue, somebody had ordered all discharges be stopped immediately, at least until a certain matter could be straightened out. This action on the part of the Headquarters meant 500 military personnel would be held in limbo.

The Major hung up the phone then apologized for the delay. "I see no reason to hold you two fellows up." He then handed us our Honorable Discharges. "Good luck to you two guys. You are no longer the responsibility of Uncle Sam."

In the eyes of our Commanding Officers, Gordon and I were AWOL. It was an offense that could easily have turned us back into privates and incarcerated us in the Guard House. My Commanding Officer was furious. He happened to pass Hamp in the hallway.

"Do you have any idea where VanNatter is, Hamp? He's AWOL, you know, and that could be serious."

Hamp looked at the officer, then quietly spoke. "I don't think he'll be coming back, sir. He's got a civilian job."

I spent the afternoon with my good teacher Raymonde Delanouis. There was a sadness and yet a happiness about my going home. We spoke about New York and things I should do to continue with my life as a singer. As I prepared to bid farewell, she went to a small desk and withdrew some letters she had written to people that might be willing to open doors into the musical worlds. There was a letter of introduction to Maestro Wilfred Pelletier at the Metropolitan Opera. Another letter was written to Rosa Ponselle who lived in Baltimore and another personal letter to Madame Elizabeth Schumann who was teaching voice at Curtis Institute in Philadelphia. As she handed each letter to me, she then reached for another letter.

It was to Dr. and Mrs. Dubrosky. In this letter, she asked the Doctor and his wife to give me a warm greeting when I arrived back home.

As a final gesture, Raymonde reached for a small pencil drawing of a woman. It was a simple drawing but as she handed it to me, she said, "I want you to have this. It was done by a very famous artist by the name of Felicien Rops. Each time you look at it, you will think of me."

It was nearing the time for the office at the Headquarters to close. I agreed to meet Hamp and Gisele at a small café across the street from the building on Avenue Kleber where we had worked and had turned our working relationship into a family affair. As we sat sipping a glass of wine, Gisele spoke. "Van—we have planned a party for you this evening—a farewell party. We are all going to Bel Tambourin in Montmartre."

Gisele had given so many parties. All of them "going away parties," but going away never happened. This party was for real. When I arrived at the famous nightclub, I discovered my entire office force was there. My ex-commanding officer was also there, but he was not invited to our party. The band played, and we danced and danced on the crowded dance floor. My right arm seemed to react like a handle bar as Gisele and I glided over the floor, and each time we danced near the commanding officer and his date, my right elbow managed to give him a jab in the side. I got my revenge. He later told Hamp, had he been able to stop all the discharges, including mine, he most certainly would have broken me to a private.

I spent the last night at the Magazin Dufayel, packing memorabilia and personal items into my dufflebag. The hours spent at Bel Tambourin left little time for sleep. As daylight lifted the darkness of night, I was on my first lap of the long journey home.

CHAPTER 54

THE TRAIN MOVED SLOWLY AWAY from St. Lazarre Station. The date was January 11, 1946. Gordon and I found a compartment where we would not be disturbed by other passengers. There were misgivings about leaving the most beautiful of all European cities. From the day Paris was liberated, Paris had been my home. The friends became more than friends; they were family. Those people included Jews, French aristocrats, people on the street—all of whom were grateful to the Americans for driving the enemy from their home land.

The journey was quiet as we passed through the Normandy countryside. Gordon was a man of few words and I wasn't one to force a conversation if the other person decided not to talk. The steward announced lunch was being served in the dining car. When we entered the dining car three cars from where our compartment was located, a French Maitre d' ushered us to a table then presented us with a menu. White table linens, a bottle of wine, and a menu neither one of us thoroughly understood, would be our farewell meal and the last chance to indulge in French cuisine.

When the train reached Le Harve, Gordon and I threw our dufflebags over our shoulders and walked toward the pier and the Merchant Marine billets. We were assigned beds. The accommodations were clean and the beds were even decked with white sheets and warm blankets. What a difference! For a few nights while waiting for a ship to take me home, it was difficult to fathom the luxury a Merchant Marine had in comparison to the years I occupied a bunk and slept on a burlap mattress at the Magazin Dufayel.

Next to my assigned bed, lay a young Norwegian chap. He spoke English well. Like me, he was waiting to be assigned a ship. Of course, he was a genuine Merchant Marine. He had traveled the high seas long before the war began. The sea was his life. He had survived torpedo hits and even spent a certain amount of time on a life raft floating on a world of water for days before being rescued by one of our Allied vessels.

"The Atlantic is mighty rough this time of year, Friend," was the way he opened the dialogue between him and me. "What's the name of the ship on which you've been assigned?" Of course, I had no answer to that question. They haven't told me yet," I replied. My new friend continued. "I hope it's not that ship, that one anchored outside this building. That's what they call one of them 'Victory Ships.' They have a reputation for splitting in half in mid-ocean., I'd sure hate to be sailing on that tub." As the Norwegian spoke, my color turned a sickening green.

My new acquaintance's description of the ocean at this time of year and the type of boat which possibly would be the one Gordon and I would be assigned, was not exactly the news I wanted to hear.

Our conversation was interrupted when someone announced a phone call for VanNatter. Making my way to the front desk, doubts circulated in my mind: "Had the army caught up with me again so they could accuse me of going

AWOL? Cautiously, I lifted the receiver of the phone. The message was the best send-off present possible. Gisele and the entire office staff in Paris wanted to wish me a bon voyage one more time prior to setting sail.

I met Gordon as he stood outside the Merchant Marine Office. It was time for chow. To get to the mess hall meant we must walk along the pier and alongside the ship anchored in Le Harve's Harbor. I related to Gordon what the Norwegian sailor told me about the Victory Ship. When we returned to our assigned beds, there was an order stating we would be sailing on the ship anchored at the pier. It was called the "Wheaton Victory."

The foreign soldier was right. It was the same ship moored at the pier, a troopship that would carry a large number of officers and enlisted men back to their homeland.

Early the following morning after consuming a hearty breakfast Gordon and I went aboard. A small cabin in the bow of the ship was previously assigned to Gordon, me, and another chap whom neither one of us knew, not until we settled into our double bunks. We were then assigned the duties we were to perform during the ten-day voyage. My responsibilities were easy. I was to make up the officer's beds each morning while they were eating breakfast.

After settling in our cabin, Gordon and I went on deck to watch the GIs and officers come aboard ship. When the gangplank was released from the pier and the anchor pulled in, a tugboat guided us into international waters and the open sea.

The ship hadn't moved from the shores of France before my gut began churning and my head went into a spin. The food I had eaten at breakfast wanted to come up. I dashed toward the railing of the ship, then tried to direct my head over the railing, hoping that everything coming up would go out to sea instead of spilling onto the deck.

The skyline of Le Harve was still in view when I heard a friendly voice from a fellow standing behind me. He was a tall, muscular, black man, a seasoned seaman who had sailed the Atlantic in summertime, wintertime, peace time and in war time. "Hey, feller - you're lookin' kinda peaked." The would-be good Samaritan reached into his pocket and pulled out a lemon. He took out a knife from his side pocket, then cut the lemon in half. "Here, squeeze some of this juice in yer mouth. It might settle yer gut." I took the lemon, then attempted to squeeze some of its juice down the back of my throat. My gut did not agree with the good Samaritan's antidote for sea sickness. I rushed to the railing and whatever remained in my stomach from breakfast spewed over the railing and went out to sea.

I finally moved away from the railing and made an attempt to reach my assigned quarters. I stretched out on the bottom bunk but the discomfort of the waves rolling in my gut continued to compete with the angry waves sweeping the Atlantic Ocean. Every roll of the ship caused my insides to rush against my gut like an incoming tide slapping against a sandy beach.

When we reached the three-mile zone and international waters, the tug boat was released from our ship and we were on our own. The huge vessel began to groan and moan like it was in more pain than the never-ceasing churning in my stomach. The ship rolled and heaved throughout the day. At noontime, I exerted an effort to rise from my bunk and put on a pretense of acting like a Merchant Marine.

The galley was located in the center of the ship. This meant going on deck, grabbing hold of a steel cable stretched from bow to stern, so I wouldn't be washed overboard. The winds whipped around the open decks of the ship like a hurricane. The swells from the Atlantic began to look like mountains as the knee deep saltwater dashed over the decks. With both hands I tightly wrapped my grip around the steel cable. I managed to reach the center of the ship and a door that would open onto a flight of stairs that would lead downward to the ship's galley. With a sudden burst of extra ordinary strength I was able to open the door in spite of the strong wind pushing against my entire body.

Once inside the vessel, I found my way to the galley. The food aboard ship was more appetizing and better tasting than anything I ever experienced from an army Mess Sergeant, but I couldn't eat. I just wanted to make it back to my cabin, curl up on the lower bunk and stay there for the duration.

The black chef watched as I attempted to put food in my mouth. "Hey feller. There's only one way to git rid of seasickness and that is to eat whether you think you can or whether you think you can't. I guarantee, if you do as I tell ya, you might just enjoy the ride. It's goin' to be a long and rough haul before we git to the other side."

Consuming food was the answer. After consuming that first meal, the discomfort subsided. Even my legs adapted to the ceaseless rolling motion of the ship.

I managed to consume two meals on that day, lunch and dinner. The following morning, like a seasoned sailor, I made my way to the galley, ate a full breakfast, then went to the officer's quarters to begin my assigned duties. The bunks were all occupied. The officers were so ill from sea sickness, none of them chose to leave their bunks. For the following ten days, the gentlemen of the army refused to eat or leave their bunks, or attempt to put any food in their stomachs. I returned to my quarters. For the duration, sailing over the stormy seas, my assigned duties were never consummated. Not because of my unwillingness to fulfill them, but because I couldn't make up beds when they were always occupied.

The angry sea defied all those who dared to sail upon its waters. The Atlantic was known for its defiance, always daring intruders to enter its realm. The high winds never ceased. Holding tightly onto the cable that stretched from stern to bow was my only salvation from being washed overboard. Like a seasoned seaman, I soon learned I could make it to the galley and then back to my quarters without succumbing to a watery grave.

With each roll of the ship as it climbed the mountainous swells, water dashed across the deck and I found myself wading in icy waters up to the mid-calf of my pant legs. The violent winds pushed against me like an impenetrable wall.

In the middle of the night and the third day at sea the ship rolled and moaned. It was sometime during that black night the troop ship was suddenly caught in a wave trough. The lights throughout the ship dimmed and then all was blackness. I was thrown from my bunk onto the deck. Gordon was tossed from his upper bunk. Our third cabin mate was thrown from his bunk causing all of us to land in one big heap on deck. Everything not bolted down fell on top of us. The ship lay on its side leaving us in a black void of darkness. The thought that perhaps the ship was sinking and had split in half passed through our minds. Frightened, we waited for the next swell that would send us to the bottom of the sea.

An eternity seemed to pass before the ship's generators returned lights to the vessel and the ship slowly righted itself.

On the ninth day, the ship sailed into calm waters. I walked onto the deck. Instead of a cold, wet, wintry morning, the sea was calm and the air was warm. We had successfully reached the Japanese gulf stream. Officers began to emerge from their bunks like prairie dogs popping up out of underground tunnels. A second lieutenant stood at the bow of the ship. He seemed to be in a trance or in deep meditation when suddenly he disappeared from sight. The ship rolled and water rushed over the deck. When the ship righted itself, bobbing up from the salty brine, a very wet and disoriented officer's hands were frozen to the ship's railing. No comic actor could depict the look on the lieutenant's face. I went into a fit of laughter. Of course, my sense of humor was not well received by the officer, but I didn't care. The man with a single gold bar on his shoulder would never again hold my fate in his hands.

Only a few hours remained before we would dock in New York harbor. Gordon and I were summoned to the captain's cabin. As we entered the inner sanctum of the man who was always at the helm of the ship, we were greeted by a good-looking man with a full head of prematurely silvery gray hair. He had a calm quietness which seemed to match the mood of the sea at that moment The captain rose from his swivel chair. Reaching out his hand, he grasped our hands with a firm handshake. "Glad to have had the honor of having you two guys aboard. Sorry it was such a rough trip, but, in spite of the wave trough, we made it and I believe we're going to anchor in New York Harbor with no further problems," he said. On the captain's desk lay two sealed envelopes. Inside each envelope were three one hundred dollar bills and one fifty. The same amount of money the army gave me on the day I re-entered civilian life. "We'll be docking about 8:00 a.m. tomorrow morning, men. There is no reason you fellows can't git off his tub as soon as we dock and the gangplank is lowered. There is no purpose for your waiting until the troops leave the ship. I know it's been a long time since you were home. I'm glad we have been some help in getting you there."

With military politeness, Gordon and I stood at attention and gave the officer a final salute. He smiled. "You're not in the army now, so cut the crap. Get outta here."

It was the sounds of Manhattan that awakened me. I realized then the ship was no longer moving and we had reached our destination. We had failed to see the Statue of Liberty when we sailed three years prior and now that we were docked, we failed to see her again.

Gordon and I threw our dufflebags over our shoulders, rushed down the stairs to the gangplank and for the first time in three years, our feet touched American soil.

Like ships passing in the night, Gordon and I parted with a handshake. It would be the last encounter we would share. As for the stormy journey across the wintery Atlantic, that would forever remain embedded in our memory.

CHAPTER 55

"Taxi! Taxi!" I yelled as if I were an ordinary New Yorker. A yellow cab pulled up to the curb. "Take me to Penn Station," I ordered. I tossed my dufflebag onto the backseat of the cab then crawled in beside it.

"It didn't take ya long to git off that boat, Soldier. How long has it been since you was home?"

"It's been awhile," I responded. I was no longer a soldier even though I continued to wear Uncle Sam's uniform which displayed a number of battle stars.

The cab zipped through the heavy Manhattan traffic like a football player headed for a touchdown. Crosswalks and traffic lights had little or no respect in the City of New York. It was obvious: it was every man for himself. People on foot darted in and out of the moving cars like millions of undisciplined ants. The speeding cab in which I was a passenger would slightly touch the coattails of pedestrians who dared to go from one side of the street to the other amidst bumper-to-bumper traffic.

Although the ride in the taxi was almost as threatening as the ten-day sea voyage on the *Wheaton Victory*, I was able to observe America's prosperity. Department store windows displayed the latest fashions in clothing. Women actually wore leather high-heel shoes—not the wooden clodhoppers worn by the French girls in Paris. Meat markets displayed fresh cuts of red meat and small markets exhibited an array of fresh vegetables. Fruit stands overflowed with an abundance of melons, fresh oranges, grapefruit, bananas, all available, provided one had money to buy. It was a vast contrast to the empty shops in Paris where food continued to be at a premium. The Parisian windows formerly displaying elegant fashions prior to the war remained bare. Les Halles, the Parisian market for fresh produce remained as deserted as most war time train stations. The black market was the only business that flourished during and after the war. It was the only source of food for the French people until a peace time economy could be established. It was obvious from my first glance at America after three years absence that the United States had not been touched for lack of comforts and luxuries known only to Americans. America's greatest loss during the most devastating war in history were the thousands of young American soldiers who died on foreign soil so the land of plenty could thrive.

The taxi came to a stop at the curb in front of Penn Station. Placing my dufflebag on the sidewalk, I reached in my pocket for the correct change needed to make the taxi driver happy. "Keep it, Soldier, and welcome home." With those words, the cab pulled away from the curb looking for a more lucrative fare.

When I reached inside my pocket for change, my fingers touched a tiny packet tied with a silk string. I lifted the packet from my coat pocket and when I untied the string and opened the tightly wrapped paper, there was a pearl in it. It was a parting gift from Gisele. On the paper, she had written:

To my dear Van—this little gift I would like you to have made into a ring for Gerry. Every time you look at this pearl, you will think of me.
Gisele

Carefully, I wrapped the paper around the pearl, then tucked it inside my coat pocket.

The Gothic structure of Penn Station and its magnificent marble pillars overshadowed the surrounding buildings on Seventh Avenue. Across the street stood the Hotel Statler. My eyes roamed up and down Seventh Avenue then across 34th Street toward the East Side of Manhattan. There it was, the tallest building in the nation, the Empire State Building. The only time I'd seen the building was in a photograph. At the time, a heavy fog had settled over the city causing an airplane to crash into the top floor. It was international news. In awe, I stood on the steps of Penn Station and marveled at the Empire State building and all the surrounding skyscrapers rising upward toward the heavens until they touched the clouds. Streets hummed with automobile traffic. People, people, and more people! Rushing somewhere, looking but seeing nothing. The war was over and for the New Yorker, it was business as usual.

The military uniform was a pass to wherever a soldier wanted to travel. This was a gratuity offered by the railroad free of charge. I had no opportunity to purchase civilian clothing since my discharge from the army. Consequently, the uniform continued to cover my body as it had for three years and would continue to do so until I reached Akron and could make my entrance into the civilian world by donning the proper attire that would make my peacetime status official. My army uniform had to be my passport to get me to my hometown of Akron, Ohio.

I stepped onto the escalator to the lower level of the station. As I stepped off the moving stairway, I heard the conductor's last call. "All aboard, all aboard for Princeton!" I reached the steps of the train just as the train began to move away from the terminal. The conductor reached for my dufflebag then politely tossed it above the seat where I would sit. I removed my overcoat, then quietly relaxed in anticipation of the ride to Princeton. The train made its way under the Hudson River via the Holland Tunnel. When we ascended from the darkness, the skyline of New York City faded into oblivion. We rolled over the tracks of New Jersey, never stopping until we reached a picturesque village to take aboard more passengers or let people disembark that had reached their point of destination.

Elizabeth! Rahway! Tenafly! Each village train depot displayed its own quaint personality. The scene had not changed since my first visit to the East Coast at the age of 14. I knew my destiny was to someday return to New York and to New England where I would find my niche in the world of music. Potbellied stoves warmed the waiting room of each picturesque train station. People had time for a few minutes of friendly, congenial, and caring conversation before continuing on to wherever they were going. The world, at that time, was not a world of automobiles. Many depended on the train to go from one place to another.

Princeton, New Jersey, is a pretty university town. It is not only the home of the famed university, but within a short walking distance from the Ivy League school, stands the world-renown Westminister Choir College.

Westminister was founded primarily as a source for supplying the Presbyterian Church with highly trained choral directors. Dr. Williamson recruited many of the finest vocal teachers and singers in America to teach at his school. I had a flashback to the time I was 14 years old and had spent one summer at Westminister Choir College Summer School, conducted at Mount Herman in the foothills of the Berkshire Mountains. Dr. Williamson, at that time, had given me his valuable time to teach me how to pronounce "L," a speech impediment that had plagued me since the day I was born.

The train began to slow as we entered the town of Princeton. The conductor passed through the aisle announcing, "Princeton! Princeton!" My eyes searched the platform for the girl I had longed to come home to, the girl who never missed a single day during the three years of my absence to write a letter, even though there wasn't much to write about on the home front.

As if the young woman standing alone on the platform were an apparition, one even more beautiful than she had been the day I went off to war, I knew there was no mistake as I glanced at the girl who was still in her teens when I went away and who had become my first real love. Gerry was no longer a teenager. She was now a mature, magnificent specimen of female beauty.

I reached for my dufflebag, then pushed my way to the open door at the end of the car. I sat my dufflebag on the steps, waiting for the train to come to a halt. Stepping from the train onto the platform, I opened my arms. Her embrace and tears were the assurance I needed. There was no doubt our love had more than withstood the sands of time.

The village of Princeton and Princeton University is a town of celebrities and world-renowned dignitaries. Albert

Einstein roamed the campus and the village like any normal American. People's faces whose photos appeared daily in the nation's newspapers were as common as next door neighbors. It was the home of the famous scientific brain of Albert Einstein, a brain that caused our nation to give birth to one of the most destructive weapons of war known to mankind. It was true: the deadly weapon of war brought a terrible conflict between two nations to an abrupt end, but that same weapon also became a monster far beyond the control of its human creators.

I planned to spend only a couple days in Princeton, hoping to make some connections in New York City before returning to Akron and abandoning my army uniform. Gerry walked me to the residence whose occupants agreed to let me stay with them during those two days.

Gerry had prearranged this accommodation, which gave me access to a telephone. Leaving my dufflebag in my room, I walked Gerry back to her dorm at Westminister.

My first telephone call to New York City was to telephone Maestro Wilfred Pelletier at the Metropolitan Opera House. The voice I heard over the phone was like that of an old friend. "How soon may I see you, Van? I want to hear you sing."

"Could I see you tomorrow, sir? I just arrived this morning and I am in Princeton visiting my girlfriend."

"Why, yes. I think that is possible. How about tomorrow morning, say 11:00 o'clock? I will be waiting for you at the stage door."

There was no problem. I was certain Gerry could be away from school for one day. She could accompany me to New York.

My second telephone call was to Madame and Doctor

Dubrowsky. A cheerful voice answered the phone. As I had done during those long war years, I was a go-between for communications between Maestro Pelletier and Madame Dubrowsky by utilizing my APO address. It was during Madame Delanouis' tenure at the Metropolitan as a leading diva that the Dubrowskys opened their home to the young singer from France.

"Van, we are so anxious to see you. Just this morning the postman brought a letter from Raymonde saying we should expect you to telephone. Please come to dinner tomorrow night. We are most anxious to have news of Raymonde and also to hear about your audition with Maestro Pelletier. We have been devoted friends to the Pelletiers for many years. As you probably are aware, his wife, Rose Bampton, is a leading diva with the Metropolitan."

"Would it be too presumptuous, Madame, to ask if I could bring my girlfriend? We have been separated for such a long time and even now our time is short since I must leave for my home in Akron, Ohio." There was no hesitation in Madame Dubrosky's response.

"Of course, dear. You must bring your young lady. We are most anxious to meet her. We'll expect you then, say, at 6:00 o'clock?"

I could barely contain the good news from Maestro Pelletier. I wanted to tell someone, but Gerry would be in class until late afternoon. I began a leisurely stroll through the Princeton campus. Large shade trees dotted the magnificent grounds and an occasional park bench under one of the trees seemed to say, "Come, young man, take a load off your feet and sit here." Students were either away because they had not returned from the Christmas holidays or they were involved in curricular activity inside the university. The campus was totally void of other human beings as I quietly sat down on the bench.

Waiting for the time to pass so I could be with Gerry, I noticed a tall, handsome, familiar looking gentleman dressed in military uniform laden with medals and battle stars approaching me. As the man drew closer and approached my bench, I suddenly realized it was General Pleas B. Rogers. Quickly I stood at attention and extended a salute. The general was first to speak "Well, Sergeant, when did you get back? I am so happy to see you again. I have often thought about you and have not forgotten the beautiful music you and the Glee Club so unselfishly gave to the troops in London and in Paris. What do you plan to do with your life now that the war has finally come to an end?"

I was burning with excitement over the morning telephone conversation with Maestro Pelletier and I wanted to tell somebody. The general listened with intent interest and when I finished, he held out his hand and with a firm handshake he quietly said, "I want to wish you the greatest success, Sergeant."

The general who'd led 13 men into Paris under cover of darkness before Liberation Day continued, "Those performances you gave so many times in the chapel near Grosvenor Square, the concerts and radio broadcasts in London and in Paris shall be remembered for a very long time. I also vividly recall your performance with Glenn Miller's Orchestra on VE Day."

Standing at attention, I gave the general a final salute. A gentle, sincere smile flashed across his chiseled face and the vision of the man standing on the beachhead at Omaha Beach in Normandy as he greeted the 13 men of the Forward Echelon Company was suddenly relived. It was like two ships passing in the night, never to meet again as we continued our journey into uncharted waters.

As the image of my war time protector and leader faded into memory, I reached inside my pocket and touched the small packet Gisele had given me as a going-away gift. I decided not to tell Gerry about the pearl. Not until I had the stone mounted into a ring.

Gerry and I had a quiet dinner together that evening. We reminisced about the war. I told her about my phone call to New York and begged her to cut classes so she could spend the day with me. She agreed to accompany me to New York and also to the audition. We would spend the remaining part of that day sightseeing until it was time to arrive at the Dubrosky home for dinner.

The building at the corner of 39th and Broadway appeared to be more of a well used warehouse than a facility housing the world's greatest singers, musicians, and conductors. Raymonde often spoke about the opera house in non-glowing terms, saying it was undoubtedly the most drafty and cold building in which she had had the privilege to sing. At no time did she mention it as an ancient tenement. The Metropolitan Opera House could not compare with the elegant opera houses in Europe with their marble staircases, elaborate chandeliers, and rich thickly hand-woven rugs displayed on the magnificent marble floors.

The immortal names passing through the door of the Metropolitan Opera House encompassed not only Raymonde Delanouis, but famous sopranos, mezzo sopranos, tenors, baritones, and basses plus a large chorus of singers that would turn a Cecil B. DeMille production into a close second with all its grandeur. Enrico Caruso and Martinelli reigned as kings in the tenor wing. Tibbett, Scotti, Leonard

Warren, although never getting to sing the romantic roles with the leading divas, were household names in the baritone wing. Geraldine Farrar, Kirsten Flagstad, Rosa Ponselle, Grace Moore, Rise Stevens and a host of others reigned in the minds of opera lovers and would never be forgotten. Having one's name on the Met roster was comparable to winning an Olympic gold medal.

A Canadian tenor by the name of Edward Johnson had replaced Galli-Gassetti and Herbert Witherspoon. He had sung numerous roles during his tenure as an artist on the same stage as other famous tenors, but when he was appointed general director, he opened the door for many American singers. Even though many were only assigned compramario roles, twists of fate occasionally brought small part singers fame and fortune when they were given a chance to prove to the world their exceptional talent.

Lawrence Tibbett was a typical example. The young baritone from California, through the efforts of a vocal coach and accompanist by the name of Frank LaForge was able to get an audition for his young protégé, Lawrence Tibbett. As a result, the young singer was added to the roster, singing insignificant and ungratifying roles such as Valentine in "Faust."

Frank LaForge was a superb pianist and accompanist. He was probably the most notable vocal coach and accompanist within the classical circles of New York City. He patiently coached the leading divas, tenors, and baritones in their respective roles they would perform on the world-renown stage. So it was with Lawrence Tibbett. He coached the young singer in all the small parts as well as leading baritone roles, and one of those leading roles was the character of Ford, in Verdi's "Falstaff." It was destined to be this particular operatic role that would bring LaForge's young protégé into international prominence.

The Italian baritone, Antonio Scotti, was the king of the baritone wing of the Metropolitan. He was well schooled in Verdi operas. Not only did he sing Verdi extremely well, he also created a memorable interpretation for the role as Scarpia in Puccini's "Tosca." It was always Antonio Scotti who was given first choice of roles until one fateful afternoon matinee when the man awakened only to discover he had an unforgiving case of laryngitis. He was slated to sing the role of Ford in Verdi's "Falstaff." He couldn't sing! Only one baritone on the Met roster knew the role of Ford. It was the comparably unknown singer by the name of Lawrence Tibbett. The Metropolitan Opera was not inclined to reimburse money for tickets that were purchased far in advance of the opera. The management had no choice but to let the young baritone from California sing the role in the stead of the great Antonio Scotti.

The Italian baritone was incensed. His ego and jealousy caused him to stand in the wings, waiting for the young baritone to fall on his face. As Lawrence entered the stage, he had found his way home. His voice began to resound like a brilliant angelic trumpet. His rendition of "The Credo" brought the Shakespearian classic story to life, setting a precedence that even to the present day there has been no equal. The audience rose from their seats in standing ovation as the curtain fell. Lawrence Tibbett was a star.

When the gold curtain closed at the end of the act, it was always traditional for the stars to take bows and receive their laurels from the audience. Senore Scotti stood in the wings, graciously parting the curtain aside for all his colleagues, except one. Lawrence waited in the wings, waiting for the great singer to open the curtain for him. Scotti refused to let the youthful artist take a deserved bow. The audience waited and cheered, "We want Tibbett! We want Tibbett!" Totally dejected by the actions of the famous Italian baritone, Lawrence quietly made his way to his dressing room and began removing his costume. He removed the wigs, beard, and grease paint from his youthful face. The sound of the audience penetrated his dressing room and he could hear the stomping of feet and the loud shouts, but he could do nothing.

There was a knock on his dressing room door. Lawrence opened the door: It was the stage manager. "Sir, you must come now; they want you to take a bow. It's the only way the opera can proceed. We must bring some sanity to this audience; they have gone crazy!"

The young singer glanced at his image in the lighted mirror over his dressing table. Quietly, half undressed, he rose from his chair and followed the stage manager to the wings of the opera house. The gold curtain parted and for the first time in operatic history, a young American took center stage to acknowledge his well-deserved accolade.

Scotti's selfish display of jealousy literally caused the audience to stampede. There was stomping of feet and loud boos overshadowing any claque Scotti may have hired to encourage bravos and applause. The king of baritones would no longer reign on his sacred pedestal.

Lawrence Tibbett's matinee success appeared on the front page of every American newspaper the following morning. Radio stations broadcast the news of the phenomena into each American home. Every management company within the City of New York arrived at Lawrence Tibbett's doorstep begging to be his personal manager, promising him a long career on the opera stages of the world, concert stages, and a movie career. Deciding on Evans and Salter as managers, Lawrence began his long, fruitful career. Offers flowed from every direction, including Hollywood. The world's concert and movie sound stages belonged to him.

Gerry and I strolled along the sidewalks of New York from Penn Station to 39th and Broadway. It was true: the building looked more like a tenement building than a house for the greatest musicians, singers, and opera divas in the entire world. The stage door was open. A rather short, gray haired gentleman appeared. It was Maestro Wilfred Pelletier. He extended a firm handshake and a warm welcome as he ushered us into his dressing room. Before I could sit down, the great musician took his place at the piano. Gerry sat on the sofa.

"Well, Monsieur Van, what are you going to sing for me?"

I had no operatic repertoire. All the time I worked with Raymonde my literature consisted of Brahms, Fauré and Debussy. These were considered art songs. The nearest piece I had to offer that would be of an operatic quality was a song written by Brahms entitled "Der Kirchoff."

Before I had a chance to get a good breath, the great musician struck chords on the piano I never knew existed. He played with such bravissimo, it was as if I were suddenly working with a large orchestra. Raymonde had trained me well. I had learned all my repertoire with her sans accompaniment and had learned to count the value of every note. I could hear her say, as she had spoken so many times, "Van, you learn the music this way, and you will never have to worry. You will always be right."

My voice took flight and as I finished the final note of the song, Maestro Pelletier complimented me. "Now, Monsieur, what can I do for you?" I knew I had to go to school, but aware of my academic record, I was certain no college or university would accept me. I only knew how to sing. "I want to go to school, sir," I answered. The Maestro was quiet for a moment, then he spoke. "Well, would you consider going to Juillard?"

My mouth opened like I had just swallowed a canary. Stuttering a bit, I responded. "Do, do ya think that's possible?"

Wilfred Pelletier reached for the telephone. He dialed a number and I could hear the voice of another person speak on the other end of the line. Wilfred Pelletier spoke. "Let me speak to George Wedge, please." The efficient voice of a receptionist quietly asked. "Whom may I say is calling?" With a firm answer, the maestro replied, "It's Wilfred Pelletier at the Metropolitan Opera."

Within a second, a resonant voice projected through the telephone receiver. "This is George Wedge. Pelly! My God, it's been a long time since I spoke with you. What's new? And why do I have this unexpected telephone call?"

"George, I know it's been a long time since we talked but I have a young singer here, an ex-GI who just returned from France. He worked with Raymonde Delanouis during the time he was stationed in Paris. You do remember Raymonde, don't you?"

I could hear George Wedge's response, "Well, who could forget that beauty?"

"George, I believe this fellow has a talent worth developing and I think he is someone you should take a listen to."

"Pelly, you know that's no problem. If you say this young man is good, tell him I will see that he is matriculated into our school at the beginning of the summer session. Tell him I will expect to see him in mid-June."

My life changed within one morning on that cold January day. I couldn't believe my good luck. I was accepted into Juilliard School of Music!

Gerry and I left the opera house and walked toward 59th Street. It was lunch time, and within a short distance from 59th Street was Central Park and a restaurant called Tavern on the Green. We had a quiet lunch then moseyed toward the zoo in Central Park The afternoon passed quickly. As daylight began to fade and nighttime turned on the millions of lights, we walked toward Central Park West and the address Madame Dubrowsky had given me the day before during our telephone conversation.

The Dubroskys lived in a pretentious-looking apartment building whose canopy stretched from the entrance to the edge of the sidewalk A uniformed doorman stood like a wax figure until a taxi or a Rolls Royce pulled up to the curb. We entered the luxurious lobby. A black, uniformed elevator man greeted us. His clothes were neatly pressed and his congenial manner expressed the elegant manners one would expect from a servant serving the chosen elite who could well afford the lifestyle of the rich. We entered the elevator and when we reached the floor on which the Dubroskys resided, the elevator man stood aside while Gerry and I moved from the elevator into the hallway. "It's the apartment at the end of the hall, sir. They're expecting you."

A bit nervous, I pushed the doorbell. A slightly built, middle-aged Jewish man with a thinning white hairline opened the door. "Well, well, you must be the young singer we have anxiously been waiting to meet. And this must be your beautiful lady friend." Without further ado, Dr. Dubrosky ushered us into an entryway which opened into a large living room. An elegantly dressed matronly woman stood at the entrance to the living room. She was a bit taller than her husband and she exuded a rare, radiant beauty and sophistication. Her voice was musical and warm as she greeted us then motioned for us to sit on the long down sofa placed in front of a large picture window that overlooked Manhattan's skyline and Central Park. She reached for Gerry's hand as she spoke."My, you do have a beautiful young lady friend, Mr. VanNatter. May we call you 'Loy' or do you prefer 'Van'? Raymonde always referred to you as Van." It was a good feeling, knowing our new acquaintance was ready to accept us on a first name basis.

"A letter arrived just this morning from Raymonde, telling us to expect you to call. She mentioned how anxious you were to return home, primarily because of this young lady. Now I under stand why."

Dr. Dubrosky interrupted our conversation. His blue eyes sparkled and danced as he spoke. "I believe this calls for a celebration. How about a cocktail before dinner?"

Gerry was far more educated in this kind of protocol. She had often experienced what we referred to as "the Happy Hour" or "the Cocktail Hour."

Madame Dubrosky rang a small bell that was placed on the coffee table. A servant appeared dressed in a black dress laced with a white collar and a white cap on her head. In her hands, she held delectable looking hors d'oeuvres.

There was a toast to my arrival home and to Gerry's and my future. The evening was turning into what the Germans referred to as a "gemutlich" evening. Our conversation centered around my audition with Monsieur Pelletier and how he made it possible for me to be accepted into the finest music institution in America and probably the best in the entire world.

The good doctor and his wife were strong supporters of the Metropolitan Opera long before Raymonde arrived to take up residency in their home during the opera season. They often entertained many of the great singers and conductors. As we discussed the musical world, I felt as though I already stood on the threshhold that would lead me into the great world of music.

"Dinner is served, Madame," I heard the maid announce as we tipped our glasses for one more toast. We entered into a formal dining room and for the next couple hours, we dined on one of the finest meals I had consumed in a long time.

The hour was late as Gerry and I bid goodnight to the Dubrowkys. There was just enough time to catch the last train to Princeton. Reaching Princeton, I escorted Gerry to her dorm then walked slowly as in a dream world to the home that let me have a room and a bed to sleep in for those two short days after the return to my homeland. My mind was in the clouds. I knew where I was going. The metropolis of Manhattan was going to be my Mecca.

Chapter 56

THERE WAS NO SPECTACULAR GREETING when I stepped off the train in Akron on a very cold winter afternoon; nothing to compare with that warm day in June of 1943. No familiar faces met the train.

I took a taxi from the depot to the house on Malacca Street. The name of the street was changed to Frazier Avenue but the house looked the same. The open porch and the old swing attached to its rafters were just as inviting as they were during those pre-war years when I was a teenager. That swing was often my refuge where I would swing for hours visualizing what it would be like when I reached manhood and could fulfill my dreams. It was where I courted Marietta, thinking she was the right mate for me. I even thought of marrying her before I was drafted into the army, but, fortunately, Gerry came back into my life and those ideas were quickly abandoned. The neighborhood hadn't changed. The only missing part of my past was the death of my dog, Toby.

During my absence, Toby transferred the affection he loyally bestowed on me to Claude. He became Claude's dog. Everywhere Claude went, Toby was at his heels. It was a heartbreaking day when Claude left the house and didn't realize the little black and white terrier anxiously waited to tag along. Without closing the front door leading onto the porch, Claude made his way down the four steps to the driveway. The car was parked near the steps and without realizing Toby was close at his heels, Claude climbed into the driver's seat of the unlocked car. He closed the car door, started the motor, and put the car in reverse. As the car moved, the body of Toby was caught under the back wheel. Not even a whimper was heard as the last breath of life was snuffed from the body of my friend.

Claude Rainbolt was a big man with a heart as big and tender as his physical stature. Losing Toby was like losing a child. I knew it wasn't an easy task to inform me while still in London, that Toby, the dog who followed me home when I was still in grade school, was dead.

Those who stayed behind during the war earned a bundle of money in defense plants. Since they couldn't spend as readily as in pre-war years due to rationing, their bank accounts grew. Only the inconvenience of rationing beset the comforts of middle-class America. Across the street, the Wiggingtons never deviated from their Wednesday night Holy Roller prayer meetings. Our next door neighbors, the Hamiltons, would come and go from their house to our house as if it were their own and vice versa. Doors were never locked. Mrs. Brannon's body was tortured by a few more beatings from her alcoholic husband and Ted Anglin, who had the prettiest daughter in the neighborhood, periodically fell off the wagon. His gentle, patient spouse quietly endured the drinking sprees and when Ted reached his saturation point with Barley Corn, it was the usual rush to the altar at the Nazarene Church, begging forgiveness. As he did so many times throughout the years, the preacher stood over the kneeling man, his hand firmly planted on the repentant's head. His voice would rise toward the heavens and with the brilliance of a golden trumpet the man of God sent upward a prayer of contrition for the wayward soul kneeling at his feet. The prayer was endless. The pleading never ceased until the good Reverend was certain Satan was on the run and had thoroughly and completely departed from the soul of the sinner man.

I returned to the church I chose to attend during those pre–war teenage years. The preacher and his wife never altered their dull preaching of the gospel every Sunday morning and evening. I reclaimed my place in the choir as I had done from the time I was 14 until that day in June of 1943 when I went off to war. Clarence Thompson's hands moved in the same one-two-three-four manner as he led the congregation in singing the hymns. Although worn and tattered, the hymnals were of little use since the congregation sang the songs so many times, they knew them by memory. Frances, the choir director's daughter, never married. She continued to sit on the organ bench she had occupied since the organ's installation. She spent so many hours on that bench, her derriere was eternally imprinted into the oak seat.

My salvation for returning home was brought about by the devoted who helped me endure those difficult teen adolescent years which would have been totally unbearable without the guidance bestowed upon a young lad whose life had been disrupted by the death of his mother.

Many young men from the congregation caught in the draft as I had been, returned home and once again joined the church's fold. Some were severely injured, but the majority came back with their bodies intact.

Norm Simpson, my buddy, was shot down over Germany

long before the invasion of the European continent. No one was certain of Norm's fate, not until the day he came home and suddenly appeared at the church. Norm loved music and he was a good musician. Of all the people I knew and grew up with in Akron, I received more enthusiasm from Norm than anyone at home or the congregation when I told him I had been accepted at Juilliard.

When the Allied bombers were plentiful enough to make it across the English Channel and into Hitler's air space, Norm was one of the first Americans to be sent on a bombing mission. The squadron of planes took off from Great Britain like migrating birds. They flew across the Channel and within minutes, the sound of bomber engines rocked the skies as they flew over Holland, Denmark, then Germany. As Norm's plane crossed the border into Germany, his plane became surrounded by German Messerschmitts. They buzzed around the Allied bombers like a swarm of mosquitoes. Anti-aircraft artillery on the ground pounded the open sky with tons of flak. It was like a meteor storm in outer space. Norm's plane was hit. The plane burst into flames. Norm and his buddy ejected from the aircraft seconds before their plane exploded into a ball of fire then plummeted to earth like a fatally wounded bird. The two airmen fell several hundred feet before their parachutes engaged and brought them to an open field surrounded by a grove of trees. A German farmer tilling his crops rushed toward the two unexpected guests. He kindly helped the two enemy airmen untangle their bodies from their deflated parachutes. No one spoke English or German, not until they reached the farmer's house. It was then the two American airmen discovered their captor spoke a perfect English.

The farmer and his wife were kind. They offered the two

enemy airmen a place to bathe and food to eat. They were then bedded down in a small bedroom where they slept until the following morning. As Norm and his buddy ate a hearty breakfast, the German farmer informed the two Americans he would have to turn them over to the authorities. Norm and his buddy were destined to spend the rest of the world conflict as prisoners of war in a concentration camp somewhere in Germany.

Art Robinson was the fair-haired boy in the church choir. Reminiscing a bit about those teen years, I was probably jealous of Art because Clarence Thompson assigned all the solos incorporated in the church anthems the choir sang to him. Art was good looking and blessed with a beautiful singing voice. He married one of the church girls prior to being shipped off to war. Shortly after he married, he was drafted and sent to an infantry basic training camp. Here, like all other able bodied young men, he was trained to kill the enemy. He was eventually shipped out to the front lines of battle. I don't know how many battles Art engaged in, but the most devastating was the one where he was struck in the head by enemy fire. The lead penetrated his helmet then exploded, creating a wide open gap in the man's skull. His injuries were pieced together and a steel plate replaced his shattered skull. For the remainder of Art's life, he would be obligated to live with a metal plate covering a gaping wound in his head. The sun became his enemy. At no time for the remainder of the veteran's life would he dare venture into the sunshine without a head covering. The sun's heat could quickly bake his brain.

Julius and Hilda Marion were my mentors. Julius or J.C. as we often referred to him, represented the kind of father figure I desired but never had. Hilda, his wife, was gentle and kind. She had a rare knack for understanding teenagers as they made their transition from adolescence into adulthood. Their young daughter, Phyllis, who appeared so immature and childlike when I went off to war was no longer a child. She had grown into an attractive young woman. Shortly after my enrollment in Juilliard School of Music, the Marions sent me a train ticket to return to Akron and sing for Phyllis' wedding.

Julius was too old to be drafted when war started, so his contribution to the war was laboring in one of Akron's many defense plants. He was a good man and throughout his life he walked the straight and narrow and lived his religion. His religious bent was the only characteristic which sometimes annoyed me. Quoting the Book of St.John was J.C.'s answer to all the woes of the world. Nevertheless, the Marion influence helped to mold my life to where I could guide my own ship as I left the adolescent years and entered into manhood

I had no intention of spending much time in Akron, just long enough to have several meetings with my good friend and teacher, Mabel Todd. Her thinning white hair and strong, determined face only accentuated the strength exuding from Akron's most productive and prestigious teacher. Mabel Todd was my lighthouse in the eye of many storms since the first day we met. She understood my burning desire to sing and never wavered from her belief and trust that music would be my contribution to society.

"Do you think you are making the right decision, Loy?" She asked when I told her about my acceptance at Juilliard. "There are undoubtedly good vocal teachers in New York but from singers I have listened to over the years coming out of Juilliard causes me to have deep reservations as to whether that is the best place for you to continue your studies. I had hoped you would consider going to Westminister."

Doubts about my decision to matriculate at Julliard were planted. I began to wonder if Mabel might not be right and perhaps I was about to make an unchangeable decision. It was a known fact that performers were not necessarily good teachers. Of course, there were exceptions as in the case of Madame Raymonde Delanois. Dr. Arnold Smith, at the Royal Academy of Music in London, was not a singer, yet singers came from all over the world to study voice with him. Dr. Williamson, the founder of the Westminister Choir College was not a singer, yet he produced some of the finest vocal sounds to ever come from the human throat.

Gerry remained in Princeton finishing her last year of schooling. I spent many evenings in the Gerraghty home with Mom and Pop Gerraghty. Being a dental technician, Tom Gerraghty agreed to fix the space between my two front teeth. One of the last statements Maestro Pelletier said as I was leaving his presence at the Metropolitan Opera house was to have my teeth fixed. The process meant extracting two front teeth whose protrusion was undoubtedly caused from sucking my thumb as a young child. The teeth had to be pulled in order to attach a permanent bridge. Tom, at first, said he would prefer the extraction be done by an oral surgeon, but after studying the project at hand, he said he could accomplish the same job and it wouldn't cost me any money. Making dentures was Tom's business, and even if I was asking him to do something for which he wasn't licensed, I said, "Okay, Tom, it's a go!"

Tom pulled my two front teeth then attached the new bridge to my remaining teeth which served as anchors. He then gave me exercises to speak in order to pronounce the f's and a few other consonants plus telling me to read out loud until I got used to my new cosmetic appearance and feeling.

Leaving Tom Gerraghty's lab, I began walking down Main Street. There was the familiar Lowe's Theatre, Bond's Clothing Store where I worked as a stockroom boy, and then my eyes glanced toward a jewelry store next to Polsky's that displayed the most magnificent jewelry I had ever seen on display. The precious gems were encased in a large wooden display case whose top was a very thick slab of heavy beveled glass. It rested near the door as one entered the store.

It was a sunny day although it was January and the depth of winter. The beauty of the brilliant diamonds, emeralds, and other precious stones glistened, being enhanced even more by the sun's rays piercing through the large window in front of the store. I stood in front of the store gazing at the jewelry, but nothing amongst the display suggested what kind of a ring I could have created from the gift Gisele had so generously given me.

I entered the store. The proprietor was occupied with another customer, although he did acknowledge my presence. I walked to the nearby showcase. I perused the gems. Diamonds burst forth with an indescribable brilliance, more so than any other item. The recall of when I purchased an engagement ring for Marietta and how those plans turned to dust flashed through my mind. The thought of buying another ring presented doubts. It was not a long wait before the proprietor was ready to give me his undivided attention.

The jeweler moved down the narrow passageway behind the jewel cases separating the seller from the buyer. He reached across the counter to shake my hand. "Hey, welcome home, Soldier! Say, you're the young kid who used to do all the singing around this town? Remember? I presented you with a gold loving cup trophy a few years ago for winning that singing contest that was broadcast over WABC."

I was embarrassed. "Yeah, I'm that guy. I just got out of the army. Only been home a couple days, then I'm gonna head back to the big city. I was accepted at Juilliard."

The proprietor's eyes opened as wide as saucers. "Congratulations! I just knew you were something special when I first heard you sing. Sure glad you made it home, Buddy. What can I do for you?"

I withdrew the packet from my pocket, then carefully unfolded the paper in which the pearl was encased. I laid the pearl on the counter. The sunlight penetrating the front glass window facing the street beamed toward the pearl and as the reflected light reached the surface of nature's creation, it turned to a pastel yellow. Carefully, the jeweler picked up the pearl. Pulling his loupe down over his right eye, he began examining the gem. "Very interesting," I heard him say under his breath. He then took the pearl and placed it between his teeth. He laughed as he removed the pearl from his mouth then placed it on the counter. "I jes' bet ya thought I was goin' to swallow it, didn't you? A real pearl has the taste of sandy grit. This is one way of telling whether the pearl is real or if it's made of paste. You have a rare gem here. Where did ya get it?"

I related the story about my parting gift from Gisele. When I finished, the man laid the gem on the glass counter top. "This pearl would make a magnificent ring and I would like to make it for you. You see, pearls are a very special gift of nature. They are alive, and unless they are worn, they lose their luster and die. Are you planning to get married?"

I attempted to bypass the question. "Well, I don't know

that it's an engagement ring. I don't know whether the girl to whom I plan to give the ring would even consider me as a possible mate. Oh, by the way, how much is this going to cost?" I didn't have much money and I still had to return to New York. I knew, when I got back to New York, I was going to have to get a job, something I could do even after I enrolled in school. My acceptance into Juilliard didn't include room and board.

"Don't worry, Soldier. It won't cost much and when I finish setting this stone, any girl would be more than proud to wear the ring. Come back in a week and you'll see what I'm talking about."

I left the store wondering what the jeweler meant when he said, "It won't cost very much." I did know it would be different than any other ring and it would belong to Gerry.

Next to the jewelry store, Bond's Clothing Store displayed a huge sign advertising men's suits which included two pair of trousers. I eyed the garment being neatly fitted on a manikin standing in the display window. I knew the wearing of my uniform had just about worn out its welcome. Up to the present time, no one questioned my status as a soldier and I made no effort to tell them otherwise. The face of the man dressing the manikin, making certain each fold of the suit on the phony body fell at just the right angles was familiar. He was almost as wax-like as the figure he was dressing. Only his eyes moved, casing every movement of a young stock boy executing his duties as he darted from one rack of clothing to another. I recalled having a strong dislike for the all too familiar face of the proprietor. The passage of time had not caused that dislike to abate. There was a flashback to only a few years prior when I too was a stock boy and stood on my feet from the time the store opened until lunch time when I was permitted to sit on a cardboard box in the stockroom to indulge in my peanut butter sandwich. I could feel myself inside the young stock boy as I watched him move about the store making certain each suit was hung to the precise demands of the store's proprietor.

Entering the store, there was no visible sign of recognition as the man with the stone-like face finally asked, "May I help you?"

"I just got out of the army, sir, and I need some civilian clothes, like a new suit, some shirts, and an overcoat." The stoic faced man pointed toward a rack of men's suits. "I don't want anything in brown, sir. That's been the color of my clothing including my shoes for the past three years, and now that I'm a civilian, I finally have a right to choose any color I want."

The proprietor, making no comment to my statement, removed a tape measure from his pocket. He placed the tape across my shoulders then proceeded to measure from the nape of my neck to just below my buttocks. "You'll take a 40 long." At least the man knew how to talk, I thought. He walked over to a rack of neatly hung suits and removed a blue gaberdine coat. Underneath the coat on the hanger were two pair of trousers matching the coat. The coat was a perfect fit. "Remove your coat, please," the man said. I obeyed the man as if he were an inspecting officer telling me to bend over and spread my cheeks apart. He took his tape measure and with his right hand, he reached for my crotch, letting the measure fall to just the right position on the shoe where a cuff would fold. He marked his measurements with a piece of chalk.

"The dressing room is over there." He pointed to the cubicles I knew so well. When I worked in this same store as a stock boy, I had removed many discarded suits customers left lying on the floor or on the bench. My job was to pick up after those slobs and put the clothing back on hangers then into their proper places on the rack Of course, the pants had to be folded to the precise specifications and the coats were wrinkle free or they would never have passed the proprietor's inspection.

The pants fit perfectly around the waist. Other than having the cuffs tacked into place, there was little alteration necessary. I stood in front of the full-length mirror just outside the dressing room. I smiled at the image staring back at me revealing an engaging smile and two perfect front teeth. "By golly! I do look good!" I whispered under my breath. I returned to the showroom and the proprietor quickly marked with a chalk any other alterations necessary to make my wardrobe a perfect fit including the width of the cuffs.

Near the racks holding the suits were overcoats. They were hung in precisely the same detailed manner as the suits. Over the overcoat rack were men's hats, but the one that really struck my fancy was a Homburg. I wanted a Homburg. "Let me try one of those hats, sir. I'm leaving for New York City soon and I'm sure I'm gonna need one. I also need an overcoat. What have ya got that'll go with this new suit and this Homburg?" It was like talking to myself as I glanced at my reflection in a mirror stationed near the overcoats and hats.

The proprietor pulled an elegant top coat from the rack. It fit as if it had been tailored just for me. "I'll take everything, sir, including a couple shirts and this tie. I do want, however, to wear these clothes home. If you don't mind, perhaps you could tuck in the cuffs on at least one pair of trousers."

I returned to the dressing room and took off my blue gaberdine pants, replacing them with my uniform trousers. I was dressed when the man reached over a half door and gave me a box. "You can put your army uniform in this box. Your suit will be ready in just a few moments." I undressed again. I folded my pants, neatly folded my Eisenhower jacket with its battle stars, ribbons, and sergeant's stripes then placed the costume that had been a part of my life for almost three years into the box.

A pair of altered trousers suddenly appeared over the top of the half door. Donning my new suit, my overcoat, and my homburg, I proudly left the dressing room. I took one more glance at the man standing in front of the full-length mirror. My army days were at an end. I was ready to challenge the world in peace as I had done during the time of war.

Chapter 57

When Mom died, my sister Betty and my sister Ruth attempted to keep the family ties strong even though we had all been separated and farmed out as children to other families until we were mature enough to strike out on our own. Two sisters and one brother lived in Muncie. They were Edna, Betty, and my eldest brother Francis. All my siblings married and had created their own families. Harvey never moved far from Gaston. He would remain in that vicinity until the day he died.

At no time during the war years had I heard from my father. He had remarried and divorced by the time I returned home. One of my priorities prior to leaving for the Big Apple was another visit with my siblings who had never moved far away from the Midwestern town of Muncie, Indiana.

It was early morning when the train pulled into the train station in Muncie. The city which was always considered a metropolis in the mind of a child now seemed no more than a village after being exposed to cities like London, Paris, and New York. The streets and boulevards which I envisioned as being wide were narrow and people easily could conduct a conversation while standing on opposite sides of the street. No buildings were more than two stories. What a contrast to the elegant department stores and office buildings in London and Paris where the buildings could boast of having at least six floors.

Muncie was still a town of foundries and of course Ball Brothers, the home for the production of glass canning jars. The company had created employment opportunities for many of the town's permanent residents. The glass company contributed much to the town of Muncie and to society. They built a substantial hospital and eventually founded with their financial contributions what is known as Ball State University.

Numerous foundries also dotted the city where scrap metal was melted and recycled. Ball Brothers and the foundries kept the economy afloat for many during the Depression when there seemed to be nothing there for the poor people of this Midwestern town. These business enterprises provided a light in the tunnel of darkness during the long years of homelessness for many and others who had no way of providing for their families.

I got up from my seat as the train began to slow. I removed my luggage from the rack over my seat and moved toward the exit door of the car. Standing on the platform was my sister Betty, her husband Bob, their three children Bobby, Jr., Jim, and their baby sister Susan. They had all grown so rapidly during my three year absence. As Betty gave me a warm embrace and a kiss, tears welled in her eyes, she said, "We're glad you're home, Loy." My brother-in-law firmly shook my hand then grabbed the suitcase which I'd purchased in Akron so I wouldn't be lugging the dufflebag which like the uniform was forever put away like all the other memorabilia collected during the war. Bob placed the suitcase in the trunk of the car and I climbed into the back seat with the three kids.

My sister Betty inherited many of mother's traits. She was warm and always ready for laughter and fun. She had a genuine concern for helping others. All during the war, other than the daily letters from Gerry, I could anticipate a letter from my sister updating me about my other siblings. It was always Betty and Ruth who communicated via V-mail during those dark and hopeless days of the war. I heard nothing from my brother Harvey or my brother Francis. Occasionally I might get a short note from my oldest sister Edna. As far as my father was concerned, there was never a note nor did he inquire about his sons who had gone off to war.

My first inquiry about the family regarded my brother Harvey. I wasn't even certain Uncle Sam had drafted him as he did me and certainly didn't know he had been sent to the South Pacific where he ended up on the Godforsaken island of Guam.

As we chatted away about all the changes that had taken place, I brought up Harvey's name. "Loy," Betty said, "We ain't heard a word from Harvey. I think he must be home by now. I don't know why he ain't come to see us. We were always pretty close. Maybe it's his wife, Edna Grace. I always had a feeling she resented the family. When we get home, I wonder if you'd mind tryin' to reach him by phone. I'd like to see him. I've spoken with Ruth and we think it would be a good idea to have a welcome home get together at the farm. If it's all right with you, we'll do that this comin' Sunday. Maybe you can persuade Harvey to come if he's home."

Betty continued chatting away. "Ya know Dad and Lily got a divorce, don't you? I think I wrote you about that while you were in Paris. Ain't seen hide nor hair of Dad for quite a spell. He stayed with us for a time after he and Lily called it quits and they separated. It was all okay until I discovered he was using our address to make his connections with a Lonely Hearts Club. He made me so mad, I sat down and wrote him a letter on a roll of toilet paper. It took the whole roll to git what I had to say off my chest. I guess when he received a roll of toilet paper in the mail, which by the way was delivered back to our house, he felt it was time to move on and I ain't seen 'em since."

Prior to the war and when I was settled in Akron, Dad made a visit to show off his bride to Urith and Claude. It wasn't a visit to see how I was doing, but just the idea of introducing his fat wife into the family circle. He had married this woman within three months after Mom died. That in itself was enough to stir up resentment within my soul that he had no more respect for Mom that he couldn't wait just a bit longer before taking on another spouse. I wasn't exactly keen about having what they call a stepmother.

Lily was indeed very heavy and I wondered how she would ever fit in the front seat of the Model T and still leave room for Dad to manipulate the steering wheel of his old jalopy.

I suppose it was due to my upbringing to "honor your father and your mother" that I felt obligated to make an attempt to see Dad. At any rate, it was more out of respect than love. There was no more conversation about Dad, not until the following morning.

At breakfast, Bob, who was a man of few words, always letting my sister have center stage, spoke. "Loy, let's take a ride over to the foundry. I heard Abe was workin' there. If he ain't there, they might know where he's stayin'."

Pulling into the parking lot of the foundry, Bob guided the car toward an open door where I could easily observe men standing in front of roaring furnaces, their eyes covered with goggles, their hands protected with heavy gloves. Both hands grasped huge tongs that picked up heavy pieces of discarded metal for recycling. The scrap metal was then tossed into a blazing inferno and melted into liquid. Near the entrance to the foundry stood an elderly man. His body, worn and bent from years of hard labor, slowly moved a long-handled broom which he held in his withered hands as he swept the residue of scrap metal from the earthen floor. The silhouette of the man bore no resemblance to my father or the father I knew. My Dad was like the eternal oak tree that remained deeply rooted in the earth, its branches reaching toward the heavens. He had endured heavy rains, sleet, snow, drought, tornadoes, and poverty, and like the giant oak, he refused to bend or be uprooted from the source that gave him sustenance and life.

When the car came to a stop, the old man lifted his tired head to gaze in our direction. I got out of the car and walked toward my father. He stared at me with those cold, steel blue eyes. He knew it was me, yet there was no attempt to recognize my presence. His head dropped and his hands continued to move the broom in a pretense of sweeping away the metallic residue.

"Hi Dad." Slowly Dad lifted his bent head upward then gave me that direct stare I recalled so vividly as a small child. That look was more effective than being reprimanded with a slap on the face or a beating with the razor strap.

"What do ya want, Loy? I see ya made it outta the army and I cain't see where it hurt ya none. Hope they made a man outta ya." Dad stopped sweeping long enough to let his body rest against the broom.

"I just wanted to see how you're doin,' Dad. I understand you and Lily got a divorce."

Dad's weak voice caused by age and poor health returned to his sweeping. Almost in an inaudible whisper I heard him say. "Yeah, I finally got rid of that woman. She was the meanest critter God ever created."

In an attempt to keep some kind of conversation going, I said, "I think Harvey's home from the war, too, Dad? I'm gonna call him when we get back to Bob's house. We thought you might like to see him."

The old man made no acknowledgment to my statement. As I spoke he rubbed his leg and a painful grimace flashed across his face. "What's wrong, Dad? What's wrong with your leg?" He leaned the broom against the trash bin then lifted his pant leg covering his long johns.

"My leg hurts," he said as he carefully pulled the leg of his long underwear up toward his knee.

The flesh on my father's leg was hard and black, almost to the point of looking petrified. "Dad, I think you'd better see a doctor. I don't think yer leg looks so good. It could be serious." Dad let his pant leg drop until it fell just below his shoe top. He reached for the broom and resumed sweeping.

"Maybe I can help ya out, Dad. I have a little money. Not much—but enough to git ya to a doctor."

"I cain't afford no doctor, Loy! I ain't no rich dude like some people I knowed and I don't wear them fancy clothes neither."

It was obvious Dad was referring to my new pair of pants shoes, sweater, and the Homburg. "I don't need yer help, Loy and I don't want something fer nothin' neither. I gotta git back to work."

"I'm not gonna be here long, Dad. I'm headin' fer New York City. They accepted me into Juilliard School of Music. That's just about the best music school in America and maybe the entire world, Dad. Remember how we used to make music, Dad? You'd play the French harp and Harvey would play the Jews harp. The only thing I could do was sing."

Dad could never visualize or appreciate my good fortune. All of his waking hours were spent shucking corn, gathering metal junk that could be sold to foundries, and now in his latter days sweeping dirt floors in a foundry.

"How about comin' out to Ruth's on Sunday, Dad. Ruth, Betty, and Edna decided we should have a get together, sort of a celebration for a couple soldiers returnin' from the war. I'm gonna try to see Harvey if I can git Bob to drive me to Gaston."

Dad continued pushing the long-handled broom over the earthen floor, letting the bristles of the broom push the metallic residue into a pile so it could easily be picked up and placed in the trash bin. I knew he was in excruciating pain and I wanted to help him, but he wasn't willing to be helped. I prepared to leave, and for one brief moment as I turned toward the open door, Dad stopped sweeping.

"Loy." I turned to face my father. "Is Lily gonna be there? If she's comin', I ain't comin'. I never wanna see that varmint again."

"No one knows anything about Lily, Dad. She's not been in touch with any of the family, not since your separation and divorce. You always told us not to stick our nose into other people's business and I consider your problem with Lily your business. No Dad, Lily won't be there. I'll be shovin' off now. I know yer supposed to be workin'. I would appreciate it though if you would consider comin' out to Ruth's place on Sunday."

As I took a couple steps toward the open door, I heard

Dad's thin voice flutter in my direction. "I jes might see ya Sunday, Loy. Thanks fer comin'."

That afternoon, Bob, Betty, the children, and myself drove to Gaston. Harvey was home and he was glad to see us but there was an unsettled coolness I never experienced in all the times I shared with my brother and his wife Edna Grace.

"I'm glad ya got home safe, Loy. That war brought about a lot of changes in all of our lives; I know it did mine. Let's go out in the yard and swap a few war stories."

We left Betty, Bob, and the children inside the house as we moseyed to the outside. Harvey was the first to speak. "I thought about ya a lot during these past years. I came home to a mess and I don't know how I'm goin' to resolve it. I'll have to tell ya about it later. Jes' wanted you to know though the kids and me will be at Ruth's on Sunday, but Edna Grace will not be there."

CHAPTER 58

THE PAYNE FAMILY—I.E., RUTH AND Luther and their four children—lived in a typical simple Midwestern farmhouse. The nearest town was a junction in the road they called "Keystone." The house, the barn, and the outer sheds including the pig sty was surrounded by 40 acres of rich Midwestern farm lands. A gravel driveway circled a huge elm tree. A front porch spanned the width of the house, facing a manicured carpet of grass extending to the edge of the gravel road leading to Keystone. It was indeed a picture postcard setting with the typical red barn and a silo erected only a few feet from the house. It was what one would consider an ideal place for my sister and her husband to raise their family in a healthy and safe environment. In the years to come, it would be my sanctuary away from the noise and the fast-living pace in New York City.

Many changes had taken place in the way farmers tilled the soil—much different than the pre-teen years I spent in the country hiring myself out at harvest time. The tractor replaced a team of horses who pulled the plows and drags that broke up the moist clumps of dirt. There were, however, several cows to be milked twice daily, chickens to be fed, and hogs to be slopped.

Behind the barn near the pig sty, Luther created his own horseshoe arena. The popular game became a regular Sunday afternoon pastime for the men folk while the women sweat over a wood-burning store in the kitchen preparing a mountain of food.

Harvey and his children had already arrived at the farm when Betty, Bob, myself, and their three children pulled into the circular driveway. Harvey walked toward our car as we came to a stop. "Come on, Loy, let's take a walk. We might want to share a few private moments we don't want the others to share."

We walked along the country road in silence until Harvey finally spoke. "Loy, as I told you, Edna Grace and me are have'n trouble. I came home from the war only to find she was shackin' up with someone I thought was my best friend. She took the kids and even moved away from the house we'd lived in since we got married." My brother then began the saga about his homecoming.

"It was a cold winter day when the train I was on that was bringing me home slowed then came to a stop. Anticipation and excitement flowed through my veins as I left my seat and prepared to take my dufflebag from the rack above where I was sitting. I rushed off the train hoping to place my arms around my wife and my two kids, but there was no one there. I thought perhaps they might be inside the depot since there was a light snow falling and the air was cold. I walked inside the depot and still no sign of Edna or my two kids. I rushed out of the depot and began walking toward the old house where Edna and I were married and had brought our two youngins' into this world. I noticed the house was dark when I stepped on the porch. As I was about to open the door, I heard the voice of our neighbor echoing through the night air.

"'Hey, Harve, is that you?' the voice said. 'Yeah, it's me,' I answered. It was the voice of Jim Williams, our next-door neighbor.

"'I think you'd better come over and come inside, Harve. How about a beer?'

"The first question I asked Jim was, 'Where's Edna Grace and the kids? I ain't heard from her for a couple of months, but the last letter I got said she and the kids were anxious for me to come home and they'd be at the train to meet me.'

"Jim said nothing, not until he went to the icebox and withdrew two bottles of beer. It was then he began telling me bout Edna Grace.

"'Edna moved out of the house a good month ago, Harve. Said she found a cheaper place on the other side of town. She left a note for me to give ya." He withdrew a piece of paper from his pocket. 'I think the least the woman could've done was tell ya she moved. I was quite upset with her.'

"I took the paper from Jim. The only words written on the paper indicated an address on Mulberry Street. Jim knew Edna had been shacking up with some guy almost as soon as I went off to war. The entire town knew. There was no such thing as a private matter in Gaston. The slightest bit of gossip had the capabilities of blowing a situation into a major disaster. A person's sex life and what they did in bed was as common as eating bacon and eggs every morning for breakfast. Tongues wagged faster than a dog's tail. 'Did it happen at his house or her house? What about the kids? You'd think they'd at least have respect for the kids if none for themselves.' Edna Grace's indiscreet sexual escapades became public knowledge as soon as I left for overseas duty. Everyone knew with whom she was sleeping—everyone except me, the father of her two kids.

"I could feel the blood rush to my face and anger began shaking my body. Leaving the half-finished bottled of beer on the coffee table, I put the dufflebag over my shoulder and rushed out the door."

The echo of Jim's voice rang through the night breaking the silence of the deserted Gaston street. "I'm really sorry, Harve. You don't deserve this," he said.

"My head was as if someone had suddenly hit it with a sledge hammer. That bitch! That God damn bitch! What about my kids? Oh, my God! Anger rushed through my entire body.

"I turned onto Mulberry Street. It was only a couple blocks to No. 110. As I approached the house, I could see Edna Grace through the lace curtains sitting in a rocking chair. Next to her stood a small child; I could only presume it must be my daughter who was just a mere infant when I went off to war. I stormed upon the porch. I'm sure Edna Grace heard my heavy footsteps. I rapped on the door but I got no response. I heard the little girl speak, 'Mama! Mama! Ain't ya gonna see who's knockin' on the door?'

"I gave one shove and the door opened. 'Well, this is one helluva home comin!' I said. 'Ain't nobody here glad to see me?'

"Edna still didn't move from the rocking chair. She was like she was in some kind of a trance. Her cold, blue, unblinking eyes were totally void of tears or recognition.

"My daughter became frightened. 'Who's that man, Mama? Who is he, Mama?'

"The sound of my voice caused my son Jerry to rush out of the bedroom into the parlor. 'Daddy! Daddy!' He ran toward me and wrapped his arms around my waist. 'I missed ya, Daddy! I'm sure glad you're home!'

"My daughter Diane broke away from her mother and ran toward me. I lifted each one of the kids in my arms and held them close. 'Tomorrow will be better, kids, but now I think it's time you were in bed. Yer mom and me have some talkin' to do.'

"I followed Diane and Jerry into the bedroom then closed the door. I could feel my six-foot frame begin to tremble with anger. 'Ya got a lot of explain' to do, Edna, and I think you'd better start talkin' and I mean now!' I wanted to pick up my wife and shake her like a terrier shakes a rat. My fists were always my source of protection but to strike my wife was an unthinkable act. 'Okay, Edna, what's been goin' on?'

"My wife's lips began to quiver and in an almost inaudible voice, she finally spoke. 'I—I've been havin' an affair, Harve. It ain't right—I know'd it ain't right...' Her voice trailed off into silence.

"Like a dog ready for an inevitable attack, my voice seemed to drop to a deep growl. I leaned my body toward my wife until I eyeballed her stone face. My two muscular arms grabbed each one of her shoulders. 'Who's the son-of-a-bitch, Edna? I wanna know and I wanna know now!' I picked her up, stood her on her feet, and began to shake her as I looked at her at eye level. 'Who is he, Edna?' By then the sound of my voice had reached the shout of a sergeant.

"Edna's cold, blue eyes no longer looked downward. She raised her head and tears started to flow over her pale cheeks. 'I needed a man, Harve. I needed a man! You were gone for such a long time,' she said.

"Then there was a sudden change as she wiped away the tears from her cheeks. As quickly as the crocodile tears flowed, they ceased. Her face took on the appearance of a cat in heat. 'I'm sure ya didn't go without any, with all them native girls on that island. Why should I suffer here alone while yer fuckin' yer way around the Pacific?'

"With each statement my wife made, I became even more angry. 'Who's the son-of-a-bitch, Edna? I'll kill the bastard! I was trained to kill the bastards who tried to take our country away from us and to kill one more son-of-a-bitch who has done a good job of destroying my family ain't gonna hurt my feelin's one bit.'

"The steel grip I tightened around my wife's shoulders that had brought her to her feet were now used to slam her back into her chair. Edna began looking scared. She knew only too well I never made idle threats. 'I don't wanna tell ya, Harve. I jes' don't wanna tell ya!'

"The anger boiling in my veins turned to rejection. I turned toward the door then walked out into the cold night air. I could hear my feet crunching on top of the snow-covered ground as I began to walk the empty streets of Gaston. It must have been around midnight when I stopped at a local saloon, one Edna and myself often catered during the pre-war years. The scene hadn't changed. The same swingers we partied with before the war were still boozing it up and trading wives at the town's popular watering hole. Before the war we'd been party to a few of their games, but now it was different. I thought I had settled down when we had kids.

"As I opened the door to the saloon, a voice at the bar greeted me. 'Well, look who's here? Welcome home, buddy! Let's buy this hero a drink!'

"I ignored the invitation then sat at the far end of the bar. 'Gimme a beer and a double whisky,' I ordered.

"As I was about to take my first sip, another drunk sitting at a table not far from the bar yelled. 'Hey, Harve! Understand yer best friend's been fuckin' yer wife while you've been away.'

"I leaped from the bar stool like a tiger determined to pounce and conquer its prey. I grabbed ahold of the inebriated drunk, raised him from his hair then stood him on his feet.

"'Keep yer God damn mouth shut, buddy, or I'll shut it fer ya fer good. Do you hear what I'm sayin?' I yelled as I shoved him back into his chair then returned to the end of the bar. It was then I knew the whole town knew about my wife.

"The saloon closed for the night and I began walking the snow-covered, deserted streets of Gaston. Thousands of thoughts rushed through my troubled mind, even going back to the days I just missed graduating from high school.

"Edna was always easy in bed and my sexual urges at that time jumped to their highest peak. Once Edna opened those pearly gates, I knew it was the point of no return and marriage was the only way out.

"I know I disappointed the Rogers family. They'd been my family and my haven from the time I was 12 years old and I was treated more like their son than their own son.

"After I married Edna Grace, I got a job working for Warner Gear. It was a factory job that would support my wife and soon my first child then my second child. All was fine until the Draft Board summoned me for military service.

"Daylight began to filter through the soft falling snow. I returned to the house on Mulberry Street and stepped on the porch of the house I never knew. I didn't bother to turn on a light. I just removed my clothing down to my underwear, then lay on the daybed that served as a sofa during the day.

I must have drifted off to sleep. It was the soft touch of my son Jerry's hand that awakened me. Next to him was Diana. Both children placed their tiny arms around me. 'We're so glad you're home, Daddy,' Jerry said.

"I held each child close to my body and finally spoke. 'Kids, it's goin' to be all right,' I said as I gently placed a kiss on each child's forehead."

I listened until I was certain Harvey had nothing more to say. There was really nothing I could say that would relieve the hurt and pain my brother was enduring. He was in deep thought as we started our walk back to the house. It was at the bend in the road when he spoke. "I'm gonna fergive her, Loy, for the kids' sake. I'm probably pretty much to blame for this mess. We used to play the fast game particularly with the gang we hung out with when we first got married. Wife swapping was the vogue and our Saturday night wild parties usually ended up with being in bed with someone else's wife. If Edna got pregnant by the bastard, that baby will be mine. I will never know that I was not its father."

My brother was true to his word. A baby girl was born and she became just another addition to his family. When the children were grown, except for the baby, Harvey divorced his wife and when the baby also graduated from high school, it was only then he waited for the chance to find another wife.

The sound of my dad's Model T sputtering to a stop as he pulled into the driveway brought attention from the men playing horseshoes. When Dad got out of the vehicle it was obvious he was in great pain. Other than saying, "I'm glad to see ya made it home, Harvey," he slowly limped his way toward the house. I followed Dad as he entered the house. "I think you'd better sit down Dad," I said as I opened the door into the kitchen. I ushered my dad through the kitchen into the parlor. A rocking chair was placed next to an ornate upright piano. I pushed a hassock in front of the chair so Dad could elevate his leg.

The entire family was there except Mom, my oldest brother Francis, and my half brothers and half sisters. It would be our final get together before death would take each member one by one.

Dinner was ready and the men folk came in from the horseshoe arena. We all gathered around the kitchen table except Dad. After the usual blessing and prayer of thanksgiving, my sister Edna prepared a plate of food for Dad while he sat in the rocking chair with his lame leg propped up on the hassock. The old man contributed nothing to the ceaseless chatter ringing throughout the farmhouse. While the womenfolk cleared the table and prepared to wash the dishes, Luther said, "How about another game of horseshoes, y'all? I bet I can make more ringers than any of ya."

I stayed close to Dad. I hadn't touched a piano since leaving Paris. I sat down on the piano bench thinking Dad might like a little music. "Remember when we used to make music, Dad, when we all lived under the same roof?"

Dad made no response to what I was saying. I noticed on the piano rack the old standard "Love's Old Sweet Song." I let my hands touch the keys, and after playing a brief introduction, I started to sing. I thought somewhere in the recesses of my father's mind he would recall some of those better days. My sisters gathered in the doorway separating the kitchen from the parlor to listen. None of the family was indoctrinated to the sound of opera or the sound of a singer unless it came from the *Grand Ole Opry* in Nashville.

When I finished the first verse and began to sing the

second, Dad suddenly removed his leg from the hassock, stood straight as a poker, and with the all too familiar cold stare, he spoke, "Loy, ya ain't nothin' but a dude and ya ain't worth a hill of beans. I don't think you'll ever amount to nothin'! You've been nothin' but a dude since the day you was born!"

With that final statement from my father, I watched the old man storm from the parlor. He pushed my sisters aside who were standing in the doorway. Those words spoken by Dad would be engraved eternally in my memory. Through the window I could see the old man limping toward his outdated Tin Lizzie. I could hear the crank turning in the crankcase. The engine sputtered and began to purr. When the rickety Ford reached the gravel road, I knew it would be the last time I would see my father. The sad part of this story was, I really didn't care.

My world had expanded from the confinement of a small world into a huge world, and although I went to war as a young boy, I returned a man. I was now captain of my own ship and ready to sail into uncharted waters.